D1145054

THE MIDDLE CLASSES
THEN AND NOW

THE MACMILLAN COMPANY
NEW YORK · BOSTON · CHICAGO · DALLAS
ATLANTA · SAN FRANCISCO

MACMILLAN & CO., LIMITED
LONDON · BOMBAY · CALCUTTA
MELBOURNE

THE MACMILLAN COMPANY
OF CANADA, LIMITED
TORONTO

CITY OF WESTMINSTER
PUBLIC LIBRARIES

"Truly I don't know how they were at Austerlitz, but they could hardly have been better."

So reflects a vain bourgeois citizen, dressed in the bright uniform of the national guard, as he preens himself in self-admiration before a mirror. The cartoon is by Honoré Daumier (1808–1879), a famous French caricaturist.

THE MIDDLE CLASSES
THEN AND NOW

By

FRANKLIN CHARLES PALM

New York
THE MACMILLAN COMPANY
1936

323.32

RD/39784

Copyright, 1936, by
THE MACMILLAN COMPANY.

All rights reserved—no part of this book may be reproduced in any form without permission in writing from the publisher, except by a reviewer who wishes to quote brief passages in connection with a review written for inclusion in magazine or newspaper.

Set up and printed. Published August, 1936.
First printing.

PRINTED IN THE UNITED STATES OF AMERICA
BY THE STRATFORD PRESS, INC., NEW YORK

TO MY FATHER

who did not live to see it done

and

TO MY MOTHER

who yet lives and encourages

It matters not how strait the gate,
How charged with punishments the scroll,
I am the master of my fate:
I am the captain of my soul

(W. E. Henley, *Invictus*).

PREFACE

Who are the "middle classes"? Where did they come from? What are their characteristics? What effect have they had on the tide of human affairs? What of lasting value have they contributed to civilization? What is their status today? Where will they be tomorrow?

No one book could hope to answer such comprehensive questions and certainly this volume makes no pretense at being a detailed and exhaustive history of the bourgeoisie. Indeed, before such a work can be written, a vast amount of documentary material will have to be evaluated, many contributory books, pamphlets, and periodicals will have to flow from the presses. The present volume attempts only to serve as an historical introduction to the study of the middle classes by giving a brief, simple, factual account from the earliest times to the present. It is the hope of the writer that this preliminary investigation will pave the way for more intensive research and additional publications on the same subject or specific divisions of it.

A chronological and political, not a functional and economic account of the part played by business men in the development of Western civilization, this book is not predicated upon any preconceived personal idea of historical interpretation or social evolution, but is based simply upon the general thesis that our modern society, with its political, social, and economic institutions is dominated by the great middle classes, whose genesis, ascendancy, and place in European history constitute a story so far largely untold. *The Middle Classes,* therefore, is an attempt to fill the gap.

Much material is available, dealing with the middle classes directly and indirectly. Novelists, poets, essayists, and other literary craftsmen drawing inspiration from within themselves have penned compositions shedding oblique light on the bourgeoisie; and though such material can not be accepted as history, nevertheless its value is such that it ought not to be excluded and therefore the author has incorporated in the text four chapters on "Literature and the Middle Classes," chapters necessarily sketchy but otherwise indicative of the possibilities for further elaboration. In this connection it should be clear that a complete account of these people would include a discussion of bourgeois influence in painting, sculpture, music, and the sciences.

Of direct material, perhaps the first volume purporting to give a history of the middle classes was a book, published in 1833 by an English journalist and muckraker, John Wade, and entitled *History of the Middle and Working Classes.* Despite the author's intention to trace and account for the "origin and progress" of these classes, he merely offered a digest of facts culled for the most part from Hume's *History of England.* It is significant, however, that the term "middle class" got into the title of a book at that early date. A few years later (1838) a work was published in Paris bearing the same title: *Histoire des classes ouvrières et des classes bourgeoises.* Written by Granier de Cassagnac, a French journalist, romanticist, and conservative, it consisted for the most part of a highly doctrinaire elaboration of the thesis that the first free workers and burghers were descendants of emancipated slaves.

In the light of our present knowledge on this topic we may well realize that a satisfactory study of the middle classes was not possible until Marx and Engels wrote their works. Certainly they were the first to develop the idea of the class struggle and to define the position of the bourgeoisie with relation to the other groups. Moreover, Marx made men "middle-class conscious" by showing how the Industrial Revolution had created a *new* middle class—"the petty bourgeoisie." Inspired by these concepts, such scholars as Werner Sombart in *Der Bourgeois* (Duncker and Humblot, Munich, 1913) and Thorstein Veblen, in *The Theory of the Leisure Class* (The Macmillan Co., New York, 1899) brought out especially well the economic importance of the middle classes.

Recently, a number of excellent works have appeared to

testify to a rising interest in the bourgeoisie. Of these, Joseph Aynard's *La bourgeoisie française* (Perrin, Paris, 1934); N. A. Berdyaev's *The Bourgeois Mind* (Sheed and Ward, London, 1935); John Corbin's *The Return of the Middle Class* (Charles Scribner's Sons, New York, 1922); Lewis Corey's *The Crisis of the Middle Class* (Covici, Friede, New York, 1935); R. W. Gretton's *The English Middle Class* (G. Bell and Co., London, 1917); W. B. Pitkin's *Capitalism Carries On* (McGraw-Hill, New York, 1935); Evelyn John Strachey's *The Coming Struggle for Power* (Covici, Friede, 1933); E. C. Wingfield-Stratford's *The Victorian Tragedy* (G. Routledge and Sons, London, 1930); and Louis B. Wright's *Middle-Class Culture in Elizabethan England* (University of North Carolina Press, 1935) are especially suggestive.

To facilitate further investigation a formal bibliography of the middle classes is contemplated by the author. No attempt has been made, therefore, to list all the material used in the preparation of this volume. For the present, the reader will find quite helpful a short, well-selected bibliography at the end of Alfred Mesuel's excellent article, the *Middle Class,* in the *Encyclopedia of the Social Sciences* (The Macmillan Co., New York, 1933) volume X, page 415.[1]

In the preparation of this book the writer takes pleasure in acknowledging the assistance rendered by certain members of the younger generation to whom the fate of society is of more consequence than to those of the passing age. First and foremost must be mentioned Theodore Ginsburg, without whose valuable aid in the improvement of matter and style this volume would not have been published at the present time. Victor Norman read parts of the manuscript and the proofs and made many pertinent suggestions. William Chaiken, Carter Jefferies, Mary Ross, Albin Anderson and Beverly Fisher also examined various chapters, and enabled the author to detect minor slips, errors, and omissions. Gordon McWhirter and Edward Willis read the proofs and saved the author from many pitfalls. Yet

[1] In *The Middle Classes,* especially in chapter XX, "The New Revolution," the author has incorporated material from his *Europe Since Napoleon* (written with the assistance of F. E. Graham) (Ginn and Co., Boston, 1934).

none of these friends is to be held responsible for any of the defects of the book. For mistakes the author takes full responsibility.

FRANKLIN C. PALM.

Berkeley, California.

CONTENTS

THE MIDDLE CLASSES
THEN AND NOW

CHAPTER I

PROLOGUE

WHO ARE THE MIDDLE CLASSES?

The higher and middling orders are the natural representatives of the human race (Lord Macaulay in the Edinburgh Review, *March, 1829).*

OUR prehistoric ancestors may or may not have been class conscious. We do not know, for though the Eolithic, Paleolithic, Neolithic, and other members of our family tree have left us a plentiful legacy of axes, daggers, knives, swords, pottery, statues, urns, hammers, mallets, needles, horns, and paintings, they have inconsiderately neglected to include an accompanying commentary on their social status and organization.

A far cry from that age is civilization today. Capitalists! Bourgeoisie! Proletariat!—Upper Classes! Middle Classes! Lower Classes!—Plutocrats! White Collar Slaves! Laborers! These connotative phrases have become the glib stock-in-trade of our contemporary historians in their multifarious publications dealing with the political issues of the day. Yet, though they have filled the library of history with many an argumentative, descriptive, and "definitive" study of the class extremes in our social strata—the upper and lower classes—they have left a gaping space on the shelves for a general history of the broad society in between, the middle class—or to use the internationally recognized French equivalent for this phrase (which shall be employed interchangeably in this volume henceforth), the *bourgeoisie*.

Who are these middle classes and these bourgeoisie?

The philological heritage of the untranslatable word *bourgeoisie,* for which "middle class" is an inexpressive English substitute, goes back to the ninth and tenth century Germanic word *burg*. The upper classes—the nobles, clergy, and knights—lived in their well-nigh impregnable strongholds, while those freemen, not so fortunate as to be well-born, dwelt in towns and villages nestled in the formidable protection of the baronial castles to which they ran for shelter when threatened by danger. Thus, in the Germanies when the townsmen wished to hide *(bergen)* they scurried to the near-by shelter or stronghold *(burg)*. Consequently a definite association began to be built up between the *burg* and a certain class of people—dependent, not "gentlefolk" or of good blood, and with stabilized residences.

In these so-called Dark Ages, the *burg* possessed a very small mercantile population, if any, but by the twelfth century, as a result of renewed trade, the *burg* lost its connotation of a military and administrative center and earned the significance of "a privileged urban community," its members becoming known as *burgers* or *burghers*. Soon, by those language processes which respect no boundaries, the words invaded foreign territory until in the ensuing centuries there came into international usage the French *bourgeois* and *bourgeoisie*.

Historically, as we have seen, the middle classes originally consisted of freemen and townsmen, as distinguished from the privileged aristocracy and from the peasants riveted to the land. In the early modern period (1500–1789), however, social readjustments necessitated a more elastic definition, a definition concisely expressed by Gretton as "that portion of the community to which money is the primary condition and the primary instrument of life." Under this category came the commercial, industrial, and professional groups as distinguished from the nobility, the peasants, and the wage-earners. Today, all class boundaries have become even more difficult to define, because traditional privileged persons for the most part have disappeared, groups have moved from one stratum into another, individuals have risen and fallen in status, modern society has become so complex that persons may belong to more than one class at a time. Consequently, a certain section within the old bourgeoisie is now called the middle class. It refers, as Harkness puts it (in *John Calvin; the Man and His*

Ethics, Henry Holt and Co., New York, 1931) to the "not-so-rich and not-so-poor individuals between the proletariat-labor group and the wealthy capitalist and social aristocracy." Such a "sandwich" definition indicates how difficult it is to characterize the middle classes. Anomalous, mutable, with tenuous fringes, the middle classes never have been and are not now a fixed entity, to be encompassed by a simple, rigid definition. The "middle" cannot be defined in terms of itself or *per se;* it cannot avoid dependency upon its relative extremes. Thus, the meaning of middle classes is likely to remain with good cause in a state, so to speak, of suspended definition. However, though a precise definition is virtually impossible, nevertheless, one can characterize its membership in a general way.

Two rules of thumb can be applied as measures for the social stratum. One attempts to classify bourgeois society on a basis of income earned; this we may call the *How Much Theory.* The How Much Theory labels one a member of the bourgeoisie if one earns above a stipulated amount, the advocates having suggested seriously such exact sums—one wonders by what Einsteinian formula—as $729 and $1500. Such a yardstick seems superficial; more to the point is the second method, which we may call the *Where From Theory.* The Where From Theory divides society on the basis of the economic source from which the individual derives his income. Applied, this theory results in a threefold division:

1. *The Upper or Capitalist Class.* Its income is based upon hereditary status, applied privilege, self-recognized superiority in intelligence and opportunity, control of the means of production and distribution; in short, upon invested capital. This class, at a rough estimate, comprises only about two per cent of the people. Looking about, we can readily include bankers and financiers, industrialists, large stockholders, and great landowners—any possessors of vast wealth or great power.

2. *The Lower or Working Class.* Now tending to become known as the *proletariat,* this group defines itself by the negation of the capitalist principle; the working class is such because of its lack of capital and because its income is derived from labor. A more inclusive way of putting it is to say that

the working class consists of those persons who receive wages—the wage-earners. Theirs is a stipulated income based on the sale of labor for a set price. Included is thus a homogeneous section; to name a few, factory workers, farm hands, machine operators, clerical employees, artisans, mechanics. These may number over sixty per cent of the population.

3. *The Middle Classes or the Bourgeoisie*. Between the upper and lower classes we have the middle classes. The derivation of their income is a compromise; it comes from a combination of their own labors plus invested capital. Examples are the farm-owner, the small business man, the small manufacturer, the average professional man. In our social groups perhaps thirty per cent of the people fall under this category.

All this may appear to be too simple, a contradiction of the original premise that a definition is impracticable. But complications enter to distort these seemingly clear images. Different countries, different nations, even different sections, have divergent class distinctions. The hobgoblin of caste confuses the sober analyst of society. Sudden changes leave a disturbed scene; indeed, on account of commercial, political, and religious movements, particularly of the eighteenth century, people have begun to view society through a concept significantly expressed by the French: Liberty, Equality, Fraternity. Around this motto centers the instability of the class structure. In the present day it has taken another form through Marxian class concepts. Karl Marx's clarion cry: "The history of mankind is the history of class struggles," has awakened a resounding echo and some people of today are beginning to think of a classless society, or rather a society of one class—the proletariat. With such a vision in mind, they actually hope to eliminate the opposing classes, the capitalist by annihilation and the bourgeois by conversion. Thus the militant leaders of the proletariat, hearkening again to Marx—"The rich are becoming richer and the poor poorer; between the upper and the nether millstone, the middle class will be ground out!"—attempt to make clear to such petty bourgeois groups as teachers, civil service employees, physicians, and all sorts of salaried workers that they too are wage-earners, that the white collar has a tendency to become very easily stained with the soil. With pitiless logic they point out: first, how virtually impossible it is becoming to rise out of one's class; second, how similar the laborer and the white collar slave are in one only too vital respect—both must work or starve. To derive a conclusion, it becomes evident that under social pressure the boundaries of the definition are continually crumbling and shifting.

The middle-class individual is not only to be objectively classified by the process of identification with a group; he also has subjective impulses—in short, he can be analyzed as an individual personality with characteristic attributes. He prizes education because he firmly believes that education is power and because he thinks it essential to democracy. He boasts of impartiality in politics and often observes a suicidal neutrality; but he is easily swayed by demagogues, for deep within him are biases and prejudices. He wishes to be known as a self-made man, capable, independent, self-reliant. Sober forethought and intelligent ambition are his guides of action. He is steady, stolid, and industrious.

Above all, the middle-class man is acquisitive—money is his god, financial success his goal. To this passion he brings that spirit of capitalist enterprise which has been defined by Werner Sombart as "the resultant of the combination of all the qualities of the soul necessary for the successful consummation of an undertaking." This same writer lists some of those "qualities of the soul" as that of the conqueror, shown in mental energy; that of the organizer, shown in the utilization of many people's work; and that of the trader, shown in the art of distribution. He writes again, "The gaming passion and the pleasure of winning naturally turned to such enterprises as were capitalistic in their character," and he quotes a couplet from Goethe to illustrate still further:

> and that a mighty work completed stands,
> one mind suffices for a thousand hands.

In addition to the desire for gain, the bourgeois character contains certain qualities generally described as "middle-class virtues." These, writes Sombart, "include all the views and convictions (and, of course, the actions and conduct based upon them) of a respectable citizen and head of a family, no less than of an honest tradesman." His personal standards of morality, however, are variable; and he frequently divorces business ethics from them. His is the doctrine of "Let the buyer beware." He craves social distinction and likes to belong to a society, a lodge, an order, a political party. Decent living is his habit. He is often complacent, conventional, correct, snobbish. His home is his castle, his family his whole life. Altogether, he hopes to create a world in his own image. America knows him as Babbitt.

Another definition may be made from the commercial point of view. According to this definition, "holy economy," subdivided into thrift and industry, is perhaps the basic bourgeois characteristic. Expenses must not exceed earnings, and something must be saved—the more the better. "Be mindful, my sons, never to let your expenditure exceed your income," wrote Alberti, the fifteenth-century Florentine capitalist, and his advice has reëchoed down the centuries. Furthermore, time must not be wasted any more than money, for "time is money."

A distinction must be made, however, between the "holy economy" of the old style bourgeois individual and that of the modern business man. This change from old to new, as will be shown, occurred during the early part of the nineteenth century. The old style middle-class man did not consider wealth an end in itself; its virtue lay in the creation or preservation of life values. Furthermore, the business pace of the old bourgeois gentleman was slow; he worked leisurely and nurtured the ideal of retiring from business and living in the country; he preferred a small volume of trade at high profits. Quality goods were considered as a matter of course. Advertising was scarce and very conservative. Custom hunting and price cutting were disapproved, and so were technical improvements and changes in business processes if they involved loss of employment to workers or other capitalists.

Very different is the modern business man. Whereas his predecessor considered the commercial life a friendly ramble down the lane toward comfortable retirement, the modern business man often considers business a steeplechase—devil take the hindmost—toward Profit. Obstacles—competition, labor, capital, modernization—he takes for granted and trains for hurdling them. He is indeed as efficient as a race horse. Profit has become the center of his thought and every action is in terms of that one purpose—to make money. His business must be made to flourish. Size, speed, and novelty are but a few integral factors. To decrease expense in order to increase profit is but one of his axioms. Stock exchange transactions are essentially characteristic of this new phase of capitalism. Because capitalist enterprisers' activities are now so many-sided, and because trading and contracting are now so complex, calculation so delicate and difficult, business is rationalized and cold-bloodedly systematic. Customers are ferreted out, sales resistance lowered and overcome, and the products scientifically distributed. Characteristically, production for exchange is the rule rather than production for use.

How do the middle-class virtues fare among the modern bourgeoisie? Industry is now a necessity, not a matter of choice. Frugality is still practised in business dealings, but in private life the new standard of "conspicuous consumption" has arisen. Honesty in commercial transactions, that is, the fulfillment of contracts, is demanded as a matter of course, but individual personal honesty is now of secondary standing. However, all these characteristics of the modern business man apply largely to Big Business. In the small and middle-sized enterprises the principles of the early days of capitalism frequently prevail.

The above, then, is a brief analytical picture of the middle classes. It will well serve its purpose if, in reading the chapters to come, it will assist us to recognize the part played by them in the unfolding of our Western European civilization.

Chapter II

EARLY SELF-MADE MEN

Of what avail were battle in that day?
No profit was, no wealth for which to fight,
But cursed was the evil time, I say,
When sweating men began to dig to light
Metals deep-lurking in the earthly night,
And first knew gems, and in the rivers sought them,
Alas! then sprang to life the cursèd blight
Of avarice, and their first sorrow brought them

(*F. E. Hill,* Chaucer's The Canterbury Tales, *Longman's Green and Co., New York, 1930*).

Babbitt can trace his genesis and genealogy back a long way; in fact, his ultimate ancestors are the early self-made men of Babylonia and Egypt. That active bourgeoisie existed about 2500 B.C. is indicated by definite records which describe the presence of a society of numerous levels, fundamentally divisible into two extremes, the nobility and the proletariat, between which there was a middle section of merchants, ambitious and prosperous, drivers of shrewd business bargains, hard taskmasters, and loyal servants of their ruler.

The presence of a commercial middle class in the rich Mesopotamian valley is amply shown by the law code of the Babylonian king, Hammurabi (2067–2025 B.C.), which has numerous provisions dealing with merchants and the carrying on of commerce. Typical of such legislation is the following:

> If the merchant has given to the agent corn, wool, or any sort of goods to traffic with, the agent shall write down the price and hand over to the merchant; the agent shall take a sealed memorandum of the prices which he shall give to the merchant.

Similarly, Egypt, which prospered during the early period of the Empire (1580–1150 B.C.), had energetic bourgeoisie.

As Thebes, her main metropolis, became a market center for commerce from all parts of the known world, she waxed prosperous, her free landowners, artisans, and merchants accumulating great wealth. Although they rose in power and prestige, thereby strengthening their social organization, they exerted little control over political affairs. Their state of well-being was destroyed by a depression which descended during the latter period of the Empire. These commercial classes suffered as trade declined, as Egyptian territories broke away from the weakening parent state, and as invaders from the North, about 1150 B.C., destroyed the power of its kings. A tendency to regard hard work as a degrading occupation also checked the initiative and ambition of the trading groups. Despite these prevalent obstacles, artisans and merchants constituted a well-organized part of the population of Egypt when Alexander the Great conquered the Empire in 331 B.C. Thereafter, the business classes became merged with those of neighboring countries to form, in the Hellenistic Mediterranean world, a sort of international middle class—typified by the Levantine merchant and artisan—which still exists today.

But it was Phoenicia, rather than Egypt, which was the top bourgeois state of the ancient world. A nation of traders, its citizens demonstrated astonishing initiative and persistent progress in domestic manufactures, ship construction, foreign colonization, and general commerce. They exhibited qualities which we have come to think are solely products of our present successful self-made men, qualities such as perseverance and real audacity in enterprise, acuteness of intellect, and a practical utilitarian sense of values; nor did they allow honesty to interfere with business. On the industriousness of these Phoenicians Hebrew literature sheds considerable light. The *Holy Bible* reveals that between 1250 B.C. and 900 B.C., Phoenicia enjoyed great prosperity from her industry and trade. Her workmen and craftsmen were extensively occupied in Jerusalem; in the *Holy Bible* (I Kings, 7:13-51), for example, we read of Hiram, a master workman, who helped to plan and build Solomon's great temple. But Hiram and his fellows did not confine their talents to neighboring regions; exchanging the products of the East and the West, they visited all parts of the known world.

Although the rise of the Assyrian Empire checked Phoenician prosperity, by 630 B.C. the latter again was experiencing an era of marked economic well-being. At this time Tyre was its foremost commercial city. As described by the prophet Ezekiel:

> Judah, and the land of Israel, they were thy merchants: they traded in thy market wheat of Minnith, and Pannag, and honey, and oil, and balm.
>
> Damascus was thy merchant in the multitude of the wares of thy making, for the multitude of all riches; in the wine of Helbon, and white wool (Ezekiel, 27:17-18).

Ezekiel goes on to mention Arabia, Egypt, Babylon, Mesopotamia, Asia Minor, Lyons, Greece, and a number of other lands; and he states that Tyre was "a merchant of the people for many isles . . . [she] didst enrich the kings of the earth with the multitude of [her] riches and of [her] merchandise."

Although conquered by the Persians and by Alexander the Great, Phoenicia managed to retain for a while the leadership she had built up in trade and industry. Aided by their knowledge of navigation and geography and by their monopoly of such products as tin and dyestuffs, her middle classes, despite increasing competition, were able to prolong their prosperity until, finally, other peoples, especially the Greeks, began to follow Phoenician routes, thus destroying the exclusive control. In time the Phoenicians, like the Egyptians, became merged with their neighbors and were absorbed as a part of the Levantine trading and artisan groups.

By the fifth century B.C. the economic as well as the political leadership of the Ancient World had passed into the hands of the Greeks. Originally an agrarian people, the Greeks had gradually developed commercial and industrial interests, and soon there appeared between the nobles and peasants a middle class, concentrated in towns, and consisting of artisans, craftsmen, and merchants. At first this urban population, ruled as it was by the landed aristocracy, was not self-assertive; but during the so-called Archaic Period (1600–1100 B.C.) the situation gradually changed as trade between cities and even with foreign lands expanded rapidly and the business classes accumulated great wealth. As Glotz tells us in his *Ancient Greece at Work* (Kegan Paul, Trench, Trubner and Co., London; and Knopf, New York, 1926):

> A merchant class grew up, active, keen, and enlightened. It formed guilds . . . which stoutly defended their interests. It demanded written laws, and brought democracy into the constitutions; when it met with too strong resistance it set up a tyrant. It even placed its stamp on the intellectual life of the new Greece.

The landed aristocracy at first opposed the political aspirations of the middle classes. As early as the sixth century B.C., however, the tradesmen endeavored to break the power of the nobility by making wealth and not birth the basis of social distinction. At that time Greek political life was centered in the strong independent city-states. In many of these small political entities the bourgeoisie throughout the sixth and the fifth centuries B.C. revolted against the aristocracy. Often, when the landowners did not give way voluntarily, the middle classes reached their objectives by supporting tyrants. These dictators, usually from the aristocrats themselves, as recompense for such support, would modify the franchise of citizenship so as to include their backers, the rich element of the bourgeoisie. In Athens, Solon, one of these dictators, did this by arranging a new classification of the citizenry according to income, an early application of the *How Much Theory*. He also attacked the privileged position of the landowners by permitting the sale of land and by allowing an owner without direct heirs to will his property to whomsoever he pleased. Cleisthenes, another tyrant supported by the merchant classes, weakened the power of the landowners by wrecking the political influence of those old aristocrats.

Many prosperous Athenians harbored ambitions to play a part in politics some day and often their hopes came true. In 460 B.C. a gifted young noble named Pericles was elected general-in-chief of Athens. He placed himself at the head of a bourgeois party and for thirty years opposed the conservative aristocracy. Pericles dreamed of a new, beautiful, and wealthy city as the center of an Athenian Empire which should dominate the Greek world.

Athens, during the Periclean democracy which followed, became a bourgeois state. With birth no longer a qualification for political preferment, the business classes played a foremost rôle in the selection of governmental officials. Many of the prominent leaders were of bourgeois origin, as for example, Lysias and Demosthenes, two great orators, both of whom were sons of armorers.

Great riches, amassed by the middle classes as a result of economic expansion, explain the political rise of the Athenian bourgeoisie. In Solon's time and in the days of Pericles, Athens was a world market. The center of economic life was the *Agora,* the market place, the following description of which is from Calhoun's *The Ancient Greeks and the Evolution of Standards in Business* (Houghton Mifflin Co., Boston, 1926):

> At the foot of the Acropolis, crowned with the temples of the Gods, lay the noisy, crowded, ill-smelling retail market; not far away were the thronging wholesale districts and the dockyards of the *Piraeus,* and the grim industrial district about *Laurium,* where the air was polluted by the noisome fumes from innumerable smelters.

The *Agora* was the social as well as the business center of Athens. There all classes of Athenian society met and discussed the topics of the day. Among those to be encountered in the *Agora* was the new type of Greek social leader—the newly rich bourgeoisie, "forerunner of many modern 'self-made' men," described by W. A. Becker in *Charicles; or, Illustrations of the Private Life of the Ancient Greeks* (D. Appleton and Co., New York, 1866):

> Look at that man advancing towards us, followed by three slaves . . . His robe reaches to his ankles. . . . He talks loudly with his slaves of silver goblets, drinking horns, and bowls, so that the passers-by may hear, and puffs himself out, till the city seems almost too small for him. Now who do you think he is? A fellow of the meanest extraction, who has lately emerged from extreme indigence to great riches. . . . Not long ago I saw him in sordid garments. . . . At

present he would be vastly indignant if a badly dressed person presumed to address him.

Increase in the number of the bourgeoisie was encouraged during and immediately after the Periclean age as a result of a period of economic prosperity. The Greeks had traders in all parts of the known world who corresponded with one another. They had bankers in the key commercial cities who exchanged letters of credit. They had sailors in every great harbor who stood ready to carry out orders. In the industrial centers the small shops were still the general rule, but elsewhere were factories and mines in which hundreds of men were employed and in which great fortunes were invested. "The abler and more fortunate employers were doubtless accumulating capital with a ruthlessness characteristic of an age when men see or think they see avenues to unheard of wealth open to them," says Grundy in his *Thucydides and the History of His Age* (J. Murray, London, 1911). And Glotz amplifies this, declaring that

> Understandings were formed, cartels were created. The boatmen of Smyrna combined to abolish the disadvantages of competition and to raise prices, until the city came down on them with a crushing decree. Speculators had the inspiration of limiting production in order to impose their own prices.

Greek merchants, always alert to swell profits, recognized the value of advertising. In India, for example, they frequently made donations to the local temples. To reward them, statues, decorations, and other ornaments were prominently displayed with acknowledgments and commercial self-boasting quite evident, it naturally being expected that sales resistance would be lowered and good will engendered when the populace read the inscriptions. In such early fashion appear our modern methods of "smart" business.

In cultural as well as in economic life the Greek bourgeoisie played their part. Believers in education and individualism, they glorified Greek culture in all its forms, producing as a result many prominent members of the Greek intelligentsia from the middle classes—a preëminent example being the philosopher, Socrates, who, like his father, was a stone-cutter by trade.

Social reformers appeared in this Greek bourgeois society to oppose the privileges enjoyed by the nobility and by the wealthy business classes. The opposition was manifestly noticeable during periods of economic depression and especially after costly wars. Certain intellectuals openly criticized social conditions and often advocated almost revolutionary changes in order to better them. A few liberals, Plato, for example, even advocated the empirical establishment of a perfect social order. Plato's *Republic* is the written exposition of his ideal. Most thinkers, however, merely criticized the current situation. Aristotle did this in a very practical way when he wrote in his *Politics:*

> Men are easily induced to believe that in some wonderful manner everybody will become everybody's friend—especially when someone is heard denouncing the evils now existing in states, suits about contracts, convictions for perjury, flatteries of rich men and the like which are said to arise out of the possession of private property. . . . Ruined fortunes and revolutions go together.

Despite these criticisms and warnings, the bourgeois Greeks refused to give up their economic and political individualism. Living in small city-states they engaged in a number of civil and foreign wars which finally culminated in the Roman conquest of Greece. Greek business men now were deprived of political power save as Roman administrators. Excluded from politics, they increased their influence, however, in the fields of commerce and industry. Membership in the Alexandrian and later the Roman "Empires" opened the whole territory of the Mediterranean and near-by regions to their activities; and Greek economic expansion into Egypt, Syria, Persia, the Balkan peninsula, and even into Rome itself, reached tremendous proportions. In time Greek economic and cultural influence in the Roman Empire was so strong that the central part of that state was shifted in 330 A.D. to Constantinople, capital of the Eastern or Byzantine Empire. There Greek teachers,

Greek soldiers, Greek artisans, and above all, Greek merchants became the most vital elements.

In its early period of development Rome, like Egypt and Greece, was an agricultural and pastoral country, inhabited on the one hand by great landowners and on the other by poor shepherds and farmers. By the first century B.C. it had changed from a pastoral and agrarian to a trading and industrial state. The center of economic activity was the city of Rome with a population estimated at from several hundred thousand to eight million people. Commerce and banking were the outstanding pursuits. The prosperity of that metropolis rested largely on a profitable trade carried on with all parts of the ever-expanding Empire. Little heeded at first, colonial revolts and the attacks by enemy powers threatened the maintenance of this vital commerce, but leaders arose urging the Roman people to repel these invaders, arguing, as did the self-made orator, Cicero, when Rome was threatened by the Persians:

> If some lose their whole fortunes, they will drag many more down with them. Save the state from such a calamity; and believe me (though you see it well enough) that the whole system of credit and finance which is carried on here at Rome in the Forum, is inextricably bound up with the revenues of the Asiatic provinces. If those revenues are destroyed, our whole system of credit will come down with a crash. See that you do not hesitate for a moment to prosecute with all your energies a war by which the glory of the Roman name, the safety of our allies, our most valuable revenues, and the fortunes of innumerable citizens will be effectually preserved.

The "innumerable citizens" mentioned by Cicero constituted the Roman bourgeoisie of the late Republic and of Imperial Rome. They were concerned, for the most part, in the tremendous commerce which supplied the varied needs and luxuries of Rome, and had only supercilious scorn for those industries which were limited to the making of everyday essentials, carried on as they usually were by the lower strata of the population.

During this period the bourgeoisie were composed of three types. There were the nobles, who ranked just below the Senatorial group in the political and social system. A considerable part of their wealth was derived from the tax-farming companies and other concerns which contracted for government business. These men did not carry on business directly; agents managed their enterprises. A second section of the middle classes consisted of the free tradesmen who were in direct control of their enterprises. Like the nobles, they owned great tracts of land and a large number of slaves, and like them they were also interested in tax-farming and state contracts. The chief difference between the nobles and the business men was the relatively lower social standing of the latter. A third element of the middle classes included the freedmen. At first they suffered a certain social inferiority because of their servile origin, but in the second or third generations most of the distinctions disappeared and the grandsons of former slaves possessed the same social standing as that of the upper classes. Frequently they became as rich as the wealthiest nobles.

Most Roman business was conducted in a central place—here called a *Forum*—a combined Wall Street, Produce Exchange, Social Club, and Debating Hall. As in the Athenian *Agora,* large crowds collected to hear the latest news from all parts of the world. Another great center of trade was the *Emporium,* a wholesale trade and warehouse district. Oliver pictures the *Emporium* in his *Roman Economic Conditions* (University of Toronto Library, 1907):

> Here were boatmen shouting, stevedores loading and unloading, drays carting away the newly arrived merchandise, commission dealers buying and selling, and, ubiquitous as at the present day, customs officials.

There was also in Rome a Fifth Avenue, called the *Via Sacra.* It was filled with jewelers, metal founders, sculptors, artists, and other dealers in luxuries. Inasmuch as they obtained good prices for their products they were financially much better off than were the merchants who dealt in those necessities for which the price was relatively fixed and the profit necessarily small.

Outside the city the middle classes, composed of wealthy merchants, manufacturers, and retired capitalists, were even more authoritative than were the bourgeoisie in Rome. In that metropolis the nobility remained a powerful social and political force, but in the provinces the old aristocrats were so few in number that the tradesmen gained complete domination. They held all the central and lucrative municipal offices, and since in the Empire the cities were the provincial centers of government, they played an outstanding part in the administration of the entire state. Theirs were lives of ease, of power, of luxury, and of social supremacy.

Both in Rome and in the provincial cities the bourgeois standard of living was equal if not superior to that of the highest aristocracy. Scions of rich merchants were as well educated as sons of senators, and daughters of successful officials wore as fine trinkets as the haughty ladies. Possessing more money than the aristocrats, the shopkeepers became the leading patrons of art and connoisseurs of the various refinements of life. The luxury and debauchery which characterized the Roman Empire were largely the results of bourgeois extravagance. Morally the nobles were no better than the business classes, but financially they were unable to compete with their pleasure-loving countrymen. Indeed, the low moral standard of the bourgeoisie was reflected in their unethical business methods. Horace nicely expressed the bourgeois philosophy on this matter when he wrote:

> Seek money first, good friends, and virtue next;
> Each Janus lectures on the well worn text.
> Lads learn it for their lessons, gray-haired men
> Like school boys drawl the sing-song o'er again.

As in other states, the Roman merchants were not united. During the Augustan era (31 B.C.–14 A.D.) the rich business men who owed their wealth to the exploitation of the resources of the state and their political power to their wealth, joined with the semi-feudal landowners in the governing of the Roman Republic. The lesser middle classes and the proletariat, however, united in support of ambitious politicians and military leaders. In return these two groups were aided by the obligated emperors who adopted the senate, the body representing the municipal business men, as an advisory council.

Three definite stages mark the evolution of the rich bourgeoisie. In the first, lacking prestige, they were willing to cooperate with the landed aristocrats in the conduct of the state. In the Republican era, which was the second, a shift in policy took place, for as commerce, industry, and scientific agriculture developed and the lesser merchants became wealthier, they took over direct control of the city governments and supported leaders who would cater to their desires. But the municipal middle classes were unable to maintain their control, for rising cost of government, growing corruption, and continuous wars brought on such heavy taxes that the taxed became restive. When the big bourgeoisie tried to wring revenue out of the masses by means of merciless exploitation, they completed a destructive economic cycle by thus constricting the purchasing power of the workers. Small farmers began to find it unprofitable to till the soil as large estates cultivated by slaves, and the importation of cheap foreign wheat, lowered prices to sub-profit level. Out of jobs, thousands of peasants and workers became dependent on the community. In failing to remedy this ugly economic situation, the government was forced to establish a dole and thus to support the unemployed at public expense. Meanwhile, the petty bourgeoisie were crushed by the financial burden of taxation thrust upon them by the selfish landed and commercial aristocracy who refused to pay their share.

Unable by law to open their ranks to the lower classes, the big bourgeoisie paved the way for the third stage in their evolution—their decline. This began in the second half of the third century A.D., when a bitter civil and social war occurred between the property-owning groups and the masses. About the same time an acute economic depression was signalized by a rapid diminution of business activity in the various cities of the Empire. A desperate attempt was made to bring about economic recovery by setting up a form of state capitalism with full power lodged in the hands of a dictator. Gradually, however, the collapse of bourgeois business enterprises weakened the Roman Empire, and when the Barbarians swept across the frontier in the fourth and fifth centuries A.D. they encountered a state economically as well as morally and physically unable to offer real opposition.

Reduced in area after the Barbarian invasions, the Western Empire experienced a prolonged depression. The government, a Roman-Oriental fusion, refused to accede to the economic and political demands of the bourgeoisie; meanwhile, the nation began to go to seed. In what had been the great Roman Empire of the West, civilization reverted to its original state of agrarian simplicity. Crushed by German territorial conquests and Moslem control of the Mediterranean Sea, Western Europe became an agricultural area populated by small economically independent rural communities with a few minor towns. Once again the peasant and the landed proprietor had to break the ground for another bourgeois civilization.

Fortunately, the Barbarians failed to destroy the civilization of the Eastern or Byzantine state, which, although assailed on all sides by Slavs, Normans, Italians, and Turks, attained a period of real greatness. "The Empire," said a chronicler, "old woman that she is, appears like a young girl, adorned with gold and precious stones." Socially, the Byzantine Empire consisted of a theoretically absolute emperor, a bureaucracy, a landowning class, the bourgeoisie, and the working classes. Of all these groups the middle classes were the most vitalizing. Inhabiting the various cities, they were occupied with commerce, banking, and industry. To them, largely was due the rapid prosperity of the country. They were aided by the government, which, recognizing the need for economic development, intervened in business with the purpose of facilitating its expansion. Under the supervision of a governmental official, the Prefect, the various trades were organized into closed guilds, whose membership, wages, methods of manufacture, conditions of work, and prices were minutely regulated. Industrial life in all its aspects was carefully and frequently autocratically watched over by the government, so much so that Nicole, in his *Le Livre du Prefet,* described the great Byzantine metropolis, Constantinople, as "the paradise of monopoly, of privilege, and of protection."

The central administration not only protected and encouraged guild members, but also aided the consumers. Provision was made to maintain a "living wage" for the worker, to check the avarice of the capitalist, to eliminate the unproductive middleman, and to prevent the control of industry by a wealthy minority. Food regulations were especially detailed. The state, for example, determined the price at which food was to be sold and the price at which raw materials were to be bought. Moreover, the guilds could purchase materials in certain localities only; and to facilitate state control all sales were public and in general could be made only at prescribed places. Violations of these regulations were severely punished by exclusion from the guild, confiscation of property, fines, floggings, mutilation, or exile.

Our apparently "modern" economic ailments had their counterparts in the Byzantine Empire. Wealth tended to concentrate in the hands of a few; prices, especially of foodstuffs, soared; wages lagged behind. The public suffered. In search of a solution to these problems the government proceeded to regulate business, at the same time doing everything in its power to stimulate industrial activity. As a result, the Empire, during the early Middle Ages, was the economic as well as the intellectual center of the Mediterranean and Western world. Therefore, during the Renaissance, when Western Europe awakened from her winter of hibernation and ended her period of rural isolation, she received from the Eastern Empire not only the intellectual heritage of the Ancients, but also Oriental business methods, bourgeois concepts, and the model for future self-made men.

CHAPTER III

MEDIEVAL MAIN STREET

A Haberdasher *and a* Carpenter,
A Weaver, Dyer *and* Upholsterer. . . .
Each of them seemed a burgess proud, and fit
In guildhall on a dais high to sit;
And in discretion each was qualified
To be an alderman, and had beside
Income and goods sufficient for the station
Which would have filled their wives with jubilation
(*Hill,* Chaucer's The Canterbury Tales).

MEDIEVAL Main Street, with its bourgeois homes and small businesses, had no place in Western Europe during the first part of the Middle Ages, roughly from the fifth to the twelfth centuries A.D. For Western European society, consisting in general of the clergy, the nobility, and the serfs or peasants, was organized in small self-sufficient economic units—the agricultural manor villages—which had little need for business men to serve as economic go-betweens. Labor, industry, and agriculture were the prerogatives of the serf or slave class; few artisans and professional men hung out their shingles solely to attract upper-class patronage.

But, by the end of the twelfth century, the initial cobblestones werc laid for the medieval streets of Europe as the middle classes began to grow and to attain power and permanency. Of the steps or causes in their origin and development, although these are neither fixed in number nor easily analyzed, five seem outstanding: first, agricultural overproduction; second, trade guilds and town government; third, the Crusades; fourth, ravages of nature; fifth, formation of powerful kingdoms.

Agricultural overproduction was the open sesame to freedom and to consequent gain in status for an increasing number of serfs. According to the feudal system they were obligated to pay their lords certain fixed duties in return for the use of a definite allotment of land. Bountiful crops not only permitted them to pay the annual interest on this mortgage on their lives but also, by selling the surplus in the open market, to accumulate enough so as to cancel the contract—to purchase emancipation. With their newly gained economic liberty, they were free to start on the highroad toward elevation into the upper class strata.

Sometimes these peasants were so busy raising a surplus that they were not able to provide for themselves all the essentials of life; consequently, fairs and markets sprang up; artisans began to cater to this new trade; and soon certain places, called towns, were established about those trading centers that had attained a degree of permanency. The middleman fashioned himself a secure place in the affairs of trade. Thus we see the genesis of a laboring bourgeoisie and also of somewhat higher artisan-merchant classes.

Without coöperation and organization, however, these latter groups would have been in constant danger of dissolution by being pushed down among the lower brethren. Living in small and active towns, with similar interests and specialized talents, these people early learned the lesson of coöperation for the common good. A spirit of democracy arose, long to endure as a class characteristic. Resulting from identity of attitudes, the medieval guild solidified separate elements. These "associations of all persons enrolled in a particular craft or guild" provided coöperative facilities for the development of medieval commerce and industry by controlling the number of workers in the shop, the conditions of labor, the size of the output, and the quality and price of the goods.

Stemming from the guilds were the rising town governments, for the middle classes, having learned the power of collective effort, sought and obtained freedom from the control of the feudal lords and set up their own independent town administrations. Northern Italy seems to have been the birthplace of these burgher cities, largely because trade never fully died in Italy even with the devastating invasions of the barbarian hordes, and also because the Italian towns, being at the head of the Adriatic Sea and just south of the Alps, were the first to experience the revival of trade with the Orient. In addition to a favorable geographical location the Italian towns were aided by the struggles between the Holy Roman emperor and the pope, for both rulers, aware of the wealth of these cities, granted concessions in order to win their support. As a result, by the opening of the twelfth century, the Lombard cities were practically independent of outside control.

During the twelfth and the thirteenth centuries independent town organizations also appeared in France, in the Germanies, and in England. In some instances freedom was purchased from the rulers; frequently the townsmen won their charter by the sword; occasionally they obtained independence upon their lord's death. Many a small town, however, was established by a prince in coöperation with interested business men. He would select the site and lay out the market place, the streets, and the district for homes, then induce people to settle in his town by offering them in a solemn charter such inducements as exemption from arbitrary exactions and from all tolls within his realm. Although most of the citizens in the twelfth century lacked actual political control of the towns, they were promised equal justice, protection, and economic and legal freedom by their king. They were satisfied, for these were the things that they chiefly wanted. By the beginning of the fourteenth century the middle classes, through their position in these cities, were recognized legally as a class different from the serfs, peasants, and other townsmen.

The third influence in the evolution of the middle classes was a great religious and military movement—the Crusades (1096–1291). For one thing, to finance these expeditions, nobles and knights would often obtain the necessary funds by selling towns freedom in the form of charters; then, when many of these noblemen failed to return and their estates were broken up, those peasants who did not succeed in purchasing part of the land migrated to the cities to obtain work, thus swelling the population of these independent communities.

A greater and more permanent effect of the Crusades was

the tremendous acceleration of trade. Before these campaigns, commerce with the East had been mainly for the purpose of satisfying the needs of the church and the nobles. The demand, therefore, for goods was limited. But, as a result of the Crusades, silks, spices, and a wide variety of other products of the Orient became familiar to the people of Western Europe and the growing demand created a large market. Cities, concerned with the passage and handling of goods, appeared in various parts of Western Europe. In the interior of Northern Italy, towns controlling the Alpine passes leading to France and Germany benefited through this commerce. Later, cities in France and Germany along the trade routes north and south increased in wealth and in size. The Crusades, furthermore, did much to stimulate business enterprise. Great opportunities offered maritime commerce by the transport of Crusaders and by the increasing trade led to the formation of corporations and the development of complex forms of business administration. In brief, the mechanism of modern commercial life under which we live came into being in the commercial towns of Italy during and shortly after the Crusades.

Of the Crusades, the Third and Fourth are especially relevant. Desirous of earning greater profits by eliminating the Greek middlemen, the merchants of the Italian cities induced the Crusaders to forego the direct conquest of Jerusalem and instead to take possession of parts of the Levant. Then, in these cities Venetians, Genoese, and Pisans, among others, established trading depots and thus obtained direct access to the East. The Fourth Crusade was also primarily economic, rising out of the desire of the Venetians to control the valuable trade of Constantinople. In these undertakings the Italian bourgeoisie were aided by many noblemen who were financially interested in the business enterprises of these cities. Indeed, the Crusades, originally an attempt to regain the Holy Land for the Christians, had degenerated into an imperialistic struggle to conquer the East.

The fourth factor, an indirect one, contributing to the rise of the bourgeoisie, was the depletion in the ranks of the nobility through the numerous plagues, epidemics, and famines which afflicted Europe. Frequently their property was taken over by kings and transferred to small independent peasants who could be taxed. Moreover, their serfs, as mentioned before, often obtained freedom and went to the cities, where they added to the free labor supply which the middle classes needed in their activities. The decline of the privileged classes helped the bourgeoisie in another way. Monarchs, unable to rely upon the nobility, frequently summoned tradesmen to occupy administrative positions.

Formation of powerful kingdoms during the latter part of the Middle Ages also facilitated the rise of the business man. Eager to end the frequent wars, to abolish the numerous tariffs and tolls which hindered the development of commerce, and to see political and social order reëstablished, he supported the attempt of his king to extend the royal prerogative at the expense of the feudal lords. As these rulers gained in power they reciprocated by encouraging and promoting the advancement of commerce and industry, especially by raising armies and navies strong enough to safeguard traders on land and sea. By the close of the Middle Ages many kings consciously realized that the power of the monarchy was dependent, partly at least, upon the formation of a prosperous state and that such prosperity was furthered by the active commercial class. Therefore, they took a lively interest in trade and industry. Commercial treaties were negotiated; certain industries were encouraged by offering the workers and *entrepreneurs* attractive wages, privileges, and concessions. Ship owners were given protection against pirates. Some shippers even advocated the unification and standardization of the weights and measures used in their territories. In fact, these medieval sovereigns, desirous of promoting economic prosperity, sanctioned a policy of state intervention. Consequently, the tradesmen gladly supported the authority of their kings and willingly paid higher taxes.

As a result of these and other causes, by the thirteenth century Western Europe had a well-established, prosperous, independent middle class. During this and the succeeding century it began to consider itself as good as the privileged nobility and clergy, an attitude mirrored in such medieval poetic satires as the *Roman de la Rose,* the *Fabliaux,* the *Romans de Renard, Piers Plowman,* and the *Canterbury Tales.* "The rehabilitated merchants and artisans," writes Boissonnade, "escaping from the prison of serfdom, had become freemen. Better still, they had set themselves up as equals of the landed proprietor, the knight, and the clerk." An early fourteenth-century *Renard le Contrefait* praises the bourgeoisie thus:

> It is the best of all estates; they live very nobly, can wear clothes fit for a king; they have falcons . . . fine saddle horses. . . . when the knights are obliged to go to the army, the bourgeoisie stay in bed; when the knights go to be massacred in battle, the bourgeoisie go on swimming parties and picnics.

In the allegorical *Roman de la Rose* the royalty and nobility are regarded as creations of the people, chosen by them to provide protection and justice for the whole community. If the upper classes fail to carry out these duties, the people have the right to rebel by refusing to pay taxes. Thus the poem expresses the bourgeois doctrine of popular sovereignty. In *Piers Plowman* one finds exhibited a modern spirit in its outcries against the harsh and unjust social order, the worldliness of the church, and the cruel indifference of the ruling classes.

But it was Chaucer, himself an excellent example of a bourgeois citizen, who gave the best and most truly human picture of medieval life. Nowhere is there to be found a better portrayal of medieval society than in his *Canterbury Tales.* In them one finds a representative cross section of medieval England. His graphic portraits of the grave and courteous knight; the gay young squire; the dainty prioress; the worldly monk, friar, and pardoner; the humble parson; the coarse and vulgar shipman; the garrulous wife of Bath; and the studious clerk of Oxford, make the period live for the twentieth-century reader. Most members of the pilgrimage were from the middle class. Such was the Host himself. Such, too, was the Doctor, a thorough and perfect practitioner, and Alice, "the Good wife from near Bath":

She was a worthy woman all her life;
Five husbands had she had at the church-door,
Not counting other company in youth.

Such, too, were the Weaver, the Upholsterer, and the Dyer, all "clothed in liveree." Truly middle class was the Merchant:

There was a *Merchant* with a forked beard,
In motley dressed, and high on horse he sat,
Upon his head a Flanders beaver-hat;
His boots clasped fair and elegantly.
His words he spoke full solemnly,
Sounding always the increase of his winning.
He would the sea were kept for anything
Between Middleburg and Orwell.
He gained by the exchange when he did sell.
This worthy man employed his wit full cunningly
So that no one knew he was in debt,
So stately he was of demeanor
With his bargaining and his borrowing.
He was a worthy man withal,
But, in truth, I know not what men call him.

Turning from literature back to the public weal, we find that political influence as well as economic prosperity contributed to the dignification of the middle classes. In Northern Italy, as will be shown later, they dominated many of the prosperous city-states. In other countries of Western Europe they constituted the Third Estate in the various national assemblies created during the Middle Ages. Towns in Spain began to send representatives to the assembly, called the *Cortes,* about 1188. These delegates were expected by the king to help raise money for the needs of the state and to support him in his opposition to the powerful feudal nobility. In England, the towns did not obtain general representation in Parliament until 1265. As in Spain, the delegates from the towns were required to give the ruler financial support for his wars against France, Wales, and Scotland. In France the communes were represented in the

Estates General, first called by King Philip IV in 1302 in order that he too might obtain the backing of his people. In the Germanies, where a national state did not exist, and where the Holy Roman emperors actually exerted little influence, the burghers formed associations of towns, like those in Italy, at first for economic purposes, but soon also for political action. The greatest of these leagues was the Hansa, which rose out of certain minor commercial agreements made in 1241 by Hamburg and Lübeck. Inasmuch as the Holy Roman Emperor was unable to furnish the protection necessary to maintain trade, the merchants of the German trading centers had formed an organization designed to protect and to encourage commerce, especially in the Baltic. By the end of the fourteenth century the Hanseatic League had a written constitution and included in its membership eighty-five towns. In the fourteenth and fifteenth centuries this greatest of early middle-class economic organizations dominated the commerce and industry of Northern Europe.

Whereas in Germany the bourgeois classes were dominant in the political, as well as in the economic life of many cities, in France and England a different situation developed. As a result of the rise of a centralized monarchy, the towns in these countries lost their independence through the absorption of certain functions of local government by the royal officials. In return for this extension of royal power, the kings frequently augmented the political influence of the bourgeoisie by taking their representatives into the administration. During the reign of Louis XI of France, for example, business men filled most of the key positions in the internal administration.

In the late Middle Ages the general character of commerce and industry changed. Individual enterprises located in one city began to give way to business on a national or even on an international scale. By the end of the fifteenth century capitalistic production was beginning. Wealthy bourgeoisie organized banking associations with the purpose of advancing money to industrialists and merchants, rather than of doing business directly. This changed economic policy was exemplified in the rise of such great bourgeois families as the Welsers, the Baumgartners, and the Fuggers. Here is Gustave Huard's account of the Fuggers from *L'Évolution de la bourgeoisie Allemande* (Alcan, Paris, 1919):

> These Fuggers began to enrich themselves in the fourteenth century as weavers. In the following century they gave up their silk and wool business to deal only in banking and mining. Bankers to the princes, they were the Rothschilds of that day. The Hapsburgs . . . borrowed from them repeatedly; Maximilian and Charles V were their clients and ennobled them. Montaigne mentions them in connection with his voyage to Germany: "One of that family, dying several years ago, left the equivalent of 2,000,000 écus to his heirs, for the prayers for his soul, gave the Jesuits there thirty thousand florins, for which they accommodated him very well."

In their private lives members of the middle classes were tremendously influenced by the great wealth which they accumulated from their capitalistic, commercial, and industrial enterprises. On their Medieval Main Streets, especially in the Germanies, they constructed magnificent houses. According to Montaigne, buildings in Augsburg were "much finer, larger, and higher than in any city in France, and the streets were much broader." The dwellings of the rich bourgeois inhabitants compared favorably with the palaces of kings. It was said of Antoine Fugger that he could lodge the emperor and the emperor's entire retinue in his house. The shopkeepers, claims Boissonnade, often "adopted the magnificent and luxurious ways of the high aristocracy. Men such as the patricians of Venice, Jacques Coeur, or the Portinari at Bruges dwelt in palaces or mansions worthy of princes."

The rise of these able capitalists, as Boissonnade points out in *Life and Work in Medieval Europe* (Knopf, New York, 1927), had its ugly side. Into the medieval economic organizations was brought "unrest and pernicious ways, reckless speculation, the practice of rings and monopolies, even of cartels, the most complete absence of scruples, and a contempt for every law of morality." As a result of these practices a great part of the bourgeoisie sank to a status equivalent to that of the modern proletariat. In the fourteenth century the poor apprentice had no hope of becoming a master, for the guilds demanded large fees and long, costly masterpieces from these men; while the way was made easy for the sons and relatives of the master. This exclusiveness of the guilds gave rise to a class of industrial workers who did not own the shops in which they worked and sometimes did not own their tools. Consequently, they lived on the daily wages they received from the master. In other words, they sold their labor to the highest bidder in the open market.

All through the century from 1340 to 1450, group antagonisms made themselves felt within the middle classes. "The last century of the Middle Ages," writes Boissonnade, "is *par excellence* the century of urban revolts." Oppressed by the very rich merchants and industrialists who controlled the municipal administrations, the petty bourgeoisie and working men frequently revolted in order to gain control of the cities and to force concessions from the wealthy oppressors. These uprisings occurred in every part of Europe, but they were most violent and frequent in the great towns of Flanders and Lombardy.

Twice the lower classes in Flanders united in inter-city leagues to oppose the designs of their wealthy persecutors. In 1338–1345 under the leadership of James Van Artevelde, a man of good family, they vainly tried to better conditions. In 1378, led by Philip Van Artevelde they began a second attempt, this last revolt ending in a great battle in 1382 in which 26,000 of these petty bourgeois and proletarian "radicals" were said to have been killed by the troops of their powerful opponents. Medieval Main Street ran with blood.

In the cities of Lombardy a series of revolts occurred about the same time. The lower classes rose up, terrorized their rich enemies, took power into their hands, and attempted radical reforms. All during the fourteenth century the Lombard and central Italian towns were torn by civil wars, with the upper middle classes losing their position of dominance in almost all of the cities. Unable to combat successfully the alliance between the petty bourgeoisie and the proletariat, the wealthy groups often gave their support to despots. These so-called tyrants, frequently military leaders, rewarded their rich backers by rigorously suppressing radical movements and disarming the lower classes. Thus the despotism and tyrannies of the Renaissance, to be discussed later, were primarily the result of the struggle between the well-to-do upper bourgeoisie, and the masses.

In France, the Holy Roman Empire, England, and even in Spain, similar agitations by the lesser middle classes and the proletariat against the wealthy bourgeoisie occurred. In these countries the internal conflicts of the business men, however, enabled the kings to bring all groups under control of the state as the monarchs forced various classes to subordinate their antagonisms for the general welfare of the monarchy. But the establishment of the modern absolute state did not signify the political and economic downfall of the middle classes. Instead, the disruption of the old feudal order, which accompanied the rise of absolutism in the Middle Ages, was an integral step in the formation of our modern bourgeois and capitalistic society.

In retrospect, as we survey the conditions out of which the middle classes evolved, the obstacles which they surmounted, and the prestige that they attained by the end of the medieval period, we cannot help but second the assertion of Boissonnade that the gradual rise "of millions of men belonging to the commercial and industrial classes, to whom the marvelous expansion of urban life was due, is one of the capital events of history."

Chapter IV

TIDES IN THE AFFAIRS OF MEN

There is a tide in the affairs of men,
Which, taken at the flood, leads on to fortune;
Omitted, all the voyage of their life
Is bound in shallows and in miseries.
And we must take the current when it serves,
Or lose our ventures

(*Shakespeare,* Julius Caesar).

In the affairs of the middle-class men at the inauguration of the modern period (c. 1500), there were two tides, taken at the flood, which led them on to fortune. These were the Italian Renaissance and the Commercial Revolution, the first two of a series of changes which had their origins deep in the late Middle Ages, and which, with their successors, the Religious Revolt, the Mercantile System, the Technological Revolution, and the Industrial Revolution, resulted in fundamental economic, intellectual, and religious modifications in the whole social macrocosm. Whatever the effects were on society as a whole, in particular they consistently contributed to the continued growth of the middle classes.

Of these early revolts, the Italian Renaissance meant most to the bourgeoisie for within it were the germs of economic prowess and of social respectability, both so ardently desired by the struggling upstarts, and of a rebirth of individualism, so essential in their political economy. A town movement, the Renaissance was essentially middle class, participated in at the beginning by those burghers of the Lombard cities of Northern Italy who refused to remain "common men." Wide awake, they observed the possibilities of profits inherent in the perceptible revival of trade and industry after the Crusades. With these profits they supported financially an intellectual revolution—the Renaissance. As we shall see, this revolution, by sanctioning their economic pursuits, made them more than just middle-class men; it made them gentlemen, patrons of the arts.

At the time of the Renaissance, the Italian bourgeoisie was divided into two main groups—the capitalist or large property owner, and the lesser middle-class man or small property owner. Both consisted of merchants, shippers and carriers engaged in the transportation of merchandise, builders of boats and wagons, and many varieties of artisans. Lawyers, doctors, musicians, artists, writers, teachers, and mercenary soldiers also belonged to this social order. The bourgeoisie, in brief, was the money-making class.

As a result of their financial ability the Italian business men of the fifteenth century dominated the economic life of Europe. They were pioneers in the formation of commercial, industrial, and banking organizations; in the invention of the double-entry system of bookkeeping; in the management of colonies; and in the advancement of navigation. In 1450 there were few financiers to compare with the Medici, Portinari, Sassetti, and Guidetti. Commercial arithmetic and bookkeeping were in use in Italy during the fourteenth century, Florence alone having six schools of commercial arithmetic, regularly attended by 1200 pupils. Italian merchants and bankers also introduced into European countries the bill of exchange and other instruments of banking and economics. The number of Italian words in current economic use, such as di*sconto, netto, deposito, fòglio,* and *bilàncio,* indicates the extent of Italian influence on business.

Italy became the fountain of economic knowledge and activity. Italian bankers helped to organize the finances of kingdoms and to spread the knowledge of economic practices throughout Europe. Venice was for many years the training school for the merchants of the South German cities. Jacob Fugger, for example, learned his business in Italy, where his brothers had warehouses. English merchants gained the knowledge of commercial methods from Italian traders and bankers, and the latter were encouraged to bring their ideas to the French court and to the French industrial centers. Italian traders and bankers also played leading rôles in building up the prosperity of the burghers of Bruges, Antwerp, and Amsterdam.

Owing largely to bourgeois demands, Italian universities as early as the twelfth century revived instruction in Roman Law. This legal system had been originated in a capitalistic age and its spirit was capitalistic. It permitted the taking of interest; it sanctioned the profit system; it recognized the sanctity of private property; and it emphasized the authority of the secular ruler. As a whole, it tended to undermine the medieval system which stressed the idea of a just price, and therefore it was not only introduced in Italy but it was also adopted in most capitalistic states.

Even though they possessed great economic power, the Italian bourgeoisie were always self-conscious over living in a social order which looked down upon them and disdained their enterprises. For, during the Middle Ages, men were more interested in theological and philosophical problems than they were in political, economic, and social matters. Man was supposed to devote his mundane bodily existence to preparing for an eternal life of the spirit. The worldly career of winning a living and piling up wealth was, at best, a necessary preoccupation. Usury was frowned upon, and the fair or just price in commercial transactions was considered all that a merchant should expect. Production, as a rule, was for immediate consumption. Men were restricted by the feudal system, by the church, and by tradition.

As society became more orderly a sense of security developed. The influence of the established order lessened, for a gradual rise of personal confidence quickened the interest of the bourgeoisie in the world about them. Boldness supplanted fear; individualism replaced feudalism; and optimism triumphed over apocalypticism.

The thirteenth and fourteenth centuries marked the rise of the Italian business men. They overthrew the rule of the hereditary nobility and set up a democracy; gradually this new government gave way to a body politic dominated by a plutocracy of successful merchants who frequently substituted the tyranny of money for the despotism of birth; finally the plutocrats created their own hereditary nobility. Florence and other Italian cities conferred titles on their illustrious "self-made men." The bourgeoisie had made possession of money a mark of personal merit.

Determined to establish their economic practices as legal and their social positions as respectable, the Italian business classes welcomed the revival of learning in the fifteenth and sixteenth centuries as the means to these ends. In their opinion the attempt to imitate the ancients, who were interested in worldly things, meant a justification of bourgeois standards. Consequently, most wealthy men took keen delight in becoming patrons of a learning which would sanction worldly rather than spiritual ways of living. The Greek and Roman freemen enjoyed the material and sensual sides of life. Why shouldn't the Italians do likewise and develop a great materialistic civilization?

Many comforting concepts appeared to substantiate this aim. In his popular works, L. B. Alberti, for example, maintained that expenditure should never exceed income, that saving is a virtue, and that idleness and extravagance are two cardinal sins. Diligence and application are the source of all power. The Renaissance, indeed, gave business men an opportunity not only to justify their earthly doings but also to build up an aristocracy determined by wealth and education rather than by land and blue blood, a social status based upon attainment rather than upon birth. To their satisfaction, Renaissance scholars discovered that in his *Politics* the great Aristotle had defined nobility as resting upon excellence and wealth. In later times their own Dante dissociated *nobile* from the condition of birth and placed it upon capacity for moral and intellectual eminence. He considered his own nobility as a mantle from which time was ever cutting something away unless he added fresh worth to it. Niccoli, an eminent scholar, completely satisfied the ambitious bourgeoisie when he wrote that he believed the Roman word *nobilis* (remarkable) was more appropriate than *nobile* since it would make man's social position depend upon his deeds. In general, these Renaissance writers made one outstanding contribution to the business men in their opposition to aristocracy—they justified achievement as the real criteria of nobility.

Individualism in the political, economic, and intellectual world was the one distinguishing characteristic of the Renaissance. Scholars glorified the dignity of man. They honored man as a rational, volitional being who was free to shape his career according to his abilities. As such, individualism was well brought out in Machiavelli's *The Prince,* throughout which he paid glowing tribute to personal merit, honorable or otherwise. Those, he said, who came to power by their own efforts found it possible to preserve with "little trouble what it cost . . . infinite efforts to gain." No group welcomed this emphasis upon individual success in politics, as well as in literature and in art, more than did the middle classes. A passion for personal freedom and political glory inspired them with the desire to scale the heights of political and social power. Francesco Sforza, a peasant, became Duke of Milan; Benvenuto Cellini, whose *Autobiography* symbolizes Renaissance individualism, boasted in having been born humble and of having laid a greater foundation for his family than if he had been born of great lineage; Lorenzo de Medici took time from the business of statecraft and from his commercial pursuits to write poems that "would form a creditable tale of production for a life of leisure."

Individualism helps to explain many contradictions and characteristics of bourgeois life. As a tradesman the Italian was determined to attain success at whatever cost; as a patron and lover of the humanities he was a finely civilized person. Torn between the claims of nature and those of humanity he often forgot the idealism of Plato and frequently tortured and murdered innocent rivals who stood in his way. By so doing, rugged individualist of rugged stock that he was, he rode successfully the ruthless currents of that period.

Unbounded egotism and astounding versatility were often the results of this Renaissance individualism. Cellini, for example, was a law unto himself; even Pope Paul III, when he heard that this disorderly genius had committed murder in the streets of Rome, calmly said: "Artists of the valor of Benvenuto are superior to communal laws." This braggart also typified the unusual versatility of his age. Artist, soldier, musician, and writer, he well represented that bourgeois ambition which caused Renaissance merchants, bankers, and politicians to express themselves in many fields of endeavor.

Despite this individualism the Italian business men imitated the nobility in many ways. For example, like the aristocrats they enjoyed amusements and all kinds of entertainments. Elaborate arches, gates, and columns were set up to greet distinguished guests; and the projections of houses and roofs were pulled down because they interfered with the advance of glittering processions. Games were many and popular. Football, known as *calcio,* was played by two teams arrayed in brilliant colors. Volley ball, or *pallone,* was so irresistible to middle-class men that many of them, as today with golf, neglected business affairs for it. Gambling and music were common parlor amusements.

Since Renaissance culture stressed social life, bourgeois men and women wanted to look well. Both sexes wore wigs and corsets and used cosmetics to improve their appearance. Clothes became so elaborate and costly that the more frugal business men banded together to pass ordinances regulating expensive details in dress.

Influenced by this emphasis upon personal achievement, many successful men were especially eager to assume the rôle of patrons of the Renaissance. "Every man of position," writes the historian Sismondi, "from mercenary captain to the merchant, spent an income on scholars that would serve today . . . to carry a family through the artificial conventionalities of a London season." Although prudent and often frugal, these bourgeois patrons had a sincere and intelligent love of refinement. The Medici family of Florence was typical. Rising from obscurity as pawn brokers, this family came into prominence in Florence through the successful business dealings of Cosimo de Medici (1389–1464), a shrewd Florentine, who, having accumulated great wealth, tried to displace a member of the noble house of Albizzi as the leader in Florentine affairs by liberally patronizing the Renaissance scholars. Exiled by his rivals, he later returned to Florence and made it worth while for scholars and artists to take up their residence in that city. For instance, through his influence, a scholar, Poggio by name, with his illegitimate family of fourteen children, was exempted from taxation because he had come to Florence to live by study and not by traffic in merchandise; Vespasiano, a bookseller, was commissioned by Cosimo to establish a library in Florence; and Fecino, son of Cosimo's physician, was made head of the Platonic Academy founded at Florence by this famous Medici patron. Merchants, travelers, and missionaries were lured by rich rewards to be on the lookout for manuscripts.

Lorenzo the Magnificent, another member of the Medici family, was perhaps the leading patron of the Renaissance. No individual in Florence was able to amass such a vast treasury of books, antiques, paintings, and bric-a-brac. Proud of his bourgeois origin, he had the satisfaction of bestowing his money as a patron of art and learning in such a way as to bring prestige to his class. "A considerable sum," wrote Lorenzo with reference to the amount of money he had spent on buildings and alms, "but I do not regret it. Many think it would have been better to have kept some of it in our pockets; but for my part, I regard it as an honour to our house."

The culture which they so freely bestowed to some extent clung to the givers. If not genuine, the social polish of the ambitious bourgeoisie had at least as fine a glitter as that of the nobility. At first the members of this social class had considered education only as a means of fostering the money-making powers of their sons, for as bankers, traders, manufacturers, and landowners, they could readily see the practical value of education; consequently, children were hastily schooled in the rudiments of business and put directly to work at the occupations of their fathers. But, as the bourgeois gentleman grew wealthier, he came to rely more and more upon hired assistants; thus it became less and less necessary for his son to go to work at an early age. Therefore, the ambitious father, wishing to match the abilities of his offspring with the prowess of the nobility, sent the youngster "to college," where he became familiar with languages, literature, music, the fine arts, and such frills as the hitherto upper-class pastime of dancing and the delicate, psychological art of love-making. In general, the boy was to ape the gentry by becoming proficient in all noble sports; willy-nilly, he was to be pumped full of a little medieval chivalry.

Fixed rules of etiquette were set up by the new learning. Determined to possess fine manners, the wealthy classes tried to polish what manners they already possessed and to become "perfect gentlemen" by acquiring new ones. Numerous "What Every Gentleman Should Know" handbooks were published. Castiglione's *The Courtier,* for example, described the real society man as an urbane, suave person, familiar with the study of the humanities; Casa's *Il Galateo* was devoted entirely to telling the business man what to do in polite society; Bonvesin da la Riva, a professor of rhetoric at Milan, wrote on "the courtesies of the table."

Italian middle-class people tried to attain social distinction by personal achievement in art and literature as well as by good manners. Most of the Renaissance artists and scholars were of the business classes and the proletariat. Raphael, Leonardo da Vinci, and Cellini, for example, in their personal lives and also in their works of art, revealed such bourgeois characteristics as versatility, worldliness, and individualism.

Perhaps no writer of that period understood the money-makers better than Boccaccio. In his famous *Decameron* he describes Italian society just leaving the Middle Ages. Only a few of the bourgeois characters have put on the finer garments of culture. These few are accepted in Boccaccio's intellectual group; the others, who have wealth but nothing else, are ridiculed by the author. Especially does he delight in poking fun at the selfish merchant who has failed to achieve culture and refinement.

Despite these invasions into the realms of politics, learning, and society, the Italian self-made men were unable to make their economic livelihood respectable throughout Western Europe. Banking, commerce, and manufacturing, they realized, were not recognized as genteel occupations. Money gained by hard work was tainted, while hereditary wealth was estimable. Therefore, the European bourgeoisie as a whole retained an inferiority complex which often intensified their hatred of the two primary forces opposed to their social ambitions—the feudal nobility and the Christian hierarchy.

By another early modern upheaval, the Commercial Revolution (c. 1400–c. 1700), the middle classes were granted a second helpful opportunity to weaken feudal and religious opposition and to advance socially. Called a revolution because of the primary alterations it made in business, in trading, in shipping, in the financial aspects of commerce, and in the theories underlying economic practice, this transformation brought with it a growing recognition of the rôle of the merchant classes in the quickening of business activity.

Revival of trade with the East, the establishment of strong monarchical states, and the decline of the self-sufficient life of the Middle Ages prepared the way for the Commercial Revolution. But the Age of Discovery, in which Vasco da Gama visited India via the Cape of Good Hope and Columbus discovered America, precipitated this economic resurrection. Accompanying the establishment of overseas empires, the center of economic activity passed from the ports around the Mediterranean to the Atlantic sea coast. As markets expanded, commerce flourished and shipping tonnage increased. Spain, Portugal, France, the Spanish Netherlands, and England engaged in extensive commercial and colonial undertakings. Such cities as Lisbon, Nantes, Antwerp, and London became the economic centers of Europe.

Many were the products that began to appear for the first time or in greater quantities in these market centers. Gold and silver were brought from the New World. Tea, sugar, and tobacco were introduced. More cargoes of pepper, spices, and cloves were imported from the East. Demand was stimulated until soon luxuries had become necessities. Moreover, as cities grew in size, the exchange of stable goods such as fish, grain, and timber expanded.

This revolution, resulting in the establishment of colonial empires, filled the coffers and augmented the power of the bourgeoisie in Western Europe. Shrewd merchants were very quick to see the profits of coöperation. In the Middle Ages business had been carried on for the most part by individuals, the guilds, strictly speaking, not being "business" associations, and what few partnerships existed being on a small scale. Colonial trade, however, now needed considerable capital to purchase goods, to build ships and warehouses, and to hire workers. As a result, men began to pool their resources. Various trading alliances were organized, including the chartered companies. These organizations were granted privileges and frequently subsidies by the home government. In these firms the idea of defining rights and privileges, found in medieval communities and in modern constitutions, was applied to business undertakings. In this way the small investors were able to join the wealthy individuals in a business project. A community of interests arose between the two groups, a factor not to be underestimated, for it meant that all elements in society participated in this commercial expansion of the individual national units.

By making necessary a money economy, the expansion of trade promoted the commercial calling of the bourgeoisie. Barter and local coinage were acceptable in the Middle Ages when trade was limited and goods were sold at a just price based on cost of production rather than on supply and demand; during the early modern period, however, commerce became international, and so some universally satisfactory medium of exchange had to be devised. Another imperative reason for a money system was that governments, forced to maintain large standing armies, found it difficult to pay their soldiers and officials in goods. Taxes in the form of money were needed. The great influx of gold and silver coming into Europe at this time led to the establishment of the modern coinage systems. Whereas in the Middle Ages most of the small supply of precious metals was held by the church, in the sixteenth and seventeenth centuries gold and silver became the common medium of exchange. Barter practically vanished. By possession of these precious metals traders were able to have warehouses built, boats constructed, and workmen hired for wages. Governments found it possible to collect taxes in the form of money. For these reasons, the number of persons engaging in various enterprises and securing their livelihood by wages in the form of gold and silver steadily multiplied.

Money economy and modern capitalism insured the supremacy of the bourgeoisie. The profession of banking, involving the creation of credit and the taking of interest, enabled business men to accumulate fortunes. The Medicis of Florence, the Coeurs of Bruges and Paris, and the Welsers and Fuggers of the Germanies, were a few of the wealthy self-made men of this era. Connected with banks, trading companies, mines, and other forms of economic enterprises, these "millionaires" of the sixteenth century by means of loans to kings, for instance, exerted indirect but tremendous political power.

As these traders and bankers waxed wealthy, their exploitations were followed by a rise in the cost of living. High prices, it is true, were largely due to the increased amount of bullion made available through importation from the New World and through extensive mining in Europe; but they were also the result of monopolies set up by grasping merchants and money changers. By the early sixteenth century these bourgeoisie in certain towns, especially in the Germanies, were able to boost the cost of necessities as well as of luxuries by controlling the entire supply—"cornering the market."

This rise in the cost of living enabled the wealthy business men to profit at the expense of the other social classes. The landed proprietors—the nobility—found it difficult to enjoy the advanced scale of living which the Commercial Revolution was making available. As farmers their incomes were limited. They could, of course, add to their revenues slightly by levying in violation of previous agreements additional fees upon their peasants; but this procedure did not augment their incomes enough to permit them to vie with the upper bourgeoisie in the "art of living," while at the same time it antagonized the workers. Many German lords raised their feudal levies upon the peasants, and this was a contributory cause for the Peasants' Revolt of 1524–1525. In this uprising the peasants protested against these obnoxious taxes and requested their lords to abide by the contracts which had been in existence for many years. Faced by this problem of diminishing income, numerous French noblemen gladly accepted governmental positions and sinecures as a means whereby they could retain the social supremacy they had long enjoyed.

Not only the wage-earners, but also the small merchants and artisans, suffered as a result of the higher cost of living. Consequently, in the sixteenth and seventeenth centuries they became distinctly hostile to the great commercial enterprises organized by such capitalists as the Fuggers and the Welsers. The petty bourgeoisie claimed that the great trading concerns built up monopolies which were responsible for "huge prices, scarcity of money, adulteration of foods, and corruption of officials charged with enforcing the laws against monopoly." The capitalists also were accused of ruining the small freehold farmer by advancing him money on his land at usurious rates of interest and then foreclosing when he could not pay. Being unable to compete with the large companies, the small merchant was either forced out of business entirely or compelled to buy his goods from the big concerns.

The monopolists in the Germanies, as will be shown later, were especially powerful. To secure relief from these forces of economic strangulation, numerous schemes of reform were proposed: some revolutionary, others reactionary; some local, others universal. Few were carried out. Moreover, in opposing the monopolists, none of the petty bourgeoisie thought of winning allies by elevating the wage-earners to their level and conferring upon them the advantages which they themselves possessed.

In the Germanies and in Italy, the Commercial Revolution, in the long run, injured the big bourgeoisie, as well as the other economic groups. Up to about the middle of the sixteenth century the German plutocrats had prospered and were a recognized leading element in society. Then a period of decadence took place. One of the chief causes of this economic decline was the discovery of America and the opening of new trade routes to India and the Orient, for henceforth the cities of Western Europe became the great commercial towns, and such trading centers as Hamburg, disadvantageously located, experienced a general commercial depression.

At the same time a significant financial crisis occurred. The drop in the value of money, which took place in Europe during the latter part of the sixteenth century, hit the German bankers hard. In addition, the failure of many speculations and the bad faith of a number of rulers to whom the bankers had lent money resulted in disastrous bankruptcies. Even the wealthy Fugger family lost most of its fortune in a few years and was saved from total ruin only through the possession of great rural domains.

This depression helped to bring about the dissolution of the Hanseatic League. Moreover, after the Discoveries, trade in northern waters could no longer be monopolized by the Germans. Attacked by the superior Dutch and the strong British navies, threatened by the rise of hostile Slavic states, and unable to find political support in a disunited, weak empire, the Hanseatic League disintegrated rapidly.

The Thirty Years' War (1618–1648) was the final stage in the steady decline of the early German bourgeoisie. Prior to this conflict, the internal market offered the merchant some hope of salvation. But the terrible, long struggle, fought largely on home soil, ruined the Germanies. At least one half of the population was destroyed, and the loss of property was disastrous. Meanwhile, the center of gravity in European trade and industry had gradually shifted from the Mediterranean and the Baltic to the Atlantic seaboard.

In Western Europe, strong kings, wealthy traders, and shrewd money-lenders were the chief beneficiaries of the Commercial Revolution. Monarchs, often backed financially and politically by the middle classes, were able to exert strict control over their feudal subjects and at the same time to defeat their royal neighbors. Increased taxes, the result of economic prosperity, permitted the enlarging of military and naval forces. With this, various rulers became power-conscious, determined to make vast empires out of their little kingdoms.

The bourgeoisie were able to obtain a slight degree of political and social as well as great financial power from the Commercial Revolution. Some of them gained governmental positions, which frequently accorded them a certain social distinction that they very much desired. At the same time they were expected to support by their trade and industry the privileged hierarchy of nobles and clergy as necessary parts of the absolute monarchy. Thus, despite their commercial and intellectual advances the middle-classes, nevertheless, remained a part of "the forgotten men of the Middle Ages"—the Third Estate.

Chapter V

MESSIAHS OF THE MIDDLE CLASSES

For nothing is more unseemly than a man that is idle and good for nothing—who profits neither himself nor others, and seems born only to eat and drink. . . . It is certain that idleness and indolence are accursed of God (John Calvin).

In the time of the Roman Empire the Christian church smiled upon the middle classes who were oppressed by intolerable taxes, but in the Middle Ages it frowned upon these ambitious men. Staunch defender of the established order, it favored the hierarchy of classes and feared the anarchy of individualism. Subordination of the material to the spiritual side of life was its constant aim; therefore it tended to oppose usury and to advocate such medieval economic beliefs as the "just price." Despite this emphasis upon "other worldliness," the church itself possessed great wealth and so laid itself open to overt criticism. Something had to give, and the result was the Protestant Reformation. Its guiding spirits, Luther and Calvin, by their doctrines deserve to be known as the Messiahs of the Middle Classes.

Political decentralization in Central Europe made the Germanies a logical place for the uprising to begin; there the Holy Roman Emperor exerted little real authority and in that section there existed a definite desire on the part of many local rulers to promote their own independence by obliterating his influence completely. Besides decentralization, materialism, often the twin brother of "prosperity," also explains the Germanic origin of the Protestant Revolt. At the opening of the sixteenth century, German merchants in Venice handled a major portion of the goods imported from the East. "Germany," wrote Jacob Wimpheling, a famous scholar of that time, "was never more prosperous than today, and she owes it chiefly to the untiring industry and energy of her people, artisans as well as merchants." During this period of prosperity the accumulation of wealth became the all-absorbing passion. "All the world is running after those trades and occupations that will bring the most gain," said the popular preacher, Martin Butzer, in denouncing this materialistic spirit. "All the clever heads which have been endowed by God with capacity for the nobler studies are engrossed by commerce, which nowadays is so saturated with dishonesty that it is the last sort of business an honest man ought to engage in" (quoted in Schapiro's *Social Reform and the Reformation,* Columbia University Press, 1909).

Augsburg was the center of trade in Central Europe. From here eastern goods were distributed. In 1503 the Welser firm of Augsburg secured privileges and established a warehouse in Lisbon. Huge profits were made. The capital of the Fuggers rose from 196,761 gulden in 1511 to 2,021,202 gulden in 1527 and yielded a yearly profit of fifty-four and a half per cent on the investment. With the increase of trade via the Atlantic, the German traders had to transport goods in large quantities and in big ships. More capital was necessary, and therefore organizations of rich merchants for transporting and selling goods came into existence. The small merchant found himself crowded to the wall. Martin Luther, in his pamphlet *On Trade and Usury* (1524) indicted the sordidness of Big Business, saying: "The monopolists succeed in driving out the small merchants by buying up large quantities of goods, and then suddenly raise the prices when they are left masters of the field. So, these monopolists have everything in their hands, and whenever they wish, raise and lower prices at will, and oppress and ruin small dealers." Lucas Rem, the merchant chronicler of Augsburg, wrote a very enlightening description of a wealthy German trader. "This man," said Rem, "had the reputation of being a good Christian, yet he often oppressed the common man. He would buy up at good bargains all the ashwood, corn, and wine, and keep them in storage until a great demand arose for them when he would sell at very high prices. . . . No merchant worth less than 100,000 florins could compete with him."

At first monopolies were largely confined to goods imported from the East, but before long, large companies began to control domestic products. This, together with the fall in the value of money, caused prices to skyrocket. High prices led consumers to grumble against the unchristian monopolies of merchants. According to the fiery German patriot, Ulrich von Hutten, there were four classes of robbers: merchants, jurists, priests, and nobles—and the greatest of them all were the merchants.

Despite these complaints, the monopolists had their defenders. Replying to a committee appointed by the Diet of Nuremberg in 1522 to investigate monopolies, the city officials of Augsburg declared that great companies were necessary to business and that business was the foundation of every powerful state. Regulation of these companies would cause them to go elsewhere and the country would suffer. Moreover, any attempt to limit the profits of these concerns would injure the widows, orphans, and other innocent people who lived by investments in these enterprises. "How then can one say that the rich trample down the poor when they actually save them from their own incompetence and misfortune?" As a result of this investigation a decree limiting and regulating trade in eastern goods was passed. It was never effectively enforced. The great companies were so wealthy, the cities they controlled so powerful, the central government so weak, and the relations of political office holders and companies were so close (the former often shared in the profits of the companies or were bribed) that the monopolies continued unchecked.

Antagonism between the great traders and the petty bourgeoisie indicated the social unrest which existed among all classes in the early sixteenth-century Germanies. Nobles, peasants, and wage-earners, as well as the lower middle classes, were dissatisfied. High prices naturally lessened the purchasing power of their revenues and their wages. Determined to better their economic status they were ready to oppose any institution or individual which stood in their way.

The Christian church became the focal point of opposition.

Not only did many men envy the wealth of that organization, but also they opposed the heavy taxes exacted by it. One source of church income was especially unpopular—the indulgence, whereby a man by payment of money hoped to escape punishment for his sins. A crisis was reached when the church, through the sale of indulgences, was involved in the fight between the wealthy merchants and the petty bourgeoisie. The former often advanced money to individuals who sought positions in the church. They loaned, for example, a sum of money to Albrecht of Brandenburg which enabled him to become archbishop of Mainz. In order to regain this money, plus a good rate of interest, the capitalists who had made the loan sent an agent to accompany the churchman John Tetzel on his money-raising campaign.

As the story has it, when Tetzel began his rather promiscuous sale of indulgences in the vicinity of Wittenberg he stirred the ire of Martin Luther (1483–1546) a young, recently consecrated doctor of divinity, who was preaching in the castle church. It was Tetzel's showmanship to carry a chest with him; when a person dropped a coin, the ringing sound as it hit the bottom was supposed to signify the departure of the soul from purgatory on its route to paradise. "God willing," said Luther, "I will beat a hole in his drum." Angered, Luther nailed his ninety-five theses attacking Tetzel on the church door. In less than a fortnight they were known all through the Germanies. Even the pope read them, for he invited Luther to the Vatican, an invitation which the reformer decided it might be safer to decline. In the revolt which resulted, the petty bourgeoisie, believing that an unholy alliance existed between the capitalists and Rome, rallied to Luther as to a Messiah.

The revolt which followed, however, was not merely economic in its origin. There were in the Germanies many sincere individuals who, as Christian Humanists, believed that the church had drifted away from its original purity, and consequently they sought a return to the "original church," just as the Italian Humanists advocated the revival of classical times.

Martin Luther, therefore, in breaking with the church, had the support of diverse elements. These groups accepted with enthusiasm his belief in justification by faith rather than in sacramental observance. Some intellectuals welcomed this as an attack upon the false doctrines and rituals of the "materialistic church." Others regarded this belief as a religious justification of political and social liberty. Many practical German rulers supported Martin Luther in his attempt to establish the Lutheran church because this revolt gave them a chance to gain control of church property within their states and thus to weaken the influence of the Holy Roman Emperor, right arm of the papacy. Aware of this royal support, Luther in his first popular pamphlet, *Address to the German Nobility,* "called upon the rulers, especially the knights, to reform the abuses." He appealed to German nationalism as opposed to Roman internationalism. Inspired by his belief in the "priesthood of all believers," the lower classes, especially the peasants, maintained that, inasmuch as God above was sovereign, they had a right to rebel against the nobles who exacted illegal dues from them.

Luther, however, was not a social radical, for while he was willing to appeal to the political ambitions of the local rulers, he was primarily concerned with spiritual salvation rather than with social justice. True, he was aware of the social and economic inequalities of his time, and he denounced the wealthy capitalists, including the Fuggers, who through their monopolies artificially raised prices. Moreover, he criticized the "worldliness" of trade, money-making, and other aspects of economic enterprise. But at no time did he approve of social revolution. God above, he claimed, would punish the wicked; therefore, the downtrodden should suffer on earth and wait until the day of resurrection when the wicked would be found guilty and the good would prosper. The downtrodden, however, refused to wait; they revolted time and again. Thereupon Luther, now an outspoken advocate of law and order—"the authority of Caesar"—denounced the peasants and sided with the ruling classes.

Many unprivileged elements in society found much to stimulate their ambitions in the program of the other leading Protestant Reformer, John Calvin (1509–1564). A Frenchman by birth, he set forth his religious ideas in his famous *Institutes of the Christian Religion* (1536) and tried to carry them out in the bourgeois city of Geneva. There, by taking advantage of political decentralization, he made himself a virtual dictator. His influence, however, was not limited to this one city. During the sixteenth and seventeenth centuries hundreds of thousands of people accepted his beliefs and established Calvinist churches in France, in the Netherlands, in the Germanies, in the British Isles, and in the Americas.

In most of these countries Calvin's religious ideas appealed especially to the middle classes. Desirous of finding some religious justification for their money-making predilections they soon discovered in Calvinism a Christian religion which would not only defend their practices but would make them respectable. No wonder Calvin was hailed as a Messiah of the Middle Classes!

Calvin did not consciously advance views of economic significance. His tenets by chance coincided with the economic changes ushered in by the Commercial Revolution. Furthermore, Calvin was a reactionist and as such he accidentally expressed views which later took on economic meaning. Determined to revive what he considered "the original Church," he accepted two great ideas which characterized early monastic asceticism. These were: first, the leading of a sober, frugal, industrious life; second, the unremitting, indefatigable pursuit of one's calling. By these marks could be distinguished the elect, and by such conduct could the Christian glorify God and prove the fact of his own redemption.

According to Calvin, one's calling in Scripture meant a lawful mode of life ordained for him by God. Therefore it was the responsibility and duty of man to pursue his calling on earth wherein he would "hammer out his own salvation." Inasmuch as "thrift, diligence, and discipline" were forms of duty, Calvinists saw no reason to deny that these qualities should be as valuable and justifiable in commerce and industry as in agriculture. Indeed, a sober, frugal, and a busy life usually meant that a man was of the elect in worldly goods as well as in spiritual power. Many Calvinists logically concluded that the glorification of work and of thrift rather than of pleasure and leisure constituted not only a sure road to heaven but also a dependable way to economic independence.

Calvinism, therefore, placed the responsibility for economic security as well as for spiritual salvation squarely upon the shoulders of the individual. By stressing the sole right of a person to work out his own destiny and by rationalizing the failure of the many and the success of the few by means of the doctrine of predestination, Calvin actually justified economic as well as religious individualism. This religious sanction of economic activity explains perhaps why "most of the shining lights of Calvinism arose from the mercantile classes" and why "among Calvinists business ability and piety have always gone together."

Emphasis by Luther and Calvin upon the responsibility of the individual before God and before his fellow men dealt a death blow to the hierarchical view of society in both its spiritual and its economic aspects. Calvinism, although at first authoritarian, became, by the seventeenth century, the vehicle of a virulent utilitarian individualism. It would be incorrect, however, to maintain that economic individualism—the *laissez faire* doctrine—sprang from Calvinist teachings; nor is it true that Calvinism deliberately justified political liberty. Calvin, himself, was not consistent in his political views; he was an opportunist. In Geneva he was an able autocrat; and, wherever his followers prospered under absolute government, he counseled loyalty to the established order. But when kings opposed his followers—in France, for example—he advocated the right of men to oppose tyranny. God above was their sovereign. The pressure of economic necessity caused Calvinists, unconsciously perhaps, to support, whenever necessary, individualism in business as well as in politics and in religion.

Calvin's defense of usury also tended to justify business pursuits. During the Middle Ages and even in his own time the taking of interest had been in disrepute. Calvin, however, maintained that inasmuch as the Scripture nowhere prohibited it and modern business conditions required it, the taking of interest was justified, "except it be repugnant to justice and charity." Apparently he recognized the danger of interest taking, for he attacked all methods which men might employ to gain additional interest under other names. "Such coverings," he said, "are of no more avail than Adam's fig leaves." A man, he maintained, must always bear in mind two considerations: What can the borrower pay? How useful to him was the loan?

With the spread of the Calvinist movement over Europe and the New World, the religious justification of middle-class occupations was assured.

"It is not wholly fanciful to say," wrote Tawney in *Religion and the Rise of Capitalism* (Harcourt, Brace, and Co., New York, 1926), "that on a narrower stage but with not less formidable weapons, Calvin did for the bourgeoisie of the sixteenth century what Marx did for the proletariat of the nineteenth. He set their virtues at their best in sharp antithesis with the vices of the established order at its worst, taught them to feel that they were a chosen people, made them conscious of their great destiny in the providential plan, and made them resolute to attain their ends."

Calvinism, perhaps more than any other religious doctrine, gave adequate sanction to economic activity in the sixteenth and seventeenth centuries. Strictly speaking, however, the capitalist-bourgeois spirit—the pursuit of gain as a principle of conduct—was not a product of any religious sect. Rising "rather from the material conditions of civilization than from some religious impulse," this profit ideal in the seventeenth century influenced Catholic as well as Protestant thought. Jesuits, writes Dr. H. M. Robertson in his *Aspects of the Rise of Economic Individualism* (Cambridge University Press, 1933), became the leading Catholic exponents of the commercial spirit—not because they were particularly favorable "to the encouragement of the capitalistic system," but because, "as the most prominent casuists and confessors," they were most in contact "with the lay world, with its aims, and its difficulties." [1] In short, all religious sects were moved by the materialistic enthusiasm of the early modern age.

[1] But J. Brodrick, S. J., in his volume, *The Economic Morals of the Jesuits* (Oxford University Press, 1934) attacked Robertson's thesis. "As everyone knows," he wrote, "it used to be a favorite Protestant objection against the Catholic Church that the countries under her influence had the poorest trade returns. But, of course, *laissez-faire* and capitalism were in honour then, whereas now their glory has departed."

Nevertheless, while the pursuit of gain was not necessarily an offspring of Protestantism, it should be evident that its sects, especially Calvinism, more than any other, added "a halo of ethical sanctification to the appeal of economic expediency." Calvinism first pointed the road toward a reconciliation of true Christian living in and with the evolving bourgeois capitalistic system. Moreover, it encouraged as the social basis of the new order—an active, aggressive middle-class element and an exploitable proletariat. Although on the one hand it preached a gospel of social and economic betterment to the upper groups, on the other it gave to the workmen a gospel of obedience and service. Unable to improve their social positions here, they were to receive their rewards in heaven. Meanwhile, honest service was to be their lot.

Both Luther and Calvin had as a cardinal tenet that of freedom of conscience, an idea enthusiastically accepted by the bourgeoisie. The right to private interpretation of the Scripture was a real help to bourgeois enterprise, for the middle-class man, like the priest, thus was able to justify almost anything; now lawyers, politicians, and business men, as well as theologians, were able to use the Bible like an Ouija board. Sympathetic theologians satisfied the consciences of the most unscrupulous men of affairs. Thus, the "needle's eye," which Christ said a rich man would have to go through in order to get into heaven, was said to have been an open gate in Jerusalem. Pious business men perhaps found satisfaction in discovering many bourgeois passages in the Old Testament. They must have appreciated the story of Jacob, of how he defrauded his uncle Laban and then piously ejaculated: "Except the God of my father, the God of Abraham, and the Fear of Isaac, had been with me, surely now hadst thou sent me away empty . . ." (Genesis, 31:42). They probably enjoyed reading about Abraham, rich in cattle, in silver, and in gold!

Reactions against long-standing ideas of poverty, chastity, and obedience were among the principal social effects of the religious revolts. Bourgeois individualism can be seen in the attitude of the Reformers toward poverty. Frequently neglected was the idea that wealth entailed social responsibility, for after the Middle Ages "men no longer held, they owned." Too often a beggar was despised; poverty was considered disrespectable; the poor were not deemed "blessed." In the opinion of the self-satisfied middle-class men, the benign hand of God was not raised over these, "our brothers."

The business classes actually considered themselves to be the "chosen people." Flattered by Luther's famous doctrine of the priesthood of all believers, they became the backbone of many Protestant churches. Frequently in control of the selection and dismissal of clergymen, they enjoyed a certain degree of practical power in the church. Congregational singing, the use of the vernacular, and responsive reading also further enhanced their position in the religious service.

During the sixteenth and seventeenth centuries the religious revolts did much to strengthen the middle classes politically. Internationalism, aiming at a commonwealth under the dual authority of pope and emperor, was broken, and in its place rose the concept of nationalism, supported by the bulk of Protestants and a spreading number of Catholics. This nationalism marked the beginning of a new era, and the assertion of Latimer that "God hath showed himself the God of the English" was typical of the new patriotism. National religions and national states, which became definite ideals in the sixteenth century, were partly inspired by the views of Luther and Calvin. In Catholic monarchies, such as France, the bourgeoisie became extreme patriots.

In other fields of political theory the Reformed teachings exerted indirect influence. Divine right of kings and representative government were favored by Protestant leaders whenever by so doing their interests could be advanced. But behind these views rose the fundamental concept associated with the new society—the lay state, dedicated to the principle of nationalism and devoted to the welfare of the middle classes.

CHAPTER VI

MERCANTILISTS: SEEKERS FOR GOLD

If you would know the value of money, go and try to borrow some (Benjamin Franklin).

MERCANTILISM—a new doctrine of political economy, adopted by sovereigns shortly after the Medieval period—buoyed up the bourgeoisie, economically and politically. In essence, this policy is primarily a money theory of wealth, its basic tenets being, first, that gold and silver are the sources from which the prosperity of the state is derived; second, that the acquisition of this money can most effectively be accomplished by the state through the promotion of foreign trade and more particularly by the establishment of a favorable balance of trade. Succinctly, the mercantilists were seekers for gold whose object was to sell the maximum of goods to foreign countries but to buy the minimum from them.

To attain a favorable balance of trade, and to acquire the precious metals, sixteenth and seventeenth-century governments contrived many expedients, a principal one being the establishment of colonial empires which were expected to supply their mother country with cheap raw materials and to buy from her expensive manufactures. Spain's leadership in this sphere was preëminent. Another plan was to encourage the development of their country's shipping so that no money should accrue to foreign merchantmen. For instance, Britain's Navigation Acts were aimed directly at the Dutch who had become prosperous by obtaining a near monopoly of the carrying trade of the world. Again, the home governments often prohibited the importation of manufactures and foodstuffs from foreign countries so that "infant industries" could be started and home agriculture stimulated. Taken as a whole, mercantilism, fundamentally, was state building on the economic side.

As a result of these economic doctrines, all classes found commercial and mercantile pursuits of great concern. Kings, attempting to become little Caesars in their dominions, saw in mercantilism a way to economic prosperity and political power through greater tax revenues, revenues which would then supply finances for huge military and naval forces, to fight dynastic as well as colonial wars; for the construction of beautiful palaces, equal if not superior to the buildings of classical times; and for a standard of living appropriate to a modern affluent potentate.

To the nobility, mercantilism constituted new life blood. In France, for example, more taxes enabled the ruler to preserve feudal society by granting pensions, military positions, and governmental jobs to his "poverty-stricken aristocrats." In return for this "dole" he was able to deprive the nobles of their political power and to make them servile. Thus mercantilism with its golden prosperity was to be the means whereby the absolute monarch could subsidize the decadent privileged nobility, who were otherwise unable to afford to live in the style to which they had long become accustomed. In England, however, the effects of mercantilism upon the nobility were somewhat different. Unlike many trade-loathing aristocrats of France, the British lords were perfectly willing to invest in commercial undertakings. By so doing they were able to retain for a while their social supremacy and to live in the usual grand style.

But it was to the upper bourgeoisie most of all that mercantilism mattered. To them it was a political and financial Horn of Plenty. Everywhere the state by restrictions and privileges supported great merchants in the establishment of powerful commercial monopolies. In England and the Netherlands, such legislative bodies as Parliament and the States General enabled the wealthy landowners and the commercial classes to control the government. In absolute monarchies, such as France, men of money were able to obtain political offices, governmental subsidies, and exemptions from certain taxes. These benefits tended to amplify the subservience of this group to the monarchy, so much so that the European bourgeoisie of the seventeenth century had few standing rights, and were usually dependent upon the good-will of the king for advancement and protection in their economic activities. "As long as rulers, therefore, favored mercantilist policies for building up the state, a close bond connected the business classes and the monarchy."

During the seventeenth and eighteenth centuries the policy of mercantilism was adopted by nearly all countries engaged in commerce and industry. Spain used it to foster great prosperity. Italy and the Germanies applied it with success. But it was in England, France, and the Netherlands that mercantilism experienced its greatest triumphs.

England rose rapidly as a modern commercial and industrial state. In the train of the mercantilistic expansion of commerce there followed the prosperity of the sixteenth and seventeenth centuries. The old aristocracy was practically destroyed in the Wars of the Roses of the fifteenth century—the new was primarily bourgeois. A London Burse, or Royal Exchange, built in 1569, saw many men become merchant princes. Soon the sun rose over the English colonial empire, never to set. From King Henry VIII's confiscation of church property the landowners and merchants gained still more wealth. Theirs was a golden era.

After the death of Queen Elizabeth in 1603, the wealthy commercial bourgeoisie entered politics. Determined to curb absolutism, to reduce the cost of government, and to establish a state which would conform to their economic interests, the nobles of the market place precipitated, in the 1640's, the Great Rebellion. Originally they intended to bring about moderate reforms; but their backers, the more radical Puritans and Independents representing the lesser business men, insisted upon more drastic changes. Led by their strong man, Oliver Cromwell, these defenders of small property overthrew the monarchy, beheaded the king, and in 1653 established a republic. Dominated by the Independents—shopkeepers, artisans, craftsmen, and yeomen—Cromwell's army, having ousted the Presbyterian moderates, then set up a dictatorship.

As dictator, the crusading Cromwell endeavored to govern England, to conquer Ireland, and by means of Navigation Acts, to destroy Dutch commercial competition. At the same time he planned a moral and spiritual kingdom of God in England, perhaps superior in principle to the one established by Calvin at Geneva. Uncomplaining toil, constant thrift, extended patience, sensible thinking, perennial prayers, and fierce warfare (always on the side of right), Cromwell believed, would result in the creation of a powerful and perfect political and social order. This bourgeois régime would replace the monarchy, which, neglecting the sterner virtues for unholy corruption and immoral indulgence, was doomed.

Cromwell soon faced powerful radical as well as conservative opposition. Encouraged by the success of the revolution, a section of the Independents, called Levellers, insisted upon the establishment of a democratic republic and the formulation of a program designed to obliterate extreme wealth and poverty by making England a land of small property owners. Staunch defender of the rights of private property, Cromwell brutally obliterated the Levellers, admitting that he feared the dominance of the poor more than that of the rich.

Calvinism, as interpreted by Cromwell, however, soon bore heavily upon the wealthy merchants and aristocrats. Its sternness grew tiresome. Men who had gained riches in business wanted to enjoy life. They began to hanker for "the good old days," and, consequently, they welcomed the restoration of the gay monarchy in 1660 and the end of the puritanical dictatorship. Henceforth, according to Gretton, the wealthy merchants no longer tried to create a bourgeois state; instead they dominated whatever government was in power.

Autocracy, however, was never completely reëstablished. In 1688, when James II in his diplomacy, wars, religious policy, and expenditures ran counter to the wishes of the ruling commercial and landowning classes, there was another bourgeois revolt—the Glorious Revolution. Invoking the current concepts of popular sovereignty and the Calvinist belief that "Kings are of the same dough as others. . . . People were not made for kings, kings were made for the people," the tradesmen, in control of Parliament, deposed James II and called his daughter Mary and her bourgeois Dutch husband, William of Orange, to the throne. Complete "justification" of the act appeared shortly in the work of John Locke (1632–1704) entitled *Treatises of Government,* the first great political tract to represent the position of middle-class property owners who had been the chief instigators of the revolt and were the chief beneficiaries from it. In it he favored a government which would be limited by a bourgeois charter of rights—a constitution—and would be elected by the people. These ideas were expressed later by such political interpreters as Rousseau and Jefferson. Indeed, "well into the nineteenth century Locke has remained the vaunted oracle of these groups not only in England but throughout the world."

As a result of the Revolution of 1688 the wealthy upper middle classes united with the nobility in the exercise of political power and in the direction of culture. These great merchants and financiers often married descendants of the citizens of Cromwell's Puritan Republic and rose to social prominence. Contact with the refinements of aristocracy, as well as with the conservatisms of wealth, caused them, unlike their ancestors, to respect social discipline and tradition. Gladly they supported the nobility in maintaining an aristocratic-bourgeois compromise wherein the privileges of great wealth as well as of birth were maintained. The prestige of blood continued; high positions were still reserved for ancient families; and the court remained crowded with aristocrats obtaining royal favor. But the wealthy merchants also had a chance to enter this exclusive circle by marriage or by royal grant.

Despite this alliance between the nobility and the upper middle classes a complete merger of the two groups did not eventuate. Cultivated and polished as they became, the merchants and financiers simply could not think and feel in common with the aristocrats. Calvinists for the most part, they found it impossible to get away from the piety, the simplicity, and the sentimental moralisms of their ancestors. The aristocratic emphasis upon pleasure did not appeal to them; they preferred to work—to acquire, not to spend—to be busy workers in the hive and not merely ornamental queens.

Like Albion, France also was the nation wherein the mercantilist system "found its most celebrated application" and the bourgeoisie an improved but still a subordinate social station. By the end of the fifteenth century she also possessed a strong national feeling. Every one, both high and low, recognized and obeyed her king. Catching the spirit of the Italian Renaissance, Frenchmen, especially in the seventeenth century, developed a unity of feeling which had as its basis, according to Guérard, the "Rationalism of the Classical Age, rather than the revelation of the middle ages; the benevolent absolutism of Caesar, rather than the chaotic feudalism which rose after the invasions; and finally classicism in literature, rather than medieval spiritualism." This emphasis upon ancient culture, for all that, did not lead to the complete overthrow of the feudal system. A feudal-classical compromise was arranged, wherein the absolute monarch, backed by the bourgeoisie, deprived the nobles of their intrinsic political powers, but permitted both nobility and clergy to retain their basic social and economic privileges and distinctions.

Only against great opposition was the feudal-classical compromise effected in France. During the sixteenth century, many feudal lords participated in the French religious wars in order to weaken the king and to regain their political powers. Both the Catholics and the Huguenots (French Protestants) advocated at various times the limitation of the power of the king by the Estates General. Bourgeois Huguenots in many French towns attacked the monopolistic and restrictive policies of the king and the guilds, demanding political autonomy and economic liberty. Frequently foreign countries, Spain and England, for example, threatened to intervene in French affairs. Social unrest, accentuated by the high cost of living and the general economic stagnation accompanying the civil wars, also threatened to result in complete chaos and anarchy.

At this critical juncture a group of patriots, called *Politiques,* advanced the classical and Fascist concept of the supremacy of the state and advocated the subordination of all individual purposes to that of the monarchy. Henry of Navarre accepted the leadership of the group, and as King Henry IV of France, became a modern bourgeois dictator, reviving not only the political but also the economic phase of absolutism. Prior to his reign (1589–1610) a number of Valois rulers had preferred such mercantilist policies as the promotion of commerce and of colonial expansion; but it was not until the time of Navarre that mercantilism became a definite policy whereby the feudal-classical state could be sustained by means of economic prosperity.

In his exploitation of the economic resources of his kingdom, Henry IV was aided by an efficient statesman, Sully, a stern, gloomy, penurious Huguenot and an exponent of Calvinistic thrift and economic enterprise. To obtain money and to gain the support of the very wealthy traders he established the Paulette tax whereby an ambitious middle-class man could purchase a hereditary position as magistrate or judge and thus become a nobleman of the robe. Meanwhile, this minister improved the collection of taxes; by reducing expenditures and by decreasing the amount of corruption he stored a surplus in the treasury. Believing that land was the source of all wealth, he also did much to promote scientific agriculture. Decreased taxes on farming was only one incentive to the producer. By draining obstructive swamps, planning a system of canals to connect with important rivers, building bridges, and constructing roads, transportation was vastly improved. The silk industry was greatly stimulated by bringing mulberry trees to central France, Lyons especially becoming a leading silk center. Sully also encouraged the manufacture of glassware and pottery.

Following the death of Henry IV in 1610, France under a weak government experienced another period of economic decline and financial corruption. The sound policies of Navarre were abandoned, and France seemed headed toward bankruptcy and economic chaos. During this critical period a French economist, Montchrétien, published his *Traicté de l'Œconomie Politique* (1615), in which he prescribed economic as well as political absolutism. In the opinion of this mercantilist, benevolent despotism should have as its chief aim the economic growth of the state. He recognized the middle classes as the group largely responsible for this undertaking and urged the king to support them in the promotion of trade, industry, and colonization. He believed in the accumulation by the state of a great amount of gold and silver. He also maintained that the rich economic resources of France, if developed, would solve all financial troubles and contribute to the "public welfare."

Mercantilism, as advocated by Montchrétien, had the welfare of all groups as its objective. The king would benefit because economic prosperity would make it possible for him to collect more taxes and thus enable him to carry on his plans to enlarge his military and building programs. The nobles, in turn, could look forward to lucrative positions in the army and government, or to larger pensions. Middle-class men naturally would prosper through improved business conditions, better opportunities in governmental service, and exemptions from taxation. Peasants and wage-earners, however, were to get the milk after the cream had been removed; to them would be left only the "blessing" of harder work at the same wages.

The reëstablishment of strong government by Cardinal Richelieu between 1624 and 1642 paved the way for the adoption of the mercantilist plan. Accepting both the feudal-classical compromise and economic nationalism, this astute statesman during his brief administration established in France an efficient centralized monarchy, and made that country again one of the great European powers. He died, however, before he could carry out the economic phase of his program and make France a prosperous and commercial monarchy.

During the reign of Louis XIV, 1643–1715, France became the classical example of an absolute and mercantilist kingdom, owing largely to Colbert, the king's brilliant economic statesman. Son of a dry-goods merchant of Rheims, he typified the progressive leader of the bourgeoisie. With no landed estates, class interests, pride, or tradition to prejudice him against the crown or to make him disdain hard work, he was able to give his king undivided loyalty and to devote himself wholeheartedly to the financial and economic betterment of the state.

Colbert was one of the early modern exponents of "bourgeois efficiency." Having little sense of humor he took himself very seriously. Known as the "work-ox" of Louis XIV, he labored sixteen hours a day and encouraged the king and all office holders to do likewise. "Work was his passion and his obsession." To him monks, nuns, and priests were useless to the state because they did not work.

Colbert had but one objective—a strong and prosperous kingdom. As a business man and as superintendent of finances, he first set out to balance the budget. Disregarding the sufferings of the tax-payers and their appeals for consideration, he proceeded to levy and to collect heavy taxes. Himself a typical self-made man, he was in his own private life a very good spender; for he lived well and gave money, positions, and lands lavishly to his relatives.

Like most economic statesmen of his day, Colbert adopted the mercantilist prosperity program. Like them he regarded gold and silver as the life blood of the state; and, therefore, he proposed that trade, industry, agriculture, and colonization should be stimulated so as to secure as much bullion as possible. His measures reached such extremes that holidays were abolished whenever possible so as to augment the output of goods.

This earnest statesman was concerned with all phases of governmental activity. Despite the strenuous resistance of "individualists" Colbert established numerous codes designed to regiment industry and commerce in such a way as to bring prosperity and gold to France. Finances, the navy, public works, commerce, agriculture, education, colonies, foreign affairs, art, literature, were just a few of his numerous interests; while the upbuilding of the navy, the development of transportation, and the growth of agriculture, of commerce, and of industry—in short, the economic expansion of the empire—were definite examples of his achievements.

Louis XIV, however, refused to be king of the middle classes; he wanted to be Caesar—king of France by Grace of God. He was willing to work many long hours daily for his people; but as king of this great nation—the second Rome—

he believed that he had to dedicate himself to the task of making his monarchy superlative in all phases of human endeavor. France, he maintained, must be the cultural center of the intellectual world. France, politically, must be the dominant nation in Europe. France, economically, must surpass her competitors. She must attain her destiny—acquire her "natural frontiers"—even if expensive and destructive wars were necessary.

Colbert's policy of making the monarchy powerful by means of economic development and the accumulation of precious metals did not interest Louis XIV. The king inwardly disliked the dull Colbert and other government officials. He enjoyed the comradeship of his brave generals and his gay courtiers. He preferred to visit military camps, to hold sieges, and to give parties at Versailles, rather than to inspect manufacturing establishments, to confer with committees, or lend his presence to bourgeois social functions. Colbert might devote his time to establishing a uniform currency, abolishing internal tariffs and tolls, building roads and canals, stimulating trade, commerce, and agriculture; but these "lowly" pursuits were not of great significance to the king; he, Louis XIV, was the Grand Monarch, he was everything—the very state; he was the pinnacle of the classical ideal.

Colbert died before the "Grand Monarchy" collapsed. Two years after the able statesman's passing, Louis XIV made probably the worst of his numerous mistakes. Determined to carry the classical concept of unity to its logical limit, he revoked the Edict of Nantes (1685), which had given the Huguenots a degree of religious toleration. Inasmuch as a considerable number of the exiled Huguenots were artisans and business men this act deprived France "of the very sinews" Colbert had striven to strengthen. Meanwhile, the king exhausted the treasury, and almost ruined industry, commerce, and agriculture by engaging in a series of wars designed to establish the "security of France by making that nation dominant in Europe." The great continental states and England opposed this particular phase of the classical ideal; France was defeated; and the Caesarian ambitions of Louis were squelched. To his infant successor, Louis XV, the "sun king" left in 1715 a bankrupt, poverty-stricken, restless kingdom. Later the absolute monarchy—this feudal-classical compromise—was to be subjected to the attacks of the apostles of feudalism and the exponents of bourgeois enlightenment. This time, however, a revolution was in the making.

CHAPTER VII

HOLLAND: CENTER OF BOURGEOIS SELFISHNESS

Learn, my son, with how little wisdom the world is governed (Attributed to Count Axel von Oxenstierna).

NOT England and not France but Holland, the largest province of the Spanish Netherlands, became the foremost bourgeois state of Western Europe during the early modern period. Holland attained this position by a series of political incidents culminating, just prior to this time, in the so-called Great Privilege, concessions to the aristocrats and bourgeoisie from their ruler by which the States General, representing the propertied classes, obtained the sole right to coin money, to raise taxes, and to undertake wars; political positions in the Netherlands were to be awarded to natives; decrees of the imperial government which conflicted with the privileges of towns were void; no one could be summoned to justice outside of his province; and the States General could meet when and where it pleased. These concessions were by no means gifts from the skies showered without reason upon the upper and middle classes by benevolent monarchs. No, the rising tide of bourgeois prosperity had so engulfed the Dutch state that the Hapsburg rulers were only too glad to see that the commercial classes were conciliated and treated gently.

Even in the Middle Ages, that part of the Netherlands which is now Belgium had become a great commercial center. First, the city of Bruges experienced economic prosperity; later, due to the shift of trade from the Mediterranean to the Atlantic, to the introduction of more modern business methods, and especially to its better harbor facilities, progressive Antwerp took over economic leadership from backward Bruges. Located on the broad Scheldt River and inhabited by burghers who possessed a strong belief in liberty and progress, Antwerp soon became one of the main commercial centers of Europe, merchandise coming to it by land and sea. The port illustrated an amazing variety of commercial and industrial life. Men of every race, speaking all languages, thronged the streets. Their ships were as different as their merchandise. The Portuguese brought spices, silks, and medicinal herbs from the Orient; Germany and the Baltic states supplied the market with grain; England furnished wool for the great textile mills; and Portugal, Spain, France, and Germany provided wines. Industries flourished. Besides being known as a weaving center, Antwerp was famous for her manufacture of munitions. All the nations of the world depended on her for military supplies. Truly the proud member of the bourgeoisie of that city could say truthfully that almost every industry was represented in his "hometown."

In the train of Antwerp's thriving industrial and commercial development followed its rise as a financial mart. Antwerp became the money market of the world. The Fuggers, the Welsers, and other great banking houses had their representatives in that city; governments kept local agents there to borrow money on short notice. Most loans contracted in Antwerp or in other cities of the Netherlands acted as a boomerang, for not only did the bankers reap wealth from high rates of interest, but also the country as a whole benefited, as the borrowed money was usually spent in the Netherlands. During the late Middle Ages Antwerp did not count her assets in guilders, but in tons of gold. Later, a considerable part of the precious metals from the rich mines of the New World flowed to Antwerp, where it furnished the necessary bullion for credit.

Antwerp's economic prosperity attracted large numbers of people. As this metropolis grew, a gilded throbbing city rose out of the complex of tar smells, ships' bells, and factory smoke. Buildings, factories, houses, and a new city wall expanded its proportions and rejuvenated its appearance. Under the spell of the Dutch Renaissance, the bourgeois gentlemen bought or built finer homes furnished with artistic and beautiful tapestries, paintings, plate, and furniture.

This prospering middle class became the dominant element in all "Low Country" life. Even in the inland provinces, where the nobility and the clergy enjoyed greater privilege, according to Geyl's *The Revolt of the Netherlands* (Williams and Norgate, London, 1932), "the urban middle classes, enterprising, well educated, keen on their privileges and liberties, played an important part in economic, intellectual, and political life."

A cardinal tenet of the bourgeois economic philosophy was the belief that the efficiency of all would result in the comfort of all. As a result, the bourgeoisie were instrumental in transforming the economic technique of the country. Communication was facilitated, one innovation being a postal service; and transportation was so advanced that in the middle of the sixteenth century even a rapid transit system was instituted for the quick delivery of fresh fish from Ghent to Paris. A luxuriously built Bourse, founded in Antwerp in 1531, led to considerable speculation, gambling, and high interest rates. To curb various practices an edict in 1540 declared as usurious "all interest above a legitimate gain in honest trade." The social counterpart of speculation also existed. Fashionable clothes, brilliant feasts, and sumptuous banquets distinguished the social life of the rich bourgeoisie. Ostentation became the marked characteristic of their brilliant and gaudy society.

But in the midst of this plenty there was poverty. Growing concentration of wealth in the hands of the rich burgher class led to the impoverishment of large sections of the lower classes, especially among the artisans. Class distinctions began to appear as the gulf widened between the successful trader or business person, frequently a self-made man, and the worker or artisan whose standard of living was steadily declining. The streets of Antwerp were crowded with vagrants, transients, and professional beggars. So vital to the welfare of the state did the problem of the poor become that it was necessary to transfer control of all charity from the church to the government.

Unfolding of the bourgeois commercial supremacy was attended by an inevitable disagreement with the established Catholic church. Loath to recognize even the authority of their own councils, these early masters of trade looked with growing disfavor upon papal church interference in secular matters. Although they desired salvation, they did not believe that it was necessary for them, in order to be eligible for salvation, to sacrifice their rights as individuals and their possessions as prosperous business men. In their opinion material success on earth should be a recommendation rather than a black mark in the Book of Judgment.

The Dutch merchants gave at least tacit assent to intellectual criticism of the church. Erasmus, the great humanist, for example, in advocating a reform of that institution from within, had the support of many intellectuals of the upper bourgeoisie. Antagonism toward the church was also harbored by the lower classes. The radical sect, the Anabaptists, rose largely out of economic conditions and, by advocating a complete social and religious regeneration, appealed to those who had failed to accumulate worldly goods. To the poor this promised earthly as well as heavenly salvation. But inasmuch as this sect appealed to the powerless downtrodden rather than to the omnipotent rich, it failed to develop real strength, and gave way to Calvinism, with its fighting creed, its organization and discipline, and its profit-making philosophy.

An economy so nourishing to complete freedom and individualism as was the Dutch proved propitious to the growth of Calvinism despite early opposition from the Hapsburg autocracy. Naturally, the Holy Roman Emperor, Charles V, as the great secular defender of the church, opposed this reform movement. Placards were posted in the Netherlands prohibiting the printing, sale, and reading of heretical books. Death by hanging, beheading, quartering, or burning was meted out to those guilty of offenses against the church. The rack became as much a Dutch institution as the windmill. By 1575 the Inquisition was in its iniquitous heyday. The testimony of one witness could convict an accused person, and once found guilty, his property was forfeited to the church or state.

When Charles V began enforcing the "loss of property" provision, he at once faced stubborn hostility. The bourgeoisie would rather lose their heads than their hard-earned possessions, for loss of property deprived them of their honorable standing. They were further angered when they saw to whom their confiscated belongings went—to none other than the hated clergy who promptly proceeded to enrich themselves even by engaging in tax-free trade. Resentful of such treatment, the Dutch burghers found it consoling to support a revolutionary movement such as Calvinism, which could be used against the privileged position of the obnoxious clerics.

Upon the abdication of Charles V (1556) and the accession of Philip II as ruler of Spain and the Netherlands, the ill-feeling between the Calvinists and the Spanish Catholics came to the surface. Philip II, an ambitious and fanatical king, was determined to root out heresy at any cost. His repressive measures led to riots, in many instances either instigated or participated in by the middle classes; whereupon Philip II sent troops to restore law and order. An orgy of destruction ensued, in which whole cities were destroyed and their inhabitants massacred. Aroused by such atrocities, William, Prince of Orange, a German who had once been a representative of Charles V in the Netherlands, raised a body of mercenary soldiers in Germany and rushed to the defense of the Netherlands. To his chagrin the Hollanders failed to furnish the supplies his troops needed. Each city delayed sending aid because it did not want to give more than any of the other towns. Moreover, the united support of the Dutch Calvinists and Lutherans was not forthcoming.

Unable to make much headway on land, the German leader incited Dutch privateers to prey upon Spanish shipping. In 1572 the seaport of Brill was captured by "sea beggars" and the Dutch, believing that fortune was smiling on William's cause, gave him better backing. At no time, however, could he rely upon their individual support. Each Protestant group thought that the Prince was partial to the other, while both often believed that he actually was for the Catholics. All of them claimed that the money they gave him went into his own pocket. With such suspicious allies William found it more than difficult to carry out his military program. Before he could attack a town under Spanish control, he had to obtain the consent of the burghers in that city. If he captured it, the middle-class citizens, tired of war, often would not allow him to maintain a garrison. They seemed determined to assert their political rights and yet to protect their economic interest—both to have the cake and to eat it.

Apparently force alone could induce the tradesmen to change their minds. This was the Spanish method, and it was well illustrated by the fall of Antwerp. Antwerp, like the other cities ruled by selfish, short-sighted business men, had opened her gates to Spanish mercenaries, at the same time refusing to support William. With bold independence she relied upon her local military forces consisting of hired troops to defend this "splendidly isolated" city. The folly of this method of defense was soon made evident. In November, 1576, about 5000 soldiers in the Spanish army revolted, and in order to secure booty in lieu of their unpaid back wages, attacked the city of Antwerp. This "military strike" led to the capture and the sack of the city of 200,000 by the Spaniards. Over five hundred homes were burned—the total loss, including silver and gold taken, amounted to over fifteen million dollars! The bourgeoisie were the victims of their own selfishness.

Moved by this misfortune, the burghers of the Netherlands decided to combine their forces under the leadership of William of Orange. But William, before long, discovered that he was not the head of a united army. The Protestants in the Northern provinces began to feel pangs of conscience because they were associating with the Catholics of the South. Moreover, they were jealous of the economic supremacy that region had enjoyed and did not propose to see it revived. Consequently, the two groups engaged in a fratricidal war. Thousands were killed, while William stood by helpless to stop the struggle. Little wonder that France, England, and the German princes, though opposed to Philip II of Spain, lost interest in William's cause.

Quick to see the advantage of this civil war, Philip II, with bribes and religious arguments, had induced the Southern provinces to break away from the opposition. Meanwhile, in 1579, the seven Northern provinces organized a government under the Union of Utrecht. This new government was a typical bourgeois republic. William actually controlled two of the provinces, while the others had their own private armies and military leaders. So long as its own province was not threatened, the local burghers would not send their armies to help the other provinces, even though the latter were in danger. However, they did coöperate enough in 1581 to declare their independence from Spain.

In 1584 William was assassinated, and the middle classes, realizing that he had indeed been their real leader, selected his son, Maurice, as Captain General of the Netherlands, but executive power remained in the Estates. Eighteen years of age, Maurice, the burghers expected, would defend their national independence, but would not interfere with their local rights.

Philip II, meanwhile, sent a large army to end the revolt in the Netherlands once and for all. Antwerp was besieged in 1585 and before long was made to suffer a serious food shortage. To meet this situation the bourgeois citizens of Amsterdam sent boatloads of supplies; but inasmuch as it was dangerous to run the Spanish blockade, they raised the price of their foodstuffs to cover the risk. The thrifty burghers of Antwerp, however, refused to pay the higher charges, whereupon the business men of Amsterdam stopped running the blockade. The "penny-wise" citizens of Antwerp now had to tighten their belts as food became scarce, and when they could tighten no more they decided to capitulate, so that they could return to work, war being decidedly unprofitable.

With the capture of Antwerp in 1585, the Southern provinces came under the rule of Philip II. High taxes now ruined what little trade and industry there was. As a result, several hundred thousand people migrated to Holland, England, and other countries. Fields were overgrown with weeds. Whole towns were deserted, while in others packs of wolves and of wild dogs attacked men in the streets. Trade practically ceased and industry stagnated. Thus ended six years of selfish bourgeois rule in these provinces.

In the Northern districts, however, young Maurice, proving to be a competent military leader, repelled the attempts of the

Spaniards to invade Holland and the North. Meanwhile, behind the lines the burghers built up a political system of the worst type, an oligarchy of the middle classes in the guise of democracy. Burgher politicians deprived the people of all participation in the government. Self-governing provinces and towns were administered by twenty-four, twenty-eight, or thirty-six men, and inasmuch as these boards perpetuated themselves by selecting their own members, the rulers of the Dutch democracies were, in reality, self-appointed.

Burgher influence even invaded the army, going to such an extreme that representatives were sent by the States General to advise Maurice on military tactics and generalship. Much to his disgust, when he would determine upon a battle, these lay advisers would delay operations until the States General had been consulted. Often it was then too late to act. In 1600 these bourgeois commissioners managed to place the army in so untenable a position that the Spaniards trounced the Dutch vanguard. Whereupon the advisers fled, taking a goodly portion of the army with them as a guard. With these liabilities absent, Maurice proceeded to win battles and thus to add to his popularity among the common people. Despite the backing of the masses, he was forced by the solid, selfish, burgher political group, at the moment when he was in a position to expel the Spaniards from the Southern as well as from the Northern provinces, to accept a twelve-year truce.

Despite the war, the Northern provinces had prospered. Supported by England and France, they had strengthened their position on the sea as well as on land so that by the end of the sixteenth century Holland was extending her shipping business to all corners of the globe. With the chartering of the Dutch East India Company by the States General in 1602, the Dutch left the age of small business and entered the era of great corporations. As a trust or monopoly the Dutch East India Company had limitless power; for example, it obtained control of pepper from the East and boosted the price until it made a profit of 3000 per cent on this single article. Dividends multiplied—in a single year they often amounted to 60 per cent of the original investment. To all appearances the East India Company was a state within a state.

The Dutch West India Company was another noteworthy corporate venture. Trade was chiefly in slaves and tobacco, which did not pay the huge profits obtained from spices. After the expiration of the twelve-year truce with Spain, the West India Company made its chief gains out of piracy. Capturing Spanish treasure ships, this powerful organization frequently earned huge dividends for its stockholders, and the admirals responsible for the seizure of the Spanish vessels were accorded enthusiastic receptions by their bourgeois admirers and investors. The company secured a foothold in Brazil, while in America it established, quite appropriately, a city in its own image—New Amsterdam, now New York.

By 1620 Holland was not only the leading commercial power, but also the only state engaged in trade on an international scale. In 1591 she had entered the Mediterranean markets and soon dominated them. She carried nearly all the grain from the Baltic ports. It was said that when Europe suffered a short crop for one year, Holland was enriched for seven years. Her canal system was perfected to transport all products, and barges ran on timed schedules as do trains and airplanes today. She had trade agreements with nearly every nation.

Prior to this era of prosperity, Dutch traders had frequently borrowed from Jewish moneylenders to finance commerce; but now they obtained control of financial affairs for themselves. The Bank of Amsterdam was established in 1609, and an insurance company was organized to carry the risks of business. But a merchant could insure ships and cargo only up to 90 per cent of the "turn-in" value, this maximum being established because frequently ship owners, wanting new vessels, insured their ships up to the original value and sank them. The dependable Dutch burgher was weakening in character before the temptation of economic prosperity. "Success had turned the heads of the Dutch," says Barker in his *Rise and Decline of the Netherlands* (Dutton, New York, 1906):

The cautious spirit which had been formerly one of their chief characteristics was again rapidly disappearing. As gold could be obtained without trouble, the mercantile class had to some extent become demoralized. Everybody wanted to be rich quickly. The rage for money-making had bereft men of their reason; prudence and common sense were thrown to the winds, and the younger generation did not heed the warnings of the older men who had become rich by hard work. The Indian merchants and their friends were rolling in wealth; the Dutch spirit of thrift had disappeared, and legitimate business was being replaced by speculation, and speculation by gambling.

Individualism prevented the rise of an efficient centralized state until it was too late. After the truce of 1609 with Spain, Maurice, the military leader and stadtholder of the provinces, received the enthusiastic backing of the nobility and the lower classes and became the national leader of the union. But he was opposed by Oldenbarneveldt, Advocate of Holland, the largest province, who in turn was backed by those bourgeois individualists who placed faith in states rights and republicanism. A religious issue, centering around the question of predestination, involved the two groups. By means of this dispute, Oldenbarneveldt split the followers of Maurice and prevented the formation of a central government. In his attempt, however, to gain complete independence for Holland, Oldenbarneveldt failed. He was arrested and executed by the Nationalist forces.

In 1618, at the Synod held at Dordrecht, the Dutch Calvinists proceeded to oppose State rights and to support the idea of a strong central government. By that time, however, the middle classes were firmly in the governmental saddle, and so allowed Maurice, prior to his death in 1625, to dominate the government. After that, even though the Northern provinces were recognized as an independent state by the peace treaties which ended the Thirty Years' War, a strong central government was not established. In theory the provinces were ruled by a stadtholder, who had very little executive power, being a military leader responsible to the States General. To complicate matters the Advocate, or Pensionary, of Holland, the largest province and the center of bourgeois individualism, possessed great influence. He helped to prevent the rise of a strong unified government until the reign of William III of Orange (1672–1702). Personally powerful, the latter did become an absolute king, but by that time the Dutch could not benefit through strong government, for they had lost their commercial supremacy to England.

Perhaps of more consequence than any other factor in the decline of the Netherlands was the persistence of bourgeois selfishness. Middle-class politicians, in carrying their money-grabbing tactics into the field of foreign affairs, succeeded in earning for their country the ill-will of both England and France. Queen Elizabeth of England, for example, helped the Dutch in their wars against Spain to the extent of almost four million dollars. This loan had not been paid when James I became king of England in 1603. Pressed for money, the monarch finally arranged a settlement with the Dutch for one million three hundred thousand dollars. The burgher politicians thus saved their tax-payers much money, but James I of England never forgave the Hollanders. The French king looked with hostility upon the Dutch because they sold arms to his rebellious subjects; he did not consider that France had given the Netherlanders some aid in the war against Spain. Obviously, the shrewd business men of the Netherlands were always willing to make money, even at the expense of friends. Unfortunately, their short-sighted methods brought unpopularity to their country and thus contributed to its gradual territorial and commercial decline.

European wars benefited the Dutch bourgeoisie. During the Thirty Years' War (1618–1648), the Dutch furnished war materials and food to both sides. Merchants of other countries tried to obtain business by cutting prices, but the Dutch used cartels to dump products, ruin competitors, and then to raise prices. When the Netherlands and Spain were at war, the business men sold food and supplies to both sides. They opposed the plan of their leader, Frederick Henry, successor of Maurice, to bring the Southern provinces of the Netherlands into the Union; consequently, he was unable in 1638 to capture Antwerp because the Dutch merchants were sending supplies to the very people he was besieging. Barker illustrates the official attitude of one of the traitors:

> When Frederick Henry returned from his fruitless expedition to Antwerp, a merchant of the name of Byland was at his request arrested by the authorities for having sent a large quantity of gunpowder into Antwerp. When he was told that he had been a traitor to his country Byland declared "Trade must be free to all, and must not be interrupted by war. We men of Amsterdam have a right to trade wherever we please. If I should have to sail into hell in order to make a profit, I would do it even if I should risk burning my sails."

So he sailed frequently into hell!

The burghers were individualists *par excellence*. In the Treaty of Münster (1648) they forced the Dutch states to agree to a peace with Spain, whereby the Northern provinces were recognized as independent. In doing this, the Dutch deserted their ally, France, for they had promised to remain in the war until the Southern Dutch states had been conquered and divided between France and the United Netherlands. France, left in the lurch and finding her northern frontiers endangered by the Spaniards, indignantly canceled the trade privileges which had been extended to the Dutch. This cancellation contributed directly to the decline of the Dutch Republic.

After the Treaty of Münster the program of the Dutch bourgeoisie was "peace and economy." In order to save money the middle classes of Amsterdam forced the States General to adopt the principle that preparedness even for defense should be abolished. Despite the growing commercial competition with England and the evident antagonism of France, the Hollanders, now independent, hoped to maintain and even to augment their material prosperity by clever economic practices.

When Cromwell's party came to power in England, however, the Dutch were faced by a group just as concerned over trade and just as unscrupulous as they were. Henceforth it was another example of "Greek meeting Greek," with the English "Greek," blessed by foresight, winning the rivalry. Confident of their economic strength and of their ability to outwit their rivals, the Dutch, to save expenses, reduced their army and navy, and negotiated treaties of amity with neighboring states. Possessing a naïve confidence in the sanctity of written agreements, the Dutch actually believed that they were secure. They soon learned, however, that written promises were genuine only so long as both sides benefited. Therefore, when in 1652 war broke out between England and Holland as an aftermath to the English Navigation Acts, the Dutch soon found out that the other nations, having little at stake, kept out of the controversy, while they, practically defenseless, were unable to fight the British alone.

True enough, the Dutch had sufficient powder, guns, and ships to put up a fight; but foolish economy, rampant corruption, and squabbling coöperation prevented these from being utilized effectively. Their navy consisted for the most part of merchant ships manned by middle-class seamen instead of by trained professional officers and sailors. They had no united navy, for each province had its own admiralty. Eventually, in the need for naval unity, a colonel of the cavalry was made admiral of the combined fleets. But the Dutch could offer no resistance to Cromwell's strong fleet, empowered as it was by the Navigation Acts of 1651. Soon realizing that they could not protect their commerce, they decided to sue for terms of peace.

Meanwhile, the masses demanded the restoration of the House of Orange and the continuation of the war. Peace negotiations instituted by the burghers of Amsterdam (behind the backs of their "brothers" in the other provinces), whereby they hoped to obtain better treatment than the others, finally resulted in a general settlement. According to the terms of the peace, Cromwell promised never to allow the Prince of Orange to govern the Netherlands. Thus, though the Dutch bourgeoisie retained their political supremacy at home, it was at the cost of resigning their commercial supremacy abroad.

This capitulation was only temporary. In 1658 John De Witt, acknowledged leader of the middle classes, attempted to rebuild his country's commercial fences. Interest rates were reduced, and trade was fostered in various ways; treaties of commerce and friendship were renewed. Holland again courted prosperity. This prosperity, however, was short-lived. Clever middle-class propagandists began to harp on the thesis that the House of Orange was a liability, and that the bourgeois oligarchy alone could bring riches to the people. In 1664 England, determined to rule the seas, again worried the Dutch. Once more the latter found themselves unprepared and their allies cool; again the burghers decided to take charge of the navy, only to discover that most of their ships had been sold to the English. By 1667 Holland was thoroughly beaten, peace being concluded by the Treaty of Breda.

France, as well as England, contributed to the downfall of the commercial Dutch Republic. During the seventeenth century that country, owing to her great statesmen, Richelieu and Colbert, became a ranking sea power. On the European continent she was one of the leading political and economic states. In fact, both England and France, because of their marked economic progress, attracted thousands of ambitious artisans from foreign lands, especially from Holland. This weakened the middle classes in Holland and strengthened these groups in England and in France. During the reign of Louis XIV, France also engaged in economic warfare with the Dutch Republic. Later, the French king, encountering Dutch opposition in his attempt to annex the Spanish Netherlands, decided to punish this state by means of a war. It was the same old story; again the Dutch were unprepared. Meanwhile, they argued among themselves as to what policy to pursue and sent letters to Colbert complaining about French treatment. In the war which followed, the Dutch fleet, commanded by civilian leaders, was defeated; and on land her forts, with rusty guns fallen to the ground, offered little protection. At this critical juncture, the Prince of Orange, despite bourgeois opposition, was made commander-in-chief of the army. Aided by German mercenaries, he was able to hold back the French. In 1678 the business classes, tiring of a profitless war and eager to rebuild their trade markets, ended this conflict, as they had so many before, by deserting their German allies and giving up. By so doing they definitely lost their commercial supremacy.

Just as Louis XIV looked only through the eyes of a dictator, so the Dutch middle classes saw only with the eyes of a tradesman. In France everything had to be subordinated to the personal desire of the king to carry out the feudal-classical compromise. In the Netherlands all interests had to be secondary to those of the business men, and their desires were confined to the immediate rather than to the distant future. Consequently, in trying to reap quick profits at the expense of others, the Dutch middle classes stirred up real hostility, especially in France and in England. This, in the course of time, ruined them.

Political corruption also contributed to the downfall of the Dutch republic. Other governments, it is true, were not free from this form of dishonesty; but the bourgeois oligarchical republic seems to have been the worst offender on this score. Moreover, the Dutch concept of economy was childishly naïve in an era of political jackals. Instead of realizing that pacifistic ideals were not the mode and that it might be more profitable in the long run to pay taxes for the maintenance of adequate military and naval defenses, they tried to economize by resorting to a hazardous confidence in the intentions of their neighbors and rivals as expressed in treaties and agreements. The confidence usually turned out to be misplaced, for when the Dutch sent long letters to their "friends" objecting to acts which were construed as "unfriendly" and illegal, no answers, much less any action, resulted.

Despite their shortsighted policies and their eventual inferior status, the Dutch bourgeoisie did contribute much to Western civilization. In commerce and in industry they were among the pioneers of the early modern period. Dutch agriculture led in scientific progress, Dutch scientists and mathematicians were unequaled. In the sphere of maritime law the United Netherlands were supreme. In education, the University of Leyden was one of the leading centers of Protestant learning in Europe.

In art the Dutch painters produced some of the world's greatest masterpieces. Rubens of the Spanish Netherlands (Belgium) was perhaps the most celebrated painter in the first half of the seventeenth century. He was also a good business man, "employing a number of student assistants and accepting numerous lucrative orders" from such influential and wealthy patrons as Henry IV of France and James I of England. His 2200 compositions indicate that his art was a profitable business. In the seventeenth century the Netherlands was the center of the school of "realistic" painting. Interested more in the "common men" than in the aristocrats, such artists as Jordaens, David Teniers, Frans Hals, and Rembrandt depicted the life of the middle classes and the peasants. As a result, their pictures of country fairs, urban carousals, meetings of guildsmen, of corpulent burgomasters, beautiful landscapes, and stern scenes from that fountain of "rugged individualism," the Old Testament, give us an excellent idea of Dutch burgher life in those golden days.

The greatest importance of the United Netherlands lay in the fact that it was the only place where complete intellectual freedom existed. Consequently, it became a prominent haven of refuge for thinkers of various nationalities who were oppressed at home. From Spain and Portugal came many exiled Jews; from Germany, Calvinists; from France, Huguenots; and from England, Puritans and Pilgrims. These persecuted people showed their appreciation of the freedom the Dutch offered by working indefatigably for the good, not only industrially of Holland, but intellectually of the whole world. Great thinkers were cradled in their foster home. Spinoza and Descartes, for example, found in Holland freedom to express ideas which in other countries would have been censored or suppressed.

French despotism and Dutch oligarchical republicanism thus well illustrate the two types of government which accompanied the rise of the bourgeoisie in the seventeenth century. In both France and the Netherlands mercantilism was the accepted doctrine. In France, however, economic interests were in the final analysis subordinated to a state dominated by a narrow, ambitious king; while in the Netherlands the interests of the state were subordinated to a short-sighted, selfish bourgeoisie. Therefore, in both countries economic prosperity was temporary. During the eighteenth century business leadership passed to England, where the middle classes were able to create a more workable politico-economic concept of the state.

Chapter VIII

BOURGEOIS ECONOMIC REVOLUTIONS

The essence of the Industrial Revolution is the substitution of competition for the medieval regulations which had previously controlled the production and distribution of wealth (Arnold Toynbee, Lectures on the Industrial Revolution, *The Humboldt Publishing Co., New York, 1884).*

THE eighteenth century saw England close to the zenith of bourgeois power. No other nation challenged her commercial or industrial supremacy; even France, which for centuries had been England's bitter colonial and maritime rival, was prepared to award the palm of victory to her small neighbor across the channel. England was rapidly becoming the workshop of the world.

For this newly acquired sovereignty of the English middle classes many factors were responsible. Politically, through the control of the Whig party, the wealthy commercial classes were able to dominate Parliament whenever that party held the reins of government. Geographically, England's insular location made it possible for her to ignore European affairs not her immediate concern, to depend upon naval rather than upon military power for security, and to concentrate upon domestic matters. Her colonies were in the temperate zone, suitable for colonization. Financially, she was bolstered by the powerful Bank of England, which was prepared to support her at any time and to any extent in domestic or imperial undertakings. Economically, she was prepared to make the most of those economic revolutions which had their genesis in the eighteenth century.

England was fortunate too in the fact that no medieval institutions were present which could inhibit economic advancement. At no time had the guilds been dominant. The nobility exercised no adverse powers; indeed, the nobility and the tradesmen often united, as they did in the Glorious Revolution of 1688, in common opposition to the despotic authority of the king. Before the eighteenth century religious orthodoxy had vanished and intellectual freedom had been attained, an accomplishment unequaled in any other country. Political stability was the gratifying consequence of insistence on the part of the middle classes and the nobility upon the fundamental rights and concessions granted in political contracts. Parliament saw to it that no arbitrary taxation by the king afflicted the landowning and commercial groups; the establishment of the cabinet system gave them direct control of the government.

Confidence in the established government was further enhanced by the English judicial system. A well-defined code of laws guaranteed that all men could be tried free from political interference. The bourgeois beliefs in law and order, and in the sanctity of property and of investments were better regarded and upheld in England than in any other country. Progress along legal and constitutional lines, rather than by revolutionary methods, characterized English policy.

The concrete results of the new emphasis upon economic matters were apparent in early eighteenth-century England and France. Both nations experienced an era of commercial and colonial expansion, which in turn led to a period of artificial prosperity. By the Treaty of Utrecht (1713) with Louis XIV, England secured for her famous South Sea Company the lucrative monopoly of importing slaves into the Spanish colonies. As a result, South Sea stock boomed almost over night from $500 to $5000 a share. Similar concerns were organized which followed the lead set by the South Sea Company. In the era of speculation that followed tremendous paper fortunes were made. Swift, in his *Gulliver's Travels,* alluding to the state of the public mind under the excitement of the many schemes and speculations which came out during the years 1719–1721, termed these investments "bubbles." "The people in the street," he wrote, "walked fast, looked wild, their eyes fixed, and were generally in rags." Practically every one, he intimates, was absorbed in the pastime of gambling, for the neglect of the houses and the absence of cultivated tracts were evidence of the inattention to the legitimate pursuits of commerce and agriculture. Chimerical adventures in trade trapped the unwary. Companies were formed not only for fisheries, for insurance, for working mines, and for almost every type of ordinary commercial enterprise, but stock was sold to establish concerns "for making wigs and shoes, for making oil from sunflowers, for importing jackasses from Spain, for trading in human hair, for fatting hogs, and for a wheel for perpetual motion."

France, too, was building up a glittering prosperity. John Law, a clever Scottish financier, in 1716 convinced the French government of the great advantages of credit and in short order established a government bank, issued bank notes, and formed great trading companies, directly supported by the government. As shares in these companies soared, France rose on the crest of a great speculative wave to heights of frenzy not reached again until 1929. Prices of stocks rose to fabulous highs. Princes, priests, doctors of the Sorbonne, and shaven friars mingled with money-changers, shopkeepers, valets, and coachmen in the orgy of buying and selling. Women jostled for shares with men. Ladies of fashion went to the stock market as they went to the opera. The cafés were full of gentlemen and ladies who sipped their wine, played quadrille, and sent their servants out to execute their buying and selling orders. Almost fantastic were some of the incidents of those hectic days. It is said that owners of houses on the streets where stocks were sold grew rich from enormous rents which they obtained. A cobbler put chairs in his little shed, and had pen and ink ready for those who wished to seat themselves and deal in stocks. A hunchback hired himself out as a human desk, pleasing the crowd to such an extent that he became rich from gratuities.

Fortunes were made over-night by people of all classes. John Law was crowned a financial wizard, and people followed him whenever he appeared on the streets. Meanwhile, the cost of living "went sky-high." To buy a roast chicken cost 200 livres. Successful speculators lived in a grand manner. Gold and silver dishes, luxuries from all parts of the world, expensive ornaments—then as now the *nouveaux riches* expressed themselves in unrestrained orgies of flagrant expenditure.

Immorality and crime accompanied this false prosperity. Upon becoming rich, the fortunate one who had always been poor and respectable now showed himself as good as his superiors by having as many mistresses as the aristocrats, by drinking as much wine, and by swearing as great oaths. Murders, robberies, and assaults were more and more frequent. An organization of eighteenth-century gangsters composed of both men and women spread its nefarious villainies to all parts of France. This "brotherhood" generously adopted a code of ethics, stipulating that those robbed were not to be robbed a second time. A card was therefore presented to the victim when he was first relieved of his riches and after that he was immune from further robbery.

But the prosperity of France rested on quicksand, not on the solid foundation of commerce, agriculture, and industry. It was a prosperity founded on *what might be*—not on *what actually was*. It was a wishful gambling, with prayers frequently thrown in. By 1719, many Frenchmen, especially envious noblemen, were questioning Law's methods. Meanwhile, the ambitious financial wizard was issuing bank notes recklessly, was undertaking too many business enterprises, and was paying frequent unearned dividends. Some shrewd speculators, aware of the possibility of a crash, decided to realize their profits, then to send their money abroad, or to invest in real estate. In the face of the selling wave which followed, Law tried to sustain prices by giving out favorable statements, but to no avail. Paper money began to depreciate rapidly. Again Law attempted to restore confidence in his currency by issuing edicts ordering coins to be used only in small amounts and persons to possess only a limited supply. Use of diamonds, gold, and silver plate was forbidden. The value of coins also was changed frequently to make them comparable in value to paper currency. Moreover, hoarding of jewelry and precious metals was prohibited.

Law, however, could not maintain the credit and stability of his house of cards. In the midsummer of 1720 came the crash.

Stocks went into a fatal tailspin. The streets were full of delirious people milling about, wringing their hands, trying to sell their holdings. In the rush around one of the banks of Paris five women were suffocated. One unfortunate speculator wrote: "Alas, alas, a week ago I was rich; now I am poor and have not enough money to pay my servants." John Law fled, leaving the panic to continue unchecked. Not only the people but also the French government was affected. In vast measure it lost the confidence of many of its people because of its connection with the banks, the trading companies, and the paper money put out by John Law.

Thus, the Commercial Revolution had culminated in an era of Big Business and of speculative prosperity succeeded by a financial panic and a depression. What with her huge national debt, the loss of the major part of her empire in the Seven Years' War (1756–1763), and the failure of the feudal-classical compromise (absolutism) to function efficiently, France was set for a period of "hard times" and the way was paved for the French Revolution.

Frightened by the debacle in France, the British government acted to strangle its wild-cat companies. Confidence was undermined in the South Sea Company, and a panic ensued. Thousands of investors were ruined; and their only consolation was a parliamentary investigation as a result of which, in the modern manner, corruption and fraud were discovered and a few individuals punished while most of the real criminals escaped.

England, however, did not suffer to any comparable extent. Her commerce continued to flourish, and her merchant aristocrats continued to make high profits. The desire for additional colonies was intensified. Robert Walpole (1676–1745), the first prime minister of England, encouraged commercial expansion as a way out of the depression. Under the sway of mercantilistic ideas, he embarked on a policy calculated to add to the amount of money in England. Imperial expansion culminated in the French and Indian War (1754–1763) and English supremacy in North America. Meanwhile, two additional economic revolutions—the Agricultural and Industrial Revolutions—made England the industrial as well as the commercial center of Europe.

In agriculture, before the eighteenth century, agrarian processes had improved very little. For centuries it had been the custom to sow seeds broadcast, a wasteful method, as many seeds failed to take root and others were too close together to grow. In the middle of the eighteenth century the invention of the drill, which deposited seeds in straight furrows with sufficient space between to assure growth, considerably multiplied a farmer's potential wheat yield. Study of soils also resulted in the introduction of clovers into the rotation of crops, because these were found to add atmospheric nitrogen to the soil. By this improved rotation, which changed the crops each year in a four-year cycle, the farmer was able to use all his land without impoverishing it. Another innovation was the use of artificial fertilizers. Manure had long been used to restore the fertility of exhausted soil, but in the nineteenth century science produced artificial means of nurturing wasted or poor soils. These new techniques, together with irrigation and drainage, improved not only the crops but also made available more lands upon which products could be successfully raised.

Scientific methods were applied to other phases of farm life. Careful breeding produced finer cattle. Farm tools were better made. In the eighteenth century the horse hoe and the threshing machine were invented. In 1826 a climax in agrarian progress was reached when the famous Bell reaper appeared. These various machines revolutionized agriculture.

This Agricultural Revolution completely changed the English landowning system. For centuries most farmers had owned or rented lands consisting of strips located in various parts of local estates. This situation made it difficult for the great landowners to introduce the new methods of farming and stockraising. Therefore, aided by parliamentary support, they gradually took over the land which had been tilled by the peasants; consolidated and inclosed their holdings; and proceeded to drain and fertilize the soil, rotate crops, and introduce careful breeding of cattle and sheep. The small farmer found himself at a disadvantage. Frequently he could not show clear title to his strips and was forced off the land. Often he was too poor to construct farm-buildings or to purchase tools, seeds, and stock. Giving up his property, he became either a city factory worker or a landless agricultural laborer. His discontent was voiced in such lines as

> The law locks up the man or woman
> Who steals the goose from off the common;
> But leaves the greater villain loose
> Who steals the common from the goose.

This reorganization of agriculture enabled the various capitalistic proprietors to introduce machinery, to get along with less hired laborers, and yet to produce more crops. At the same time the Agricultural Revolution inflicted but temporary unemployment on most of the peasants. Deprived of their land, many of them flocked to the cities to look for work. This they secured. For a transformation, as great or greater than in agriculture, had taken place in industry. Where, previously, there had been a decided scarcity of work to be done, there was now an actual lack of laborers to do the work. Responsible for this new scheme of things was the coming of the so-called Industrial Revolution.

In industry down to the middle of the eighteenth century, only small-scale manufacturing had existed. Under the guild system, which predominated throughout the later Middle Ages, production, not extensive as yet, was carried on in small groups. A master gathered around him a band of craftsmen and apprentices "who were all employed together in the friendly operation of a common work-shop." By the fifteenth and sixteenth centuries a different type of organization appeared in certain industries. This new kind of industrial order was called the domestic or putting-out system. It "involved the intervention of a capitalist or organizer between craftsman and consumer—a man who owned the raw materials, and often the tools, hired the workman for wages and made his living by marketing the goods at a profit." A man with capital might own the materials and tools with which to make cloth. Knowing where to obtain the raw materials and where to dispose of the finished articles, and with capital to buy the former, he could parcel the work out to families, pay them wages, and later sell the finished products to the consumer. In some parts of Europe there were weavers who, owning tools and materials, worked in their own cottages and disposed of the goods which they produced to merchants in markets. The latter either sold or exported these commodities.

But the domestic system, in fact the complete structure of industry, began about 1750 to crumble before the onslaughts of those radical revisions which are collectively known as the Industrial Revolution. A revolution is never entirely manmade; behind it is always an intermingling variety of forces, mostly social and economic. Primarily, the Industrial Revolution had its being in the mass forces of an enormously expanding population between 1750 and 1800. This expansion had two basic causes. First was the more bountiful food supply; second was the better health of the people as a whole. The medieval plagues and epidemics had spent their virulence. A period of medical discovery evolved a better understanding of physiology, of remedies, cures, and preventatives, of such an indispensable process, for instance, as vaccination. Also, there was a sounder canon of health by the people themselves. Sanitary conditions were bettered, modes of dress less restricted, bathing at last less an aversion, health fetishes and superstitions almost bygones.

As the population grew, the demands of the people, especially of the bourgeoisie, became more pressing for those luxuries (turned necessities) which constitute a higher standard of living. They developed a taste for more varied and for more substantial foods; they fancied cotton and linen clothing instead of homespun; they wanted better homes and finer public edifices; they preferred good highways and faster transportation. Forces began to work reciprocally: as the population grew, the demand became greater, and as the demands were satisfied, the population grew; expanding markets led to increased trade, and as trade increased the markets further expanded. With the acquisition of India in 1763 by England British industrial progress was stimulated. An anonymous pamphleteer explained this economic development when in 1701 he wrote:

> The East India trade procures things with less and cheaper labor than would be necessary to make the like in England; it is therefore very likely to be the cause of the invention of arts, and mills, and engines, to save the labor of hands in manufacture. Such things are successfully invented to do a great deal of work with little labor of hands.

This prediction came true in the Technological Revolution, the immediate precursor of the Industrial Revolution. In 1769 James Watt secured the first patent for a steam engine. Soon the world was enriched by the locomotive, the steamboat, the loom, and the power machine. Nature began to be harnessed for the service of man as water power was controlled. By steam, by electricity, by chemical processes, new life was injected into industry.

Attendant upon this Technological Revolution was the culminating movement of bourgeois economic progress. The Industrial Revolution, which later spread to the Continent, originated in England for much the same reasons which had made her the leading commercial nation: the isolation from continental military and political problems which her insular position made possible, the lack of political interference in economic undertakings, the existence of banking and investment facilities, and the presence of those natural resources, especially iron and coal, needed for industrial expansion. It was no wonder that Englishmen during this period turned to machinery for increased production, instituting the great transition from man power to machine power.

Human energy could not hope to do the work of the mechanical devices which were soon enthroned in the realm of industry. Spinning machines to make yarn, run by water power and later by steam, facilitated a larger output of manufactured goods. With the development of mechanical power came factories, making possible the production of greater quantities of goods in huge shops instead of in private homes as under the domestic system. Arkwright, called the father of the factory system, not only used machines but anticipated contemporaneous specialization by having men work on particular phases of certain articles.

A marked gain in the output of manufactured goods came as a result of the discipline and supervision of men in factories. Indeed, the factory, whether worked by steam or water power, constituted the early phase of the Industrial Revolution. To it may be ascribed the greatly multiplied production, first of woolen, cotton, and iron goods, and later of most other manufactured articles, the necessities and luxuries of today. The utilization of steam power resulted not merely in the construction of factories and the raised output of manufactured articles, but it also made goods cheaper, promoted the demand, and revolutionized transportation and communication.

With this transformation brought about by the Industrial Revolution came a complete change in the system of economy. The feudal régime disappeared. In place of a social structure in which the status or occupation of each individual had been determined by birth, tradition, and law, and under which production was carried on to meet immediate needs, or for local exchange at a "just price," there arose the system of production known as *capitalism*. This term does not mean capital goods, such as livestock, machinery, or railways, nor is it synonymous with *manufacturing*, for it also comprises the whole scheme of agricultural economy. It is not, moreover, restricted to machine industry, having begun to flourish before machinery came into extensive use. Capitalism may be considered as a system of production in which the primary concern is profit for the *entrepreneur*. Its motive is to sell on the most advantageous terms, that is, for the maximum amount of profit to the owners. The scope of its operations seems almost unlimited. Indeed, under the capitalistic system, the amount of wealth accumulated, the number of men and women employed, would seem to be capable of almost unlimited expansion.

By making possible the rise of a very powerful, aggressive, and efficient industrial group, the Industrial Revolution paved the way for the complete political and social triumph of the bourgeoisie. At the same time it contributed also to the rise of the so-called "common man"—the wage-earner. It did this by making him class-conscious. Only for a short while was the worker willing to submit to the evils as seemingly brought about by the mechanization of industry. Conscious of his sufferings, he and his fellow-workers organized with the purpose of bettering their conditions. To obtain these ends, the wage-earners joined the middle classes in their opposition to the political and social restrictions of the feudal, aristocratic society. As we shall see, the Industrial Revolution, by contributing to the rise of these two groups, was chiefly responsible for the downfall throughout Europe of the old régime.

Chapter IX

LITERATURE AND THE MIDDLE CLASSES

I. Those Bourgeois Gentlemen: Defoe, Molière, & Co.

Our political protégés, especially in England, did not break into print by name for centuries after they had shown themselves to constitute a distinct class. True, there are, as the New English Dictionary shows, isolated examples of their notoriety. About 1564 or 1565, for instance, Mary Queen of Scots is reported to have told Lord Randolph: "I sent for you . . . to see how like a bourgeois wife I live." A century later Lord Clarendon, in his *History of the Rebellion* (1671), remarked about a certain personage that he "liv'd in a jolly familiarity with the Bourgeois and their Wives." The word *bourgeoisie* has no English record before 1707, when the *London Gazette* quoted a statement addressed "To the Council of the City, the Clergy, and Bourgeoisie of Vallangin." The English equivalents, *middle class* and *middle classes,* had first notice in 1812 when the *Examiner* reported on "Such of the Middle Class of Society who have fallen upon evil days," and in 1831 by Brougham in the *Spectator:* "By the people . . . I mean the middle classes, the wealth and intelligence of the country, the glory of the British name." But it was not until the middle of the nineteenth century and later that these various terms were in common usage by historians, economists, and novelists; and only today are they becoming familiar to the man on the street.

Long before, although they were not called by name, nevertheless the in-between classes were described and characterized by one of the great masters of literature—Chaucer (see pages 26-27)—in his *Canterbury Tales.* Since his time, pushed to the fore by economic, political, and religious movements; endowed with prestige and with wealth; hankering for the culture of the decadent aristocracy; blessed with a new-found leisure that threatened to lead only to boredom, this new nobility set out to impress itself on the literature of the people as it had on their politics. As theirs was a growing part of the national life, so they made themselves, their ambitions, characteristics, opportunities, frustrations, successes the theme for a divergent literature, a literature of the middle classes, for the middle classes, and gradually by the middle classes.

In England and in France—these countries being in the forefront both politically in middle-class expansion and culturally in literary genius—in these, therefore, we find the best and most representative works by or about the bourgeoisie, making their national literatures in general an embodiment of the national life. Such works serve a useful purpose in this story of this new society by shedding indirect light on the political, social, and economic ideas of the people and by building up in silhouette a portrait of the early Babbitt. Such light and characterization, as we shall observe, is keenest when directed by great masters, like Defoe in England and Molière in France.

In England the men of the middle classes were deeply absorbed in the varied phases of Elizabethan and seventeenth-century life and avidly grasped at all literature both out of the prevalent curiosity of the age and from a desire for knowledge and self-improvement. Busy men with little time for the dilly-dallying road to culture trod by the upper-class dilettantes, they followed short cuts to bourgeois perfection by patronizing authors of handbooks, pamphlets, and miscellanies. As an example, "Guides to Godliness" were very popular among them, for the business men, tempering business with religion, believed that books teaching morality made possible earthly as well as heavenly salvation.

History, too, began to take root in the consciousness of this new social section as its members became more aware of the well-springs of nationalism from which they drew their sustenance. To the tradesman history was both utilitarian and avocational, for he believed it developed culture, virtue, and patriotism in the reader, contributing thereby to a man's success in social circles or across the counter. Crude and elementary, history was written as often to amuse as to inform; it was credulous in its use of sources and in the artless presentation of facts bearing doubtful marks of authenticity; also, it lacked a social sense or any definite perspective. But it bubbled over with enthusiasm for tradition and achievement, with pride for the great men of the past, with hope for the future. Pioneers all were such writers as Michael Drayton (1563–1631), who wrote a long rhymed concoction of legends, stories, descriptions of battles, of kings, of countryside, known as *Polyolbion;* Edward Hall (d. 1547), John Stow (1525–1605), and Raphael Holinshed (d. 1584?), whose *Chronicles* were widely read and used by politicians and writers; Sir Walter Raleigh (1552?–1618), who set out to write a *History of the World* while awaiting execution; and Lord Clarendon (1609–1674), whose *History of the Rebellion* in sixteen volumes is a comprehensive record worthy of preservation.

Biography followed in the train of history. Well-known to students of literature are such representative works as Izaak Walton's *Lives* (1670) of his contemporaries, Thomas Fuller's *History of the Worthies of England* (1662), and John Foxe's *Book of Martyrs* (1563).

Travel and exploration were fascinating to the commercial classes, and duly popular were such geographies and compilations as Richard Hakluyt's *Principal Navigations, Voyages, Traffiques and Discoveries of the English Nation* (1599) and its continuation by his assistant, Samuel Purchas, as *Hakluytus Posthumous, or Purchas his Pilgrimes* (1625).

All in all, this interest in history, biography, and exploration testified to the expansion and liberation of the human personality which was the dominant characteristic of the period. Such interest in nationalism, combined with the eagerness to look beyond Britain's frontiers across oceans to foreign lands also presaged the future day when the sun would never set on the British Empire.

Of the Titans of Literature up to and including the eighteenth century—Chaucer, Spenser, Shakespeare, Milton, Dryden, Bunyan, Swift, Pope, and Dr. Johnson—nearly all were of middle-class stock and all had more or less middle-class careers. Despite their background, however, they invariably wrote for their superiors and about the higher circles. Geoffrey Chaucer, son of a vintner, was a royal and loyal servant who in the main wrote to and about his masters, although we can be grateful that his *Canterbury Tales* include both the high and the low. Edmund Spenser (1552–1599), son of a clothmaker, also served the nation and his betters, his *Faery Queene* and other works being obviously directed to the court circles. William Shakespeare (1564–1616), allegedly the son of a butcher, wrote for the pit only on occasion and consequently to find bourgeois elements in his plays is the task for a research analyst; of his dramas only his *Merry Wives of Windsor* offers any clear reason for being regarded as a middle-class play. John Milton's *Paradise Lost* (1667) with his other poems may justify the ways of God to man, but the man they are directed to is of the aristocracy, at least of intellect. Although the greatest poet of the Puritan period and although in his public life he supported the bourgeois Oliver Cromwell in the cause of religious and political reform, Milton yet seemed to resent the prevalent bourgeois tendencies of the time, as evidenced by his *Areopagitica* (the world's boldest and most uncompromising demand for free speech and a free press) in which he shows how the middle-class man entertains his "guest religion" lavishly on Sunday, but on Monday, "religion walks abroad at eight, and leaves his kind entertainer in the shop trading all day without his religion."

The aristocratic John Dryden (1631–1700) too refused to accept the social aspirations of the middle classes, and so we find his poems filled with trenchant satire against the ambitious, revolutionary bourgeoisie. In *Absalom and Achitophel,* for instance, he characterized one of these gentlemen who

> Did wisely from expensive sins refrain,
> And never broke the Sabbath, but for gain:
> Nor ever was he known an oath to vent,
> Or curse, unless against the government . . .

John Bunyan (1628–1688), son of a tinker, in life and in writing contrasted strongly with this attitude, his *Pilgrim's Progress* occupying a place unequaled as an exposition of middle-class religious belief.

Jonathan Swift (1667–1745) took up the cudgels for the downtrodden in his shafts of satire against politics and religion, and such of his efforts as *The Battle of the Books, A Tale of a Tub, Letters of M. B. Drapier, A Modest Proposal,* and *Gulliver's Travels* stimulated the attention of the middle classes and later influenced Addison and Steele, Pope, and Fielding. Alexander Pope's main contribution was to make the man of letters a man of bourgeois social standing, although the writings of the little giant himself were generally of a classicism not essentially suited to the commercial mind. Similarly, Dr. Samuel Johnson's works were not as important to the world as his life itself. This "Leviathan of Literature" would live, it is said, if he had written nothing; his personality, as related by James Boswell, reflects a Main Street character of fine proportions.

More than any of these great men, however, it was one of those in the secondary rank of literature who was the great apostle of the middle classes. First of the modern press-agents, an opportunist in a day of many opportunities, a master of the journalistic approach, Daniel Defoe (1661–1731) wrote over 350 distinct publications and earned the sobriquet of "mouthpiece of the middle classes of his day." "His works," says Louis B. Wright, in *Middle-Class Culture in Elizabethan England,* "concentrate into a sort of essence all the burgher philosophy that has been gathering force for the preceding century and a half." A London business man, social philosopher, and journalistic hireling for any side, Defoe wrote, among other things, *The Complete English Tradesman* and *The Complete English Gentleman,* in which he favored the modern conception of the aristocracy of wealth rather than that of birth. He had no patience with the hostile attitude of the gentry toward trade or toward those tradesmen who had entered the upper rank through self-initiative and sheer ability. He would, for instance, disagree with Edward Chamberlayne (1616–

1703), an exponent of aristocracy, who upheld the traditional upper-class view by saying:

. . . Tradesmen in all Ages and Nations have been reputed ignoble in regard to the doubleness of their Tongue . . . without which they hardly grow rich. . . . So by Imperial Laws, a Tradesman is not capable of any Honourable Estate, nor to be a Commander over Soldiers.

He would have found more in common with Chamberlayne's own son, John (1666–1723), who wrote that "Amongst Tradesmen, in the first Place are Whole-salemen, then Retailers; Lastly Mechanics, or Handicrafts-Men. These are capable of bearing some Sway or Office in Cities and towns Corporate," or with Bishop Burnet (1643–1715), who in the conclusion to the *History of his Own Time* remarked that "As for the men of trade and business, they are, generally speaking, the best body in the nation, generous, sober, and charitable." Himself, Defoe also extolled the good sense and Christian charity of the bourgeois landowners by contrasting in his *Journal of the Plague Year,* a probably fictitious account but clothed in pungent realism, their humanitarianism with the callousness of the nobility. In defense of the commercial classes, he wrote in *A Plan of English Commerce:*

Pride, in Conjunction with Abundance of Ignorance, is frequently in Arms against the peaceable trading World about Precedence, and in a Plea of Antiquity: They would divide the World into two parts only, the Gentry and the Commonalty. . . .

. . . .

This Family Jargon, *for it is no more,* they oppose to the trading Part of the whole World, whom they divest of all Dignity, as well as of Degree; and blend together under one general, or rather common Denomination of Mechanicks; tho' by the accidents of Time and Circumstances of Things, some of them *are,* and for many ages *have been* true members of the Gentry by collateral Branches; nay sometimes by the chief Lines of the best and most ancient Families in the Nation.

Defoe was agreed, as Wright puts it, that the tradesman of the time rather than the landowning aristocrat was "the backbone of progressive enterprise" and the pioneer of a bourgeois civilization "which was soon to predominate on both sides of the Atlantic."

Versatile, Defoe took the lead in writing novels centering about persons in the middle walks of life, usually about the "bourgeois hero." *The Life and Adventures of Robinson Crusoe* was a far cry from the romance literature of knights and nobles which until then had had precedence; Crusoe and his man Friday were a direct contrast to the knight and his squire or the gentleman and his lackeys; contrasted too was the man-manufactured theme of honor with that of all nature—the instinct toward self-preservation. In his other novels, such as *Moll Flanders, Captain Singleton, Colonel Jack,* and *Jonathan Wild,* although these were of a more picaresque nature, the characters nevertheless were predominantly other than of upper station.

Others followed Defoe's lead, such masterpieces of characterization appearing as Samuel Richardson's *Pamela* (1740), Henry Fielding's *Tom Jones* (1749), and Oliver Goldsmith's *Vicar of Wakefield* (1766). Tobias Smollett (1721–1771), with his adventures of various colorful persons, and Laurence Sterne (1713–1768), with his unique *Tristram Shandy,* have a cousinly right to join the select company.

Varied as were his talents, however, Defoe was no playwright. It remained for others in the eighteenth century to raise the hitherto supernumerary bourgeoisie to stardom, or at least to featured parts. Richard Steele (1672–1729), for instance, in his *Conscious Lovers,* selected as the father of the heroine "an eminent merchant of Bristol." Aware of the new dignity of his class, this tradesman, Mr. Sealand, informed the aristocratic Sir Bevil: "Sir, as much a cit as you take me for, I know the town and world. Give me leave to say that we merchants are a species of gentry that have grown into the world this last century, and are as honourable and almost as useful, as you landed folk, that have always thought yourselves so much above us." A decade later George Barnwell, the hero of George Lillo's *London Merchant,* expressed a similar point of view when he asserted: "As the name of merchant never degrades the gentleman, so by no means does it exclude him."

Defoe recognized the eminence which his nation was attaining, calling her "the greatest trading country in the world," because her climate was "the best and most agreeable to live in" and her men were "the stoutest and the best." Even so the finest tribute to the merchantmen was paid by the *Spectator:*

> . . . there are not more useful members in a Commonwealth than Merchants. They knit Mankind together in a mutual Intercourse of good Offices, distribute the Gifts of Nature, find work for the Poor, add Wealth to the Rich, and Magnificence to the Great. Our *English* merchant converts the Tin of his own country into Gold, and exchanges his Wools for Rubies. The Mohametans are cloathed in our British Manufacture, and the Inhabitants of the Frozen Zone warmed with the Fleeces of our Sheep.

Even Dr. Johnson, in his English as rotund as himself, wrote pæans of praise about the achievements of the energetic traders and seamen.

A very definite philosophy—distinctly bourgeois—arose out of this literary glorification of trade. Defoe and his contemporaries pervaded their writings with the thought that the middle station was the best and happiest condition of life. In his immortal work, *Robinson Crusoe,* the press-agent of the middle classes brought out this belief. Here is what a youth, wishing to go to sea, was advised by his father, a wise and grave man:

> . . . He told me it was men of desperate fortunes, on one hand, or of superior fortunes, on the other, who went abroad upon adventures, aspiring to rise by enterprise, and make themselves famous in undertakings of a nature out of the common road; that these things were all either too far above me, or too far below me; that mine was the middle state, or what might be called the upper station of low life, which he had found, by long experience, was the best state in the world, the most suited to human happiness; not exposed to the miseries and hardships, the labor and sufferings of the mechanic part of mankind, and not embarrassed with the pride, luxury, ambition, and envy of the upper part of mankind.

Accepting the point of view that the middle station in life was the happiest, Defoe and other literary enthusiasts proceeded to tell how a young man could reach this earthly heaven. First, he had to be DILIGENT. Today we say, "Business before pleasure," but in his time Defoe used more words to the same point, arguing that trade is a business for life and must be followed with all seriousness at the alternative of ruin. Nothing should be allowed to interfere with business. Not only must the tradesman be diligent in his work but he must also find it as a pleasure and not "a slavery or a bondage," for, according to Solomon, delight in business leads to diligence and diligence leads to riches.

There is hardly any book of the period that does not in some way glorify diligence, either as a necessity in trade or a virtue in the contemporary fanaticism for virtue. In the glorification of womanhood in the eighteenth-century novel, diligence ranked next only to virtuous honor; and it was one of the qualities, as described in Fielding's *Amelia* and Richardson's *Pamela,* that enabled women to raise themselves from poverty and to save those who pursued them or those whom they loved from the pitfalls of avarice, indigence, and greed. Joseph Addison (1672–1719), in his portrait of Sir Andrew Freeport, described a merchant of great eminence in London whose indefatigable industry was one of the chief reasons for his success, and remarked that "I have heard him prove that diligence makes more lasting Acquisitions than valor, and that Sloth has ruined more Nations than the Sword."

To the wealthy, middle-class philosophers theorized, diligence was necessary in order to prevent their deterioration into luxury, pride, and avarice. Concerning this, Dr. Johnson wrote in the *Rambler:* "Too much wealth is very frequently the occasion of poverty. He whom the wantonness of abundance has once softened, easily sinks into neglect of his affairs; and he that thinks he can afford to be negligent, is not far from being poor."

To those without wealth, literary philosophers considered diligence was necessary to keep them from sloth and despair.

Unfortunately, this theory was rationalized into a profitable channel, the enforced labor of the poor. Work was one thing upon which the middle class did not take a monopoly; in fact, its members insisted that it was the duty of every man and woman to work, and they proceeded to make use of the regulations which had earlier been instituted for the "good of the state" by the labor legislation of the rising absolute governments. From his own middle-class stronghold, Defoe indelibly linked idleness with poverty when he declared *"That Poverty makes Sloth, and Sloth makes Poor."* Likewise, Sir Andrew Freeport, whom Addison called his wise and good friend, argued that giving alms was merely subsidizing idleness and that of all persons, merchants should be the last to encourage beggars, for by so doing they, who are dependent upon labor, are merely making labor more expensive to procure.

Diligence being the first of the potent words necessary to throw open the door to bourgeois prosperity, THRIFT was a close second. Notoriously, frugality was not a characteristic of the early eighteenth century, and the essayists were consequently continually berating society for its lack of moderation. It was a time of considerable cynicisms, of avarice, of ostentatious display among the aristocracy. Young Samuel Pepys, an example of the middle-class man gaining his fortune by use of his government position, painted sordid pictures of court and society life, of vast expenditures for pleasure. He himself was, like others of his class, influenced by such an example, and so we find him pitifully bewailing himself in August, 1661:

> . . . I find myself lately too much given to seeing of plays, and expenses, and pleasures, which make me forget my business, which I must labour to amend. No money comes in, so that I have been forced to borrow a great deal for my own expense, and to furnish my father, to leave things in order. . . . At Court things are in very ill condition, there being so much emulation, poverty, and the vices of drinking, swearing, and loose amours, that I know not what will be the end of it, but confusion.

This "confusion" many periodicals, among which were Steele's *Tatler*, John Dunton's *Athenian Mercury*, Defoe's *Re-*

CITY OF WESTMINSTER PUBLIC LIBRARIES

view, and Addison's *Spectator,* attempted to avert by emphasizing such tender sentiments as family affection and the virtue of moderation. Defoe, moaning over the want of men blessed with a saving grace, thus gives the gist of the matter:

> The principle of frugality and good husbandry is indeed so contrary to the general practice of the times, that we shall find very few people to whom these doctrines are agreeable. But let me tell my young tradesmen, that if they must banish frugality and good husbandry, they must at the same time banish all expectation of growing rich by their trade. It is a maxim in commerce, that money gets money; and they who will not frugally lay up their gain, must not expect to gain as they might otherwise do. Frugality may be out of fashion among the gentry; but if it comes to be so among the tradesmen, we shall soon see that wealthy tradesmen will be hard to find. For they who will not save as well as gain must expect to go out of trade as lean as they began.

This emphasis upon frugality helps to explain the attitude toward advertising in the seventeenth and eighteenth centuries. To advertise was considered "mean and shameful." The expenditure of money on decorating the front of a shop was an expense that Defoe for one could not reconcile with frugality. After warning the tradesmen that needless display would eat up too large a percentage of capital, he recommends to the young tradesman "to avoid all such needless expenses, and rather endeavor to furnish his shop with goods, than to paint and gild it over to make it fine and gay; let it invite customers rather by the well-filled presses and shelves, and the great choice of rich and fashionable goods; that one customer, being well served, may bring another."

Together with diligence and frugality, HONESTY constituted the third member of the economic trinity. Linked with the conception of honesty was the idea of the honorableness of gain, or what might be called the providential duty of the middle-class man to be middle class. It was a generally accepted theorem that it was man's duty to gain, that his station was predestined by God. It was at this point that rank became somewhat elastic, for although a man might have been born in one station God may have meant him for another. It was up to him to acquire enough money, thrift being the means, to prove the theorem and to make himself one of the elect.

Defoe was foremost among the advocates of honesty. He begged merchants to regulate carefully their relationship with the world and to guard against breaking promises, not paying bills, false money, and the unfair practices attending underselling and engrossing. Furthermore, since trade was governed by credit, and since credit was inseparably supported by honesty and industry, it was to the good of the tradesman that he perform his tasks with strict uprightness because credit once lost was hard to regain. Defoe eulogized:

> Credit, next to real stock, is the foundation, the life and soul of the business in a private tradesman; it is his prosperity; it is his support in the substance of his whole trade; even in public matters it is the strength and fund of a nation.

Therefore, the tradesman was to guarantee his credit by his honesty, for whether rich or poor, "Honesty is never out of season to a trader." Above all, the man of wealth was to be discreet in these matters because so many were dependent upon him. The greatest amount of world trade was carried on by the British, and the influence of "any stagnation of credit, any alteration of coin, any public tax, imprudently laid upon this or that branch of trade, where it is rivalled by foreigners," might spread through the whole body of the nation.

It would be easy to ignore the cloudy side of the story and lay the success of the commercial classes to these moral precepts of diligence, frugality, and honesty; but the fact is that, like business men today, those of several centuries ago used questionable means, euphemized under the term of "business ethics." They were shrewd, smart, and willing to split hairs. Anything not actually against the law or against fundamental moral principles was legitimate—if profitable. Graft was accepted with complacency; Pepys, ambitious but practical, was primarily interested in lining his pocketbook, and if at the same time he could help his fellow-men, why all to the good. His *Diary* gives illuminating examples.

Toward what was this philosophy of success directed? As a

matter of fact, the trader, although he considered himself as good as the squire, looked forward to the time when he could retire, purchase an estate, and actually live the life of a gentleman. In this period of early capitalism the spirit of enterprise was different from that of today. The idea of working just to make money was not yet a middle-class trait; money was accumulated for its trading power, its ability to purchase influence, social position, gentlemanly leisure. Retirement, consequently, was practiced to a large extent, Defoe himself advocating it and advising that a rich tradesman, "leaving off, should endeavor to quit the world of trade in peace, and go off in a calm, with the good words of the rich, and the blessings of the poor."

It was this spirit—keen curiosity for new horizons, longing for self-improvement, pride in their economic position, fidelity to the sound precepts of good business combined with shrewd ethics, and the desire to enter the upper-class circle—that enabled the commercial classes practically to rule England and made that nation the outstanding imperial power of the Western world.

Across the channel, the French bourgeoisie, like their English cousins, began to read about themselves in print and especially to see themselves on the stage in the seventeenth and eighteenth centuries. Like the English, they were boosted into prominence by the forces of industrial and commercial progress such as enlarged markets, inventive application, the use of coinage, and expanding population. Like them thereafter the principle that "power gives wealth" was reversed to "wealth gives power." In a similar fashion to the English, the French aristocracy was diminished by wars, intrigues, and excessive expenditures, the upper middle classes thus being able to take advantage of the aristocratic depression to purchase landed estates and to settle down as a new nobility. Frequently, sons and daughters of the aristocracy and of the commercial gentry intermarried and so rubbed out the obstructive social barriers. Largely because of their riches, their ability, and their respectability the business classes advanced politically; bourgeois magistrates, lawyers, and civil servants, unashamed of their vulgar origin, began to rule their fellow-men. Loans to the government tended to make that instrument more responsive to the lenders. Like the English, too, the French began to yearn for the higher things—to desire culture, satiation of curiosity, gentlemanly leisure, and the admiration of their compatriots.

Still, French business men were hampered by centuries of tradition. The aristocracy, perhaps frightened by the prospect of absorption and loss of identity, became more and more aware of its class superiority and stressed the distinctions between itself and these upstart children of riches. Resentful, and realizing their importance, the shopkeepers in turn raged at the restrictions which kept them from holding the really meaningful church and government positions. Moreover, they viewed with apprehension the mismanagement and waste in state finances, the governmental interference with industry and commerce, and the hodgepodge of courts, frequently with conflicting jurisdiction, which resulted in slow, cumbersome, inefficient, and corrupt justice. They lived with the hope that they might bring about improvement, but, deprived of effective political power, they could only look on helplessly.

From the French dramatists of the seventeenth and eighteenth centuries, more than from any of their contemporaries in any other literary métier, came a clear picture of these ambitious bourgeoisie and their fruitless, bootless quests. Almost always are they characterized or caricaturized as struggling individuals, striving to shed shop-worn crudities for aristocratic veneer, ending up as buffoons, to be laughed at and somewhat shamefully pitied. Only a few playwrights portrayed the members of the middle classes as men satisfied and even frankly proud to belong to their station.

Less a standard-bearer for any social class than a heartless stripper of shams and flogger of foibles, Molière (1622–1673) has left dramas unexcelled in conjuring up pictures of the typical bourgeois of his time. In his plays are illustrated the weaknesses and vices of this class—their aping of the nobility, their avarice and hoarding of money, their excesses of bigotry, their affectation in the professions. Truthful, however, Molière also delineated their agreeable qualities, such as "the milk of human kindness," the love of peace, the emphasis upon self-control, the belief in common sense, and the rigorous adherence to honesty.

In *Le bourgeois gentilhomme* Molière was most unflattering in his exhibition of bourgeois characteristics. Surviving today for its humorous quality more than for its allusions and representation of the contemporary scene, the play is nevertheless like a background history of a definite social type. The play abounds in scenes which bring out the foolishness, the vanity, and the gullibility of the middle-class social climbers. To bridge the gulf separating him from those of noble birth, the main character, the comical Jourdain, determines, much to the disgust of his level-headed wife, to educate himself in the finer graces. Despite the efforts of various professors of music, dancing, fencing, and philosophy, his only tangible progress is his comprehension that all which is not verse is prose. "It's prose, you ignorant woman! . . . All that is prose is not verse and all that is not verse is prose, there! That's what one learns by study." Out of sympathy with her husband's social ambitions, the commonplace but sensible bourgeois wife expresses satisfaction in her class by retorting: "You are a fool, husband, with all your flimflams; you have been like this ever since you mixed with the nobility."

In contrast to such a complacent wife, Molière in *Les Femmes Savantes* pictured the attempts of a woman to buy and use culture as one would buy and use vegetables from the public market. In this play, the long-suffering husband protests against the mania for learning which has caused utter neglect of the domestic arts. "What does it matter," he remonstrates to his wife who has fired the maid because her grammar was not good, "that she is ignorant of the laws of Vaugelas, provided she is a good cook? . . . I live on good soup and not on fine language."

Another playwright, Philippe Destouches (1680–1754), in his greatest success, *Le Glorieux*, describes with fidelity a bourgeois who actually attains the goal of his ambition by being ennobled. Although he cringes before aristocrats and purchases a title for his daughter, nevertheless he claims that his titles are simply "scraps of paper," that he is not dazzled by them. Brutal and repulsive though he is, this middle-class man is never really ridiculous. He is in a transitionary state, representing the business classes at a time when they are beginning to be on the same plane with their superiors. But the sense of values, of money over tradition, still is hard to remove. "Is money a title?" asks a nobleman. "Brighter than yours," replies the money maker. "In my desk I have bills payable to bearer which I think more of than of old parchments, mere food for rats."

Money in some theme or other was a general topic in the drama. The miser became a stock character. Molière, in *L'Avare,* took cupidity as his main theme and proceeded to describe the dissensions which greed and avarice bring into a bourgeois family. Harpagon, the father, is the type of selfish, middle-class man who places wealth above every consideration. Robbed of his buried treasures by his own son, the miser reveals, somewhat vaingloriously but otherwise in a typical cry from a sound commercial heart, his attitude toward money:

> . . . Alas! My poor money, my poor money, my dear friend! They have deprived me of you, and, now that you are taken from me, I have lost my support, my consolation, my joy; all is finished, I have no longer any concern with the world, without you it is impossible for me to live. All is over, I cannot do anything more, I am dying, I am dead, I am buried.

Other writers of the same period produced dramas which emphasized bourgeois avarice. Jean Regnard (1655–1709), in his *Le Légataire Universel,* depicts the efforts of a group of dishonest people to obtain the inheritance of Geronte, a hypochondriac, who begrudges the price of his medicine. Another dramatist, Alain Lesage (1668–1747), describes in his masterpiece, *Turcaret,* the corruption which the growing power of money was breeding in French society. These illustrations are most unflattering; they show a feverish lust for money and luxury with a corresponding callous lack of idealism and good taste.

Wealth was a fetish because it gave power. Financiers, these shrewd playwrights pointed out, refused to cringe in the presence of social superiors. Florent Dancourt, a well-known dramatist of the late seventeenth century, dwelt upon this by remarking that ". . . by shining in finance . . . one runs no risks, and one is a respected man in society." The general theme of his work indicated the confidence, the unscrupulousness, and the hardness that the "ways of finance" seemed to breed in men. Lesage, in his *Turcaret,* also described exceedingly well the cool-headed, unscrupulous, merciless financier, who quite often in the eighteenth century was the man to whom the government farmed out its taxes and who often took advantage of this office to rob the people.

Dangerous it is to deal in generalities, and so it must be admitted herewith that these mentioned characteristics did not necessarily encompass a majority of the bourgeoisie. Many there were who refused to imitate the aristocrats and preferred to enjoy rather than to worship money, to be considerate rather than harsh to their employees, to live their own lives instead of inhabiting aristocratic castles in the air. Moreover, the weaknesses attributed to them often belonged more promiscuously both to the upper and the lower classes.

As a matter of fact, the dramatists conceded the superiority of bourgeois morals. Molière, for example, in *Le bourgeois gentilhomme,* offers a telling picture of the sensible and affectionate tradesman's wife and mother of the time. This paragon, protesting against the "arranged marriage" of her daughter to a nobleman, says:

> . . . Matches with those above one's own position always lead the way to vexatious annoyance. I do not want a son-in-law to reproach my daughter with her parents, or his children to be ashamed to call me grandmother . . . I want a man in short who will be glad to have my daughter, and to whom I can say: "Sit down, son-in-law, and have dinner with me."

In another way bourgeois ethics were especially emphasized by writers. Most of them made the tradesmen faithful to their wives; slyly intimating that such was not the virtue of the aristocrats; *ergo:* a man who loved his wife was bourgeois. Voltaire, in a clever way, emphasized this very idea by describing a typical marriage between members of different classes in which the nobleman characteristically scorned his conventional wife while she faithfully and dutifully loved him. In short, some of these playwrights maintained that real home life could be found in the middle-class house while in the great manors of the aristocrats would be found only domestic discord.

On the whole, French drama in the seventeenth and eighteenth centuries faithfully described the rise of the bourgeoisie and the corresponding decline of the nobility. Usually ridiculing them in the seventeenth century, writers in the succeeding period began more and more to portray the middle classes as men satisfied with and often proud of their status. These same literary intellectuals began to emphasize the sound sense, self-reliance, and class-conscious dignity of these people.

At the same time many dramatists, in the manner of Beaumarchais (1732–1799) tended to ridicule the nobility instead of the business classes. One of the leading bourgeois intellectuals, in his plays, especially in the two comedies, *Le Barbier de Seville* and *Le Mariage de Figaro,* he revealed the weaknesses of absolutism and clearly portrayed the middle classes, their traits and beliefs. Moreover, through the lips of the different actors he interpreted French society as it existed before the Revolution, placing its leaders, the business men, in the foreground, as they were in real life. In *Le Mariage de Figaro* Beaumarchais was especially bitter in his attacks upon the accident of aristocracy. Says Figaro:

> Because you are a great seigneur, you believe you are a great genius. Nobility, fortune, rank mean all that renders you proud. What have you done for so much wealth? You have only given yourself the trouble of being born and nothing more. As to the rest, you are an ordinary enough man. While I, curse be it, lost in the obscure crowd, I have had to show more sagacity and calculation to live than one has needed to govern all Spain for the last hundred years.

At the same time, Beaumarchais was not unconscious of bourgeois weakness. A world of meaning is packed in Figaro's exclamation: "Gold, good heavens, gold! it is the fortitude of intrigue."

Aside from the drama, during the seventeenth and eighteenth centuries a great number of books dealing with commerce were published in France. Though no account of these can be given here, nevertheless the most important, *Le parfait négociant* by Jacques Savary (1622–1690), must be mentioned briefly. In order to obtain clarity of presentation, the author adopts a simple but effective device; he takes a child at the beginning of his apprenticeship and leads him by degrees into the intricacies of all branches of trade. Throughout the work Savary continually emphasizes the vitality of commerce. "It is," he says, "this continual exchange of all the commodities of life that makes commerce, and it is this trade also that makes the sweetness of life, since by means of it there is everywhere an abundance of all things." Running into at least nine editions and being translated into German, Dutch, English, and Italian, this monumental work became the generally accepted contemporary authority on commercial affairs.

All in all, whether by Chaucer, Defoe, Shakespeare, Molière, or lesser lights; whether in England, France, or countries less commercially prominent; whether in plays, novels, or periodicals, it was evident that the middle classes by the eighteenth century were an accepted subject for the various national literatures.

Chapter X

HERALDS OF PROGRESS

There can be no revolution until the ideas of men become the conscience of the mass, and until the passions of men become a living form, because "it is men and not events which constitute the world" (Bartolomé Mitre).

"Antiquity deserveth that reverence that men should make a stand thereupon and discover what is the best way; but when the discovery is well taken, then to make progression." In thus begging men to cease worshipping the past and to look forward to a new day, the far-seeing Francis Bacon (1561–1626) was but one of the heralds of progress who caused an intellectual revolt against cultural tradition and so paved the way for the French Revolution and the triumph of bourgeois individualism. This attack upon "authority" was aided by such seventeenth-century scientists as Newton and Descartes. In thought Descartes left no place for the "authority of tradition." Not believing in the "wisdom of prejudice," he substituted for it faith in the power of our thoughts today. If we use the proper method, he wrote, we shall be able to outstrip our ancestors. The golden age is not behind us. Not only is progress possible, but there are no limits that can be assigned to it in advance. Such a philosophy could not help but appeal to a large part of the middle classes of his day.

Scientific progress gave impetus to the revolt against the established order. Tracing *The Life and Death of an Ideal* (Charles Scribner's Sons, New York, 1928), Guérard asserts that "The seventeenth century was in some respects the golden age of mathematics, the age of Descartes, Fermat, and Leibnitz, leading up to the grandest triumphs of the mathematical mind of Newton. Gradually, through astronomy and physics, studies in which observation and experimentation were combined with mathematical formulation, the sciences of the concrete were reached and developed." These researches were very vital not only because of their intrinsic values but also because they made the scientific method the tool of the current intellectual exponents of reform. The technique of analysis and synthesis used by the scientist of the concrete was found to be equally explicable to the man-made organizations of law and custom known as society or government. To the enthusiastic critics and writers, therefore, the scientific revolution was not, as many nobles superficially labeled it, a passing fad or fancy. Inspired by its achievements, they adopted a practical approach to political, social, and economic problems, and by so doing ushered in the so-called "Age of Enlightenment."

Popularization of the scientific method greatly aided the "modernist" movement. Although artists, writers, and philosophers found it expedient to worship tradition, the scientists were well aware of the limited knowledge of the ancients and could not adhere to this accepted attitude of blind reverence. Charles Perrault in 1687 read a poem at a meeting of the French Academy in which he expressed this opposition, saying: "Noble antiquity ever was venerable, but I never believed that it was to be worshipped. I view the Ancients without bending my knees. Great they are . . . yet men like ourselves."

The scientists initiated a constructive instead of a destructive movement. It is true that their successors, as we shall see later in this chapter, demanded the overturn of those institutions, consecrated by the past, which in their opinion were unjust. But at this time there existed the "idea of progress as a guiding principle in seeking solutions for the difficult problems which were harassing the minds of men." This progressive idea was gladly accepted by the pragmatic middle classes, who realized that before they could attain a position in society satisfactory to their ego the idea of Providence, the basis of the aristocratically organized society of the Middle Ages, must be obliterated. In its place must be substituted the belief in growth, "which included the gradual enlightenment of man's nature, the evolution of his intelligence, the expansion of his moral sense, and the improvement of his well-being."

Possessed by this view, the publicists (the so-called philosophers of the eighteenth century) strove for intellectual and religious freedom, for political rights, and for economic independence. Desirous of well-being, they fostered above everything else the conception of the dignity of the individual as achieved through self-determination and self-expression. This assumption was primarily utilitarian, an outgrowth of the Puritan view that an individual should mold his own destiny. The inevitable result was the acceptance of the idea of success measured in commercial enterprise and in the attainment of economic liberty.

In adopting this concept of progress, men were at first cosmopolitan. They did not think in terms of national entities. According to intellectuals such as Kant and Schiller, humanity would benefit by obedience to the dictates of social expediency; thereby man in the future would enter upon his rightful heritage and enjoy the inalienable rights of life, liberty, and the pursuit of happiness. This belief spread rapidly and became highly characteristic of the middle classes. Art, science, and literature, religion and politics, the family and the state—all were examined by the interpreters of social progress with a view to bringing them into conformity with the new thought.

Withal, the middle classes soon found that it was the economic foundation of their social order that had to be reoriented; in essence, economic factors lay at the basis of the multifarious political, social, religious, and intellectual institutions. In some new way they had to enhance the life of labor, to raise it far above the supercilious life of the dilettante aristocrats. For practical reasons, too, they deemed it necessary for the expansion of their businesses that the regulations which maintained the old order be swept away or greatly altered. Opposition to the barrier of classes became more pronounced. The erection of an ideal civil society became an absorbing purpose. Having reached the conclusion that economic aspects dominated all phases of earthly existence, they welcomed most enthusiastically the birth of a new social science, economics, which explained and justified their position, a theory which they hoped would enable them more than ever to supplant the old régime by developing national governments under their own control.

This new theory began as an attack upon the prevailing acceptance of mercantilism as the life-saver of the state. Mercantilism, whereby governments regulated and encouraged economic development, had been the backbone of bourgeois success. In the eighteenth century, however, intellectuals in France and England began to question the value of the seeking-for-gold policies. In their opinion governmental regulations often did more harm than good; for example, in industry new inventions of value frequently were not adopted because governments forced the continuation of out-of-date methods. In agriculture they maintained that all governmental restrictions placed upon the sale of grain aggravated famine. Believing in fundamental or natural laws which no one should try to change, they rejected mercantilism, even questioning the belief that gold and silver were wealth and that prosperity necessitated a favorable balance of trade. In place of this doctrine these economists advocated a policy of *laissez faire* ("let things alone"). If the governments remained on the sidelines, they declared, the people could play a better economic game. One of the early exponents of the *laissez faire* idea was Vincent de Gournay. Richard Cantillon, a contemporary and an Anglo-French banker, also developed this point of view in his *Essay Upon the Nature of Commerce in General.* His work was especially significant because it paved the way for another group of economic thinkers in France—the Physiocrats.

The Physiocrats were perhaps the first to point out the meaning of the economic life of the country from the political and social point of view. Their ideas were so significant that they were adopted by many of the revolutionary thinkers. While these concepts were not middle-class beliefs in origin, coming as they did from nobles and other members of the privileged classes, their direction was such that the Physiocrats came to be identified with the bourgeois revolutionary movement.

Most of the Physiocratic social and political concepts rose out of the relationship established between liberty and property. A man with the free use of property was actually free, they said, while a person with no control over property was in reality a slave. According to the Physiocrats, the object of society was to maintain the security and the inviolability of property or, as the solid middle-class business man of today phrases it, "the protection of property and the maintenance of law and order." In view of this definition of the function of the state, the Physiocrats maintained that only property owners could be citizens. As Mirabeau, the "friend of man," put it: "le souverain et les propriétaires . . . voilà ce que compose l'État" (the sovereign and the propertied persons—they are the ones who compose the State).

Monarchists in theory, the Physiocrats really were as liberal as some of the most advanced thinkers of their time. They wanted to maintain the monarchy for the same reasons advanced by English bourgeoisie: it was convenient; it was dangerous to change; and, above all, the king was bound to realize that his advantage lay in the same direction as that of the propertied classes. But, at the same time, the Physiocrats wished to clear away all obstacles to what they conceived to be the natural course of the development of society. They stood for economic freedom, as against governmental regulation; for freedom of thought, freedom of press, and religious toleration. François Quesnay (1694–1774), the leading Physiocrat, emphasized in his works "the natural phases of life and wealth as against the artificial and complex regulation of life." He believed that the *laissez faire* doctrine conformed to nature; mercantilism did not. In his opinion the individual must look out for himself in trading. A true Physiocrat, he regarded agriculture as the natural source of wealth, the wealth which in turn was so fundamental to the progress of any state. According to Quesnay, commerce and industry were essential only as they were related to agriculture. Prosperity, in his opinion, was dependent, not upon the mercantile favorable balance of trade, but upon the *Profit Net* (net profit or yield), to be derived from the soil.

Turgot (1727–1781), one of the leading French economic statesmen of the pre-revolutionary period, was influenced by

Physiocratic ideas. An exponent of the doctrine of *laissez faire,* he believed that the government should always protect the natural liberty of the buyer to buy and the seller to sell. But the government should not interfere in the transaction between buyer and seller. ". . . Every seller," he wrote, "it being his chief interest to merit preference over his competitor, will sell in general the best goods at the lowest prices at which he can make a profit in order to attract customers. The merchant or manufacturer who cheats will be quickly discredited and lose customers without interference of government." Turgot also proposed a plan of representative government, based on many Physiocratic ideals, by which eligibility for election would depend upon property qualifications so set that he expected a large majority of the votes in the assemblies would be controlled by a solid bourgeois group.

A semi-Physiocrat like Turgot, Voltaire (1694–1778) at the same time was a radical intellectual and a bourgeois standard-bearer. His political, social, and economic ideas did not follow, like an arrow to a bull's eye, directly to a definite theory or program. He had in himself diverse elements. Theoretically, for instance, he desired the equality of man; but in his *Dictionnaire Philosophique,* he so writes only to conclude with a practical reminder:

> Every man has a right to entertain a private opinion of his own equality to other men, but it follows not that a Cardinal's cook should take it upon himself to order his master to prepare his dinner. The cook, however, may say, "I am a man as well as my master; I was born like him in tears, and shall like him die in anguish, attended by the same common ceremonies. We both perform the same animal functions. If the Turks get possession of Rome, and I then become a Cardinal and my master a cook, I will take him into my service." This language is perfectly reasonable and just; but, while waiting for the Grand Turk to get possession of Rome, the cook is bound to do his duty, or all human society is perverted.

Apparently Voltaire regarded equality as an ideal, an end to be reached in the distant utopian future. In the meantime, law and order must be preserved, and the status quo must be maintained. Voltaire's enthusiasm for these ideas probably rose out of his financial situation. Always on the lookout for chances to make money, he became a very rich man, few in the eighteenth century amassing such a fortune. One of his favorite investments, it is said, was the *rente viagère* (a kind of annuity), for, because of his sickly appearance, Voltaire managed to get high rates of return. It has been thought that he intentionally bruited about the idea that he had one foot in the grave so that he could obtain rates as high as 15 or 20 per cent on his capital. His debtors became financially ill while he lived to a ripe old age. A smart bourgeois investor was this literary giant! The realization that equality, once attained, might mean the loss of his "hard-won" fortune undoubtedly made Voltaire apprehensive. Even a superficial glance at his program shows how moderate and conservative it was.

No writer of the eighteenth century equaled Voltaire in the expression of bourgeois ideas. Although he attacked kingly tyranny, he never advocated the substitution of a French republic. What he tried to do was to clear the way for the rise of the business classes by restricting the sphere of the church to non-secular matters and by limiting the function of the state to maintaining the status quo in property relations. An ardent exponent of religious toleration, Voltaire outlined the position of the church in the modern capitalist nation, when he maintained that the church should be subordinate in temporal affairs to the state, not to the clergy; marriages should be controlled by secular authorities; and the clergy should pay taxes to the state—not to the pope—as does every one else.

In the political field, Voltaire's visions were limited to an abiding faith in benevolent despotism; at no time did he attack despotism as an "unnatural" form of government. Here he contrasted with other intellectuals, notably John Locke of England, who in the seventeenth century maintained that the ultimate source of the government was the people or their representatives, rather than a king ruling by grace of God. Voltaire's countryman, Montesquieu (1689–1755), supported Locke's views and, in his *Spirit of the Laws,* praised the English type of limited monarchy. His books made such institutions as parliament, the right of the legislature to control finances, and the *habeas corpus* proceedings familiar to the middle-class men throughout the continent. Despite the limitations of his political ideas, Voltaire, on the whole, believed confidently in enlightenment and progress through reason rather than through tradition. To the middle classes his ideas were very welcome.

To Jean Jacques Rousseau (1712–1778), more than to Voltaire, went the honor of being the peerless prophet of bourgeois democracy. True enough, Rousseau, in urging a return to nature, that is, in turning his back upon the forward movement of arts and sciences and demanding the overthrow of the existing civilization which, he believed, had demoralized mankind, was more radical than the average member of the middle classes. If, however, he meant the overthrow of the obsolescent, decadent, feudal-classical compromise—the absolute state—as the "degenerate Athens" of the eighteenth century and desired the establishment of a Sparta, where men would lead sober, industrious, and thrifty lives, then he was bourgeois. Rousseau's emphasis upon "the simple life" appealed to the middle classes, for the bourgeoisie necessarily led basically simple lives. Theirs was the applause of rationalizers. Above all, his belief in the sovereignty of the people earned for him popular commendation. By "the people" Rousseau, according to the business classes, meant those unprivileged but ambitious individuals who had money but lacked blue blood. They, not the king, were to make the laws.

Rousseau, like Voltaire, therefore, was essentially a bourgeois philosopher. That his *Social Contract* is not to be taken as a statement of practical aims but merely of principles was proved by Rousseau himself. Twice he was given the opportunity to apply his principles when the progressive elements in Poland and Corsica appealed to him for a constitution. Face to face with actual situations, Rousseau's chief suggestions were patience and, above all, moderation; by no means were radical changes to be attempted. For instance, when he analyzed Poland's troubles, he frankly agreed that serfdom was contrary to justice; but he recognized the difficulties of change and concluded by urging that nothing be done, for a time at least. When, in another case, he constructed a constitution for Corsica, it contained few radical departures. He did, however, counsel the Corsicans to beware of cities and the evils of civilization.

Unlike Voltaire and the other philosophers who represented the interests of the wealthy business men, Rousseau opposed bourgeois as well as feudal aristocracy. An ardent petty middle-class radical, he wished to see a country made up of independent small tradesmen, farmers, and artisans without poverty and without great riches. "The ideal for him was a society of comfortably situated private owners and artisans." He merited the title—prophet of the petty bourgeoisie.

Legal reforms, as proposed by the Italian economist, Beccaria (1735–1794), in his *On Crimes and Punishments,* also received the hearty approval of the bourgeoisie. As members of the unprivileged classes they were subject, at the instigation of their rulers and nobles, to arrest without definite charges; trial, if any, without impartial procedure; and imprisonment without clemency. In his treatise, Beccaria urged public trials in which the accused should be confronted by those who accused them. Nobles and magistrates should be subject to trial the same as the lower classes. Confiscation of property should be abolished. These reforms strongly appealed to the bourgeois desire for law, order, equality, and security.

But Adam Smith (1723–1790) was by far the outstanding bourgeois philosopher of the eighteenth century. Maintaining in his *Wealth of Nations* (1776) that the true strength of a nation lay in the prosperity of its citizens, Smith contended that unrestricted enterprises promoted the accumulation of riches by the individual. In direct opposition to mercantilism, he asserted that restrictions were useless and even harmful; each man knew best how to acquire wealth; and if he were permitted to adopt a policy of self-interest, the nation would become rich. The individual, therefore, should be allowed freedom in business unhampered by governmental regulation. To its advocates this doctrine of *laissez faire* constituted the expression of economic liberty.

Smith was the agent for a concept which arose out of many

intellectual streams of thought. From the theologians came the doctrine that there was no need for the state to intrude in every-day life. From the political teachings of Locke and Rousseau came the theory that the state had no right to intervene in economic matters. From the French Physiocrats came the assertion that it was inexpedient for the government to interfere with or regulate business. To some economic writers governmental interference was not only unwise but immoral. Man had natural rights, which it was criminal to deny. Every individual, for example, had the right to make money, unhampered by political and social restrictions. No rules or regulations should stand in the way of a man engaged in the production of wealth. At the same time private property was sacred and inviolate. Once wealth was in his possession, no one should have the right to deprive him of it against his will. This, in essence, was the shrewd economic philosophy of the right to have and to hold.

Bourgeois capitalism was endangered by such wholehearted acceptance of individualism. The workers soon announced that these so-called rights included that of possessing employment and of receiving a larger share of the fruits of their labor. Thereupon the employers invoked the concept of "natural law" to defend their position. According to this philosophy, inasmuch as natural physical laws had been formulated for the movements of the stars, planets, and in fact all forms of nature, did it not follow that certain natural laws should determine social conditions? Such deduction, of course, had all the falsity of reasoning by analogy. Natural laws explained why some nations and individuals were wealthy and others were poor. Poverty would always exist, for if poor men were given larger wages, they would have larger families and more mouths to feed; *ergo,* poverty would persist. Man-made regulations, maintained the orthodox advocates of this philosophy, could not overcome the law of supply and demand. It was a natural law. How could wage-earners be saved from poverty if some were predestined to be rich and others to be poor? The exponents of *laissez faire* left the solution to the individual. Bourgeois individualism made economic salvation possible through the practice of thrift, self-denial, and hard work. Other things being equal, a self-made man who followed these precepts could enter the paradise of the middle classes. If by cleverness, shrewdness, or good luck, he obtained a large share of the wealth of a nation, then as a rich man he was entitled to a place in a special section of paradise reserved for monied aristocrats.

To the fringes of the middle classes, to the lesser bourgeoisie, and to the wage-earners, all these theories, these ideas, these revolutionary concepts, were roseate rainbows over somebody else's garden. To them life was always much the same, dull, drab, workaday. Great movements such as the Renaissance and the Commercial Revolution, the establishment of Christian sects in the sixteenth century, and the beginning of modern science did not drastically affect their daily lives. Nevertheless, the heralds of progress having sounded the call, it remained for France to lead the way toward a more promising future.

CHAPTER XI

THE GREAT BOURGEOIS REVOLUTION: COMPROMISE

Bliss was it that dawn to be alive,
But to be young was very Heaven! O times,
In which the meagre, stale, forbidding ways
Of custom, law, and statute, took at once
The attraction of a country in romance!
(*Wordsworth,* The Prelude).

THE French Revolution, in essence a great bourgeois revolt against the constrictive forces of the old order, sounded the death knell of feudalism in Western Europe and was the clarion call for pioneers of a new society. "Revolution," Victor Hugo has said, "is the larva of civilization." Toward this new society the first steps were taken in the distant past and were clearly apparent by the eighteenth century, when attempts, as we have seen, were made to overthrow the established order. The pre-revolutionary social system, through its legal sanctions, had become the responsive instrument of the aristocratic and wealthy cliques, which at the most never exceeded ten per cent of the total population. Both law and custom saw to it that noble families retained amongst themselves large estates and lucrative government sinecures by allowing these to be handed down as legacies to their eldest scions or by prohibiting the partition of property. Thus was insured the perpetuation of a privileged nobility, thus kings, nobles, clergy, and bourgeois aristocrats possessed a monopoly of lands and of offices. The other classes were either underprivileged or more nearly unprivileged, for feudal, Roman, and church law all recognized the prerogative of wealth and position.

Before the advent of the Revolution, however, many European rulers of the eighteenth century, under the sway of the reformers, had decided that it was politically expedient not to oppose social and economic progress. Frederick the Great of Prussia, embodying the Hohenzollern tenet that the monarch was the chief servant of the state, devoted his energies to the end of strengthening his dominions by acquiring territories, by fostering economic progress, and by advocating a policy of religious toleration. He also desired the abolition of serfdom, but the junker landowners balked his designs. Catherine the Great of Russia attempted to establish a great assembly of her people by instituting religious freedom, establishing schools and hospitals, and advocating the growth of nationalism. Joseph II, Holy Roman Emperor, strove to unify the private Hapsburg possessions, to encourage secular education, to oppose the privileges of the church, and to abolish serfdom in Bohemia, Moravia, Galicia, and Hungary. In Spain, Charles III attempted to secure a prosperous middle-class régime by encouraging industry and agriculture. All of these eighteenth-century benevolent despots appreciated the advantages of economic enterprise and adopted policies designed to help the bourgeoisie. But, despite these traces of social idealism, these rulers refused to limit their own personal authority through the granting of political reform.

In France, following the death of Louis XIV in 1715, benevolent despotism made little headway. During this period the nobles endeavored in vain to abolish the feudal-classical compromise and to restore the feudal state; but it was too late, for France had experienced a great social change—the rise of the bourgeoisie—and the bloody terror was taking on its red tinge.

During the reign of Louis XIV the nobility had eclipsed all other classes in distinction. It is true that the king gave high civil and military positions to successful business men, but at no time did the fetish of wealth surpass the social supremacy of blood. Louis always regarded himself as a monarch ruling by divine right, and resented the title—king of the bourgeoisie. After 1715, however, wealth gradually replaced blood as the chief token of distinction. Accumulation of riches became to many the chief goal of life. This change of attitude found embodiment even in the connotation of words. In the seventeenth century, "speculation" was ordinarily construed as philosophical meditation; in the eighteenth century, the term was applied to gambling on the rise and fall of money and stocks.

Even the nobility engaged in the struggle for gain. According to one contemporary writer, they adopted the vices of the middle classes, and the latter returned the compliment by frequently assuming many immoral activities hitherto monopolized by the aristocrats. As a result of their attempts to enjoy modern luxuries, the nobles cheapened themselves. They became a speculating group, pursuing money "more passionately than the middle classes pursued titles." Love of gold, passion for material pleasure, vulgar pomp—all replaced the qualities of dignity, honor, and disdain for business which had hitherto characterized the nobility. A mad scramble for intermarriages ensued in which the nobility sought money and the bourgeoisie, titles. Thus was presaged the decline and fall of the aristocracy.

The middle classes profited by this "decay." Sons and daughters of rich business men married aristocratic lords and ladies and obtained social distinction. Petty bourgeoisie in France, as in England, gladly joined Masonic lodges which worshipped science, promoted progress, and permitted social equality. At the same time, the bourgeoisie were securing a potential monopoly of governmental positions. Consequently, as office holders and as financiers this class was in a position to demand and to receive respect. "The aristocracy is losing from day to day more land," writes Brunetière in his *Les époques du Théatre Français* (Hatchêtte, Paris, 1896), "and the bourgeoisie, the Third Estate, becomes richer in importance, takes on a new feeling of its rights. The inequalities appear more shocking, the abuses more unbearable. Their hearts are 'full of hatred,' as the poet would say, and 'hunger for justice' —or for equality."

A financial crisis finally forced the middle classes to act. They now realized the need of a unified and impartial legal and financial system. Many of the provinces had their own laws and their own taxes, and these tended to hinder commercial and industrial progress. Social groups enjoyed various exemptions from taxation. The nobility and the clergy, for example, usually avoided the payment of money to the government, while they had the right to collect tolls from their peasants. Many of the aristocrats were "tax-eaters," holding lucrative sinecures granted by the king, or possessing valuable governmental or military positions. Wealthy business men participated in this "spoils system" by purchasing governmental positions, especially in the parlements, and by being excused from the payment of certain taxes. As a result of these exemptions the major elements in the Third Estate—the petty bourgeoisie, the artisans, and the peasants—paid most of the taxes. In the Middle Ages the nobles as fighting barons justified their privileges by giving protection; in the eighteenth century most of them had become proud parasites. Quite natural, therefore, was the resentment of the middle classes; the outlet for their reaction was interest in radical reforms and flirting with the idea of a revolution.

Actual revolution became a menace only after the threat of bankruptcy appeared in 1789. Expensive wars, governmental extravagance, and corruption in the collection of taxes had greatly endangered the national credit. Business men realized that this financial collapse would greatly injure economic activities. In their opinion reform was imperative.

Even so, recent historians of the French Revolution admit that economic and social conditions in France were actually improving before the uprising occurred. Commercially and industrially France was on the upgrade; the peasants were much better off than were their brothers in Austria and in the Germanies; foreign trade had nearly doubled between 1750 and 1789; old guilds and handicraft organizations were disintegrating, their numerous regulations receiving little consideration from a growing number of independent merchants and artisans; inventions in transportation, communication, and agriculture promised a brighter future. These economic assurances caused people, especially the bourgeoisie, to see further progress ahead and to demand political and social reforms which would facilitate that development. The French Revolution was, therefore, in reality an act of faith on the part of the business groups, because they realized that economically France was on the upgrade and that real prosperity would be attained, provided pertinent reforms could be enacted.

In the year immediately preceding the calling of the Estates General, elements in all classes favored economic reforms. The king was primarily interested in fiscal changes. In the past the government, to obtain money, had sold numerous political positions to members of the bourgeoisie. Consequently, a large, expensive, and unwieldy bureaucracy had been built up which could be reduced and made efficient only through the repurchase by the government of these offices. To achieve this end the king favored a reorganization of the finances, involving, however, no drastic political or social changes.

Representative members of the privileged nobility and clergy, recognizing this need for financial reform, were willing to give up their fiscal immunities. So, too, many great landowners agreed to the abolition of feudal rights. This change, they believed, would enable them to obtain the communal lands and, like the English squires, to build up large estates scientifically managed and worked by tenants and hired labor. Without the necessary capital for the exploitation of their estates, and dependent upon the feudal dues of the peasants, the lesser noblemen fought these drastic financial and feudal proposals. As "patriotic" Frenchmen they were willing to make certain sacrifices for the good of the state; but they wished to reduce them to a minimum. Moreover, they demanded the restoration of their political power and the diminution of central authority through the reëstablishment of the provincial estates and Estates General, controlled by the privileged classes.

While reform to the royal government and the upper classes had only limited connotations, to the unprivileged groups it meant great change. All of the common people—bourgeoisie, peasants, and proletariat—desired the destruction of fiscal immunities. The business classes were especially interested in the tax problem because they had loaned money to the government and feared that a monarchy, undermined financially, could not continue to guarantee a prosperous business activity. They well knew that an insolvent government jeopardized their profits. Moreover, many of them saw clearly that the acceptance of fiscal equality would probably lead to the establishment of legal and political equality. Once these objectives were gained the bourgeoisie would be in a position to remove all restrictions on trade and industry which stood in the way of their prosperity. Abolition of feudal rights, as demanded by the peasants, however, did receive the hearty support of the bourgeoisie. In general the business classes wanted to coöperate as much as possible with the nobility.

There were men in France capable of bringing about these changes without threatening the very existence of the established order. For example, Turgot as financial minister had urged a policy of governmental economy, reforms in the system of taxation, and individualism in business calculated to restore prosperity and thus to increase taxes. But elements in all groups—nobility, clergy, middle classes, and even the peasants—refused to coöperate. Consequently, Turgot failed. Another minister, Necker, had tried to clarify the financial muddle by a policy of economy; but when he published a report on the financial condition of France which showed how the king and his "noble" parasites wasted government money, he promptly became an *ex*-minister. Calonne, following Necker, tried to court an artificial prosperity through a lavish spending of public funds. He destroyed what little credit the government had and brought France to the verge of bankruptcy.

By 1787, Louis XVI realized that reforms were necessary, so he vaguely advocated religious toleration and popular participation in the government. In short order, he called an assembly of his notables and laid his troubles before them. Meanwhile, he issued several edicts enacting certain pressing financial reforms and sent them to the various parlements to be registered. The chief judicial body, the Parlement of Paris, consisting of rich bourgeoisie, jealous of the nobility and the king's ministry, refused to register the edicts and informed the king "that only the nation assembled in the Estates General can give the consent necessary to the establishment of a permanent tax." A few days later, this Parlement "respectfully requested the king to call a meeting of his Estates General, consisting of representatives of the clergy, the nobility, and the Third Estate."

At first Louis XVI and his ministers tried to get rid of the Parlement of Paris. The latter loudly announced that it was representing the welfare of the nation against cruel, selfish despotism. This "battle cry" was quite effective, even though the bourgeois members of the Parlement were in reality advancing only their own individual interests. Unable to overthrow the Parlement, Louis XVI was forced to receive its statement of an "unwritten constitution" limiting the power of the king, and to admit his responsibility to the people in financial matters by calling the Estates General to meet in May, 1789. Demonstrations, some fostered by the various parlements, now occurred in different parts of France, the participants in these maintaining that they alone had the right to grant taxes and indicating that they were ready to do so.

The calling of the Estates General gave the middle classes, particularly the small country lawyers, their first real opportunity to engage in politics. Elections and meetings were held in all parts of France, where delegates representing the three estates were selected and lists of grievances *(cahiers)* were drawn up. Inasmuch as the bourgeoisie, liberal noblemen, and paternal village priests were primarily responsible for the preparation of these *cahiers,* practically all of the representatives of the Third Estate were selected from these groups, especially from the bourgeoisie.

A bourgeois-aristocratic compromise was the objective of the great majority of the delegates representing the Third Estate. To attain this objective a program was constructed which included a constitution wherein the rights of all should be defined and maintained by law, and an assembly which would meet in national crises and expostulate if necessary against any violations of the proposed charter of liberties. The delegates did not intend to abolish monarchy or to deprive the nobility and clergy of their social and feudal privileges; they merely desired reforms which would insure political, legal, and financial equality to all groups.

In 1789 the Third Estate in the Estates General was made

up almost entirely of bourgeoisie. Half of the members were lawyers; of the remainder there were a number of provincial and municipal officials, nobles, and clerics, and a large delegation of merchants, industrialists, and *rentiers*. The peasants and urban proletariat were not represented directly, although some of the members of the Third Estate were determined to make the Estates General a National Assembly in which all the groups would meet at stated times. In their opinion this reorganization was necessary in order to carry out such physiocratic reforms as the abolition of fiscal and legal privileges, and the improvement of the financial situation by policies calculated to swell revenues and diminish expenditures. Louis XVI had paved the way for this move when, before the assembly met, he doubled the membership of the Third Estate. This enlarged representation, the country lawyers who had been chosen as representatives realized, would not count for much unless the three groups—the clergy, the nobility, and the Third Estate—could meet together rather than in separate bodies. Only then would the 600 delegates of the "unprivileged classes" be equal to the combined clerical and aristocratic representation, and only then would they be in a position to bring about these vital reforms.

But to these finely devised plans of the Third Estate, there developed a very considerable opposition. Prior to the assembly of the Estates General the "repentant government" seemed to be on the side of the lower classes and had gone so far as to promise a constitutional assembly and a ministry responsible to the assembly; but the speeches delivered in the opening session of the Estates General, when all groups met with the king, proved conclusively that the government proposed to consider in the Estates General the matter of finances only. Ignoring the bourgeois demands for political and legal reforms, the king turned away from the middle classes and asked for the support of the conservative nobility. This change was unfortunate, because both the monarch and the aristocracy had, prior to this time, assumed a conciliatory attitude when confronted by such bourgeois demands as a constitution, individual liberty, and legal and fiscal equality.

In the face of such enmity the Third Estate, very wisely concluding that nothing further could be gained by a conciliatory policy, itself proceeded to proclaim a National Assembly and invited the other orders to join. Unwilling to assume the responsibility for a violent upheaval, the king and the upper classes finally gave way; and the nobles and clergy with the Third Estate now formed the National Assembly. Superficially there appeared to exist again a feeling of coöperation and good will; in reality, there was lodged in all the groups an intense bitterness, resentful and indignant. Many of the nobles even decided to leave France.

Dissatisfaction was not limited to the various groups in the National Assembly. In 1789 unrest was developing in the city and country districts of France. Parisian "soap-box" orators harangued the petty bourgeoisie and working people and told lurid tales about the king and his noble henchmen. On July 14 this agitation culminated in an attack by a mob upon the Bastille, a government prison. The peasants, dissatisfied because the feudal régime had not been immediately abolished by the National Assembly, began to take matters in their own hands. Insurrections broke out in various parts of France; charters, containing lists of feudal dues and rent tolls, were destroyed; property was damaged; and blood was spilled.

Panic-stricken as a result of these riots, the wealthy middle classes took immediate action. Many of the towns, large and small, organized armed forces (national guards) to protect and preserve "law and order." On August 4 the National Assembly declared for the abolition of feudal dues in principle. In actuality, the bourgeoisie intended to give the nobility adequate compensation, and laws were later passed fixing the mode of abolition, whereby feudal dues were not to be abolished, but were to be redeemed by a high money payment. The peasants disapproved but were powerless to counteract the strong bourgeois-aristocratic alliance in control of the National Assembly and the government. In time the business classes realized that the peasants could not make the payments nor could they pay the feudal dues; consequently, the Convention in 1793 abolished all feudal dues and money payments.

Between 1789 and 1791 the National Assembly, dominated by the upper bourgeoisie, drew up a new constitution and strove to clear up the financial confusion. In August, 1789, it voted the famous middle-class declaration of independence, called the "Declaration of the Rights of Man." In this document it proclaimed the sovereignty of the nation and its control over the laws. It also enunciated the rights of man: liberty of thought, liberty of expression and association, religious toleration, and trial by jury. The declaration further recognized legal and fiscal equality and the inviolability of private property.

While in theory the National Assembly declared for democracy, in practice it evolved a constitutional monarchy controlled by property owners. The constitution made the king a figurehead, and the nation was henceforth to be governed by a single legislative body elected by those who paid direct taxes. The citizens who could vote—the taxpayers—were the "active citizens"; the others—little less than half—were the "passive citizens." Thus excluded from participation in the body politic were many petty bourgeoisie, the peasants, and the urban workers; insured for the wealthy bourgeoisie was complete control of the government.

The capitalistic and physiocratic character of the new régime was clearly shown by the treatment accorded property and economic rights in the Declaration and in the Constitution. Under the absolute monarchy there had been no protection for the property rights of the individual against the claims of the government. Every phase of economic activity had been regulated in the interest of the state, and the government at all times had reserved the right to pass laws designed to protect industries, to prevent high prices of necessities, to designate the kind of goods to be manufactured, and to interfere with economic undertakings in various other ways so as to strengthen the monarchy. Against this governmental right to intervene in business the bourgeoisie in the days of absolutism could offer little resistance.

In the National Assembly, however, the wealthy classes undertook to protect themselves. With this end in mind, in the

Declaration of the Rights of Man they proclaimed the sacredness of private property by asserting that the state could not confiscate a man's belongings save for the public weal and even in that event the owner should be paid adequate compensation. In the matter of state control of economic enterprise the principles set forth in the Declaration of the Constitution were very clear; man has certain fundamental rights; the function of society is to protect each man in the exercise of these rights; and should the government go further in its control, the individual has the right to revolt.

While making a constitution the bourgeois National Assembly was faced by certain distressing difficulties. The permanent deficit, which was one of the great weaknesses of the old monarchy, was first handled by the abolition of fiscal immunities. With all groups, including the clergy and the nobility, paying taxes, it was felt that the government would be enabled to meet its current obligations. Liquidation of the national debt was less easy, for it required the obtaining of a tremendous amount of money on short notice. The government, however, made such an attempt by proceeding to confiscate the lands of the French Catholic church. Striving to do this the government encountered the embattled resistance of the church, but did not find justification of its policy difficult. In theory, claimed the state, the lands of the church had been given by individuals to assist that institution in carrying out its functions. Inasmuch as this property did not belong to any individual because of the purpose for which it was donated, it belonged to the nation as a whole. Therefore, why should not the government take over these lands, guaranteeing the church sufficient funds for carrying on its work? Smacking of nationalization was the added justification that many of the functions of the church, such as education, charity, and hospital service, should really be handled by the state.

From the point of view of the church, however, this confiscation was illegal and an attempt to bring that institution under the control of the state. Despite this disagreement, the bourgeoisie, realizing that this transfer would throw fertile lands upon the market and would provide an opportunity for investments and speculations, warmly supported the plan, claiming that the government and the peasants, as well as the business men, would profit as a result of the attendant general prosperity. For, on the one hand, this confiscation would enable the small farmers to add to their holdings and thus to support the revolution; on the other, it would authorize the government to issue paper money *(assignats)* with the land as security and thus to reduce the national debt at the expense of the church, not of the middle classes.

These reforms only served to fan the flames of unrest in France. Numerous peasants, loyal to the church in which they had their being, stubbornly buffeted the tide of revolution. Many nobles, denouncing the constitution of '91, the laws for confiscation of church property, and the required oath of loyalty to the constitution by the clergy, emigrated to the Germanies. Arriving there, the noble "émigrés" proceeded to foment feeling against the revolutionary movement in their homeland. And quite ready were the rulers here to support the postulations of the French émigrés. For bourgeois radicalism had become a great menace to the law and order of the Hohenzollerns and the Hapsburgs. An attack upon and defeat of the French radicals would discourage any similar movements in their own dominions.

Meanwhile, the masses in France were becoming more and more restive. Many peasants were incensed because feudal dues and payments had not been completely abolished. Urban workers and numerous petty bourgeoisie objected to a property restriction upon suffrage which had placed control of the government in the hands of the aristocrats and the wealthy business men. Moreover, the lower classes resented the middle-class attempts to load the burden of taxation upon the masses through the authorization of indirect taxes on food and wine rather than upon property and income. The rise in the cost of living which resulted from the tax system increased the unrest among the consumers.

But, prior to 1791, effective antagonism against the bourgeois-aristocratic domination failed to appear. This was largely due to the general prosperity of the country. Harvests were good and consequently the cost of living was not unreasonably high. As long as the economic needs of the masses were fairly well satisfied, the bourgeoisie opposed successfully the reactionary exponents of the old régime and the extreme advocates of democracy. Meanwhile, they succeeded in carrying out their policies. On June 14, 1791, the Chapelier Law, abolishing guilds, corporations, and restrictions on trade, was passed. Unions on the part of workers to raise wages were declared illegal. As a concession to the masses the indirect municipal taxes were abolished.

Louis XVI's attempt to leave France in 1791, however, threatened to provoke trouble. Arrested by representatives of the Assembly before he was able to cross the French frontier, the king and his family were returned to Paris. Rather than run the risk of a reactionary or radical uprising, which might weaken or destroy their supremacy, the bourgeoisie announced that Louis XVI had been kidnapped and forced to flee against his will, thus ignoring the charge that the king was guilty of treason.

Fully aware of the opposition by the reactionaries and the radicals, the bourgeoisie decided to maintain the status quo at all costs until the constitutional monarchy was firmly established; they therefore encouraged the formation of a National Guard in Paris under the command of the ambitious liberal Lafayette. This "original" home guard proved its worth as the defender of "law and order" by violently suppressing the famous Republican demonstration on July 17, 1791. The very severity of this force in squelching an apparently peaceful and harmless gathering indicated how great was the fear of radicalism on the part of the new property classes.

On September 14, 1791, Louis XVI took the oath to the Constitution, and the so-called limited monarchy came into existence. A period of false calm ensued. Conditions were fairly satisfactory, the lower classes were quiet, and the bourgeoisie felt secure. But under the surface, trouble was brewing.

The counter-revolutionary activities of the king and the privileged classes finally resulted in the complete abolition of the bourgeois-aristocratic compromise—the constitutional monarchy—and the creation of a bourgeois republic. Feeling against Louis XVI became pronounced when he refused to sanction laws passed against the émigrés and the non-juring priests and vetoed the desire of the legislative assembly to establish a camp of 20,000 soldiers just outside of Paris. A crisis was reached, when, on April 20, 1792, France declared war on Austria, and Prussia, springing to the defense of Austria, declared war on France. Resentful of the famous Declaration of Pillnitz (August 27, 1791), where the Hapsburgs and Hohenzollerns told the French to restore Louis XVI to his former position and thus to reëstablish a government that "shall promote the welfare of the French nation," most of the bourgeois revolutionists welcomed the declarations of war. By that time many of them thought that they were crusaders and that to defend the revolutionary cause they must subdue the hostile monarchs. On the other hand, Louis XVI believed that war might place military authority in his hands, and, even if France were defeated, he would be restored to power.

Threatened by enemies within—nobles and clergy—and from the hostile dynasties without, the middle classes, especially the petty bourgeoisie, turned to the lower classes for support. The bourgeois-proletariat alliance which resulted served to bring the king into line. On June 20 the proletariat of Paris, joined by many members of the bourgeoisie, visited the legislative assembly, bearing with them petitions, and then "called" upon the king in the palace. Louis was forced to put on a red cap of liberty and to drink with the mob, which had a gala time until the bourgeois mayor of Paris, Pétion, appeared and easily persuaded the people to go home. Many conservative middle-class men, as well as aristocrats, condemned the whole affair and called for the punishment of the leaders. Lafayette now tried to become the head of the conservative elements and to use the National Guard to protect the royal family; but the king and queen distrusted him and refused his protection. Meanwhile, the National Guard and the greater part of the middle classes joined the radical element which was demanding a democratic republic.

On August 10, 1792, an insurrection brought about the fall

of the limited monarchy and the end of the bourgeois-aristocratic alliance. By that time the revolution was not merely a fight against the old régime but a struggle against the Germans, the historic enemies of France. Thus the revolution had become a movement not merely to emancipate the unprivileged classes but a struggle to preserve the territorial integrity of France. The arrival of the National Guard from every part of the country, singing the nationalistic hymn, the *Marseillaise*, was evidence that the revolution and patriotism were identical. Firm in the belief that the welfare of the government and also that of the masses was at stake, powerful elements within the bourgeois-proletariat alliance decided to destroy the monarchy entirely and to call for a "new deal." The old government was rung out on August 10, 1792, when the king and the royal family were arrested by National Guardsmen, "active," and "passive" citizens, and imprisoned. An assembly was called to pave the way for a republic. Throughout Paris the people cried: "The monarchy is dead, long live the republic!" The first phase of the Revolution was over.

CHAPTER XII

THE GREAT BOURGEOIS REVOLUTION: TRIUMPH

A people which has consummated a revolution should never look back (Legendre).

MONEY-TROUBLES beset harassed France, and soon the critical financial situation brought about by the war forced the bourgeoisie to go farther than they had originally intended in their alliance with the proletariat. By 1792 *assignats* had depreciated in value. The government in desperation resorted to issuing paper bills, expecting to print a limited number; but once the printing presses were started they were as uncontrollable as wild horses. Inflation now followed, and the cost of living rose sharply. War and inflation are poisons in an economic system; taken together, they are doubly dreadful. In France industry, commerce, and agriculture declined, accentuating the increase in the cost of living and also producing another real problem—unemployment. Under such conditions the peasants and proletariat became very restless. Shopkeepers in Paris were terrified when they heard reports to the effect that the mob planned to massacre those in prison and then to plunder the shops. To hold the proletariat in line, the radical bourgeoisie turned on the king, beheaded him, and promised a republic which would end the cause of all trouble, the old régime, and would restore prosperity.

Meanwhile, the war with Prussia and Austria brought most elements in France to the support of the revolutionary government. Troops were sent to meet the enemy, and revolutionary and patriotic fanaticism enabled the bourgeoisie to arrest and guillotine enemies of the revolution and of France. A Revolutionary Tribunal was set up to try political offenders while the Commune of Paris, controlled by small business men, sanctioned the massacres of September. In short, the middle classes permitted the proletariat to resort to violence because their support was needed to help defeat the enemies of France and to continue the revolution.

During these turbulent days were held the elections to the Convention, which met on September 21, 1792. Like the Legislative Assembly, the Convention consisted for the most part of middle-class men. There were a few ex-nobles and some priests, but a majority of the deputies were merchants, industrialists, *rentiers,* and members of the legal profession—the latter being the largest single group.

By 1792 bourgeois organizations were influencing the course of the revolution. A group of young lawyers of the Legislative Assembly who originally came from the province of Gironde and therefore were called Girondins proposed the establishment of a republic. At first they welcomed the declaration of war, believing that it would lead to the overthrow of the monarchy; but later, when the French revolutionary armies drove the enemy out of France, they clamored for peace so that the business men could consolidate their gains under a stable government. Many Girondins, admiring ancient Greece, wanted to reëstablish in France that individualism which had made Athens a great cultural center.

Opposed to the Girondins was the leading bourgeois society, the Jacobins. Established in Paris, this organization by 1792 had chapters in the leading towns and cities of France. During the first phase of the revolution (1789–1792), the Jacobins, opportunists for the most part, tried to follow rather than to lead the masses. At first most of them were constitutional monarchists. By 1792, however, they had become exponents of republicanism. The elections of 1792 to the Convention resulted in a marked addition in the number of Jacobins elected to that body. At the same time this organization obtained control of municipal governments, especially of the Commune of Paris.

During the early phase of the Convention the Girondins seemed to be in control of the revolutionary government. At that time they planned the establishment of a prosperous, aristocratic, bourgeois régime. This was to be managed by the formation of a decentralized republic and the attainment of economic as well as political individualism. Exponents of the *laissez faire* doctrine, they advocated free trade and independence for all French colonies. Once France had established such a liberal government, other European states, they believed, would do likewise; and Europe would consist of a federation of republics maintaining world peace.

The Jacobins, representing the lesser business men, disagreed with this individualistic program of their aristocratic republican brothers. While these Jacobins desired a republic, they were not committed to the principle of decentralization and the complete acceptance of the *laissez faire*. Instead, they gradually developed a national or patriotic spirit, emphasizing the importance of the state. Acceptance of this "new" nationalism caused them to adopt a number of policies used by the very monarchical government which they were trying to destroy. In the course of time, these opportunists became as enthusiastic exponents of protection, imperialism, and security (the natural frontiers) as were Colbert and Louis XIV. In their desire to carry out these objectives they became earnest advocates for the continuation of the revolution and of the war. Promising the complete overthrow of feudalism and the enactment of measures designed to help the masses, the Jacobins were able to obtain the support of the lower classes, especially in Paris. Moreover, as a party in favor of a war which would lead to the acquisition of the natural frontier, the Rhine, the Jacobins appealed to the patriotic as well as to the economic ambitions of many Frenchmen.

Backed by the masses and by the "patriots," the Jacobins were able to bring about the fall of the Girondins. Recklessly, perhaps, the latter opposed the death sentence imposed upon Louis XVI and the continuation of the war after the enemy had been expelled from France. Thereupon the Jacobins questioned the loyalty of the Girondins to the revolution and to the nation. Accusing them of having dictatorial ambitions, those "patriots" finally succeeded in bringing about their downfall.

The declaration of war on England and on Spain in the spring of 1793 augmented the power of the Jacobins. Now they were able to say that the struggle must go on, otherwise alien nations would conquer France. Radical and almost socialistic policies were announced in order to win the support of the lower classes. Meanwhile, the Jacobins as a whole sought the establishment of a powerful centralized government in order to meet the enemy and to continue the revolution. A constitution creating a decentralized republic was drawn up by the Convention but was not formally adopted. Instead, on October 10, 1793, the Convention decreed that "the provisional government of France shall be revolutionary till peace."

This strong government, wherein full executive power was placed in the hands of a Committee of Public Safety, consisting of from twelve to sixteen men, proceeded to maintain "law and order" in France, to continue the revolution, and to push the war against the alien states. To maintain "law and order" at home, the bourgeois government resorted to the famous "Reign of Terror." More a reign than a terror, this revolutionary device had as its purpose the prevention of a bloody civil war by the arrest and the death of representative leaders opposed to the revolutionary cause.

Bad economic conditions also justified the creation of this strong government. In order to prevent financial chaos, it passed numerous laws designed to support the faltering *assignats*. Prices of essential commodities were fixed by the Law of the Maximum, and attempts were made to feed the unemployed and the poor. While these measures quieted the masses, they, by their very regulations, prevented industrial and economic recovery.

In April of 1794, the revolutionary government came under the control of Robespierre, perhaps the greatest Jacobin and bourgeois leader. Backed by his fellow lawyers, Couthon and Saint-Just, he tried to carry out a program which was essentially middle class. Meanwhile, he was attacked by the former privileged classes, which wanted to end the revolution and the war, and by extremists, who advocated the confiscation of wealth and its distribution among the poor so as to bind that portion of the population to the revolution.

As the leading member of the Committee of Public Safety,

Robespierre endeavored to steer a middle course. He desired the complete abolition of feudalism; but he oppugned the attempts of the radicals to pass a *loi agraire* designed to confiscate property and to bring about a redistribution of all land. At the same time he urged the continuation of the war because he believed that further victories would strengthen the revolutionary cause and bring territorial gains for France. Advocating protection for industry and imperial expansion, he planned the establishment of a prosperous bourgeois republic wherein the extremes of wealth and poverty would be nonexistent.

In no sense can Robespierre's policies be considered radical. It is true that the Convention confiscated the property of the émigrés and gave it to the poor; but this was a war measure designed to give the families of soldiers some means of support while the conflict continued. Influenced by the unrest which always exists in an era of high prices, unemployment, and business depression, Robespierre was forced to return to the old system of state regulation. By the Law of the Maximum and other measures that followed in 1793–1794 freedom of trade and industry was completely destroyed. The declining *assignat* was made legal at its face value and arrangements were instituted for the fixing of prices from day to day for objects of prime necessity such as wheat, flour, meat, oil, sugar, soap, salt, and shoes. All goods were to be sold only in the market place. Moreover, should merchants and producers refuse to sell their products, the state would reserve the right to requisition and sell them at the fixed price of the day. Finally, wages were to be fixed for each locality. It was apparent that during the emergency at least the government was determined to control prices and thereby enable the wage-earners to maintain a decent standard of living.

Actually, Robespierre was a bourgeois idealist. He hoped to make France another Sparta, rather than a new Athens. In this "virtuous" state, people were to develop their bodies as well as their minds, to live moral as well as economic lives. Thus, by means of a moral awakening, wherein the people would worship the Eternal, the revolution was to reach its goal.

Frugality, stoicism, and equality were Robespierre's watchwords; and the people, to attain this classical-puritanical utopia "were to be refashioned."

Robespierre's plan to organize the political work of the nation included some very practical measures. He encouraged, for example, the establishment of a uniform legal system. He was in favor of educational indoctrination; that is, a system of public education which would make every child a devout exponent of the new order and a devoted citizen of the Republic. He advocated social legislation, such as old-age pensions. In fact, he really outlined the capitalist system as it developed in the nineteenth century.

This apostle of virtue, however, did not retain his "dictatorship" very long. With the danger of invasion removed and civil disturbances under control, the *raison d'être* of the revolutionary government disappeared. Various groups in the nation, therefore, began to break away from the revolutionary government. Royalists and their followers, who were in constant danger of arrest under the harsh Law of Suspect; middle-class merchants, who had supported the Law of the Maximum, which ruined their profits only because it was a military necessity; and acquisitive property owners, who opposed the laws which took confiscated land off the market and distributed it among the poor—all united to wrest from power the man who directed the revolutionary government. Aided by a public opinion which was tired of terror and of virtue and was desirous of enjoying the benefits of the revolution, these groups succeeded on July 27, 1794, in bringing about the fall of Robespierre and his followers.

Robespierre's execution ended the radical phase of the Revolution. Moderates, now in complete control of the Convention, proceeded to seek peace and the establishment of a conservative bourgeois republic which would maintain law and order, protect private property, and prevent the return of the old régime. Against this middle group was a radical element which sought a general redistribution of property in the interest of the poor and a conservative group which yet worked for the return of the monarchy. The moderate republicans found it exceedingly difficult to maintain the balance of power between these factions. They did succeed in weakening the radicals by destroying the headquarters of the extremist organization, "the Society of Equals," and by beheading its leader, Babeuf. But the antagonism of the nobles, the clergy, and many wealthy conservative bourgeoisie they could not overcome.

Believing that the restoration of economic prosperity would strengthen their position, the moderate republicans, mostly merchants and industrialists, removed many of the regulations and restrictions imposed upon business by the revolutionary government during the war. In December of 1794 and January of 1795 they abolished the Law of the Maximum and the provisions for the registration and requisition of goods. Liberty of trade, they believed, would lead to an abundance of goods, would foster employment, would lower prices, and would bring about general economic prosperity. Instead, prices rose, the markets remained empty, and unemployment increased. This state of affairs led to serious riots and to an attack upon the Convention by a dissatisfied mob.

During this period of economic unrest the Convention drew up a constitution establishing the first French Republic. The basic idea of this new bourgeois Magna Carta was expressed by the terms, liberty, stability, and property, and by the phrase "a country governed by the proprietors is in a state of society; a country in which the non-proprietors rule is in a state of nature." Under the constitution the suffrage was restricted to taxpayers. This limitation together with a system of indirect elections insured control of the new government by the wealthy classes. Common fear of radicalism and also of a dictator caused the Convention to create an executive body of five men (the Directory) and a bicameral legislature in which the conservative upper house would be in a position to curb any radical activities in the lower chamber.

The Declaration of Rights and Duties which accompanied the Constitution of 1795 was a bourgeois charter of beliefs. Like their predecessors in 1789, the members of the Convention reiterated in the new declaration the fundamental rights of man. Unlike the men of 1789, however, they decided that a declaration of the duties of man would serve as a check on the enthusiasm of the newly liberated masses. Therefore, they proceeded to define and frequently to limit man's rights by stressing his duties. For example, they emphasized the necessity of respect for, and obedience to, law. They insisted on the connection between private virtue and good citizenship—a purely bourgeois idea. "No one is a good citizen," they declared, "unless he is a good son, a good father, a good brother, a good friend, and a good husband." No one is a virtuous man unless he is unreservedly and religiously an observer of the laws, especially the ones pertaining to the sanctity of private property; for "it is upon the maintenance of property that the cultivation of the land, all the production, all means of labor, and the whole social order rests." A moderate bourgeois régime was brought into existence by the Constitution of 1795. Control of the new government by these men was assured when they decreed that two-thirds of the members of the Convention would have to be elected to the new government in the first election.

The non-restoration of the monarchy was one of the basic policies of the new republican government. Believing that the return of the Bourbons would mean the handing over of the lands of the church and the nobility to the former owners, the politicians refused to sanction any attempt at conciliation with the old régime. Also those who had bought the feudal and church lands with depreciated paper money did not propose to lose the property they had so cleverly gained, nor did they intend to share it with the propertyless classes. Intolerant of all attacks upon this "private property," they passed a law which punished by death:

> All those who, by their speeches or writings . . . advocate the dissolution of the national representation, or that of the Directorate . . . or the reëstablishment of the royalty, or of the Constitution of 1795 . . . or the invasion of the public properties, in the name of the agrarian law, or in any other way.

Backed by this law, the government quickly suppressed all royalist and radical movements which threatened the existence of the newly established order, making no attempt to conciliate the opposition by well-devised reforms. The government, however, did try to establish an equitable system of taxation and to improve the financial problem by repudiating paper money; but these measures and other minor reforms did not revive business, eliminate unemployment, eradicate poverty, nor reimburse the nobility and the church for the loss of their lands. Instead, the government, backed by a small bourgeois minority, resorted to political intrigue in order to remain in power. For a while these stupid statesmen were successful. Most people, especially in Paris, tired of revolution and war, paid little attention to the government and tried to enjoy the pleasant things of life. Consequently, they permitted different factions within the administration to retain power by *coups d'état* rather than by popular electoral support.

The resumption of war, whereby France again tried to gain her "natural frontier," the left bank of the Rhine, paved the way for the fall of the Republic and the rise of a dictator—Napoleon Bonaparte. Popular as a result of his successful Italian campaigns of 1796–1797, he aided the Abbé Sieyès to overthrow the Directory in 1799 by a *coup d'état*. Napoleon was then elevated to the position of First Consul in the new government, which was called the Consulate. As chief executive in this complex government, he was received at first with a curious apathy. There was little coolness, but neither was there any enthusiasm. The people simply waited.

Aware of this situation, the First Consul determined to inaugurate a policy which would turn indifference into enthusiasm. He knew that the people were tired of theories and wanted to enjoy the practical benefits of the Revolution; he realized that peace and order were ardently desired by all; and he learned that to be successful he must please the bourgeoisie, for they were the political bell-wethers in France. He also believed that the French middle classes would welcome a leader who would end the revolution and would consolidate and make permanent such changes as the transfer of property. Inasmuch as the revolutionists to advance their individual interests had condemned, confiscated, and even destroyed property in the name of the state, Napoleon concluded that liberty actually was a farce. Therefore, if he could guarantee to the middle classes the material things they had won, he could make himself the autocratic head of the French state. To achieve this end he set out to attain the principal aims of the bourgeoisie: peace, order, and prosperity.

Between 1799 and 1803, the First Consul made considerable headway in carrying out these purposes. Peace treaties were negotiated with the enemies of France. Meanwhile, the clever dictator took on the rôle of a civil administrator. He adopted a modest and conciliatory attitude and ostentatiously put away his general's uniform in order to don a civilian's frock. To the nation at large he promised order without reaction at home, and peace with honor abroad. To the middle classes he pledged governmental financial stability, the encouragement of agriculture, trade, and industry, and the attainment by them of social positions befitting their importance. Then, shrewdly emphasizing the necessity for a strong executive, he promulgated a new constitution which pretended to maintain the sovereignty of the people but in reality concentrated practically all governmental power in the hands of the First Consul.

Throwing his boundless energy into the task of fulfilling these promises, Napoleon brought about remarkable changes in an amazingly short time. It is true that his policies at times were too hasty and that regularity, unity, and authority were too often substituted for liberty, individualism, and local differences. Yet the illusion of complete success was created for at least half the period of his rule and, despite the gradual development of disappointment and disillusionment, did much to prolong his reign in France.

The establishment of order in France was one of Napoleon's great achievements. When he became First Consul, the country was in a shocking state of chaos. Owing to the inefficiency of the local units of government and of the police, large bands of brigands terrorized the country and committed almost daily deeds of murder, robbery, and looting. To remedy this situation, one of the first laws passed dealt with the reorganization of the internal administration. Elective assemblies were suppressed, and their power was placed in the hands of Napoleon's representatives, the prefects. By this change, Bonaparte not only ended local disorders, but also concentrated governmental power in his hands. "France's officialdom became a grand machine, of perfectly symmetrical design, and in which the minutest wheels received their impulse from the central motive power of Paris."

Encouraged by the revival of general optimism as a result of his restoration of law and order, Napoleon determined to win middle-class support by reforms designed to stabilize the financial situation in France. A new and efficient system of tax-collecting was installed in every department, and the assessments were fixed for a definite period at moderate rates so as to awaken public confidence and thus to secure prompt payment. A sinking fund was established to keep up the price of national bonds; a considerable portion of the public debt was refunded; a regular annual budget was established; and government officers were made strictly responsible for all public funds. The capital of the Bank of France, founded in 1800, was increased so as to make that institution an important factor in furnishing financial aid to business men as well as to the government. Financial stability was also aided by Napoleon's edicts against the further issuance of government bonds and his insistence upon a "pay as you go" policy. Moreover, he lightened the taxes on capital and real estate by placing a larger burden on indirect taxes, especially upon such luxuries as tobacco and liquors. All of these measures had a rejuvenating effect upon the condition of the country. As trade began to revive and public credit to function, the reckless profiteering invited by depreciated currency was brought to an end.

Well satisfied with his financial policies, Napoleon proceeded to back the economic interests of the bourgeoisie officially. An elaborate program was inaugurated which included such items as the establishment of new industries, aid to established concerns, encouragement of chemical and industrial experiments, and inauguration of industrial expositions. In his attempts to bring about the economic rehabilitation of his country, Napoleon also planned the establishment of Chambers of Commerce and the enactment of ordinances regulating the affairs of industry and agriculture. Schools designed to teach workers to use machinery were opened, and exhibitions with rewards for excellence in workmanship were held. The system of communication was perfected by constructing numerous roads and canals. Indeed, if Napoleon could have avoided war, France probably would have experienced a marked industrial development, for in 1801 the much-needed Belgian coal fields were inside her frontiers.

While engaged in these undertakings Napoleon also promulgated a new Civil Code for France. Well aware of the weaknesses and ambitions of the middle classes, it made the father all-powerful in the home. Labor unions were outlawed because their employers feared "a state within a state" as much as did the advocates of the old régime. One famous section thoroughly indicates the bourgeois character of the Code; this article provided that "the master's affirmation is to be accepted, with reference to the rate of wages, to the payments of the previous year's salary, and to payments made on account of the wages for the current year." In interpreting the Code, Guérard writes: "It is on a level, intellectually and morally, with the metaphysics of Victor Cousin and the literature of Casimir Delavigne. Like them it is the embodiment of bourgeois common sense, without originality and without generosity."

The First Consul assisted the middle classes in many other ways. Governmental and military positions were opened to men of talent, regardless of social or economic rank. At the same time Bonaparte disregarded the principle that all professions were open to all men. He allowed the bourgeoisie to organize themselves into monopolistic orders, although he frowned on the unionization of wage-earners. "Thus the legal and financial professions—barristers, attorneys, notaries, bailiffs, stockbrokers, auctioneers—were made the preservers of the bourgeoisie."

Even in the field of education Napoleon emphasized his bourgeois program; accepting the public-school system as advanced during the revolution, he added grade schools, high schools, technical institutions, and a University of France—

all under the control of the central government. In other words, he tried to carry out the bourgeois idea that educational facilities should be offered by the state to those who possessed talents. He also adopted the revolutionary belief that education and patriotism were closely allied; in the private as well as the public schools Napoleon insisted upon the teaching of patriotism to the youth of the land. In short, he advocated the modern system of nationalist-bourgeois education.

Napoleon settled the religious problem in a way satisfactory to the middle classes. After delicate negotiations, he arranged the famous Concordat of 1801 with the pope, whereby the latter virtually recognized the legality of confiscation of church property, and the government in return agreed to pay the salaries of the clergy. A similar settlement was also concluded with the Protestant minority. Thus, Christianity was tied firmly to the government.

Impressed by these practical achievements, the middle classes with few exceptions hailed Bonaparte as the great benefactor. He had brought peace and order to the nation, and prosperity as a result of his policies was bound to follow. Great indeed was the delight of the middle classes when the vain Consul—one of the people—decided to transform his unpretentious official circles into a court which would enable the business men to assume a place in the social order which their ambition demanded.

This social policy met with little success. The bourgeoisie were fascinated rather than conquered. By its very splendor the court made them feel like "outsiders," and this feeling was more than once enhanced by embarrassments suffered at Versailles because of their lack of social manners. Nor did the court life appeal to Napoleon's military leaders. Frequent snubs and humiliations cooled their social aspirations. As for the nobles of the old régime—most of them refused to participate in the new court life, and the few who did served their master with ill-concealed scorn and contempt. Napoleon, himself, disliked this court life forced upon him as a result of his attempt to substitute an aristocracy of brains for the old-time privileges of birth.

As a matter of fact, Napoleon had a contempt for the "average Frenchman," especially the member of the monied classes. His kotowing to the middle classes was opportunistic; he wanted to build a strong state, and knowing that economic and financial as well as military strength were necessary and that the business men could provide these, he followed the path of least resistance. At no time was Napoleon planning the establishment of a prosperous democratic, bourgeois state. "We must have eyes only for what is real and practicable in the application of principles and not for the speculative and hypothetical." In making this statement, Napoleon did not contemplate the formation of an efficient revolutionary government; instead, he planned a return to the days of Caesar and the reestablishment of another prosperous World Empire with Paris as its capital. Reviving the old *politique* doctrine of the supremacy of the state, he said: "The interest of the state is not always that of the merchant." In other words, everything should be subordinated to one thing—the establishment of a powerful French nation.

To achieve this objective, Napoleon, even before he became First Consul, accepted the historic policy of French expansion via the Mediterranean to the Orient. In fact, he visualized the appearance of a great French Empire in the East and in the Americas which would take the place of the British Empire. Moreover, he adopted Richelieu's concept of the natural frontier—the acquisition of the left bank of the Rhine. At the basis of these policies was his main economic objective—the revival of commerce, industry, and agriculture in France, a revival which would make France, rather than England, the workshop of the world. In carrying out this program, Napoleon revived Colbert's belief in protection. England, faced by economic ruin as a result of the closing by Napoleon of European markets to her goods, and opposed to Napoleon's policy of imperial expansion in the Orient, threw all of her resources into a fight to the finish. In 1803 war between these two great powers was renewed; in 1804 Napoleon frankly stated his plan to make France the center of European, even world culture, by announcing his empire.

Failing to defeat the English on the sea, Napoleon by 1805–1806 resorted to his famous "economic weapon," the continental blockade. All European markets were to be closed to the British and their colonial trade until England, ruined commercially and financially, would beg for terms of peace. But his continental system was a failure. The rise as a result of his conquests of national antagonists in Prussia, Russia, Austria, and Spain; his failure to maintain the blockade—he was forced to grant licenses to trade with the enemy in order to obtain necessary supplies, such as uniforms for his soldiers—and the financial support rendered England by the House of Rothschild and other banking concerns, all contributed to its downfall. Moreover, the continental system caused a general depression throughout Europe. People became restless. Hostility began to arise against Napoleon.

By 1814 it was apparent that Napoleon's days as Emperor were numbered. Even the middle classes, who were the greatest beneficiaries of Napoleon's plan to found a new World Empire, became discontented. Most of them judged Napoleon in the light of their losses and of the immediate future—not in terms of the grand plan he had outlined. They decided that the cost of the imperial régime in men and in money was more than it was worth. Moreover, the fear of a new aristocracy as a result of the act in 1806 establishing an imperial aristocracy and a growing disfavor toward the regulation of business activity, which indeed made economic recovery impossible, caused the great majority of the middle classes by 1814 secretly to favor the overthrow of the Emperor. They were tired of tyranny and of continual wars. Only the real fear of a reaction which would bring back the old régime caused them to suppress their hostility to the little Corsican. But they did not regret the news of Napoleon's abdication in 1814; instead, they gladly accepted the return of the Bourbons in the person of Louis XVIII, who was pledged not to deprive the bourgeoisie of their material gains.

By 1814–1815 the upper middle classes favored a government which would give them peace, would guarantee the territorial changes brought about by the Revolution, and would prevent a radical revolution. Individual liberty and equality, as urged by Rousseau, and interpreted by the revolutionists of 1789, however, had not only resulted in the political, social, and material rise of the business classes at the expense of the aristocracy, but also had threatened to degenerate into a popular uprising.

But the bourgeoisie apparently were determined to establish their social order, regardless of the claims of the masses or of the various feudal groups. Formerly there had been an aristocratic literature, a society of good taste, and a "lordly life." Now all this was destroyed and the new bourgeois order was introduced by legislative acts, legal codes, and the public schools.

This new society was consecrated by nationalism, another revolutionary contribution. Inspired by the famous watchword —Fraternity—France became a patriotic, militaristic and bourgeois "brotherhood." The middle classes welcomed this new nationalism because it gave them a weapon whereby they could defend their domestic as well as their foreign interests. Labor, they said, must not become a state within a state. Nor should any nation stand in the way of the economic interests of France. The army was to be used, if necessary, to enforce these policies. Thus, the Revolution had brought about the complete triumph of the bourgeoisie. They were the state.

Chapter XIII

REACTION AFTER NAPOLEON

There never did, there never will, and there never can exist a Parliament, or any description of men, or any generation, in any country, possessed of the right or the power of binding posterity to "the end of time," or of commanding forever how the world shall be governed, or who shall govern it (Thomas Paine, The Rights of Man).

After the fall of Napoleon, most people, especially those of the governing classes, did not immediately realize that they were living in a new era. Still firmly entrenched in power, they looked with horror upon the French Revolution, with its violence, bloodshed, and chaotic confusion. In their opinion the old régime stood for law and order, while the new spirit was for anarchy and devilment. To them the attacks upon the church signified the establishment of a "Godless Age." They maintained that the French Revolution had resulted only in bloodshed and misery. Alarmed over its violent consequences, they bitterly opposed its spread and tried to return in so far as possible to the "good old pre-revolutionary days." Few of them were able to divine that the Revolution had not yet spent itself, that the disorders would continue, that normalcy and sound prosperity would not and could not return until a definitely new and different order was instituted.

Disregarding, for the most part, the very idea of the recent changes, representatives of the powers responsible for the overthrow of Napoleon, under the leadership of the Austrian and British clever diplomats, Metternich and Castlereagh, sought at the Congress of Vienna (1815) to restore the past. They realized that the great majority of the people wanted peace above all else and were not especially interested in the creation of an earthly paradise for the future. Famines, pestilences, crime, and disease—the effects of the great wars—caused churchmen, business men, wage-earners, and peasants to place emphasis upon the present and to demand law, order, and peace. Peace could be attained, claimed the conservatives, provided the pre-revolutionary conditions, under which people supposedly had been happy and contented and had lived in harmony with one another, could be restored. Therefore, most of them opposed such revolutionary and bourgeois principles as constitutionalism, legal equality, equitable taxation, religious toleration, and intellectual liberty and proceeded to re-create as far as they were able the Europe of 1789.

In restoring the past, the representatives of England, Russia, Prussia, and Austria reëstablished at Vienna the balance of power and formed a Quadruple Alliance, consisting of the representatives of these victors, who were to meet at fixed periods to decide matters of "common interest." England was not in sympathy with the proposal to make the Quadruple Alliance a means by which the political and social as well as territorial status quo would be preserved throughout the world. In the opinion of her minister of foreign affairs, Castlereagh, her only commitments were: first, to prevent the return of the Napoleonic dynasty; and, second, to maintain the agreements of Vienna for twenty years. These limitations had their origin in England's connection with the revolutionary movement in Hispanic America. In the throes of a grave economic crisis around 1820 she was willing, even eager, to turn the revolt of the Spanish colonies to account in order to dump her goods in their markets. This was because of Spain's monopolistic colonial policies which had prevented English traders from carrying on an extensive commerce. England's refusal to make the Quadruple Alliance a reactionary instrument, however, was largely dictated by the financial houses which had made possible the overthrow of Napoleon and which now planned to reap the golden harvest. Indeed, Lord Byron in his *Don Juan* did not overestimate their power when he wrote:

Who hold the balance of the world? Who reign
  O'er congress, whether royalist or liberal?

Who rouse the shirtless patriots of Spain?
(That make old Europe's journals squeak and gibber all).
Who keep the world, both old and new, in pain
Or pleasure? Who make politics run glibber all?
The shade of Bonaparte's noble daring?—
Jew Rothschild, and his fellow-Christian, Baring.

Rulers who were at the heads of the various European governments in 1815 and who were often subservient to these strong financial barons were for the most part "little men." The monarchs surrounded themselves with conservative advisers. Of these, the Austrian minister, Metternich, was the most famous. An "enlightened conservative," he knew that changes were inevitable. "I am an old practitioner," he said in 1848, "and I know how to discriminate between curable and incurable diseases. This one is fatal; here we hold on as long as we can, but I despair of the issue." For many years Metternich had defended the autocratic government and what he called "the legitimate revolution." Improvement must come, he had often said, from above. Institutions must grow over a period of time and be cultivated by responsible and intelligent statesmen. With this in mind he had assented to Austrian participation in the economic customs union with Prussia (the *Zollverein*), to the development of industry, and to the expansion of transportation—a program which could not fail to benefit the middle classes, whose revolutionary tendencies he dreaded and whom he thus hoped to pacify.

Personally, Metternich opposed the bourgeoisie, especially the members of the wealthy group, who, he believed, were trying to take the places of the aristocracy. But Metternich's plans for the establishment of an enlightened and efficient autocratic government were frustrated in their inception by the ultra-conservatism of the emperor, Francis I, and by personal antagonism of such liberal statesmen as Count Kolowrat, an "aristocratic, ambitious, and keen reformer, eager for the rights of the middle classes and the amelioration of the peasants' lot."

England, also, benefited by the rule of partially enlightened conservatives. Castlereagh, as minister of foreign affairs at Vienna, and Wellington, as prime minister at home, represented both the landed and commercial classes and in working for these groups saved England in the early nineteenth century from undue economic distress.

In France, Prussia, Russia, and many other European states, the statesmen were little reactionists. True, Prussia, in the early nineteenth century had her enlightened Stein, and France the somewhat liberal Duc de Richelieu; but, on the whole, the ministers were narrow souls, intent upon the maintenance of the status quo. Determined to avoid the horrors of another revolution, these reactionary statesmen sternly suppressed liberal tendencies. Like Metternich, they had their police spy upon all important persons and gather information concerning "radical" activities throughout the land. People became panicky and suspicious. All persons—nobles, peasants, bourgeoisie, and wage-earners—feared and suspected one another. It was a dark day for liberalism. Even constitutional England limited the activities of the people by producing the famous Six Acts, forbidding military exercises without permission, allowing local justices to issue search warrants for weapons, curtailing freedom of assembly, authorizing the seizure of seditious writings, creating a stamp tax for pamphlets similar to that imposed on newspapers, and threatening agitators with punishment. This legislation of 1819 was the climax of an attempt to stifle political and social progress.

In addition to the governments, the leading exponents of the move to reëstablish the law and order of the old régime were the nobles and the upper clergy and, in England, often the rich commercial element of the middle classes. The nobles were especially delighted to regain their social privileges and their monopoly of positions in the naval, military, governmental, and to a certain extent, the religious institutions of the land. England, perhaps, had the most enlightened aristocracy, possibly because its peers had mingled with the commercial and banking element of the middle classes and had frequently invested money in commercial enterprises.

In Europe, aristocracy, for the most part, was less progressive than it had been before the French Revolution. Conscious of the political and social distinctions enjoyed by their ancestors, most of the European noblemen, oblivious to the fact that they were living in a changing world and, unmoved by the French Revolution, actually tried to restore medieval feudalism. Myopically, the Spaniards, the Russians, and the Frenchmen of noble estate attempted to reëstablish their little despotisms. Feudal life, they insisted, must go on—unchanged.

Unconsciously, many of these noblemen had been transformed by the Revolution. Religious fervor and a fear of radicalism had replaced eighteenth-century frivolity, wit, and love of original ideas. Most noblemen became imbued with a definite Christian mental attitude, perhaps relying upon the aid of God through His clergy in their opposition to revolutionary change. This help they were able to get, for the Catholic church and the priests, aching from the pre-revolutionary wounds inflicted by the radical exponents of enlightenment, gladly came to the support of the nobility. The clergy especially frowned upon this interference by the state in the matter of marriage, and indignantly resented the tendency on the part of the government to deal with the problem of divorce. They also condemned state control of schools and decried the so-called "practical" education.

Protestants, also, defended tradition and authority. In England the Anglican church championed the aristocrats in their drive to control the government. Even the Evangelical sects, as, for example, the Methodists, worked consciously or unconsciously for "law and order." In their emphasis upon the ideal of a Kingdom of Heaven not of this world, they completely rejected that kind of utopia on earth which could be established only by revolutionary methods. Such virtues as hard work, thrift, and decent living, they believed, would assure earthly happiness and insure heavenly rewards. In short, the Christian churches and the clergy throughout Europe in the early nineteenth century were enthusiastic exponents of the established order.

English merchants and bankers joined the nobles and clergy in opposing the extremes of the French Revolution. Moreover, they adopted, in a way, the aristocratic attitude toward existence. Money, to most of these commercial patricians, was only a means whereby a man could enjoy life. An earthly utopia was attained when the merchant could retire and live the life of a gentleman. Like the enlightened aristocrat, he was a sincere opponent of political extremes. He distrusted despotism and republicanism and was well satisfied with the constitutional monarchy which enabled his group to collaborate with the aristocrats in running the state.

The merchant or banker of the early nineteenth century was, on the whole, a benevolent and kindly soul. He was a dependable supporter of the Christian church (financially) and frequently was generous in his gifts to the poor. Like the aristocrat, however, he resented the very notion that the lower classes were entitled to special consideration. He had to look out for himself and he expected his employees to do likewise.

In France and in other continental states, the upper bourgeoisie were more hostile toward the aristocracy than they were in England. They resented the privileged positions and social superiority which the aristocrats enjoyed. Ambitious and envious, these plutocrats quite frankly wanted to assume the "airs" of the aristocrats. However, forced to make the best of an unpleasant situation, they, like their brothers in England, tried to coöperate with the nobility in the governing of the state.

Leading German intellectuals often distrusted bourgeois liberalism and aimed for an authoritative régime. They sharply condemned the destructive criticism of the eighteenth-century publicists and advocated a return to faith, to belief, to sentiment—to medievalism. The Pietists of Germany, opposing eighteenth-century rationalism and extolling sentimentalism, revived Luther's "justification by faith" and attacked revolutionary thought. Without authority and faith, society, they believed, could not endure.

Reactionary writers, inspired by a romanticism based upon emotion and upon idealized history, thought that they found in the customs, art, and beliefs of the Middle Ages the best examples of what constituted a perfect social order. Stressing the doctrine of nationalism and the submergence of the individual within the group, as expressed in medieval legends, folk songs and sagas, such German Romanticists as Schlegel and Novalis actually visualized the reëstablishment of the perfect civilization which, according to these idealists, had existed in medieval times.

The great German philosophers, Kant, Fichte, and Hegel, also turned conservative. At first they had welcomed the French Revolution, but the so-called tyranny of Napoleon in Prussia after the Battle of Jena (1806) caused these intellectuals to reject democracy and individualism in favor of a monarchical state. While they recognized the stability of "the old authoritative society," these philosophers, however, did not reject the concept of individual freedom. They appreciated the significance of personal initiative in science, in religion, and in business, but leaned towards a politically autocratic state as a means to check "arbitrary action outside of all law." To avoid chaos and anarchy, therefore, Kant believed that a strong government capable of "harmonizing general control with individual liberty" was necessary. In presenting this same idea Hegel emphasized the concept of historical evolution by which he described progress as the gradual rise of the glorious state. This idea of evolution, rather than of revolution, as the fundamental factor in social development, justified the strong Prussian monarchy in which individuals worked for the interests of all.

An appeal to tradition can be found in English and French political and philosophical writings of the early nineteenth century. During the French Revolution the famous English conservative, Edmund Burke, defended in his *Reflections on the Revolution in France* (1790) the unwritten British constitution and attacked the French Revolution because "it broke with tradition." In France such intellectual defenders of absolutism as Bonald and de Maistre attacked the French Revolution and the eighteenth-century philosophers. These men maintained that Rousseau, in claiming that "man is naturally good and is corrupted by society," paved the way for massacres, the Reign of Terror, and the cruel wars of the revolutionary era.

They argued that "man is naturally bad; original sin is the ultimate truth; and man is saved by society." Authority, therefore, was necessary; without the power of the king, the clergy, and the nobles, chaos and anarchy would result.

Despite these reactionary sentiments, a general revival of liberalism was under way by 1820. In England and France, the bourgeoisie were again attacking the old régime; while throughout Europe and the Americas, liberals, representing numerous classes, were advocating various kinds of liberty, such as national unity, constitutional government, democracy, and freedom for slaves and serfs. In England, bourgeois liberalism made its greatest advance when, between 1815 and 1830, another group among the middle classes challenged the right of the autocrats and the commercial plutocrats to dominate affairs in England and in France. These new protagonists were the manufacturers, the so-called "Captains of Industry," who, dependent for success on intelligence rather than on social position, joined the commercial classes in supporting Adam Smith's doctrine of the *laissez faire*. The Textile Revolution, offering a new way whereby a man could accumulate a fortune, made possible their success. Originally wage-earners or yeomen, these men were able to save or borrow a small amount of money; with it they purchased new machines and became the owners of small factories, each factory employing a few workmen. From these humble beginnings rose some of the powerful and wealthy manufacturing families of the nineteenth century.

During the late eighteenth century these men had the good as well as the bad characteristics of pioneers. In England a "mill owner" was a "hard-bitten north-country workingman" of no education and great force of character, taking little stock of his social or political relations with the outer world. He refused to enjoy leisure or recreation for himself, nor would he allow his workers any free time. Consequently, he managed somehow "to convert the original 100 pounds (sterling) that he had borrowed into a solvent 'mill,' the prison house of children, the hidden reef on which Napoleon's empire struck." At no time did he concern himself about the physical welfare of the children he employed, except in so far as it made or marred his own fortune.

When Napoleon was overthrown, the mill owners of the second generation were originating an "industrial bourgeoisie of a new and enterprising type." Better educated and possessing a wider outlook than "his grim old father," the young captain of industry determined to enjoy more fully the political and social benefits which, he believed, wealth should bestow on him. To achieve these ends he welcomed an alliance with the gentry and the clergy around him. Moreover, he expressed ideas which often ran counter to the view of the aristocrats. He believed, for example, in the abolition of slavery; he opposed church rites, income taxes, and the Corn Laws. Ardently he subscribed to the bourgeois ideas expressed in the *Edinburgh Review.*

The manufacturer, however, did not accept the philosophy of wealth of the commercial bourgeoisie. Adopting the puritanical suspicion of the life of leisure and personal pleasure, the mill owner stressed the godliness of hard work, self-denial, and the accumulation of wealth "for its own sake." Like the commercial patricians he balked at the attempts of labor to assert its rights. Unions received his stern disfavor, and although a few mill owners, like Robert Owen, recognized the necessity of social reform, the great majority clung stubbornly to the doctrine of individualism so far as the relations between capital and labor were concerned.

In the early nineteenth century, there were also the lesser middle classes in the various cities and towns of Europe. They consisted of the small business men, such as local shopkeepers, artisans, salesmen, and professional classes (doctors and lawyers). These elements, dependent on the profit system, soon took a personal interest in public affairs. Denied the ballot for the most part, they read newspapers, which were becoming popular at that time, and discussed the various topics of the day. The petty bourgeoisie also imitated their wealthy brothers by supporting churches and by enjoying such bourgeois comforts as vacations and social and intellectual avocations. Most of them accepted the bourgeois philosophy of individualism and worshipped at the shrine of the captain of industry—the self-made man.

Perhaps the greatest of the early nineteenth-century bourgeois liberals was Jeremy Bentham (1748–1832). A sincere exponent of Adam Smith's doctrine of benevolent selfishness as the road to social progress, he advocated in his *Principles of Morals and Legislation* and *Universal and Perpetual Peace* the abolition of all laws and institutions which stood in the way of individual economic advancement. He asserted that existing institutions should be judged not for their antiquity but for their utility in promoting "the greatest happiness of the greatest number." Since each individual is actuated by selfish motives, and since the welfare of the majority is the only sensible objective of society, the dominance of the majority is an inevitable premise to progress. He believed, therefore, that political democracy was justifiable and desirable.

Bentham did more than any other writer to put liberalism on a practical business basis. Merchants and industrialists often became inspired exponents of his utilitarianism. The sanctions of tradition and of reason were ignored and keen-minded business men decided that everything must rise, stand, or fall on the basis of its utility. Few institutions of the old régime could pass this test. Feudal laws, aristocracy, autocracy, and theocracy were now attacked by the utilitarian exponents of plutocracy who were determined to establish a bourgeois state.

But what was the bourgeois state? Primarily it was a country ruled by those who supported and were affected by the government—the tax-payers. The revolutionary slogan of "no taxation without representation" was revived by these nineteenth-century leaders of the Third Estate who were convinced that regardless of the form of government—constitutional monarchy or republic—they must possess political control. Under the tutelage of Smith, Bentham, and other writers, the bourgeoisie also had developed rather definite ideas as to the duties of the state. In their opinion the state should maintain "law and order," defend its citizens against alien attacks, and conduct certain public enterprises which private individuals could not maintain. All other governmental activities, they believed, should be abolished, especially mercantilistic restrictions on commerce, industry, and agriculture. Each person should work out his own salvation. The law of supply and demand should be observed so that capital could "find its most lucrative course, commodities their fair price, industry and intelligence their natural reward, idleness and folly their natural punishment." The function of government was merely to protect life and property "at a minimum of cost."

Freedom was the watchword of political as well as economic liberals in the early nineteenth century. Benjamin Constant (1767–1830), in such works as *The Spirit of Conquest and Usurpation,* insisted that the liberty of the individual was a fundamental of human society, for it determined morality and economic progress, and it alone made for human happiness. In his support of liberty, however, Constant did not go so far as to champion political democracy. Instead, he claimed that those who were without property were generally uninformed about state matters and certainly were not interested in them. "Wealth, and its twin brother, leisure, alone renders a man capable of exercising his political rights."

In the early nineteenth century more and more nations accepted the bourgeois emphasis upon the passion for pursuing and accumulating wealth. France and England, as will be shown, strove to attain material power by adopting economic individualism. In fact, wherever the Industrial Revolution succeeded in producing an energetic group of manufacturers and traders, the lust for money became the predominant personal and professional motive. In the Germanies a strong opposition to the junker (landowner) economic doctrine of competency arose. According to this belief, each individual should aim at earning enough to insure him the means of existence and a mode of life suitable to his particular class. The rapid strides of capitalism, however, caused a number of economists to desire a system of "enterprise" rather than of competency in German economic life.

During the French Revolution most German business men favored the elimination of regulations and other barriers which stood in the way of private enterprise. Impressed by the doctrine of the *laissez faire* as proclaimed by the Physiocrats and by Adam Smith, William Humboldt, the German writer, in his monograph on the *Units of State Interference* (1795) denounced the bureaucratic system which prevented all independent action on the part of the people. Feudal and administrative economic domination was considered intolerable. The statesmen Stein and Hardenberg tried to establish economic individualism by emancipating the serfs (1807), by enfranchising the middle classes, by proclaiming the freedom of industry and commerce, by destroying the guild system, and by granting a large degree of local self-government. In short, prior to 1848 the doctrine that the state should renounce the right of directing the economic life of the nation was generally accepted by the German liberals.

The formation of the *Zollverein,* or customs union, was one of the most notable achievements of the Prussian government during the restless years preceding the revolt of 1848. Most German states had their own tariff frontiers; therefore, for example, an article sent from Paris to Berlin, in passing through various countries, would be assessed many duties, the price to the purchaser naturally being high. Trade and industry could not flourish under these circumstances. This customs union, by abolishing these numerous duties, not only lowered the price of manufactured articles to the purchaser but also stimulated the growth of trade and industry and made possible the rise of a small but wealthy middle class, grateful for the economic unity brought about by the government.

During the period from 1815–1848 decisive material progress did not accompany the spread of economic liberalism. In fact, about 1820 the Germanies experienced a general business depression which caused a drop in land values and numerous bankruptcies. England's ability to flood Central Europe with cheap goods accentuated the hard times and caused many Germans to demand higher protective tariffs. Business men in Germany, therefore, decided that the government should help them. The middle classes, especially the manufacturers, maintained that it was well within the right of a government to boost economic expansion by granting lands to settlers on easy terms (as in the United States), or by stimulating domestic manufacturing through the establishment of protective tariffs. In their opinion state aid of this nature would benefit all individuals by creating a great material and intellectual civilization.

List, the great German economist, became the foremost exponent of this gospel of economic nationalism as against economic individualism. In *The National System of Political Economy* (1841) he declared that power should be the chief economic aim. "A country can have too many scholars and too few workmen," he said. "To make a great, rich, and mighty nation are needed manufactures, free internal intercourse, foreign trade, shipping, and moral power." Agriculture was insufficient; industry was the key to wealth and culture. Power could best be obtained if a community became self-sufficient, using its resources to the utmost. Protection, designed to foster German economic development, regardless of other nations, would, in his opinion, lead to world power. Such was the program he outlined for Germany.

In England, however, the landed aristocracy, not the middle classes, were the backers of this doctrine of protection. In 1815 Parliament passed the Corn Laws, excluding foreign grain from England, unless, as was unlikely, the price of home-grown grain should at any time rise above a certain stipulated high figure. Despite the fact that meager harvests caused the price of bread to soar far beyond the pocketbook of the English workers, the landowners saw to it that this law was enforced to the letter; meanwhile the poor were on the verge of starvation. Partly because of this situation there were, in 1821, 2,500,000 "assisted poor" in the country.

The wage-earners, who could not make ends meet because of the higher cost of living, blamed the aristocrats and joined the middle classes in a move to deprive the nobility of its political monopoly. This union of classes was not unexpected, for at that time the proletariat frequently tended to support the bourgeois system. The worker usually subscribed to the theory of individualism, especially when emphasis was placed upon freedom for slaves and serfs. Moreover, the bourgeois scheme of things offered him an opportunity to advance, even though the obstacles were tremendous. He gave credit to the accepted doctrine of earthly salvation by thrift alone and believed that if he could reduce the cost of living by abolishing the Corn Laws he might be able to accumulate property and become middle class. Indeed, public schools, savings banks, and other bourgeois institutions encouraged the worker to hope that some day his son could attain economic success and become a "self-made man."

Secular education was a prominent plank in the bourgeois platform of reform. The idea of public schools was planted in France during the Great Revolution as a result of the general belief that the schools could give all children a chance to rise in the world. In Spain, Italy, Germany, the Balkans, and in Eastern Europe, nationalist organizations in the nineteenth century advocated various types of education controlled by the state.

Churchmen and aristocrats at first vigorously opposed this secularization of education. In England, the Anglican bishops did everything in their power to check the spread of public schools. Many of them believed that education, unsanctified by religion, was wicked in its tendencies and injurious in its results. Moreover, they stated quite frankly that a public school system which took "present utility and not religious duty for its mainspring and regulating principle would lead to evils, moral and political." In short, the Anglican bishops really summed up the whole case for the church when they asserted that secular education would weaken the power of the church and of the aristocratic classes. For these reasons the ruling groups in the leading states of Europe hindered the spread of public education. Their attitude was expressed by Lord Melbourne, prime minister of England (1834–1841), when he said that education was futile, for the poor positively dangerous, and that democracy was a myth. "The whole duty of the government," he averred, "was to prevent crime and to preserve contracts."

Non-conformists in the British Isles and various Protestant sects in other countries, especially in the United States, did much to spread secular education in their Sunday schools and later in their colleges. Representing the lesser middle classes and the ambitious salaried classes, these groups tried to harmonize the business and religious concepts of education by teaching secular subjects such as science and mathematics in their church schools as well as religion. Meanwhile, leaders in the skilled trades in England fostered a purely secular education by establishing institutions in which "theology was ignored and science and history emphasized."

The bourgeois stress upon freedom was a vital factor in the spread of nationalism as well as of secular education in the early nineteenth century. At first, however, nationalism was not primarily a middle-class movement. Representatives of all classes in Italy, Germany, and the Balkans, for example, as enthusiastic romanticists went back to early times to study the origin of their national language, literature, art, law, and customs.

Gradually nationalism became firmly fixed in the public policy. Politicians took great pains to exploit it to their own advantage. It was soon apparent that nationalism, as individualism, was a middle-class ideal. Both rested on the principle of competition and both were antagonistic toward the coöperative beliefs of the Middle Ages and of modern socialism. Thus the middle classes, convinced that economic individualism was the secret of success, soon cleverly used nationalism as the means by which they as Frenchmen, Englishmen, or Germans might advance their private economic interest under the guise of devotion to the state.

Eventually the concept of nationalism replaced absolutism as the principal check on unfettered individualism. Private judgment was denounced as unsound; the opinion of the majority was believed more reliable than that of the wisest councils of individuals or of monarchs. There resulted a growing emphasis upon the rights of all nations which were ruled by majorities. The individual had to subordinate himself to the government, and political individualism disappeared. Thus, two of the primary contributions of the French Revolution, nationalism and individualism, helped to destroy the chief features of the old régime, social privilege and absolutism. Once the old order was overthrown and the new one inaugurated, those in power, the bourgeoisie, used nationalism as a means of checking other groups whenever the latter threatened their designs. Welding diverse interests, nationalism became the cohesive force of the body politic. To the people of the Western World it seemed the most inspiring doctrine of all and one of the most valuable assets of the new régime.

Between 1815 and 1848 it became impossible to disregard nationalism. The patriotic movements that had formerly stirred up the French, the Poles, the Portuguese, the Spaniards, the Italians, and the Germans in their opposition to Napoleon now influenced them to claim freedom and unity for all of their nationality. These demands could no longer be ignored, for the new political, economic, and social systems introduced into Europe during the Revolutionary and Napoleonic periods enabled the middle classes to gain political control of their governments. Their supremacy hastened the formation of new national states. After these governments were established, the liberal exponents of Western civilization were in a position to lead their nations in the conquest and Europeanization of the entire world.

This tremendous expansion of the middle-class system, however, would not have been possible without the aid of science. The early nineteenth century witnessed the real beginning of modern technocracy. According to the eminent German economist, Sombart, this modern technocracy was "founded upon the application of the natural sciences to technology and the consequent transformation of empirical experience into rational knowledge." In other words, scientific research and formulation resulted in inventions and engineering (the application of theoretical science). These developments had as their goal the "complete replacement of *Quality by Quantity*." Therefore, mechanical inventions applied to industry would enable the middle classes to emphasize quantity ahead of quality production, and by so doing extend the scope of their operations and the amount of their wealth. Furthermore, the transformation from human power to steam and electric power would completely emancipate these classes. Hitherto they had been largely dependent upon the local labor supply for their help and upon local markets for raw materials and the sale of the goods. The steam engine and the steamship opened the world to their enterprise. Markets, production, and profits seemed unlimited. They had the world to gain!

CHAPTER XIV

LIBERTY? EQUALITY? FRATERNITY?

[Louis Napoleon] . . . strutted and fretted before Europe in the part of the liberal Emperor. . . . His empire . . . in the eyes of Europe [was the] champion of that emotional and mostly middle-class liberalism that had inspired such characters as those of Lincoln, Garibaldi, Heine, and Gladstone (Wingfield-Stratford, The Victorian Sunset, *William Morrow and Co., New York, 1932).*

AFTER Vienna the history of France is the history of the triumphant bourgeoisie. The discarded nobility, politically myopic, continue futilely to beat against the strong new walls of the reconstructed order. Only after several successful minor revolutions are they able to read the handwriting on the wall, to see emblazoned the words: *Liberté, Egalité, Fraternité.*

Following the overthrow of Napoleon and the reëstablishment of the Bourbon monarchy, the aristocrats worked determinedly to regain their confiscated properties and to restore the old régime. They managed to regain only about half of their estates, the balance having been sold or given away by the revolutionary governments. Together with the lands of the church all but a very small amount of the half, which the peasants were supposed to have secured, had gone to merchants, officials, parliamentary deputies, lawyers, and other bourgeois persons. These new conservative landowners quickly allied themselves with the great bankers and industrialists against the attempts of the nobles to regain their estates or to receive compensation for them. Out of this conflict, after a series of revolutions, came the final downfall of the aristocracy and the complete triumph of the new order.

The death of Louis XVIII in 1824 and the accession of his brother as Charles X of France brought to a head the struggle between the friends and enemies of the new régime, for the new king was the incarnation of a reckless and stubborn old reactionary aristocrat. Trusting in the doctrine of divine right and saturated with a spirit of medieval mysticism, he felt that he, the anointed and the chosen of God, was destined to save the land from liberalism. As the leader of the reactionaries in France he is reported to have said, "It is only Lafayette and I who have not changed since 1789." Sixty-seven years of age when he became king, he determined to restore the old régime before his years claimed him. His cardinal objectives were to be a king by divine right, to control a unified church, and possess a feudal aristocracy.

Frenchmen, attentive to contemporary problems, were both amused and disgusted when they first heard of the king's medieval views. Before long they became bored. "Let us shut the Bourbons up in the charter," said Thiers, the liberal French statesman, "and close the doors tightly; they will inevitably jump out of the window." Charles X only looked out the window to see that he would be unable to return the land to the émigrés. Therefore, in 1825, he had the assembly vote them a billion francs for the losses they had suffered during the Revolution. To pay the nobles, the government had to fund the public debt and reduce the interest rate. This financial manipulation made Charles X more unpopular, if that were possible, with the powerful investors, the middle classes. The bourgeois citizens were soon baying for his hide; they pointed alertly for a chance to trap him.

Charles accorded them an opportunity. After his minister, Polignac, had inaugurated a foreign policy which nearly involved his country in a war with Great Britain over Belgium, this same short-sighted diplomat persuaded Charles X to suppress the French assembly. Thereupon the king issued the famous July Ordinances of 1830. These restricted the freedom of the press, dissolved the new chamber before it had even met, ushered in a new law disfranchising three-fourths of the voters, and proclaimed another election of deputies.

This tyranny alienated all classes in France except the ultra-royalists. Aroused by the ordinances, middle-class journalists, eager to check the power of the Bourbons, showered literature inciting the Parisians to revolt. They were assisted by the old veterans, Talleyrand and Lafayette, who for once had agreed upon a common program, namely, a constitutional monarchy of the English type.

The Revolution of 1830 was a political milestone inasmuch as it marked the end of divine-right monarchy and of ultra-royalist supremacy. Henceforth the people would designate their type of government and their ruler. The overthrow of Charles X gave the upper middle classes their first opportunity to assume political power on the Continent. However victory had been so sudden they were not prepared to handle the situation. Consequently, the Revolution of 1830 did not result in the creation of a republic. Led by the journalist Thiers and a banker named Laffitte, the bourgeois liberals succeeded in effecting the establishment of a constitutional monarchy. Laffitte was chosen to offer the crown to Louis Philippe, duke of Orleans and liberal member of the Bourbon family. It is reported that he did this in a typically businesslike way, giving Louis Philippe his choice between a passport and a kingship. Willingly, the practical-minded Louis Philippe selected the crown, becoming king of the French—not king of France—a subtle distinction by which he, overtly at least, acknowledged that the people had conferred sovereignty upon him. He perceived, however, that his real power was derived from the aristocratic representatives of the middle classes.

France seemed peaceful and prosperous during the reign of this ponderous king; yet the people were not satisfied. They were disgusted by the reports of bribery which involved the ruler and his ministers, and they were vexed with the government's weak foreign policy. France, they asserted, was degenerating into a satellite of Great Britain. "What has this policy of business before glory or honor obtained for us?" asked patriotic Frenchmen. Most nations, they asserted, despised France. Most Frenchmen, they insisted, bitterly opposed its plutocratic government.

As Napoleon honored his soldiers by making them noblemen, so Louis Philippe smartly manufactured a new aristocracy called the "July Nobles," bestowing titles upon bankers, manufacturers, and successful speculators. From that time on the wealthy capitalists replaced the landed aristocrats as the dominant group in France, their titles and wealth being supreme recommendations to power.

Even the army was penetrated by the middle classes. During the Revolutionary Era the feudal character of this organization had been altered. Men now fought for their country, not for the king or for a feudal lord. The duty of a citizen to defend his state superseded the voluntary quest of adventure or of material reward. The middle classes, however, were not able to gain control of the regular army until the time of the Third Republic. During the years when they were rising to power, the army was composed for the most part of dissatisfied adherents of the old nobility.

One military institution not controlled by the aristocrats was the National Guard, established during the French Revolution as a shield against proletarian radicalism. By 1848 this organization was ruled by business men and became the focus of bourgeois vanity. Service in the soldiery permitted a citizen to reconcile the pursuit of gold with the display of showy costume and fostered his belief in himself as the patriotic prop of national prosperity. Wealth helped considerably in the Guard, especially as members supplied their own uniforms; and when, under the Republic of 1848, certain crack regiments in bearskin shakos protested the admission of proletarians to their ranks, they expressed a snobbishness of caste hitherto exemplified by the nobility.

At first the petty bourgeoisie had accepted the king, believing that he would adopt a broad, liberal national policy; but soon they saw emerging a new class system, in which the wealthy element was as aristocratic and autocratic as that of the old nobility. Unable to vote, the great mass of people could exercise no power. The monied and propertied class replaced the blooded stock, claiming that all persons would benefit through equality of opportunity.

By 1835 there arose a tide of opposition, including an imperialist party bent on the restoration of the Napoleonic dynasty. To stem the tide, Louis Philippe, like his Bourbon predecessors, determined on a policy of suppression. Freedom of the press was limited, and secret societies were forced to submit their constitutions for approval by the government. But this reactionary policy only served to drive many moderate liberals into the republican camp.

In order to rid himself of his opponents for a time, Louis Philippe exerted his personal power and selected a cabinet irrespective of the wishes of the assembly. Thiers, his premier, who believed that the king should reign but not rule, was compelled to resign, and the conservative Guizot (1787–1874) assumed his place. Guizot was a firm advocate of a government controlled by property owners. He believed that extension of the suffrage to the working men was foolish. "Work, get rich, and then you can vote" was his advice. A true disciple of Adam Smith, this French statesman saw to it that his government kept its hands off all internal political and social problems. Meanwhile the rich became richer and the masses became more destitute and dissatisfied. "Behold, gentlemen, the whole system of government!" said an emotional deputy in 1847, "Nothing, nothing, nothing!"

The revival of the Industrial Revolution during Louis Philippe's reign promoted economic expansion and produced better transportation facilities. At the same time it gave cause for a number of social problems. On the one hand prices rose, while profits to the wealthy bourgeoisie multiplied; on the other hand poverty, unemployment, and hours of labor increased, while working conditions in the factories grew worse. It is no wonder that the wage-earners became bitter opponents of Louis Philippe's régime.

Thus Louis Philippe was doomed. His government was in the hands of a small group of business men who were utterly devoid of social or political idealism. As a result they brought upon themselves the fury of the intellectuals—especially of the romanticists—who saw in the government a régime solely occupied with satisfying the material desires of man. Guizot's "get rich" doctrine, in fact, won for Louis Philippe the hard hostility of monarchists, as well as of romanticists, utopians, socialists, and republicans. The monarchists and most of the romanticists, exponents of aristocracy, insisted that the old régime had stood for something more than mere material prosperity. Bourgeois republicans also resented Guizot's administration. They knew that his plutocratic government had as its objective the material prosperity of France, which also was the aim of democracy, and that the government stood for a policy of economic liberty whereby every individual had the opportunity to work, to get rich, and then to become a plutocrat. But to the republican middle-class men democracy, as well as economic liberty, was a part of the new order. Therefore, they believed that a republic was the logical form of government.

In their opposition to plutocracy the middle-class advocates of democracy were backed by the wage-earners, especially the socialists led by Louis Blanc. The proletariat, restless because of growing unemployment, low wages, and high prices, regarded democracy as the first step in the attainment of economic equality. Consequently, on February 24, vehement riots forced Louis Philippe to abdicate.

An assembly convened to draw up a constitution, announcing its determination to establish a republic. As in 1789, sharp divisions occurred among the leaders in the new Provisional Government. The republicans felt that things had gone far enough. They regarded Louis Blanc's socialist activities with suspicion, although they could not afford to antagonize him. Aware of the unfortunate inequalities brought about by the introduction of machinery into France, the meager wages, the unsanitary conditions in factories, and the evils of child labor, Blanc had outlined an economic and social utopia to be gained through the creation of national workshops. Let the people rule the state through the ballot; then the state, he said, could take over industries and transfer them to the workers.

Apparently, the French middle classes in 1848 were confronted by problems similar to those facing the bourgeoisie today. This is well brought out in the speeches of Labiche, young son of an industrialist, who in 1848 was running for the French Constituent Assembly, called to create a republican constitution. Announcing a program in which he outlined a moderate bourgeois democracy, he expressed determined opposition to kings, regents, and socialism. The last he called a form of barbarism. He also disapproved of government interference in business. Social reforms, he claimed, made it impossible for employers to run their enterprises at a profit and forced them to close down their plants and to discharge their workers. "I believe," he said, "that there should be the greatest amount of freedom between employer and workers. They alone are capable of discussing and settling their interests together; the state should not interfere in their problems. Freedom for the worker; freedom for the employer; that is my program."

Labiche conceded the existence of a real unemployment problem. In his opinion this was due to overproduction as a result of the use of machinery and of "dumping" of goods by foreign nations into France. Moreover, he admitted that somehow work must be provided for the unemployed. He said, "Work for him who asks; bread for him who works." To banish unemployment he urged that the emigration of country people to the cities should be stopped and a system of public works established. "Industry cannot give work unless it can sell its goods. France manufactures more than it consumes, because the people who surround us are self-sufficing and France lacks the world markets England possesses." He then went on to suggest that the government should form an "army of the unemployed" and put them to work digging canals and channels, building roads, constructing railroads, and improving waste areas for agricultural purposes; the government should even buy up land and place the people on it, for France should be mainly an agrarian country. By means of this policy of public works France would be beautified and enriched, the unemployed would be given jobs, and the "soldiers of strikes" would become the "soldiers of law and order" (Jules Wogue, "Une leçon politique de Labiche" in *La Grande Revue*, September, 1934, 455-459).

Labiche's suggestions were partly carried out, but the republicans, although they appointed Blanc minister of public works, did not propose to establish socialism. They announced the National Guard open to all classes and proceeded to declare for a republic, for universal suffrage, and for the establishment of "National Workshops." For the sake of political expediency they put the unemployed to work on the roads or on other public undertakings. By May 100,000 men, under the direction of a superintendent who was opposed to socialism, were earning forty cents a day destroying roads and then rebuilding them.

Meanwhile, the republicans and socialists quarreled over governmental policies. Blanc protested the manner in which the government operated the workshops, saying that the republicans were secretly undermining the socialists. Disputes over French foreign policy helped to intensify the ill feeling between the republicans and the followers of Blanc. They quarreled over the advisability of aiding the Poles in their battle against Russian oppression; the radicals favored intervention, but the moderates, being more interested in domestic matters, opposed this policy. Finally a crisis occurred. The workshops were abolished by the assembly in June, 1848, and as a result there occurred another phase of the revolution—the conflict between the socialists of Paris and the bourgeois republicans.

Barricades again appeared across the narrow streets, and bloody encounters took place in various parts of the city. In this struggle the socialist cause was doomed. Not only their enemies, the bourgeoisie of Paris, but also their antagonists in the provinces of France, including peasants and wealthy landowners who flocked to the capital, were determined to overthrow the new radicals who threatened to destroy the "benefits" of the French Revolution—private property and complete economic as well as political individualism.

Intrusting full authority to General Cavaignac, the republicans successfully suppressed the revolt. On June 26, after four days of desperate fighting, the assembly, dominated by republicans, again controlled Paris. There were ten thousand casualties and eleven thousand prisoners. The harsh suppression of this revolt caused a bitter hatred between the two factions. A National Constituent Assembly, controlled by the moderates, drew up a vague Declaration of Rights and proceeded to formulate a republican government.

Having planned this new government, the Constituent Assembly called an election for the presidency. The middle classes nominated their leader, General Cavaignac; the socialists named Ledru-Rollin; and the Catholic republicans selected Lamartine. In addition to these candidates there was a "dark horse," Louis Napoleon Bonaparte, nephew of the immortal Napoleon I. Louis Napoleon preached the doctrine of equality, prosperity, and national unity; he promised peace, order, security, plenty, and glory. But it was more the glory of the past than that of the future which decided the election. Thousands of sentimental Frenchmen, hearkening to the siren call of nationalism and captivated by the romantic association with the great Napoleon, voted for the "dark horse." He alone, they believed, would give every one a square deal.

Elected, from the first Louis Napoleon was influenced by the classical concept of a centralized state ruled by a Caesar. That all classes and all interests should be subordinated to the welfare of the state was the view of the nineteenth-century fascist. "United we stand, divided we fall," is the commonplace statement of the theory. In 1852 he assumed the title of Emperor, announcing that the empire meant peace, implying also that it would bring glory. The people were asked to vote on the question of whether or not they wanted an empire. The middle classes, although somewhat fearful of Louis Napoleon's sudden rise, were ready to support him through their more profound fear of socialism. Most peasants, desirous of retaining their property and also dreading a worker's republic or a return to the old régime, added their backing. On December 2, 1852, by a proposal of the senate, the empire was restored. Louis became Napoleon III.

To ardent followers of the emperor, another golden age was at hand. The class-struggle seemed to have subsided, apparently submerged beneath sentiments of brotherly love. At first Louis Napoleon tried to raise the power and wealth of the state by adhering to a capitalist-nationalist program. France, he said, by leading in the nationalist movement, was to carry on the work of Napoleon I and to emancipate the oppressed peoples of Europe.

Moved by such ideas, Napoleon III apparently fancied himself a modern Caesar. As a benevolent despot he attempted to bring material prosperity to all classes in France by his personal actions, his promises, and his actual achievements. He quickly endeared himself to many wage-earners. Riding in cabs with engineers, attending meetings of masons, carpenters, and plumbers, drinking their health on all occasions, he acted like many convivial mayors in prominent American cities. Constantly courting popularity, he promised to reduce the cost of living and to supply work for all; indeed, he allowed workers to form coöperative societies for collective buying and selling, to organize labor unions, and to strike. Further, the state was even willing to guarantee voluntary insurance against death and industrial accidents.

Louis Napoleon made his strongest appeal to the financiers and business men. While he was attempting to centralize all political power in his hands, he believed in a *laissez faire* policy for commerce and industry. Governmental regulation of industry was lessened, the organization of commercial companies was encouraged, a merchant marine was subsidized, and a policy of free trade was instituted. Both industry and commerce were stimulated by the construction of public works. Harbors were improved, swamps were drained, canals were dug, roads were repaired, Paris was modernized and beautified, and railroads were laid throughout the country. *Le Crédit Foncier,* a national bank, centralized French banking and provided credit for the merchant nation. Commercial treaties were negotiated with Great Britain and Prussia. A steamer service was promised to Asia and America.

The emperor also endeavored to win the support of the clericals. Handing education over to the church and sending troops to support the pope in Rome, he posed as the defender of Catholicism. By promoting French imperialism he appealed to both the clergy and the middle classes. Through the conquest of Algeria, completed in 1857, the acquisition of Cochin China and Annam in 1858, commercial concessions in China in 1860, and the erection in 1863 of a protectorate in Cambodia in revenge for the murder of missionaries, Louis gave the church an opportunity to save souls and the business men a chance to make money.

Welcome as was this new enlightened economic policy and subsequent prosperity, it was not sufficient for either the small property owners or the "large" intellectuals and radicals. These groups wanted a republic and resented the loss of political liberty and the imposition of heavy taxes brought about by the rise of this Second Empire. As the murmurs of dissatisfaction became louder Louis Napoleon established censorship of speech, of the press, and of education, and set up a system of espionage to watch the people. Acts like this served only to intensify the hostility of the emperor's enemies and to strengthen their determination to destroy his autocratic government.

A close alliance was cemented between the petty bourgeoisie and the workers. Developing a humanitarian interest in the welfare of the wage-earners, many members of the business classes supported the workers in their demands for educational facilities and the right to organize. Republican writers arranged to instruct the adults by publishing inexpensive books. Libraries were established, containing besides the masterpieces of world literature, books dealing with such "practical subjects as history, philosophy, and science." Educational societies were formed, and the first professional school for girls was opened in Paris.

At first the petty bourgeoisie tended to support the numerous plans calculated to bring about social progress through the establishment of coöperative societies. Various newspapers appeared in 1866 in which socialistic doctrines were expounded, and were eagerly read by the middle classes as well as by the workingmen. This unofficial bourgeois-proletarian alliance, however, did not last very long. After two or three years of "unconscious radicalism," the bourgeoisie, swayed by the classical economists, decided that radical philosophies were impractical and injurious to their economic future. For the time being, however, the merchants found it expedient to remain united with the radical element in common opposition to the emperor.

Resistance to Louis Napoleon was led by a young republican, Léon Gambetta. Of Italian parentage but French by birth, he devoted his unusual oratorical power to a bitter and emotional denunciation of the empire. Calling Louis an adventurer who by a *coup d'état* had risen to power and hopelessly involved his country in debt, he maintained that Louis and his followers had destroyed the good things implied by the liberal watchwords of the French Revolution—Liberty, Equality, and Fraternity. France, he said, could not be free until relieved of the vampire who was sucking the life blood of the state. Louis Adolphe Thiers also bitterly opposed the dictatorial policies of the emperor. After his dismissal from the cabinet by Louis Philippe, Thiers had retired to private life; but, with the advent of the Second Empire, he reëntered politics and became a representative in the assembly. Representing the lesser middle classes, he disapproved of Napoleon's autocratic policies, being careful, however, "to warn and not to threaten the Emperor."

Victor Hugo, the romantic literary genius, also became a severe critic of the emperor. During the forties Hugo's political opinions underwent a marked variation. Formerly a stout defender of tradition, he now sprouted liberal tendencies and in 1848 welcomed the establishment of a second French bourgeois republic. For his utterances against the dictatorial ambitions of Louis Napoleon, he was finally exiled by the emperor. Departing in wrath, he issued his satirical prose volume, *Napoleon the Little,* and did not return to France again for eighteen years. When, in 1870, he came back to Paris, he lent his moral support to the Commune of 1871 and in his great creative work, *Ninety-Three,* a novel dealing with the Reign of Terror, glorified the Revolution and the cause of the common man.

The transition from romanticism to realism in literature as illustrated by Flaubert, Zola, Maupassant, and others helps to explain the widespread dissatisfaction with the emperor. Undoubtedly the romanticists' worship of the past had facilitated the diffusion of the Napoleonic legend and the popularization of another World Empire. The new tendency to emphasize realities and outward phenomena was an indication of the trend against the "romantic" state. Under Louis Philippe the people, told to practise thrift and get rich, opposed this selfish plutocratic complacency. During the empire, urged to enjoy themselves, they objected to an autocratic government which brought repression, high taxes, and an artificial prosperity.

By 1870 the bourgeoisie in France comprised a clear-cut class group. Certain definite characteristics, such as parentage, table etiquette, education, dress, and income, separated the bourgeoisie from the proletariat and the semi-aristocratic plutocrats. Thrift and the accumulation of wealth in the form of money or property were the necessary prerequisites to be met before one could become middle-class. The dream of the petty bourgeoisie was the same: "to acquire a little property, a little house, a little business, a little income from investments." But one was generally not accepted by the "elder" shopkeepers on this basis. To be *really* bourgeois one must *have* owned. Consequently, the "newly rich" were not immediately "elected." Indeed, before one could become one of the élite, one must not only own property, but one must possess certain typical external refinements such as a degree from some university, whether worked for or not; culture, as represented by a multitude of art objects, a smattering of intellectual information, or an air of *savoir faire;* a "family tree" upon which to cast complacently retrospective glances; and leisure time, which could be used for idling, vacationing, or playing the dilettante.

Despite their passion for outward show, the bourgeoisie could not tolerate the lavish and reckless expenditures of the Second Empire. To them extravagance and squandering could lead only to financial instability, which was but one step away from the complete undermining of their individual security—security, the bourgeois ideal *par excellence.* That their alarm on this score was well founded was evidenced by the precipitation of a government crisis as a result of the disastrous war with Prussia (1870–1871).

Thus beset on all sides was the "liberal empire." Bourgeois republicans, radical socialists, and political intellectuals—all formed a solid bloc of antagonists to the hapless emperor. Prussia, resentful of the opposition of Louis Napoleon to the formation of a strong German state, completed his downfall. The result was the end of the Second Empire and the creation of a "practical" democracy—the Third French Republic.

CHAPTER XV

THE IMPORTANCE OF BEING VICTORIAN

Glory to Man in the highest! for Man is the master of things (Swinburne).

ENGLAND, like France, in 1815 was under the governmental domination of the conservatives. These Tory landowners, the same ones who fastened on to Napoleon's neck with bulldog tenacity until he gave up, held the machinery of government with an unyielding grasp. They were relentless in clinging to the power which they possessed, and for this reason perhaps more than any other refused to break with the past, preferring to rule England as had their forefathers in bygone days. They could be as generous and kind and honest as any other men in England; their donations to charity were by no means small; their patriotism and political energy were unquestionable; they were undoubtedly desirous of building a greater Britain. But they lacked the vision and the education to cope with the task of social reconstruction confronting the newly born industrial England of the nineteenth century; they were unfitted both by economic position and by intellectual aptitude for a duty of such magnitude.

The middle classes by this time were beginning to force their way into the upper level of society. Men who had made fortunes at the expense of the wretched natives of India; others who had profited through the labor of slaves in the West Indies; and captains of industry, who were accumulating fortunes through the use of machinery, demanded places in the exclusive circle. As usual, "money talked." It bought "social position" and "gentleman's honor." True, the old social barriers of dignity attained through generations of gathered traditions remained, but these were often surmounted "by men climbing on their own money bags."

An industrial revolution in the nineteenth century was bringing about a shift in the balance of financial power from the squires to the bourgeoisie; this new swing, however, was not very rapid. In the twenties and thirties the actual total value of produce and manufactures was around fifty million pounds yearly. Business was conducted on a small scale, and was perilously uncertain. Booms, panics, depression, bankruptcy, unemployment, poverty, and misery made the life of the *entrepreneur* a hectic one. Men won and lost small fortunes overnight. The struggle for existence had become an economic reality to thousands. Like the squire (the John Bull of the nineteenth century), the English business man was a fighter. Lacking polish, but full of self-confidence and energy, he rushed into the fray, determined to work out his economic salvation, regardless of the interests of others, including those he employed. It was a fascinating game he played; and the stakes were worth while—high profits and social recognition.

Nor were these materialistic burghers entirely devoid of philosophical reflection on the distinguishing characteristics possessed by their class. They were frankly conscious of their own virtuosity, if not of their superiority. For many years, in order to make money, they had regarded "all diversions as wrong, and had lived bare lives, unaffected by moral sin," but finally, they realized that they were respectable and *that,* indeed, was the highest virtue of all. Old men who had lived in the profligate days when the lords were in the saddle, viewed this new society with suspicion. Noting the sobriety of these middle-class men, one of them said that "he could recall a time when to get drunk was almost necessary if a man were not to be considered a milk sop." One can well visualize the bewilderment of these "old timers" when they heard about the first meeting of the World's temperance union in London (1846).

But with the feeling that they had assumed the cloak of respectability, the middle classes took on also a less desirable vesture—that of self-satisfaction. Especially apparent was this on Sundays when they left their neat homes and trim gardens and decorously went to church. There they sat in select pews, and in a long sermon delivered by a servile cleric heard their virtues fervently extolled. Perhaps they even "thanked God" that "they were not as other people's wicked ancestors had been." Their everyday lives were established on a principle eminently conventional. They retired early and rose early, firm believers in the solemn truth of "Early to bed and early to rise, makes a man healthy, wealthy, and wise." Moreover, they slept largely, ate largely, produced largely, but according to certain cynics, did not think largely. Such was the self-importance of being Victorian.

These early nineteenth-century bourgeoisie, however, had their amusements. There were social evenings with "sit-down" teas, sedate afternoon archery parties, and punctilious calls on stated occasions. Inevitable as the "how-d'ye-do" was the deadly dinner party, described as follows by Count Melfort:

> There was brilliant plate—reminding one of a silversmith's shop; highly spiced soups, fowl, fish, beef, and quantities of other food. It lasted two hours and one half with little chance for conversation; another hour with wine; and then coffee with the ladies and music—or you might call it that.

Frequently a cynical soul, the next day, would describe the party as "very large and sufficiently dull." This was the life of many of these English social aspirants.

Practical and independent, these social climbers soon possessed a contempt for everything that could not be measured in terms of money. Such a plutocratic philosophy of life—if one wants to call it a philosophy—encouraged selfishness. The bourgeoisie frankly recognized the idea of struggle so far as business was concerned and went into trade determined to get as much money as possible.

Religion in the early nineteenth century was just another means of justifying the new economic order. Puritanism, as we have seen, favored the middle classes in pre-revolutionary days; and after Napoleon it continued to shed warm beams of approval. Affected by the conservatism of that time, Wesleyans and Evangelicals especially taught their followers to make the best of things, for, as an English writer of hymns said:

> The rich man in his castle,
> The poor man at his gate,
> God made them, high or lowly,
> And ordered their estate.

According to these exponents of Puritanism, God was no longer the urbane deity of the eighteenth century; the new Lord was a busy middle-class God who stood ready to punish severely those who disobeyed the new virtues. Wingfield-Stratford in his *The Victorian Tragedy* expresses this view when, in discussing family discipline in the bourgeois homes, he says that young Victorians were "taught that the Lord was above, and Papa, if not listening at the door, somewhere below, and lower still, a not improbable Hell." This mid-Victorian papa, however, did not believe that he was unduly severe in his treatment of his children. In his opinion he, like father Barrett of Wimpole Street, was through his harshness really contributing to their eventual happiness. Unconsciously perhaps, he was a follower of the utilitarian Bentham, and thus believed that by bringing his children up to conform to bourgeois customs and ideas he was preparing them for a life of contentment and prosperity.

"The greatest happiness of the greatest number" became the accepted concept of utopia in the early Victorian England. To attain this objective the old conservative government of the squires had to be abolished and the middle-class régime with its solid virtues and its constructive energy substituted. Like their Calvinist forefathers, these very frugal utilitarians frowned upon aristocratic elegance and leisure, and emphasized instead simplicity and hard work. Also it was their firm belief that the scientific principles of the eighteenth-century writers would help the middle classes solve all earthly problems. Hence there was no place in the scheme of things for the "lazy aristocrat."

These ideas rose out of the bitter economic strife which the

Industrial Revolution had brought into existence. Middle-class men who were engaged in this struggle naturally assumed that the world was inhabited by millions of selfish human beings. It was not difficult for them, therefore, to conclude that in the economic sphere life was a struggle for existence and that only the fit survived. Most of them went so far as to assert that this contest was a good thing in itself. They welcomed the classical economists who defended individualism, and they especially applauded the "courageous" Ricardo when he attacked the landowner for receiving an unearned increment on the rent of his land and suggested that this effortless profit should be taxed in order to prevent the squire from getting rich at the expense of his workers. The middle classes of course welcomed the thesis postulated by the classical economists—Ricardo, Malthus, and Mill—that the acquisition of capital for the purpose of facilitating the mechanization of industry and the promotion of general prosperity is permissible and even necessary. Many of them accepted the Malthusian theory of population and believed, as Malthus did, that such "natural" things as war, disease, and famine alone would answer the puzzle of overproduction.

Business idealists decried this selfish individualism, especially the idea that social reforms would encourage vagrancy and discourage thrift. As an example of the failure of economic individualism, attention was called to the fact that while a few persons were extremely wealthy, the majority were very poor. Poverty had increased, even though the ranks of the bourgeoisie had grown. Even from the conservative middle class there was now and then heard an admission that all was not well in England; but blame for anything wrong was placed on the shoulders of wicked, corrupt landowners who ruled selfishly in their own interests.

Led by these practical exponents of individualism, middle-class reformers and workmen agitated for social and political change. Such bourgeois newspapers as the *London Times* and the *Annual Register* used much printer's ink in discussing this matter; "soap-box orators" did an unusual amount of "arm-waving"; and everywhere people quoted with delight such doggerel as

> Only to think to have lords over-running the nation,
> As plenty as frogs in a Dutch inundation.

Agitation proved effective enough when the lower middle classes and the workers united under the shrewd leadership of the upper middle class and passed the Reform Bill of 1832. But no great benefits accrued as a result either to the working men or to the lower strata of the business men; as Wingfield-Stratford comments, the masses, the real exponents of a democracy "who yelled for the Bill, the whole Bill, and nothing but the Bill—got nothing but the Bill." For they had merely exchanged one set of masters, the Tory proprietors, for another, the wealthy bourgeoisie.

But the new ruling class was sufficiently wise politically to mitigate the social evils attendant upon the financial powers it wielded. It responded to the cues of the humanitarians by a temporary zeal for social reforms. For example, in the thirties slavery was abolished, social legislation was passed, and a poor law, designed to induce paupers to work by making the Poor House a replica of Hades, was enacted. Short-lived, however, was this wave of reform, for, fearful of losing their economic dominance, the upper class stifled such advanced ideas, as for instance, proposals for extension of the suffrage into the ranks of the working class. Reflecting this conservative tendency, the *Annual Register* in 1837 commented: "Short as is the interval since the agitation of that period, the influence of property, of old connections and early prejudices have already renewed their sway."

The accession of Victoria to the throne in 1837—"I shall do my utmost to fulfill my duty towards my country. Few have more real good will and more real desire to do what is fit than I have!"—marked a milestone in the history of the bourgeoisie. Victoria, "Queen of the Philistines," ascended the throne at a time when capitalist activities and ideas were becoming dominant factors in English life. Her early career was spent in a quiet and proper atmosphere. Indeed, a study of her journal and her letters indicates that she lived an uneventful existence. Her early memorabilia could just as well have been written by the daughter of a merchant, rather than by a princess who was being trained to become a queen—certainly they exhibited bourgeois rather than aristocratic tendencies. Her reaction to a certain book, for example, was: "It is wonderful," and a play caused her to remark: "How pretty and clean." When speaking of individuals, she generally emphasized their good, solid, and upright virtues; one friend, for example, was "good humored and well-read," and another was "an honest, warm-hearted, good soul."

Victoria owed her political education chiefly to her uncle, Leopold of Belgium. Leopold had realized that Victoria was to become queen of the middle classes and therefore he prepared her for this position by tutoring her in rather well-worn ideas regarding church, country, and people, always employing the words "sensible" and "moderate." Several letters written in 1837 requested her to occupy herself "with the several questions which agitate parties," and further to talk with the Dean (Anglican) concerning them. "He is a good moderate man." In reply, Victoria said: "You may depend on it, I shall profit by your excellent advice regarding politics."

About a month before Victoria was crowned, her coming of age was celebrated with great festivity throughout the kingdom. People of all stations in life paid honor to the future queen; and, according to the *London Times,* "the club houses in Pall Mall, St. James Street, and elsewhere were elegantly and mostly appropriately illuminated . . . and the trades-people manifested devoted loyalty and affection." Victoria's reaction, as set down in her Journal, was that "The anxiety of the people to see poor stupid me was very great, and I must say that I was very touched by it." A few weeks later at the age of eighteen this "modest and proper" young lady became queen of England.

Following the accession of Queen Victoria, a steady increase in trade and industry was accompanied by the definite statement and acceptance in the forties by her government of the *laissez faire* policy with its famous commandments:

1. The state shall not interfere between employer and employee.
2. The state shall not interfere between buyer and seller.
3. The state shall place no hindrance on free development of foreign trade.

England now witnessed a great expansion of resources, population, wealth, and power. This economic development in turn affected all aspects of life. Education, amusements, morals, literature, and art were influenced by the rise to supremacy of a new industrial order which placed a value upon money as an end hitherto never equaled. In short, this mid-Victorian Era (1837–1878) marked a high point in English cultural progress and a golden age comparable to that of Elizabeth or that of Augustus.

During this period the business men, who had succeeded through rare ingenuity rather than because of social position, were evolving a philosophy to justify their dominant position. In their opinion the state should be merely a restricting or police force—and all, if not wealthy, would at least be contented and happy. Let each man attend to his own business and produce, produce, produce. Then the nation as a whole would prosper. These views of the wealthy factory owners were not justifiable to the workers or to the intellectuals sympathetic to the working class. They declared that the state should not be a cold, detached observer of the intolerable misery of the wage-earners. No man should have the right to hire women and children to work twelve hours a day, or to employ men in unsanitary factories at starvation wages. Political authority must be taken from the wealthy middle classes and given to the mass of the people before true social justice could be achieved.

These radical doctrines were crystallized in the forties in the Chartist movement—a campaign on the part of the petty bourgeoisie and the workers to attain universal male suffrage and other political and social reforms. But to oppose an energetic, wealthy, and well-organized upper middle class with military resources was an impossible task, and so the demands of the Chartists went unheeded, the agitators being suppressed. This did not offer a solution for unemployment, poverty, the waste and decay of child labor, and the employment of women in factories. As production expanded and profits piled up, the poverty of the masses grew worse. Even the wealthy suffered as a result of financial crashes and speculative orgies.

True to form, the ruling classes refused to submit to a major operation, depending on nerve-deadening pills to relieve the pain. Bitter exponents of anything revolutionary and devout exponents of compromise, they ridiculed the Chartist movement and Robert Owen's utopianism as too premature and too romantic. Finally, these practical business men produced their own solution—lower the cost of living by abolishing the Corn Laws, thus reducing the price of bread. This legislation would enable the worker to live and would deprive the "selfish" landlords of exorbitant profits.

Led by such advocates of free trade as the bourgeois Cobden and Bright and the conservative Sir Robert Peel, these benevolent "humanitarians" brought about the repeal of the Corn Laws. By this legislation the cost of living was reduced at the expense of the landowner. The middle-class employer therefore felt quite virtuous. He had aided the poor and his benevolence had not cost him a shilling.

The establishment of free trade, however, did more than merely reduce the cost of living. By this act the mid-Victorians practically abandoned the mercantilistic concept of self-sufficiency. Henceforth, England was to depend upon foreign countries as the markets for the sale of goods and as the source for food. If, for any reason, the outlet for the sale of her goods or for the purchase of wheat were cut off, then her economic prosperity was doomed. In the forties, however, the business classes, thinking their prosperity unlimited, refused to worry about the future. Only the problems of the day concerned them.

This mid-Victorian prosperity, enjoyed chiefly by the wealthy middle classes, only served to intensify the determination of the workers, backed by the petty bourgeoisie, to obtain the ballot. As time went on, they became more aggressive and more powerful. By 1866, leaders of the two dominant parties, the successors of the Tories and the Whigs—namely, the Conservatives and the Liberals—realized that they must yield to the political demands of the wage-earners. Gladstone, Liberal leader of the House of Commons, proposed a limited extension of suffrage. Many Liberals, however, disappointed because the measure was too moderate, joined the Conservatives in killing it.

The conservative politicians who now came to power also thought that the advance toward political democracy could be checked. In this they were deceived. Aroused by the rejection of the bill, the masses held popular demonstrations and demanded the extension of the suffrage. Gladstone, as the fiery apostle of political democracy, furnished the famous battle cry, "You cannot fight against the future; time is on our side." Realizing that reform was inevitable, the Conservatives, led by Disraeli, decided in 1867 to extend the suffrage and thus to gain the ballots of the new voters. Consequently, another Reform Bill was introduced in Parliament. At first it was a typically moderate measure, but Gladstone and his followers in the House of Commons impelled the Conservative government to remodel the Bill almost entirely. When it finally passed, it conformed largely to the ideas of Gladstone, the reformer. As leader of the Conservatives, however, the resourceful Disraeli, who backed the measure, was given the credit.

As finally enacted in 1867, the Reform Bill ended the political despotism of the plutocratic middle classes in England. The franchise in boroughs was given to all householders. "Thus, instead of ten-pound householders, all householders, whatever the values of their houses, were admitted; also all lodgers who had occupied for a year lodgings of the value, unfurnished, of ten pounds, or about a dollar a week." In the counties the suffrage was given to all those who owned property yielding five pounds clear income a year, rather than ten pounds as previously; and to all renters who paid at least twelve pounds, rather than fifty pounds as hitherto. The better class of laborers in the boroughs, and of virtually all tenant farmers in the counties, received the ballot. This legislation nearly doubled the number of voters in England.

The passage of this sweeping measure aroused much pessimism among Englishmen. Carlyle pictured a terrible future and characterized the reform as "shooting Niagara." Robert Lowe, who had vehemently objected to the act, shuddered at the prospect of the "uncultured in control." "We must educate our masters," he said. Despite these small grumblings, the Bill of 1867 actually marked a vital step in the political rise of the wage-earning class. Henceforth, the rivalry between the bourgeoisie and the country gentlemen was pushed more and more into the background. As the wage-earners became powerful and active, the struggle for supremacy now centered between them and the bourgeoisie. Liberals and Conservatives to the present day have been prone to form a united front against the radical menace.

Parliamentary struggles which resulted in social reforms and in the rise of the working men to political power occurred during the ministries of two remarkable English statesmen, William Ewart Gladstone (1809–1898) and Benjamin Disraeli (1804–1881). Son of a wealthy Scotch merchant, who had moved from his native land to the city of Liverpool, Gladstone was fortunate enough to inherit a considerable patrimony. On the other hand, Disraeli, whose grandfather, a Jew, had migrated from Italy to England, began work as a poor though to be sure very clever young man. Their careers were as contrasting as their ancestry. Peculiarly, the Scotsman became a Liberal, the Jew a Conservative.

Gladstone was a typically benevolent member of the rising capitalist class. An opportunist as well as a sincere exponent of the doctrines of his fellow-countryman, Adam Smith, he was wise enough to know that there comes a time when middle-class tolerance and compromise must be discarded in favor of positive rather than negative government action. This liberal statesman represented a dominant element of the middle classes—the advocates of free trade. Identified with the movement which had resulted in the abolition of the Corn Laws of 1846, Gladstone seized the opportunity to promote comprehensive industrial, commercial, and intellectual enterprises, which, in his opinion, had been made possible by such members of the Manchester school as Cobden, Bright, and Mill.

On the other hand, Disraeli became a staid Conservative. He was ambitious, eccentric, and according to many orthodox Englishmen, "common." The "proper" Liberals consequently did not approve of him personally. Aware of this antagonism, Disraeli professed at first an opposition to change, a love for the romantic past, and antipathy for the unromantic manufacturers and shopkeepers, and a brotherly interest in the poor working man.

Counted as an adventurer by many Englishmen, Disraeli, a superb example of opportunism, had managed to rise politically by joining the Conservatives and by championing in the sixties the political cause of the working men. Although not asking for full suffrage, he claimed that the House of Commons should represent varieties of classes and interests rather than mere numbers. The vote, he said, should be given to a select aristocracy of laborers.

Disraeli found it difficult at first to make much of an impression in England, save on Queen Victoria, with whom he had won great personal favor by highly diplomatic practices. He desired to gain national attention by furthering some pressing political issue. But what question could be utilized for his own benefit? The ballot for the working men was sponsored and opposed by elements in both parties. Gladstone, moreover, had already jumped into the reform camp. The cause of protection seemed a possibility, but the remarkable economic progress which attended the repeal of the Corn Laws made the Manchester school far too powerful to be successfully opposed on this score. In the sixties, however, Disraeli found an issue—imperialism. Colonial expansion, he believed, would appeal to all groups, for it would bring prosperity to every one—investors, industrialists, merchants, and wage-earners—all would profit as a result of the general stimulation of industry through the acquisition of new markets. In turn, marked prosperity would solve internal questions such as the labor problem. Finally, it would appeal to British patriotism. To prepare the way for the adoption of this shrewd policy, Disraeli attacked the Gladstonian "little Englanders" of the Manchester school and accused them of furthering pacifism and republicanism, instead of a national and truly patriotic program.

Despite this rivalry, Gladstone remained in power from 1868 to 1874. As an earnest exponent of individualism he tried to aid the oppressed Irish by means of land reforms. He also aimed to improve the general run of English life by giving greater scope of opportunity to the "common man." The exclusion of non-conformists from academic privileges was completely abolished. A civil service bill was passed, granting free competition for positions in almost all departments of government. Regardless of these liberal reforms, or because of them, Gladstone's ministry became unpopular. English landowners resented his activities in Ireland, even though he had not tried to deprive them of their privileges, especially their monopoly of land in England. Many high churchmen and non-conformists disliked his education act. Moreover, the conciliatory attitude of the government in foreign affairs was scornfully branded as tame and submissive. Actually, however, the landowners and wealthy industrialists were hostile to internal reforms and welcomed a leader and a policy of ending this "eternal" uncertainty. The beginning of a great depression in England, discussed in a later chapter, precipitated Gladstone's downfall.

In 1874 Disraeli, by becoming prime minister, obtained an opportunity to carry out his imperialist aims. His first conspicuous achievement was the purchase of Suez Canal shares (1875) whereby French control of the highway to India was checkmated. At the Congress of Berlin (1878) he helped to stop the Russian advance in the Near East and obtained the island of Cyprus for England. By these acts he succeeded in impressing upon England the importance of her position as an empire, not an insular state.

Disraeli's revival of imperialism and the high status of the bourgeoisie during the mid-Victorian period were accompanied by an extraordinary development of science. The discovery of magneto-electricity in 1831 by an Englishman, Michael Faraday, contributed to the perfection of such invaluable everyday conveniences as the electric light, the telegraph, and the telephone. Discoveries in preventative medicine and antiseptic surgery, resulting largely from a study into the causes of infectious diseases, brought the most startling advances in the field of medicine, enlarging greatly the knowledge of the causes, symptoms, treatment, and prevention of disease. Perfection of appliances and inventions was of inestimable help. The stethoscope, a French discovery, was adopted in 1819 and enabled physicians to diagnose pulmonary conditions. A clinical thermometer, an English device, allowed doctors to analyze the physical condition of patients with greater accuracy than had been possible before.

Much work was done before 1876 in the fields of chemistry, physics, and geology. During the nineteenth century a new science, organic chemistry, came into existence. Through the atomic theory great headway was made in discovering the composition of matter. In the realm of physics "the most productive of the experimental investigations of the period" were made in the fields of spectrum analysis, electricity, and magnetism. As a result of these researches, scientists not only learned something about the composition of the sun but were enabled to invent the electric dynamo and other electrical devices. Frankland's researches in the interest of a safe and satisfactory water supply and Sir Charles Lyell's contributions as found in his *Principles of Geology* indicate the amazing expansion of scientific knowledge during the Victorian age. The geological research of Lyell (1797–1875) presaged an even more important contribution. When he showed that the present form and appearance of the earth was caused not by a series of catastrophes but rather by the steady and constant operation of geological forces, he really promoted an idea which was applied in the domain of biological science—the theory of evolution.

This theory was not placed upon a scientific basis, however, until Charles Darwin (1809–1882) published his *Origin of Species* in 1859. In this work he brought out the three simple propositions of unchanging law, orderly development, and selection based on fitness and adaptability in the great kingdom of life. Later, in defense of the Darwinian theory there arose many writers, of whom the most able were Thomas Henry Huxley (1825–1895) and Herbert Spencer (1820–1902). Spencer, accepting Darwin's theory, emphasized the process of natural selection and used the striking term "the survival of the fittest." Determined to apply the evolutionary theory to all great fields of life and existence, he published a series of books, which were used by many philosophers and statesmen to explain on this basis not only the struggle for existence in nature, but also the conflict of nations and the rise of the superstate.

Middle-class intellectuals welcomed this new evolutionary doctrine, for they could easily use it as justification of the economic theory of *laissez faire.* They deduced the principle of free competition in which the weak fell by the wayside, and the strong self-made men rose to the top. By their growth they in turn would contribute to the prosperity of the nation and the welfare of all. This belief, in the opinion of many of the bourgeoisie, tallied with the Darwinian concept of the survival of the fittest through natural selection.

Backed by the scientific as well as the economic and Calvinistic justifications of individualism, the middle classes could not help but manifest certain well-defined characteristics. Determined to succeed in the struggle of life, they exhibited an earnestness of purpose and an ability to concentrate unequaled up to their time. Grimly they decided to win out in the game of life by making money, and in so doing they bred a worship to toil which is well described in Matthew Arnold's poem *Quiet Work:*

> One lesson, Nature, let me learn of thee,
> One lesson, which in every wind is blown,
> The lesson of two duties kept at one
> Though the loud world proclaim their enmity—
> Of toil unsevered from tranquillity!
> Of labor, that in lasting fruit outgrows
> Far noisier schemes, accomplish'd in repose.

This emphasis upon work helps to explain the thoroughness and frequently the length of the books of Darwin, Spencer,

Ruskin, Carlyle, the Brownings, Buckle, and other great mid-Victorian writers.

The worship of toil and the morality of Puritanism dominated family life. Mid-Victorian prudery made the sexual side of marriage mysterious and glorified the home. "To preserve the home intact and pure," writes Wingfield-Stratford, "to be fruitful and multiply were considered the real functions of the mother." Divorce and violations of sexual taboos, especially by females, were abhorred and, as pictured in *East Lynne* and in the works of George Eliot, often resulted in death. Married life was idealized. Queen Victoria's devotion to her German consort, Prince Albert, is an excellent example of mid-Victorian family life. She resented the fact that his ability was not recognized by the English people and did everything in her power to advance his reputation. Gladstone and his wife, both well along in years, furnished the classic example of the happy mid-Victorian couple, as they waltzed around the room singing:

> A ragamuffin husband and a rantipoling wife
> We'll fiddle and scrape it through the ups and downs of life!

Mid-Victorian women were not oppressed domestics. Perhaps there were just as many henpecked husbands and masterly women as there are today. Certainly Elizabeth Browning, George Eliot, Florence Nightingale, and Queen Victoria, in character, ability, and independence could equal almost all of our so-called emancipated women of today. Even in the home the wife, directly and indirectly, fought for the spiritual and material advancement of Merrie England.

Great personalities, male as well as female, were products of this period. Macaulay, Robert Owen, Palmerston, Disraeli, Gladstone, like Lincoln in the United States, were products of this age of individualism, of self-dependence, of discipline, and of optimism. It is true that some of these great characters had certain unpleasant qualities which many believed characterized the mid-Victorian age. Palmerston, for example, seemed to be pretty much of a snob and an egotist. On the other hand, Robert Owen was a generous man and a sincere idealist.

Many comfortable mid-Victorians, extremely selfish and self-centered, ignored the economic inequalities of their day, while others subscribed to that great bourgeois publication *Punch* and approved of its bitter condemnation in words and in cartoons on social injustices. Perhaps these mid-Victorians were no more selfish or snobbish than are their descendants today. Certainly they were more optimistic. They were attempting to readjust their civilization to a mechanical age and believed that they could do so by producing enough for every one to eat and wear.

In brief, during the mid-Victorian period in England, the bourgeoisie enjoyed the first sweet fruits of triumph. They influenced every cranny of English life. Scholars, philosophers, poets, historians, economists, inventors, and innovators in the various branches of human endeavor expanded under the mellowing influence of doctrines of moderation and compromise, of individualism and egoism, and used their talents to develop and to defend this system. Political liberty and equality, universal suffrage, and free education were high achievements of the age. Little wonder the middle-class man sat back complacently, satisfied with himself and his country. For such was the importance of being Victorian.

Chapter XVI

SIGNPOSTS OF PROGRESS

Why don't they leave it [revolutionary change] alone? (Lord Melbourne).

Feudal-agrarianism vs. nationalist-capitalism—this was the struggle of political attitudes enacted in Europe between 1815 and 1870. The bourgeoisie led the way in making the latter triumphant in France and in England; in other parts of Europe political decentralization, the clinging of tradition, and the lack of material resources essential to a commercial and industrial economy delayed or prevented the emergence of the new order.

During the first half of the nineteenth century significant social changes occurred in Central Europe. Feudalism was abolished in Prussia and in other parts of the Germanies, free land becoming an immediate possibility. The emancipation of the serfs removed previous oppressive social inequalities and made liberty, equality, and fraternity more than mere catchwords. Although Prussia and Austria were still predominantly agricultural, the growing middle classes by that time were large enough to become an accountable factor in the revolutions, and when these were over, they applied their experience and practicality to inculcating liberalism in their native lands.

One outstanding result of the revolts which culminated in the revolutions of 1848 was that people freed themselves from such antiquated beliefs as the doctrine of divine right. The reactionary movement did not succeed in completely restoring the old political system. Parliamentary institutions were established in such states as Württemberg and Bavaria, and even in Prussia the king was forced to grant a constitution. Moreover, nationalism persisted. The Germans, the Czechs, the Magyars, and the Slavs still had visions of independence and unity; and the desire for freedom spread to many other nationalities, including the Jews, who had suffered much in various parts of Central and Eastern Europe. At the same time the middle-class concept of religious toleration, separation of church and state, and emphasis upon education controlled by the government, were being diffused throughout middle Europe. As in France before 1789, the old régime in Central Europe was falling to pieces, and the revolutions of 1848 served to hasten the changes which seemed bound to come.

Practically every European country was touched by revolutionary tendencies between 1815 and 1848. In Russia the Decembrist Revolt of 1825, wherein a group of young officers planned the liberalization of Russia, indicated the presence of bourgeois ideas in that great empire. In Turkey the Greek revolt and unrest among the Slavic peoples of the Balkans presaged the downfall of that backward country. The Young Irish movement was also a manifestation of this world-wide liberalism. In Denmark the king, responsive to it, granted, in 1849, a moderate constitution which created a parliament elected by propertied voters. In the Netherlands the liberal movement caused King William II to give his people a constitution which widened the suffrage for the lower house of the States-General. In Belgium there was an extension of democracy which doubled the number of votes. In Switzerland the problem was that of nationalism rather than of democracy. In Spain and Italy, nationalistic democratic movements resulted in feeble uprisings. Rossetti in his poem *At the Sunrise in 1848* interpreted the significance of bourgeois liberalism when he wrote:

> God said, Let there be light! And there was light.
> Then heard we sounds as though the earth did sing
> And the Earth's angel cried upon the wing:
> We saw priests fall together and turn white:
> And covered in dust from the sun's sight,
> A king was spied, and yet another king.

Italy, after an unsuccessful attempt to expel the Austrians in 1848, experienced a quick and significant nationalist revival.

The man largely responsible for this regeneration was Count Cavour. Son of a nobleman living in Piedmont and devoted to absolutist ideals, he was at first destined for a military career. While visiting an uncle in Switzerland, however, he imbibed the liberal thoughts of his age. His relative, a disciple of Turgot and Condorcet, taught the young man the middle-class concepts of progress. Fortified by his reading and his travels, he became an ardent exponent of liberalism. Convinced of the political excellence of the British middle-class system, he decided that Italy must adopt similar political and economic ideas if she were to become a powerful, united nation. He also believed that, if Italy were to imitate such liberal states as England and France, she would win their sympathy and possibly their support. He therefore began to strive for the unification of a constitutional monarchy, and the bourgeois arrangement of a free church in a free state. Apparently he did not realize that the Italian temperament, the historic past, the presence of problems peculiar to Italy (as, for example, the presence of the pope), might make the establishment of a liberal constitutional monarchy in Italy a difficult, if not an impossible task.

Cavour proved successful at least in establishing such a government in Piedmont, which was ruled by the House of Savoy. Through his newspaper, the *Risorgimento,* he urged the formation of agricultural societies, mechanics' institutes, industrial associations, and banks to aid capital and labor. In 1852, as premier of the Sardinian kingdom, he instituted a typical middle-class régime. Free trade was encouraged, shipping was subsidized, factories were built, railroads were constructed, education was stimulated, and waste land was put under cultivation. The budget was reconstructed and taxes were more equitably distributed; financial as well as political domination of the church was destroyed; many monasteries were suppressed, the Jesuits were expelled from the country; and an attempt was made to separate church and state so that bourgeois interests could dominate the government without going afoul of the clerical interests.

Cavour next embarked on an even more ambitious program

—the unification of the Italian states. To this end he conceived the thought that physical unification of the country would facilitate political unification. He therefore planned the construction of a vast network of railroads, linking together all the sections of the peninsula; he envisioned his compatriots mingling with each other culturally and economically, mutually appreciating their common heritage of ancient Rome.

Like Bismarck, his German contemporary, Cavour believed that an enlightened economic policy together with clever diplomacy and military power were guarantees of a successful government. To achieve this objective he sought support of powerful European states. Participation by Sardinia in the Crimean War (1853–1856) gave Cavour his opportunity to lay the Italian situation before the representatives of England and France. A few years later, he succeeded in gaining the support of France in a war to force Austria out of Italy. This marked the beginning of a movement which was to result in the rise of United Italy. In February, 1861, the first Italian parliament met in Turin and in March a new constitutional decree announced that Victor Emmanuel I had assumed for himself and his successors the title "King of Italy." By 1870, the entire Italian peninsula, including Rome, had come under the rule of the constitutional monarchy.

While Cavour was unifying Italy and working for a bourgeois monarchical state, Bismarck, a typical conservative junker who was an uncompromising foe of all liberals, especially of those who advocated a limited constitutional government, was establishing the autocratic German Empire. As minister-president of Prussia, Bismarck saw an opportunity to bring about German unity under Prussian leadership. The first steps in that direction were to be the destruction of the German Confederation and the abolition by means of wars of Austrian influence in the Germanies. Liberalism would then be destroyed through the establishment of a strong German state ruled by Prussia. By 1871 these phases of Bismarck's program had been carried out; the greater part of Germany was united in an empire in which Prussia held the predominant position.

The rise of the German Empire, however, was but the beginning of the story. The triumph of reactionary forces was followed by a period of internal peace. Between 1848 and 1851, German enterprise was directed toward the economic advancement of the state. Consequently commerce expanded, prices of agricultural commodities rose, and money began to flow into Germany. All groups participated in a heightened economic activity; but of these it was the bourgeoisie who experienced the fullest measure of growth. The German middle classes had already taken an active part in the patriotic and intellectual regeneration which had followed the Battle of Jena (1806). By 1851 they had had sufficient cultural and technical experience to make Germany one of the leading economic centers of Europe.

As a result, it was not long before the foundations of the great capitalistic German state were established. Credit banks, such as the *Bank für Handel und Industrie zu Darmstadt* (1853), were founded, which furnished the financial means necessary for the organization of great industrial enterprises and means of transport. Joint stock companies enabled people in all walks of life to purchase shares in economic undertakings and thus made them observant partners of the financial welfare of the state. Between 1853 and 1857 millions of thalers were invested in banks and in railroad stocks alone. Meanwhile shares in industries, insurance companies, mining ventures, steam navigation, machinery, refineries, cotton mills, and other enterprises were sold to a great number of investors, mostly of the middle classes.

Thus, while Bismarck in building the German Empire was conforming to the traditional conservative belief in political authority, the middle classes of Germany, in shaping the country along economic lines, were following the liberal doctrine of the *laissez faire*. During these years great railways were built, connecting the leading cities and the outlying districts. Mining and weaving became thriving industries. In agriculture the same initiative which enabled the engineers and scientists to improve machinery and to invent dyes, caused them to perfect scientific processes of cultivation.

In 1870 Germany was ripe for a period of marked industrial

advancement. Thanks to the *Zollverein,* internal trade had been stimulated, transportation improved, industrial expansion begun. Moreover, in the various handicrafts, as for example, in the making of fabrics and of fine steel and cutlery, the Germans had become preëminent. Consequently, with native resources, with expert handicraftsmen, with an educated middle class, and with an efficient, centralized, and paternal government, the Germans were able to ally exact science with industry in such a way as to make their country by 1914 one of the leading industrial nations of the world.

Meanwhile, bourgeois liberalism had entered the citadel of conservatism, namely, the Hapsburg dominions. Austria under Metternich experienced an age of reaction. Attempts on the part of the Austrian-Germans to bring about liberal reforms, culminated in the revolutions of 1848. Temporarily, the old order was swept away. Mutual distrust and subsequent antagonism of the subject nationalities and also the general inability of the people to realize what democracy meant, enabled the government to put down these uprisings.

Despite the conservatism of this neo-absolutist period, economically and socially Austria forged ahead. Feudalism, in its legal if not its social implications, was practically destroyed through the principles of constitutional equality. The serfs were freed, but most of them, in view of the primarily agrarian nature of the empire, remained in economic thraldom, at the mercy of the great landowner. Nevertheless, as railways, highways, banks, and factories sprang up, capitalistic economy and the middle-class system also appeared, especially in Bohemia and in Austria proper. In 1850, a customs union with Hungary provided for free trade within the Hapsburg dominions. Gradually, economic improvements bettered conditions; but unevenness of prosperity served to emphasize the separation of the various regions of the empire and thus stood in the way of real industrial progress.

During the last half of the nineteenth century, the small European nations such as Denmark, Switzerland, and Holland participated in a common civilization with the greater states, being exposed to the same influences and to the same general movements. Most of them overthrew the fetters of the old régime and adopted capitalistic methods. Of these nations, Belgium experienced the most marked industrial expansion. At the Congress of Vienna, the Powers had united her with Holland. Objecting to this unrequested union, the Belgians issued a declaration of independence and started a revolution in 1830. Backed by England and France, they secured their freedom, set up a moderately liberal constitutional monarchy, and placed political power in the hands of the aristocracy and the plutocratic captains of industry.

Independence meant prosperity for Belgium. Free from the control of the commercially minded Dutch government, the Belgians soon became a powerful bourgeois industrial nation. Their natural resources were the means to this end. Situated on the North Sea, that country was able, by the construction of canals and railways, to connect the entire region with the great seaport at Antwerp and to develop the extensive coal beds. As a result Belgium was "the one country in Europe which kept pace industrially with England, in the first half of the nineteenth century." Her immense output of manufactured goods is best illustrated by the fact that during this period she sent "machinery all over Holland, Russia, and the whole territory of the young German *Zollverein*." By the end of the nineteenth century agricultural as well as industrial improvements made Belgium one of the most densely settled and most prosperous areas in Europe.

In contrast to Belgium, Russia by 1870 was one of the largest and most economically backward states on the Continent. Nevertheless, Western capitalism had seeped into the great empire. To strengthen national defense and to improve the machinery of government, she had to borrow capitalistic methods from her neighbors. In doing this she could not remain culturally isolated. Consequently, when railroads and the factory system were introduced into Russia, they brought with them many Western ideas, such as constitutional government, civil equality, and personal liberty. Then "enlightenment," which was a spirited ideal in the lives of the small group of educated Russians during the latter half of the eighteenth century, was revived. The principle of autocracy, the predominance of the nobility, and the value of serfdom were soon questioned by intelligent Russian intellectuals.

Economic progress after 1815 thus accelerated the introduction of Western views as well as of Western practices. Between 1815 and 1855 there was a marked expansion of Russian industry and commerce with a corresponding increase in capital. Landowners, observing this progress, tried to force greater production on their estates in order to make more money, and some even used serfs in factories. But, as time went on, it became apparent that they were a hindrance to capitalist economy. The reproductivity of serf labor was low, and a need for free workers existed. Long before the emancipation of the serfs in the sixties, many Russian intellectuals realized that the appearance of capitalism in Russia had doomed serfdom.

Ruling Russia in the nineteenth century was not an easy task. Alexander I (1801–1825) and Nicholas I (1825–1855) had inherited three traditions—orthodoxy, autocracy, and imperial unity—which they considered it their duty to preserve. At the same time they were confronted by the new tendencies which arose out of the revival of "enlightenment" and the introduction of capitalism. Both rulers tried to accept the innovations and yet to preserve the old political and social system, but these contradictory factors were practically irreconcilable.

The futility of the attempt on the part of Nicholas I to maintain the old political and social order was revealed at the end of his reign during the unsuccessful Crimean War (1853–1856). Despite the bravery of her soldiers, Russia, unprepared, was defeated in this conflict. The defeat, besides being a shock to her military and political prestige, was also a serious blow to her political and social system. Revealing the inability of the government to advance Russia's interests in the world, exposing her economic backwardness, the incompetence of her bureaucracy, the corruption of her officials, and the lack of public spirit, the war caused many Russians, conservatives as well as liberal intellectuals, to look for immediate reforms. Even Nicholas I admitted before his death that his régime was a failure. He left a badly run down empire.

The reign of his son and successor, Alexander II (1855–1881), might well be considered a turning point in the history of Russia. During that period there occurred a series of changes which had as their objective the modernization of the empire. Although the czar was not a liberal, he realized that reforms were impending. Rather than risk a revolution which might force him involuntarily to accept new policies, he decided to make a virtue of necessity and to subordinate personal inclinations to the welfare of the state. Despite open antagonism of the vested interests and the landed nobility, he profoundly changed the life of the people.

Foremost in altering the political contours of the nation was the abolition of serfdom. Indeed, Alexander's Edict of Emancipation could be classed as "perhaps the greatest single legislative act in the world's history," for millions of men and women were made citizens, authority over them being transferred from the landowners to the government. But the process of liberation was slow. Earlier the czar had indicated his intention of freeing the serfs on the royal estates but the country's landholders, who clung tenaciously to the antiquated institution of serfdom, would not follow his example. The government broke through this obstinacy, forcing an open discussion of emancipation and of a general land settlement for the liberated serfs. Eventually, spurred by public opinion and with the coöperation of a few enlightened bureaucrats, the reform was passed, and between 1861 and 1866 a series of edicts ended Russian serfdom.

Open to criticism, however, was the solution of the land problem. Generally, the serfs were given the farms from which they had made their living, the government making compensation to the nobles for the loss of this property. The peasants were expected to buy this land from the government, paying for it in installments covering a period of forty-nine years. In most cases the amount of land allotted each peasant proved too small for his needs and the annual payments too great for his purse. As a result, the problem was in very many respects intensified. The fields owned by the peasants were, as a rule, combined into common holdings, the village communes, and at intervals this land was redistributed among the heads of the families in the villages. This meant that as the sons grew up, married, and became heads of families the number of peasants eligible to receive holdings swelled, while the amount of land to be divided remained the same. Thus the individual farms dwindled in size, and it became correspondingly difficult for the peasants to eke a living from the soil.

In the train of emancipation followed a number of further reforms. With the abolition of serfdom the measures instituted by the landholders to govern their serfs disappeared, and thus a blow was dealt to the despotism of the nobility in the rural districts. The czar now had to establish an efficient system of local government to take over the prerogatives of the nobility. Reform of the law courts was the primary element in this political reconstruction. In old Russia the courts seemingly had existed in order to perpetuate injustice. Based on class distinction, the administration of the laws had been generally in the hands of corrupt, incompetent, and ill-paid officials, who were subservient to the wealthy property owners. Hearings were secret, and lawyers for the defense were not infrequently unavailable. Justice was slow, expensive, cumbersome. The reform of 1864 abolished class privileges and proclaimed the establishment of "laws equally just to all." Courts were independent of the administration, appointed judges were not removable and were paid good salaries, trials were public, and the jury system was introduced. Russia's judicial system soon compared favorably with those of other European powers.

Such was the decay of Russian feudalism, and such the new dawn of democratic bourgeois government. As the old régime weakened under the reformatory measures of Alexander, so the new order waxed stronger and stronger. Deprived of serfs and of much land, lacking initiative, special training, and capital, most aristocrats failed to adjust themselves to these new conditions. Many became bankrupt while others, unable to struggle against adverse circumstances, sold their lands and tried to live on the proceeds. The bourgeoisie profited in their turn. The acceleration of industry and commerce made them more wealthy. Favorable conditions caused their number to grow. Many received political positions in governmental departments. Economic progress caused a demand for popular education and for teachers, writers, and journalists. The doctor, the engineer, and the professor became for the first time influential members of society. This professional class in turn furnished an intelligentsia "which acquired a definite group consciousness and became the backbone of the opposition to the old régime."

By 1914 Russia seemed destined to become a bourgeois state. Her middle classes were small in number but spirited and energetic. Moreover, their number was steadily increasing as recruits came in from both the nobility and the peasantry. Many nobles, because of changing conditions, were forced to sell their lands and to earn their bread through commercial or industrial activity. A small section of the peasant class succeeded in accumulating property and used it as a means to undertake commercial enterprises. Slowly, Russia seemed to be taking on the trappings of a new order. Factories, railroads, mines, a merchant marine, and a constitutional legislative body (the Duma) indicated to many Russians the advent of a new day. Russia was looking forward.

CHAPTER XVII

"NEW WORLDS TO CONQUER"

America, thou half-brother of the world!
With something good and bad of every land
(Philip James Bailey).

"AMERICA is a fortunate country," said Napoleon; "she grows by the follies of our European nations." America indeed profited by the follies of her trans-oceanic ancestors—as well as by her own errors—in order to grow up from the intractable infant of the British Empire to the Great Power of the twentieth century, mature, aloof, austere. She was thus able to develop because, besides being blessed by the largesse of nature, she was fortunate in her population of pioneers, unafraid to make their new country the world's greatest laboratory for modern capitalism. America became the land of opportunity, not only for homeless people of other countries, but for political and economic ideas in search of expression, exposition, and experiment. Out of this complex process of evolution came the present government "with something good and bad of every land."

While bourgeois capitalism was penetrating Europe, it was being firmly established in the Americas. The revolt of the Thirteen Colonies and their organization as the United States of America was in a sense a class victory, for the wealthy traders and landowners in the North and the commercial planters in the South had a great deal to gain from independence, as it promoted their free expansion into territories over the mountains, relieved them of paying taxes to mercantilist England, and enabled them to cancel debts due the mother country.

The petty bourgeoisie, however, were largely responsible for the American War of Independence (see Corey, *The Crisis of the Middle Class,* Chapter IV). Before it broke out, small manufacturers, shopkeepers, artisans, and craftsmen made common cause with dispossessed laborers against wealthy British merchants and colonial landowning and commercial aristocrats. In Boston, Samuel Adams, the leader of the middle classes, organized a secret and illegal branch of the Sons of Liberty, originally a mechanics' society, urging demonstrations, boycotts, and violence to force changes in British laws that blocked colonial enterprisers. Because concessions were granted by England in 1770, the wealthy American bourgeoisie were not won over to the idea of independence, preferring the handicaps of British rule to the dangers of widespread unrest for which the mechanics were responsible. Consequently, the middle-class radicals, to obtain the support of the upper groups, deliberately excluded mechanics from the revolutionary councils and destroyed the Sons of Liberty. Backed half-heartedly by the wealthy bourgeoisie, the small-business men then were able to precipitate the Revolution.

Provincialism among the colonists and a struggle between the lower classes (petty bourgeoisie, small farmers, and workers) and the wealthy landowners and traders, however, hampered for many years the establishment of a unified nation. Finally, a constitution was adopted which outlined a strong federal government founded upon a property basis and controlled by the rich minority. A bitter struggle ensued during the first years of the new government, between the big bourgeois Federalists, led by the aristocratic Alexander Hamilton, exponent of strong central government dominated by a wealthy oligarchy, and the petty bourgeois Republicans, led by Thomas Jefferson, advocate of State rights and a democracy of small property owners. Not until the late twenties of the nineteenth century did "the people" come into power in the United States, through the establishment of white manhood suffrage; until then the government was definitely the tool of an aristocracy of wealth and talent—in short, of a class society.

America's metamorphosis had a geographical origin. From the original Thirteen Colonies, stretching from the Atlantic

Coast to the Allegheny Mountains, the United States, through cession and purchase, reached, in the early nineteenth century, the Pacific Ocean. Henceforth her destiny and that of Europe were interlinked. Europe, staggering under an unusable surplus of labor piled up from the changes brought about by the Industrial Revolution and the consequent inability of industry to absorb the rapidly growing population, was more than glad to find an outlet in the United States, with its great unsettled lands, its embryonic industries, its lenient magnanimity toward religion and nationality. The New World in turn eagerly welcomed this invaluable tide of population, so necessary to man the ship of state.

Expansion into the agrarian West fostered individualism and nationalism, characteristics crystallized in the election of Andrew Jackson to the presidency. His sympathies with the common man, he had no brief for the bourgeois monopolistic and industrial North. An exponent of rugged individualism and of the small business and farming interests, he proceeded to oppose large-scale business, to change tariffs, to destroy the federally subsidized bank, and to stop most internal improvements. Such business as there was, mostly on a small scale, had to struggle along without government support while agriculture was enabled to prosper.

Ample justification, however, was offered for this extreme expression of individualism. Absence of governmental restrictions, together with abundance of natural resources and cheap labor, afforded each individual an opportunity to achieve material success by the practice of such bourgeois virtues as thrift, hard work, and personal initiative. The farmer, between 1828 and 1860, became the backbone of the nation. Thousands of industrious peasants flocked into the Mississippi Valley and became independent cultivators. Agriculture in the United States boomed.

Although the American nation remained dominantly agrarian, the big industrial bourgeoisie, especially of the North, prospered as a result of Jackson's "rugged individualism." As more and more foreign and Northern capital was invested in factories and as foreign and domestic trade expanded, the North, between

1828 and 1860, became the industrial center of the United States. During this period New England, as well as the Middle West, became the land of economic individualism. "In New England, the will of the employers . . . was directed to making every cent of profit possible without the slightest regard for the welfare of their employees, or the larger social questions of Americanism in that section." Immigrants formed the nucleus of a permanent wage-earning class for whose struggles their employers had not even an academic care.

New methods of transportation hastened the industrialization of the North, tended to concentrate business in a few hands, threatened the independent farmer through the imposition of high freight rates, and helped to thrust thousands of farmers' sons into urban communities. Between 1820 and 1850, the combined population of the country's four largest cities—New York, Philadelphia, Baltimore, and Boston—rose almost 400 per cent. In the decade 1840–1850, while the population of the United States rose 36 per cent, that of the towns and cities of 8,000 or more increased 90 per cent. From the standpoint of numbers the urban movement was more vital than the migration to the West, for it marked the rise of Big Business, and presaged the supremacy of an industrial as against an agrarian society.

American inventive genius, practically revolutionizing many industries, played a leading rôle in the economic growth of the United States. Nearly 5000 patents were granted in the year 1860 alone. "The fame of the inventive Yankee waxed great." An astonished European observed: "We find America producing a modern machine even to peel apples, another to beat eggs, and a third to clean knives, and a fourth to wring clothes; in fact, there is scarcely a purpose for which human hands have been ordinarily employed for which some ingenious attempt is not now made to find a substitute in a cheap and labor saving machine."

Many of the great improvements, such as the sewing machine, the vulcanizing process, the McCormick reaper, and the use of anthracite coal in the making of steel, came into existence during the ante-bellum period. The effects of the first Industrial

Revolution on the people of the North were amazing. Northern society was transformed by such new forces as rapid transportation and public education. Immigration gave the North a cosmopolitan air.

In both the industrial North and the agrarian West rampant optimism prevailed. There were no legal classes or social distinctions. The door of opportunity was open to all. Jackson's election to the presidency had inspired every poor boy in the land. A fortune and political power, he was told, awaited him around the corner. Had not Astor, the almost illiterate immigrant, made almost twenty millions? Had not Jackson, a self-made man, been elected president? "Native or foreigner, rich or poor, learned or unlearned, the race was free for all." Thus began America's "busy" era, when thousands of earnest young men were struggling to obtain wealth and to be hailed as business Napoleons.

Sentimentalism as well as "go-get-ism" characterized this age. It was a period of noble, tender, and artistic feeling during which, writes Professor E. D. Branch, in *The Sentimental Years, 1836–1860* (Appleton-Century Co., New York, 1934), people tried to reconcile unlikes—"the humanitarian philosophy of enlightenment, perfectibility, democracy, besides the philosophy of acquisition, *laissez faire,* gratuitous benevolence. Under this aegis people had played, very earnestly, many variants of a game which may be called Effects without consequences; Religion without humility; Sensuality without smut; *Laissez faire* without oppression. Benevolence without sacrifice . . . Sacrifice without pangs . . . Femininity without feminism. Food, and a cupboard undepleted. Bricks without a straw."

During this pre-Civil War period people exhibited a real faith in perfectionalism. "Almost everybody took it for granted that each low descending sun found the world a better place than the sun which had preceded. The difference between conservatives and radicals was one of dates rather than objectives." Both held that man's lot was on the mend. The reformer wanted to help those who were "down and out," but he did not propose to make those suffer who were fairly well off. Comfort for all was the great goal.

In those days there was a closer alliance between wealth and virtue than there is today. The Reverend Orville Dewey, for example, in 1835 "opined that the value of wealth depends on the intelligence, liberality, and purity of the mind." In his opinion, men of wealth were agents of God, possessing "a blessed stewardship in the service of God and a divine manifestation of mercy to man." Another preacher, the Reverend Thomas P. Hunt, justified riches in good Calvinistic fashion by claiming that "no man can be obedient to God's will, as revealed in the Bible, without becoming wealthy." According to this doctrine, the thousands of poor people in New York in 1835 were suffering, it would seem, because of their sins.

To save these unfortunates, a Renaissance of Puritanism seemed necessary. In the fifties "the blessings of poverty" were discussed by such exponents of rugged individualism as Timothy Titcomb (J. G. Holland), who, in *Letters to Young People,* wrote: "No, my boy, if you are poor, thank God and take courage; for He intends to give you a chance to make something of yourself." There began that movement which reached its climax in the prohibition, or Eighteenth, Amendment. "Little boys and girls were urged to join the cold water brigade. Coffee, tea, and tobacco were considered only slightly less immoral than whiskey." "A young man is not fit for life," Titcomb maintained, "until he is clean—clean and healthy, body and soul, with no tobacco in his mouth, no liquor in his stomach, no oath on his tongue, no snuff in his nose, and no thought in his heart which if exposed would send him sneaking into darkness from the presence of good women." The morals of young females were matters of special concern. Writers of the pre-war days advised them to dress modestly, to speak properly, to work diligently, and to pray earnestly. In the Lowell textile mills the girls "were required to reside in boarding houses supervised by their employing companies, to be in bed at the respectable hour of ten, and at all times to observe specific rules of Christian decorum." They worked twelve hours a day, or more, and received two dollars a week, or less, but the owners "painted roses over the factory gates." A legislative committee, which visited Lowell in 1845 to investigate working conditions found numerous abuses, such as long hours and inadequate ventilation, but concluded that the legislature could not amend the situation. "We look for a remedy," they hypocritically reported, "in the progressive development in art and science, in a higher appreciation of man's destiny, in a less love for money and a more ardent love for social happiness and intellectual superiority."

In literature and art, "the slush of 1836–1860 was certainly not worse than today's slush." According to a woman writer of the time, one should purchase a new book if it promotes "virtuous and useful knowledge"; affords "innocent pleasure"; cheers "the hour of sorrow"; or consoles "the heart in its moments of affliction." Apparently, the works of such writers as Poe, Longfellow, Whittier, Emerson, and Lowell, met these puritanical requirements.

In the South, prior to 1860, a civilization existed, however, whose moral ideas, outlook, and material bases were different from those of the North and Middle West. The hustling industrial North, because of its lack of social stability, its opportunities for money-getting, its worship of material success and of work as a means to an end, had lost sight of the "abundant life." In the more ante-bellum South, on the other hand, the planter aristocrat had sufficient leisure along with assurance of economic and social security, to subordinate mere money-making to making an art of living, and his way of life had permeated the whole South. Great houses, large estates, and a patriarchal mode of living characterized the sunny South in those early days. Social life was distinguished for the hospitality, charm, and grace of the landowners. The harsh and determined puritanism which developed in New England was lacking in this aristocratic stronghold. In fact, such activities as fox-hunting, dancing, visiting, and playing cards indicated that the Southern landowner resembled very closely the English squire.

Climatic and soil conditions help to explain why the South in 1860 remained the last stronghold of the landed aristocracy in the United States. Tobacco, cotton, and rice were cultivated there on a large scale. Planters, owning extensive estates, found

Negro slavery most satisfactory. There were few large cities; therefore the middle classes and the wage-earners were negligible. People were divided into three major groups: the landowning aristocrats, the poor but free whites, and the slaves. In the North the structure of society was very different. Commerce, manufacturing, and small-scale cultivation predominated. As a result, business men, wage-earners, and small independent farmers were the three predominant classes. Slavery could not flourish in the North because the landowners and business men found it cheaper to hire free labor than to own and support slaves. Therefore, slavery was prohibited in these states, and Negroes were given a position of legal equality.

During the first half of the nineteenth century a growing antagonism over the question of slavery developed between the North and the South. Sectional feeling was also enhanced by the tariff question. A crisis was reached when the North succeeded in placing a high protective tariff on manufactured goods, thus enormously raising the cost of living in the South, while leaving the agricultural products of the South unprotected. It was thus not unnatural for many Southerners to feel that they could not obtain economic justice in the Union.

Prior to the actual outbreak of the Civil War, most Northern business men professed to minimize the growing antagonism between the two sections. As long as they continued to make profits, no sectional discord could disturb their equanimity. Threats of disunion have made their appearance before, they argued. In spite of the rantings of vociferous abolitionists, or fire-eating slaveholders, they said, our profits are growing bigger and bigger each day. The hand of Providence has led America through past crises; and, in His own good time and way, He will settle the slavery problem to the complete satisfaction of His enterprising subjects.

But the bourgeois hope of Providential intervention did not materialize. Instead of subsiding, sectional antagonisms flamed up. "Men of the North, who had risen from nothing to wealth and prominence as bankers, merchants, manufacturers, or stock-jobbers," were looked down upon by the Southern planter as "uncouth upstarts" without the manners of gentlemen. City "slickers" and business hustlers were indeed heartily disliked by the easygoing Southern aristocrats. "To have these Yankees, who drove their wage slaves twelve and fourteen hours a day in badly ventilated mills for a few cents pay and who never assumed the slightest responsibility for them when sick, old, or out of work, tell the Southerner that *his* form of slavery was immoral and thus assume airs of superiority was galling." Moreover, many of the Southerners, enjoying as they did the comforts and luxuries of the landed aristocracy, were hostile to the very nature of puritanical reform.

In spite of the warnings of the approaching storm, the business men refused to believe that a war was in the making. "If there was anxiety and resentment in the South, the North was humming with industry," and its bourgeois leaders were doing their best to muzzle the abolitionist pests, even going so far as to threaten their lives. Finally involved in war, however, the middle classes, rallying behind President Lincoln's nationalist declaration that the Union was indissoluble, rushed forth to destroy the last vestiges of the old agrarian order—the aristocratic Southerner.

Bourgeoisie vs. aristocracy—for four years the bloody warfare raged. Spirit, ability, and tradition were on the side of the South, and helped to prolong the conflict; but the superiority of their opponents in manpower, machinery, and munitions gave the industrial and commercial North its victory.

The Civil War caused the destruction of the planter aristocracy, while the Northern bourgeoisie emerged from the struggle, richer and more firmly entrenched than ever. "The ruin of the planting class," says Beard in *The Rise of American Civilization* (The Macmillan Co., New York, 1927), "was more complete than the destruction of the clergy and the nobility in the first French cataclysm because the very economic foundations of the planting system, including slavery itself, were shattered in the course of events."

Far more significant perhaps than the destruction of the planter aristocracy and of the contractual theory of government was the over-night industrial, economic, and social transformation—the second Industrial Revolution. This was to result in an abrupt change in agricultural practices, and an almost complete metamorphosis of the pre-war business men. President Johnson tried to protect the declining petty bourgeoisie and small landowners, but was unable to defeat the forces led by the exponents of Big Business. With the election of Grant to the presidency the wealthy bourgeoisie rose to power. A new revolution was fostered and aided by the government. A national system of banks took the place of those destroyed by Jackson. Generous grants of money from the central treasury to aid internal improvements, so necessary to the success of the vested interests, were made by Congress. The question of the public domain, which had long vexed Eastern business interests owing to the opposition of the South, was settled. Through the passage of the Homestead Act of 1862 farm lands were almost given to persons willing to settle in the West. Simultaneously, huge grants of land were made to individuals and corporations desiring to build railroads. Colleges "for instruction of youth in agricultural and mechanical arts" were made possible through allotments from the public lands.

While various steps were being taken in Congress to strengthen the position of the big bourgeoisie through government support of large scale business, plans were being formulated to restrain hostile state legislation of the agrarian West. The Fourteenth Amendment, supposedly designed for the protection of the former bonded class, became a bourgeois "Bill of Rights." By proclaiming that no state shall "deprive any person of life, liberty, or property without due process of law, nor deny to any person within its jurisdiction the equal protection of the laws," this amendment gave the Supreme Court of the United States constitutional power to strike down any act of state or local government menacing "sound business policies." A tariff wall so high that it shut out considerable European manufactures also was erected by Congress.

In the period following the war, says Faulkner in his *American Economic History* (The Macmillan Co., New York, 1928), "unbridled freedom and competition reigned supreme." The great majority of prosperous Americans accepted as final the *laissez faire* doctrine of Adam Smith. To the merchant prince and to the average citizen governmental regulation of private business was fallacious economic policy. Capital should be aided, not impeded. The pioneer individualism of the frontier people demanded the utmost freedom of action. As a consequence, "competition and the *laissez faire* were the order of the day."

Business men, "who had, during the war, been straining at the leashes, sprang forward as strong runners to the race." Abundant capital was at hand, natural resources seemingly without limit were to be had "for the asking or taking," thousands of cheap laborers were ready for work, a vast domestic market was assured, and obliging politicians, holding out itching palms, were ready to "coöperate." Among the contestants in the race were Jay Gould, W. H. Vanderbilt, James J. Hill, Andrew Carnegie, John D. Rockefeller, Jay Cooke, and W. H. Chambers. All were of North European bourgeois stock; all began at the bottom and worked their way to the top. Most of them were church members in "good and regular standing." Jay Cooke, the financier of the Civil War, for example, frequently advised his Sunday school class that "we must all get down at the feet of Jesus and be taught by no one but Himself."

Sustained by a beneficent government and worshipped by millions of people, these leaders of business enterprise marched from victory to victory in the decades that followed the triumph of Grant at Appomattox. "With a stride that astounded statisticians," says Beard, "the conquering hosts of business enterprise swept over the continent, and twenty-five years after the death of Lincoln, America had become, in the quantity and value of her products, the first manufacturing nation of the world."

Maintenance of the Union—the triumph of nationalism—was indeed a cardinal result of the war. Henceforth the preeminence of a central government controlled by the business interests was assured. The spirit of sentimental nationalism had won a tremendous victory in America. Moreover, the Civil War vindicated the principle and the example of modern political development—democracy, and its exponent, President

Lincoln. In leading the North to victory he justified this form of government, which through its emphasis upon political liberty and social equality, had made possible his rise. Thus, complete bourgeois individualism, legal equality, and nationality emerged victorious as a result of the Civil War. Influenced by these factors, the "builders" of America were able to continue their constructive work in the West and to make this region the bread-basket of the world. At the same time, others in the Far West exploited its great mines and added to the prosperity of the nation.

The American Revolution and the Civil War were not the only significant middle-class uprisings in the Western hemisphere. They were merely the forerunners of a series of revolts which resulted in the establishment of over twenty-five independent states in Hispanic America, all of which today are playing energetic parts in the development of modern civilization.

Protected by the world's strongest and most enduring mercantile system, Hispanic America until the nineteenth century remained secure from the full force of early bourgeoisism. Gradually, streams of liberal thought, even though deflected by strict vigilance, penetrated the intellectual circles of Spain's empire. Nourished by new philosophies, a latent restiveness, centered in the mercantile and university intelligentsia, especially in Buenos Aires, spread rapidly and culminated in the revolutionary movement of 1810–1826.

Liberal principles found an especially fertile field for growth in the Creole class of the Spanish colonial world. An American-born Spaniard possessed of all the pride of true Iberians, the Creole would not stoop to the artisan positions of the *mestizos,* or half-breeds, nor to the manual labor left to the Indians and Negroes. On the other hand, he was excluded from higher offices in church and state by peninsular Spaniards, privileged politically and socially. As Creole ranks grew, some entered the church, a few held land and became planters and cattle-raisers, others filled to overflowing the professions, while still others ventured to become dealers in contraband goods. Many, however, remained idle, becoming shiftless indigents. During the eighteenth century the Creole's position became more difficult owing to the Bourbon policy of modifying the old Spanish Hapsburg system of mercantilism. Whereas under the Hapsburgs the individual had a definite place in a system, under the new order, which attempted to reform but still to retain the old structure, he was restricted in enterprise by exact and narrow definitions of individual rights.

Dissatisfied because of his economic and social subordination, the intelligent type of Creole was quick to recognize and seize upon intellectual support for his grievances. Young men, who had the advantage of being sent to Europe for their education, absorbed in Paris and in the cultured mother country itself the stirring doctrines of French philosophers. Copies of the Declaration of Independence and of the Constitution of the United States, left behind by obliging but interested merchants, and the translations of the works of Montesquieu, Rousseau, and Voltaire were eagerly read. European newspapers, used as wrappers for imported commodities, found a wide circulation. In the intellectual centers of Peru and Nueva Granada, literary and scientific societies, composed mostly of Creoles, were active in disseminating liberalism.

The accumulated grievances and growing unrest expressed themselves in a great movement for self-determination from Cape Horn to California. Initiated in 1810 by almost simultaneous uprisings in Nueva Granada, La Plata, and Mexico, the struggle continued for a decade and a half. It was not a revolution comparable to the European upheavals of that time, for though liberal philosophies stirred Creole leaders to aspire for self-rule, these beliefs did not germinate in the peoples ideas of wholesale social leveling or of radical governmental reforms, principles entirely foreign and antipathetic to traditional Spanish character.

Victory, in 1826, meant for Hispanic Americans the attainment of the right to rule themselves. A remarkable continuity of development rather than any sudden break with the past characterized the opening of the new era. The bourgeois order was not to be transplanted immediately and in its entirety. Instead, it was to be grafted upon the Spanish tree and was only to appear finally, after slow development, as a hybrid product.

For the next fifty years, during the so-called age of dictators, 1826–1876, the Hispanic Americans were seeking to strike a balance between liberty and authority, two ideals derived from their Hispanic heritage. Intensely individualistic and proud guardians of personal rights, they believed at the same time in authority, being both convinced and willing that administration should be centered in the hands of those especially designed for it. Furthermore, while their entire philosophy was fundamentally based upon the principle of equal treatment to all classes, the idea of abolishing or of lessening social divisions was completely foreign to their intentions.

The attempts to establish a practical system for the dual operation of these two principles of liberty and authority resulted in the governmental instability characteristic of Hispanic America in the nineteenth century. Nominal republics and short-lived constitutions temporarily satisfied the desire for liberty and amply provided for legal rights. However, as a result of Hispanic reliance upon authority, the incapacity of the masses, and the sparsely populated country, governments were never democratic or representative. Preponderance of power universally remained with the executive. Thus both the spirit of the people and the conditions in Hispanic America contributed to the emergence of strong men, or *caudillos*. An outstanding individual, by promising great benefits, would be readily accorded the admiring loyalty of a group accustomed to and desirous of authority in government. But when, in the course of time, individual rights were crushed, a revolution would occur for the purpose of recovering liberty. Then the whole performance would be repeated.

Closely associated with the rise of the *caudillos* was the great struggle throughout Hispanic America between localism and centralism, which in politics manifested itself in the conflict between Federalists and Unitarians. Until the last quarter of the nineteenth century, geography, lack of communication, the temperament of the people, and the fear of group exploitation all contributed to the existence of strong centrifugal forces in the governments.

Despite political instability, Hispanic America after the middle of the century was slowly progressing economically. Many of the *caudillos* themselves, both for patriotic and for self-interested reasons, promoted material prosperity. After 1876, when men of greater enlightenment were taking the place of the old-type dictator and when foreign capital began coming to a region hitherto unattractive, progress was considerably accelerated. Railroads, steamship and telegraph lines, general encouragement to industry and commerce, and educational and social reforms all inaugurated an era of material and cultural advancement. However, such progress was limited primarily to the capitals and to a few large cities. Hispanic America was still in the main an agricultural country with large scale industry unknown. Manufacturing was centered in Mexico, Chile, and Argentina.

A view of the full course of events during the nineteenth century in Hispanic America reveals forces working both for and against the rise of a middle class. The liberation movement, emphasizing self-determination, equality before the law, and enlightenment, released the individual to work for his material welfare. From 1826 to 1876 the insistence upon the preservation of personal rights and the introduction of material improvements further encouraged individual enterprise. However, political instability and unfavorable geographical conditions discouraged economic activity. Moreover, the very temperament and psychology of the people checked the growth of bourgeoisism. As a result, in that vast region from the Rio Grande to Cape Horn, the large cities excepted, there was no strong middle class at the end of the nineteenth century.

One country in the Americas—Canada—paralleled the United States in its adoption of the bourgeois system. Unlike the Thirteen Colonies, however, Canada was able to establish this new order and, at the same time, to remain within the British Empire. Great Britain did much to preserve the union. Influenced by the loss of part of her American empire she, in 1791, complied with the demands of the Canadians for national and political rights by dividing the St. Lawrence Valley into two provinces—Upper and Lower Canada—and by creating a Legislative Council and Assembly in each province.

Political control in both the provinces, however, remained in the hands of aristocratic cliques who refused to sanction changes which would deprive them of their power. Representing the conservative shopkeepers, landowners, clergy, and officials these oligarchies maintained an endowed society which resembled in many ways the English and French aristocratic orders of the old régime. Large sections of land were held by government officials, the clergy, and "speculators." Most of this property was not under cultivation and thus was exempt from taxation. Rich sinecures in the form of pensions and salaries also were enjoyed by a privileged bureaucracy. In short, Canada seemed to exist for the benefit of the chosen few. The masses—small resident landowners, petty bourgeoisie, workers, and democratic frontiersmen—were expected to pay the bills.

Opposition to this extravagant and privileged government spread among the lower classes. In the early nineteenth century these Canadian "Jacobins" openly demanded responsible government, the abolition of sinecures, and the end of the seigniorial system. In 1837 this unrest culminated in an armed rebellion. Moved by the revolt the British government sent a commission under Lord Durham to investigate the situation. After a careful study of conditions he, in the winter of 1838–1839, issued his famous report. In it he proposed the union of Upper and Lower Canada, the establishment of responsible government, and the creation of an efficient and economical régime capable of promoting progress throughout the land.

During the next few years the British government adopted most of Lord Durham's recommendations. In 1840 Parliament passed an act reuniting Upper and Lower Canada; in 1847 the control of public offices was given over to the Canadian government, and in 1854 the Seigniorial Tenure Act practically did away with the old system of land-owning. At the same time the clergy-reserve question was settled by the handing of religious property over to municipal governments for secular purposes. By these acts the small property owners erected the framework for a potentially powerful bourgeois state. But the British government still interfered in internal affairs. This situation, so objectionable to the masses, was brought to an end when Canada, by the British North American Act of 1867, obtained dominion status. Meanwhile, the Canadians reached the Pacific, so that the new government stretched from sea to sea. In the last half of the nineteenth century this sparsely populated dominion was welded by transcontinental railroads, and the way was paved for the development of another great center of bourgeois society in the New World.

In short, during the nineteenth century the middle-class system was firmly established in the Americas. Before the close of this period bourgeois society completely dominated the most powerful countries of the Occident—the United States and Canada; while in Hispanic America, the nations, although still under the spell of the old régime, were slowly but certainly inaugurating the ideas and practices of the new order.

Chapter XVIII

LITERATURE AND THE MIDDLE CLASSES

II. The Nineteenth Century: Balzac, Hauptmann, & Co.

As today it has become the fashion to defame the capitalist class, so in the nineteenth century no class was more criticized than was the bourgeoisie. Potshots were taken at them and at every aspect of their lives by the literati, the poet, playwright, and novelist, as well as by the professional journalist, the pamphleteer and the writer for periodicals, religious, political, or economic. Even the cartoonist made the middle-class man the butt of ridicule (see frontispiece). Especially severe in their criticism of this group were the French authors, Honoré de Balzac (1799–1850), Gustave Flaubert (1821–1880), and Anatole France (1844–1924).

Of these Balzac stands preëminent. Writing with tremendous intensity and vitality, he covered an immense and very intricate range of life, portraying over two thousand distinct characters, most of them carefully individualized. His aim was to unfold a complete view of French society during the age of Louis Philippe; and though he was not entirely successful in doing this, he did present a brilliant picture of the middle classes, especially those persons of the meaner or baser sort.

In his works Balzac described the bourgeoisie as a deadly blight on all true refinement and beauty. As he saw it, life under their régime was motivated only by the baser passions, frequently disguised by subterfuge or hypocrisy. So vividly did he draw pictures of the fierce struggle, the ruthless success, and the pitiable failure of this cruel society that the reader might well conclude that Balzac saw no escape from this social order save a return to divine right, landed aristocracy, and an established church.

Dramas, short stories, and tales in the then popular romantic style issued from Balzac's prolific pen, but the great bulk of his production was the masterful collection of realistic novels which he entitled *La Comédie Humaine,* or *The Comedy of Human Life*. Divided into seven classifications, the series gives the reader an immediate insight into the scope of Balzac's conception: six scenes are of private, country, Parisian, political, and military life; the seventh section is of philosophical studies. Not all of the units in the *Comedy* pertain to the middle classes, yet certainly the major portion of the work does depict the social order of the author's time.

Eugénie Grandet, considered by many critics to be Balzac's supreme novel, has as most of its characters middle-class villagers engaged in a variety of economic pursuits. These people, however, are overshadowed by the central personage of the novel, Félix Grandet, a man who displays penurious traits carried to an extreme. Father Grandet is a usurer and thus represents the bourgeois love of money to an abnormal and pathological degree. He stands out as perhaps the greatest miser in all literature. "Financially speaking, Monsieur Grandet was something between a tiger and a boa constrictor . . ." In vivid contrast to Grandet are his wife and his daughter, who, in spite of their sordid surroundings, remain, miraculously, uncontaminated by any excessive love for money, but suffer their lot with bourgeois docility, Madame Grandet assuring her child that "there is no happiness except in heaven; you will know it some day."

In *Père Goriot,* probably Balzac's best known work, most of the action centers around a miserable boarding and rooming house, a *pension bourgeoisie,* called the "*Maison Vauquer.*" Here a nondescript group of poor students, pensioned government employees, and retired tradesmen eke out a monotonous, drab existence. Thus is shown the struggle, in the Paris of 1820, of the petty bourgeoisie to escape degrading poverty.

The *Story of the Rise and Fall of César Birotteau* is a remarkable novel of middle-class life; in fact, it deals with almost nothing else. The tale revolves around César Birotteau, perfume merchant and self-made man, a bourgeois hero if there ever was one. This Parisian Babbitt appears at the height of his glory when he is granted the cross of the Legion of Honor by Louis XVIII in return for his devotion to the royalist cause during and after the Revolution. Birotteau, in order to celebrate, has his house remodeled and gives a magnificent ball, attended by all his business associates and political colleagues. Balzac paints a vivid picture of the affair:

The bourgeoisie of the Rue Saint-Denis displayed itself majestically in the plenitude of its native powers of jocose silliness. It was a fair specimen of that middle class which dresses its children like lancers or national guards, goes on Sunday to its own country-house, is anxious to acquire the distinguished air, and dreams of municipal honors, —that middle class which is jealous of all and of every one, and yet is good, obliging, devoted, feeling, compassionate, ready to subscribe for the children of General Foy, or for the Greeks, whose piracies it knows nothing about, or the Exiles until none remained; duped through its virtues and scouted for its defects by a social class that is not worthy of it, for it has a heart, precisely because it is ignorant of social conventions,— that virtuous middle class which brings up ingenuous daughters to an honorable toil, giving them sterling qualities which diminish as soon as they are brought in contact with the superior world of social life.

Much light on the French middle classes is shed by three of Balzac's shorter novels: *The Illustrious Gaudissart, The Firm of Nucingen,* and *Gobseck.* In the first story, Gaudissart is the traveling salesman, a new figure in the bourgeois world of Balzac's time. Surnamed the Illustrious, he travels through the provinces in a gay and self-confident manner. To him, selling hats, hair oil, newspaper subscriptions, or life insurance is not work; it is tremendous sport. He prospers, largely because of his chameleon personality, which enables him to be all things to all men. *The Firm of Nucingen* is a short novel of high financial operations and intrigues, noteworthy because one of the characters, Bixiou, describes in a brief but crushing paragraph the life of the retired druggist Matifat and his family, so leaving to posterity a fine picture of bourgeois ennui when business activities have ceased. Referring to Matifat and his wife, Balzac writes:

. . . They rejoiced in the possession of a handsome ground floor and a strip of garden; for amusement, they watched a little squirt of water, no bigger than a cornstalk, perpetually rising and falling upon a small round freestone slab in the middle of a basin some six feet across; they would rise early of a morning to see if the plants in the garden had grown in the night; they had nothing to do, . . . bored themselves at the theater, and were forever going to and fro between Paris and Luzarches, where they had a country house. I have dined there.

In *Gobseck,* Jean-Esther van Gobseck, a Dutch-Jewish money lender in Paris, is a character similar to miser Grandet, although not nearly so sinister. Pitiless in his usury business, Gobseck amasses great wealth. In a moment of confidence he reveals his philosophy of self-interest; and since he dealt in the commodity which lies at the heart of middle-class civilization, his statement may well be taken as Balzac's epitome of the capitalist system:

. . . If you had lived as long as I have, you would know that there is but one material thing the value of which is sufficiently certain to be worth a man's while to care for it. That thing is—Gold. Gold represents all human forces. I have travelled; I have seen in all lands plains and mountains: plains are tiresome, mountains fatiguing; hence, places and regions signify nothing. As for customs and morals, man is the same everywhere; everywhere the struggle between wealth and poverty exists; everywhere it is inevitable. Better, therefore, to be the one to take advantage, than the one to be taken advantage of. Everywhere you will find muscular folk who work their way, and lymphatic folk who fret and worry. Everywhere pleasures are the same; for all emotions are exhausted, and nothing survives of them but the single sentiment of vanity. Vanity is never truly satisfied except by floods of gold. Desires need time, or physical means, or care. Well! gold contains all those things in the germ, and will give them in reality.

One generation after Balzac came the work of Gustave Flaubert. Of a middle-class family himself, Flaubert was qualified to make observations of the contemporary scene—France in the 1840's, '50's, and '60's—which have covered a large block of middle-class life. Flaubert, however, is not a neutral observer of the social climbers; he dislikes them and seldom paints a character from their ranks sympathetically. According to Émile Faguet, "His hatred of the bourgeoisie began in his childhood, and developed into a kind of monomania. He despised their habits, their lack of intelligence, their contempt for beauty, with a passionate scorn which has been compared to that of an ascetic monk."

In keeping with the naturalistic style of realism employed by Flaubert, the middle classes are presented in a much different manner than in the works of Balzac. In Flaubert's novels the characters do not step forward for a full length portrait—as did Birotteau, for example—and Flaubert never hangs a placard around a character's neck declaring, "This is a middle-class man." Rather, the reader becomes acquainted with the Flaubert characters very gradually, just as one does in actual experience. The peculiar traits of the individual are developed in the action of the story so that at the end—and often not before—the reader can recognize a neatly rounded bourgeois personality.

Madame Bovary, Flaubert's immortal work on the bourgeoisie, is a poignant study of provincial life in the Norman villages of Tostes, Yonville, and Rouen during Louis Philippe's reign. Charles Bovary is a village doctor who carries on his professional work in an adequate, though uninspired, manner. Success would probably be his but for the complete inability of his beautiful and energetic wife, Emma, to adjust herself to the monotony of their environment. It is a situation similar to that in Sinclair Lewis' *Main Street,* a novel which consequently has been called "the American *Madame Bovary.*" Both Flaubert and Lewis expose the dead level of mediocrity in small town life; and, although the latter author makes his exposé louder and funnier, Flaubert's is just as devastating. The utter dreariness of existence in the village of Tostes is borne home to the reader in deadly fashion. Although it seems hopeless to attempt to alter the situation, impossible to change the stultifying common everyday routine, yet Emma Bovary does resist, and it is her helpless beating of wings against the windowpanes of her environment which makes the story. Her greatest difficulty lies in the unhappy relations with her husband. Identifying him as the cause of their poverty—both economic and social—she becomes emotionally estranged from him. Her celebrated adulteries follow. This phase of the story raises the question of bourgeois morality. Emma must keep her affairs secret and maintain an appearance of virtue within the village—middle-class virtue. The final result of her intrigues is financial ruin with a threat of complete exposure. In such a situation she chooses suicide. And what is the moral of the story? Here are the conclusions of Émile Faguet:

> . . . It does not teach Vice, for Vice is not particularly successful; nor does it teach Virtue, for Virtue is not particularly successful either. It teaches a medium course which is made up of prudence and of the care to avoid excess in all things, in good as in evil. It teaches order, regularity, honesty, punctuality and foresight, all of them average qualities, not virtues.

Faguet's "average qualities" are practically identical with middle-class virtues.

In his *Sentimental Education,* Flaubert turns to portray Parisian society of the 1840's and '50's, including the revolutionary period of 1848. Three distinct levels of middle-class society are described: the circle of wealthy bankers and industrialists which revolves about M. Dambreuse; the small merchants and artists who frequent the shop and home of Jacques Arnoux; and a youthful group of students and courtesans gathered about the glamorous Rosanette. These three ranks of the bourgeoisie are linked in the story by the activities of the central character, Frédéric Moreau, who mingles in all of them. This circumstance—as well as others—shows that the various subdivisions of the middle class were not airtight compartments and that the class itself was in a formative or evolutionary state. All three of these groups, however, demonstrate, in varying degrees, such thoroughly characteristic traits as: love for money; the spirit of enterprise; calculation; and such bourgeois virtues as thrift, honesty, and respectability. And, true to Flaubert's general attitude, all the characters are dull and spiritless.

Another generation after Flaubert brings us to Anatole

France. *Penguin Island* is Anatole France's best work dealing with the middle classes. It is a social satire in which institutions and classes are indicted rather than individuals. It begins rather mysteriously somewhere back in the dark centuries of the early Middle Ages. Before the book has advanced far, it becomes apparent that the history of the Penguins is in reality the history of France. Early in Penguin history the foundations of middle-class culture are laid. Property is defined as follows:

"Do you see, my son," exclaimed the holy Maël, "that madman who with his teeth is biting the nose of the adversary he has overthrown and that other one who is pounding a woman's head with a large stone?"

"I see them," said Bulloch. "They are creating law; they are founding property; they are establishing the principles of civilization, the basis of society, and the foundations of the state."

"How is that?" asked old Maël.

"By setting bounds to their fields. That is the origin of all government . . ."

In modern times, Professor Obnubile pays a visit to the republic of New Atlantis (the United States) and observes a feature of capitalistic policy, namely economic imperialism with its warfare in the interest of foreign markets. A little later, the economic background of the Penguin state is revealed in terms which have a familiar sound:

. . . In every ordered State, wealth is a sacred thing; in democracies it is the only sacred thing. Now the Penguin State was democratic. Three or four financial companies exercised a more extensive, and above all, more effective and continuous power, than that of the Ministers of the Republic. The latter were puppets whom the companies ruled in secret, whom they compelled by intimidation or corruption to favor themselves at the expense of the State, and whom they ruined by calumnies in the press if they remained honest. In spite of the secrecy of the Exchequer, enough appeared to make the country indignant, but the middle-class Penguins had, from the greatest to the least of them, been brought up to hold money in great reverence, and as they all had property, either much or little, they were strongly impressed with the solidarity of capital and understood that a small fortune is not safe unless a big one is protected.

Social justice, as well as wealth, is discussed. At the close of the Pyrot case (the Dreyfus affair), the bourgeois Pyrotists dismiss their socialist allies with these words: "To the devil with you and your social justice. Social justice is the defense of property." At the conclusion of this great crusade to purify the republic:

> . . . The government remained in subjection to the great financial companies, the army was exclusively devoted to the defense of capital, while the fleet was designed solely to procure fresh orders for the mine owners. Since the rich refused to pay their just share of the taxes, the poor, as in the past, paid for them.

This cynical view of middle-class civilization reaches a climax in the final chapters which describe the perfection of an industrial society some time in the future. Its organization resembles modern fascism in which a small group of capitalists, directors of huge industrial trusts, exercise control over a vast proletariat. Buildings are built higher and higher to house the offices, banks, and shops of the city, thirty and forty stories not being uncommon. Tunnels drive deeper and deeper into the ground. A horde of fifteen million workers labor in the great industrial metropolis. But this super-capitalism contains the germs of its own dissolution. A series of mysterious explosions, set by anarchists, upsets the equilibrium of the complex society; it crashes to ruin. The whole country reverts to a primitive condition. Then very, very slowly, nations and cultures again grow up. Eventually, buildings again are erected in the capital thirty and forty stories high, and fifteen million workers labor in the industrial metropolis. Thus did France portray what he considered was the bitter cycle of French capitalism.

Unlike French intellectuals, German writers, prior to the outbreak of the French Revolution, paid little attention to the position of the various classes which made up the society in which they lived. They had no feeling of nationalism, because the subdivision of German territory made such sentiment rather impossible; nor were they troubled by any bitter class conflict, for Germany was untouched by the deeper forces of the Industrial Revolution. Only under the impact of French revolutionary ideas did the Germans begin to notice their own surroundings.

Unfortunately, treading on the heels of heralds of the revolutionary millennium came the troops of Napoleon. Militant nationalism and hatred of the foreigner now replaced democracy and cosmopolitanism. Even the formerly idealistic German philosophers, such as Goethe and Fichte, turned their attention away from the brotherhood of man to the new and more pressing task of unifying Germany and driving out the foreign tyrant.

Following the overthrow of Napoleon in 1814, reaction held sway in politics and high-minded men turned cynical and bitter. Of the few German writers who were not sunk in mediocrity, Heinrich Heine (1797–1856) was preëminent. Coming from a bourgeois environment, he believed wholeheartedly in liberty and democracy and desired above all the unity and freedom of Germany. But this "bourgeois revolutionary" patriot soon encountered unremitting antagonism and oppression. Bitter and disillusioned, he portrayed the feelings of many German liberals when he wrote:

> Aye, you must have lost your senses,
> Thus to speak before the people,
> Thus to dare to talk of preachers
> And of potentates and princes!
>
> Friend, you're doomed, so it appears:
> For the princes have long arms,
> And the preachers have long tongues,
> And the masses have long ears!

Despite this pessimism, there appeared in literature a new type of work which expressed a more hopeful attitude toward existence—the so-called novel of provincial life. Writers of these novels were, in the main, middle-class men. One of their chief aims, besides a fairly realistic presentation, was to elevate and educate. They dwelt on middle-class virtues and showed how well "good men" were rewarded in the end. Although these works cannot be taken as very accurate descriptions of rural life at this time (the desire to elevate and to educate caused too much distortion), they are useful in that they present pictorially the ideal of the contemporary prosperous farmer, seen mainly through the sympathetic but somewhat short-sighted eyes of the urban middle classes.

Two of these novels, which seem to be fairly typical of the whole school, are *Uli, The Farmhand,* by Jeremias Gotthelf (1797–1854), and *Little Barefoot,* by Berthold Auerbach (1812–1882). The plots of these stories are usual enough. Those who know Cinderella will see at once her resemblance to Little Barefoot, the poor orphan girl who marries the rich farmer's son, when virtue wins out in spite of lowly position. Those who remember Horatio Alger will certainly recognize Uli, who rises from the position of lowly farmhand to marry Frenali, the girl of his heart, with the blessing of the whole community, and becomes the manager of a large and prosperous farm. All the characters, of course, live happily ever afterward. Or, as the author's flowery rhetoric has it:

> Yes, dear Reader, Frenali and Uli are in Paradise—that is, they live in unclouded love, blessed by God with four boys and two girls; they live in growing prosperity, for the blessing of God is their luck; their name has good repute in the land and far and wide they stand in high esteem . . .

Although it is difficult to find a good contemporary description of the German urban middle classes in the period before the formation of the Empire, we may be sure that hard work and morality were not limited to the good farmers. A later writer, Thomas Mann (1875–   ), who looked back on the old days with some sympathy and understanding, has reconstructed the life of a rich merchant family of that time in *Buddenbrooks*. This family of grain merchants might well have taken as their motto the advice of the founder of the fortunes of the house: "My son, attend with zeal to thy business by day; but do none that hinders thee from thy sleep by night." Following this advice, the Buddenbrooks had done good business and prospered with a clear conscience. There was, however, a tendency to confuse the clear conscience with the good business. What would harm the business was felt by the head of the house to be bad. The new head of the house states this feeling clearly when at his father's funeral he says to a brother who has been cut off with little and has appealed to his sense of justice:

> In this sad and solemn moment I have offered you my brotherly hand. But if it is your intention to speak of business matters, then I can only reply in my capacity as the head of the honorable firm whose sole proprietor I have today become. You can expect from me nothing that runs counter to the duties I have today assumed; all other feelings must be silent.

Above all, this great merchant family prided itself on its stability and prosperity. On important occasions, such as the reading of the will of the deceased head of the house, the wealth of the family and the firm were piously reckoned up. The eldest son, who now became the authority, held it as his sacred duty to make good what losses had been incurred under his predecessor and to carry the family fortunes ever higher. That this should be the feeling of the active head of the business was quite natural, but it did not stop there. Even the servants and dependents took pride in the fortune and good name of the Buddenbrooks. The reactions of the daughter of Consul Buddenbrook when she hears that her husband is bankrupt, although that does not directly touch the family name, are like an echo of César Birotteau in the depths of his despair. "In that minute (when Antonie Buddenbrook realized that her husband had lost everything) all that was involved in the word 'bankrupt' rose clearly before her: all the vague and fearful hints which she had heard as a child. 'Bankrupt'—that was more dreadful than death, that was catastrophe, ruin, shame, disgrace, misery, despair."

This state of feelings and mode of life was not permanent. By the second half of the nineteenth century Germany was definitely under the influence of new forces. A new way of life was developing both in the cities and in the country. All through the nineteenth century the economic power of the middle classes had been increasing. With the growth and spread of the capitalistic economy, these good people dropped the old traditions and began a career of rapid expansion. No longer was the credit of a house a theoretical expression of its position in the community, a luxury to be brought proudly forth on state occasions and then to be put back carefully on the shelf. Credit began to be used more and more in order to increase capital. When the realization of this added power to make money came to the middle classes, a great change was wrought. The bourgeoisie now seemed to turn upon itself. Friendliness toward the lower classes disappeared; opposition to the upper classes was brushed aside. Everything was turned to piling up capital and making money as fast as possible. Gone was the old love of stability that expressed itself in the horror of bankruptcy. To make money it was necessary to take risks, to see nothing but the possible accumulation of wealth.

In Germany, as elsewhere in Europe, after the failure of the attempted Revolution of 1848, the middle classes, as a whole, lost interest in politics and turned toward making profits. Unfortunately, along with this surrender of political ambitions, went a growing lack of interest in culture. This change is described in Eloesser's *Modern German Literature* (Knopf, New York, 1933):

> . . . Every respectable house contained as warrant of culture a set of the classic writers, a history of the world, and an encyclopaedic dictionary. Nothing that had been produced in literature since Goethe was now regarded as of any value as an essential creation of the German mind, railway engines and telegraphs being considered far more valuable. . . . It is a fact that during this period, with the exception of scientific works, books were seldom or never given as presents to grown-up people.

Adding to this coolness between practical affairs and classical interests, a new style appeared in literature which turned it even more against the middle classes. This was the appearance of the so-called naturalistic or realistic school. This type of literature, which sought as its ideal an almost photographically exact description of society and all its works, had long been developing outside of Germany. At the moment its greatest master was Henrik Ibsen (1828–1906).

This Norwegian writer, who lived long in Germany, used as the basis for his plays the problems that faced all of European society, although his setting is always in Scandinavian countries. In *The Pillars of Society,* he digs sharply and deeply into the character of the grasping business man. In *An Enemy of the People,* the printer Aslaksen, chairman of the House Owners' Association and active worker for the Temperance Society, depicts most clearly the timidity and cowardice of the middle classes, as seen by the realists. Another type represented is the conservative bourgeois burgomaster who holds the reins of authority and would rather risk harming the public than endangering his own investments. When asked whether it is not a citizen's duty, when he has conceived a new idea, to communicate it to the public, the burgomaster answers: "Oh, the public has no need for new ideas. The public gets on best with the good old recognized ideas it has already."

After these plays had appeared, Ibsen wrote attacking other problems of society. Good people were outraged by his treatment of feminine independence in *A Doll's House* and his treatment of other and similar questions in such masterpieces as *Ghosts* and *The Wild Duck.* For years those who opposed Ibsen and those who admired him stormed and raged at each other. But the inevitable result of Ibsen's genius was a change in the drama of all Europe, and particularly that of Germany. There the old, conventional stage, whose best pieces were still the classics of the eighteenth century, gave way to a new realistic technique and to a concern with the actual situations of the day.

Foremost, although not the first in time of the realistic dramatists, was Gerhart Hauptmann (1862–   ). In his early play, *Before Dawn,* and in his later and perhaps most famous one, *The Weavers,* members of the middle classes are seen. They form a background for the misery of the working classes. Hoffman, in *Before Dawn* and the manufacturers in *The Weavers* are well aware of the latent or open hostility of those whom they employ, and their chief desire is to justify themselves, as much in their own eyes as in those of the workers. In *Before Dawn,* Hoffman, a former radical student turned successful business man, stresses the bourgeois argument that reforms are good, even necessary, but they must take time. Speaking to a friend of his student days who is still a reformer and who pleads for the betterment of the working conditions of the miners, Hoffman says:

> . . . Don't misunderstand me! I am the last man to be lacking in sympathy with the common people. But if something is to be effected, it must be effected from above. In fact that's the only way in which anything can be done. The people never know what they really need.

In *The Weavers* the situation is different. Here trouble comes to the manufacturers not through a bourgeois reformer but through the misery of workers themselves. Driven to desperation by want and starvation, the weavers so far forget their places as to object to the low wages and miserable conditions, and finally they break out in a fury of destruction. Like Hoffman, Dreissiger the manufacturer feels called upon to defend himself, which he does in an eloquent speech to a group of complaining weavers:

> . . . If some poor little fellow sticks in the snow in winter and goes to sleep, a special correspondent arrives posthaste, and in two days we have a bloodcurdling story served up in all the papers . . . It's all the manufacturer's fault—he's made the scapegoat. They flatter the weaver and give the manufacturer nothing but abuse—he's a cruel man, with a heart of stone, a dangerous fellow, at whose calves every cur of a journalist may take a bite. He lives on the fat of the land and pays the poor weavers starvation wages. In the flow of his eloquence the writer forgets to mention that such a man has his cares too and his sleepless nights; that he runs risks of which the workman never dreams; that he is often driven distracted by all the calculations he has to make and all the different things he has to take into account; and that he has to struggle for his very life against competition; and that no day passes without some annoyance and some loss. And think of the manufacturer's responsibility, think of the numbers that depend on him, that look to him for their daily bread. No, no! None of you need wish yourselves in my shoes—you would soon have enough of it.

And this is said to men who are overjoyed when they find a stray dog, and have meat to eat for the first time in years.

Writings of this type brought the nineteenth century to a close. Hauptmann showed the middle classes face to face with the problem of the rising proletariat. The middle classes stormed, they threatened to use force; they pled before justice and prayed to Heaven for protection of their wealth. They called the leaders of the opposition demagogues and trouble makers, and tried to split the ranks of their enemies by promising rewards to those who would behave themselves properly. But they did not ease the lot of the proletariat.

Even in backward Russia the rise of the middle classes was noted by literary lights of the nineteenth century. Of these intellectuals three writers are especially famous for their characterizations of the economic climbers—Alexander Ostrovsky (1823–1886), Anton Chekhov (1860–1904), and Maxim Gorky (1868–). In such plays as *Wolves and Sheep, The Truth Is Good But Luck Is Better,* and *Poverty Is No Crime,* Ostrovsky has given us a remarkable picture of the rich Russian merchants of the fifties who, although very few in number, aspired to be socially equal to the nobility. Once enriched, the Russian trader burned with a desire to spread about his wealth, to spill it on expensive satisfactions of his vanity, to astound every one around him, and to triumph over the spite and humiliation of his competitors. Above all, he wished to efface the traces of his humble origin by trying to work himself into a superior caste.

As depicted by Ostrovsky, pride of wealth frequently gave rise to ideas of boorish omnipotence. Many rich merchants sincerely thought that they could do everything, that they were all-powerful. And what was the use of wealth? Just this—that no matter what came into your head, you could obtain it. Therefore, all human beings were reduced to two categories: the rich, for whom everything was permissible, and the poor, for whom everything was prohibited; the ones who could buy everything, and those who could not refuse anything. In *A Cat Has Not Always Carnival,* one of Ostrovsky's characters bursts out:

Who can tell what he's up to? Just see what it is to be rich! He's repulsive to me, positively repulsive—yet he's my guest! I won't get anything out of him, and I don't expect it. But how's a person to say "Get out" to him—and him a millionaire? A pretty state of affairs! And what a mean trick in people to start such a thing as bowing to money! But just hold on! Take his money away, and he's not worth a kopek. Yet everywhere he goes he is honored—and not because they want to gain anything from him but just as if he really did amount to something! Why don't they tell such fellows, "Here, we can get along without you and your money: you're nothing but a low-down brute." But they dare not say it to his face! Women are sharper at this sort of thing. If only we had a little more grey matter! . . .

"Where there's capital, there's honor"—in the thoughts and actions of some of Ostrovsky's merchant characters this phrase meant that all those who were ill-clad, badly paid, badly lodged, had no "honor," no dignity; and such people therefore were not to be trusted or even recognized. Thus the poor were completely intimidated. Small employees, chained by their salaries or the fear of losing them, were forced to submit to the vilifications of bourgeois vanity. These particular merchants were never short of injurious and humiliating ideas. The suffering and the abasement of others delighted them.

Another trait embellishes Ostrovsky's picture of the merchant; it is a defiance of knowledge. Intellectual life was something quite foreign to the merchant; since it did not make one rich, he esteemed it but little. He judged it, as he did the law, by those who represented it, and he saw them in a position inferior to his. In the last analysis it represented progress, and he —tradition; it believed in the power of thought, and he—in the power of money; it liberated the desires and longings of the soul, and he stifled spiritual expression.

Anton Chekhov, like Ostrovsky, Turgenev, and other Russian writers, possessed an almost uncanny ability to portray the life and characters of his time. Especially successful was he in illustrating the characteristics of the professional people. Chekhov, in his works, particularly his play, *The Wood Demon,* emphasized bourgeois materialism as it existed during the last quarter of the nineteenth century. The pursuit of pleasure in youth, followed by pursuit of wealth during manhood, disgusted him; he reveals this disgust in his harsh treatment of society of all classes, especially the professional groups. That they drink, eat, and sleep, and think not of their fellow-men and of their country, seemed to be Chekhov's complaint. In many of his works he gives his readers an example of a man or woman whom he would like to see imitated. Such an example is the Wood Demon, or Mikhail Llvovich Khrouschov. He is a young doctor, whose hobby is forestry. He is industrious and hard-working; he has ideals and, what is more, he lives up to them. However, this middle-class man seems to have been the exception to the general rule. Most others were dull, selfish, and shortsighted people.

Compared to Ostrovsky and Chekhov, Maxim Gorky was the more radical of the Russian critics of the bourgeoisie. Gorky's novel *Foma Gordeyev* contains perhaps the best account of the middle classes as they lived in the early years of the twentieth century. In this novel the lives of two rich merchant families are described. The old people, who gained their wealth by hard work, unscrupulousness, and boldness, are contrasted with those of the younger generation who are well educated, speak like gentlemen, yet who also have an eye for greater wealth. The entire novel is interesting, not only because it is very well written, but because it gives the ideas and ideals of the "Merchant Class" expressed from different angles by the members of that group. Gorky's descriptions of men are also exceptionally well done. Foma Gordeyev, the hero of the novel, for example, exemplifies the criticism of the class by Gorky, who, as a proletarian writer, sees no good in the "exploiters of the people." Foma, an unfortunate example of a man who is unable to adjust himself to his environment, criticizes the whole merchant class in these words:

> O you rascals! . . . What have you made? You have not made life but a prison. You have not established order, but you have forged chains on men. It's close, suffocating, there's no place for a living soul to turn. . . . Man is perishing! You murderers! Do you understand that you are alive only through the long-suffering of mankind?

Yet Foma himself had no solution for this *long-suffering* mankind and showed his love for his fellow-men by squandering his wealth on loose women, city parasites, and weaklings in wild drunken orgies.

In Hispanic America's literature, just as in its history, are found expression of forces both favorable and adverse to the rise of a middle class. As Hispanic ideals and minds met bourgeois currents early in the nineteenth century, clearly defined concepts crystallized in a prolific outburst of verse. Later in the century, the same concepts revealed themselves in the more direct and realistic descriptions of fiction. During and immediately after the revolutionary period, literature was permeated with several of the major ideas upon which a rising middle class is nourished. Exclusive of the militaristic note, one theme predominated. All poets sang of it—the vision of a great material and cultural future for "all America."

The theme of material progress is masterfully rendered by Juan Cruz Varela (1794–1839), the great peace poet. Taking a prosaic subject, the completion of the hydraulic works through the Argentine pampas, he, in his *La profesía de la grandeza de Buenos Aires (The prophecy of the greatness of Buenos Aires)*, foretold with lyrical inspiration the future of his country. He saw the bare pampas converted into productive fields, and he visioned the day when Argentina, rather than sending all her wool abroad, would manufacture her own cloth at home in great factories. The new hydraulic works would bring to the entire country "a large fortune forever."

A bourgeois principle appearing in the revolutionary verse and even more frequently in later Hispanic American literature was that of intellectual liberty. The theme constantly rises to the top in the phrases and stanzas of much of the poetry, and there are a few poems devoted entirely to the subject. The principle of intellectual liberty is linked with that of progress in the philosophy of an eminent Argentine poet, Olegario Victor Andrade (1841–1882). In *El porvenir* (*The future*) he joyfully proclaims that the "order of the emancipated human conscience" arises in a country "tied for three centuries," the liberated peoples "embrace before the sacred altar of ideas" and then advance, for "they have in their hearts the infinite desire for progress, the love of the ideal, faith of the good." In *Prometeo* (*Prometheus*), an ode to the emancipation of human thought, Andrade makes a stirring appeal to the thinker to arise for the sake of human progress:

> Arise thinkers!
> Progress is your triumphal herald
> And truth the desired goal
> Of your gigantic solicitude.

Another fundamental middle-class concept, individual enterprise, was forcefully presented in the literature of the post-revolutionary period. However, Hispanic Americans almost always mollified the fullest bourgeois interpretation of the idea by coupling self-enterprise not only with individual returns but with the general welfare. Andrade in *Atlantida (Atalantis)* did this very thing. After reviewing in glowing terms the progress of the "Latin race" in America, he calls the individual into action, but for the purpose of promoting the future prosperity of his country.

Fiercely and powerfully, Hispanic American poets, especially Luis Palma (1863–1894), criticized the ruthless methods of individual enterprise, as well as its materialistic goal. The struggle for a material end not only seemed purposeless and far removed from the real meaning of life, but its corollary of competition, into the vortex of which humanity was drawn and injured, was especially obnoxious. Two words appear again and again, placed in contrast to each other, "egoism" and "humanity." Strong condemnation of the inhuman methods of individual enterprise was made in Calixto Oyuela's *Fantasía (Fantasy)*. Man disguises his deceit, cunning, and egoism by a royal mantle of gold and then begins a war upon his fellowman:

> The infamous scuffle
> The savage assault,
> Which man arrogantly calls "the struggle for life,"

Obliterates in his confused conscience
The desire for the deal of right.

In a society in which individuals were tending to act solely for self-interest, a strong authority was needed, whereas rule by the people was a pure farce; such was the opinion of many Hispanic American writers concerning democracy, another principle embraced by growing middle-class groups. Even at the height of the revolutionary enthusiasm, poets invariably spoke of liberty as meaning "the leadership of the wisest and best." The phrase of Esteban de Luca, "a country under the counsels of wise men," and the later expression of Bartolomé Mitre, "legislators of high intelligence," are typical. Oyuela in his *Fantasía* asserted that, as a government becomes more democratic, it almost always turns into a "perfidious ministry" where "swarms of politicians labor for their personal interests."

The Colombian Julio Arboleda (1817–1862) spoke ardently for authority as opposed to pure democracy. In his unfinished poem, *Gonzalo de Oyón,* he personifies the struggle of two opposite tendencies in America. One, the chaotic spirit of lawlessness and unrestraint, is represented by Álvaro, and the other, the traditional Spanish spirit of respect for authority, order, and religion, is symbolized in Gonzalo, brother of Álvaro. In the course of a conversation with his brother, Gonzalo explains that since humans are moved by self-interest, if authority is broken, "all in a crowd, arrogant, without check, will run after the sceptre." All will wish to be kings, and society "will seethe in mad, eternal confusion." Álvaro exclaims, "And still thou wilt respect the king!" Gonzalo answers affirmatively. The king is a useful barricade against self-interest. "Remove it—and thy right and my right and the right of all is the same."

Another concept modifying the idea of a growing middle class, and which is integrally bound up with the literary expressions against individual enterprise and pure democracy, is the Hispanic American interpretation of equality. Social leveling, however, is foreign to this philosophy. Men must have equal rights and all are brothers, but each has a different station and a different function to perform. Although most of the expressions of this kind of equality, which is durably coupled with *noblesse oblige,* are integrated with the other concepts above described, a few single interpretations may be found. Felipe Pardo y Aliaga (1806–1868) at the end of his *La constitucíon política* distinguishes clearly between that equality which promotes and that which destroys the general welfare:

> Equality, protector of progress,
> That which with vigor promotes merit
> That which with good education improves
> The wicked instincts of the people,
> That which gives and exalts, is a benefactor,
> Sacred equality, to which one should aspire;
> That which in order to equalize removes and diminishes
> Is equality which outrages justice.

It is significant that an ardent liberal and a political opponent of Arboleda, the conservative landowner, should make one of the most accurate definitions of the Spanish concept of equality. José Eusebio Caro (1817–1853), who at one time was forced to leave Colombia on account of his vehement stand for liberty, wrote *La libertad y el socialismo (Liberty and socialism)* as a tirade against the revolutionary general, José López. Here he clearly states that man is "king of himself and king of his things."

Hispanic Americans expressed bourgeois idealism in novels as well as in their poems. Although novel writing had not developed to any great extent in Hispanic America until recent times, valuable analyses of middle-class life and principles may be found in a few of the better books written in the second half of the nineteenth century. One theme predominates and is common to the point of monotony. That theme is the tragedy of marrying for money. It stands in sharp contrast to the plot, also common, based on middle-class philosophy, which pictures the poor young man who by his virtue and work rises in the face of tremendous odds, wins his lady-love, and lives happily ever after. On the other hand, this universal plot indicates the infiltration of the middle-class idea of equality into Hispanic

American society. The materialistic phase of bourgeoisism is generally rejected, but the idea of an equality which facilitates the passage from one social group to the other is gradually being accepted.

Based on opposition to materialism, most novels of this period criticize severely the capitalistic or upper middle class and sympathize with the lower middle class. A most interesting defense and analysis of the latter group was written by a Mexican, Juan Díaz Covarrubias (1837–1859). The title chosen by this author for one of his shorter novels was *La clase media (The middle class)*. The story is centered around the relations of two groups in Mexico City—one a petty bourgeois group, living in a cheap rooming house, and the other some wealthy aristocrats. The moral virtues and honesty of the former are contrasted with the extravagances and immorality of the latter. The difficult position of those who happen to be in the middle-class strata of society is very clearly pictured in *La clase media*. On one occasion, several of those living in the rooming house had taken their usual Sunday afternoon ride through the aristocratic section of town.

> They returned to the city at the close of day, and without knowing it they felt heavy of heart upon leaving behind them those beautiful vistas. For some hours they had been deluded by a happiness which is never real in the middle class of society to which they belonged. That class, being honorable, is virtuous, and being virtuous, it has to suffer a life of self-denial and martyrdom, because, situated between the upper class and the proletariat, the middle class does not have the pleasures of the first, but has their aspirations, and it suffers the afflictions of the second without having its ignorance.
>
> One of those poor women does not desire to wear the diamonds with which the aristocracy is decked; but neither can she let herself be unadorned like the proletariat, and in order to wear an ornament she has to buy it almost at the cost of her life.

An excellent satire on the upper middle class was written by the Mexican, Rafael Delgado (1853–1914). His book, *Los parientos ricos (The rich relatives)* ridicules the false affectation and mimicry of the family of Don Juan, which has suddenly risen in society. Through wise investment of his money in Paris, Don Juan had been able to increase his capital materially. Returning to Mexico from Europe, the family attempts to put on the outward show of gentility. French mannerisms are profusely exhibited. Mexican people and customs are weighed in the balance with Parisian life. The family is always bored with the theaters and operas of Mexico City, and the stores are impossible. Juan, the frivolous, insolent, and superficial son, is forever saying to his wondering, well-mannered cousins, "If you only had been with me in Paris . . . !"

The lower as well as the upper bourgeoisie received disapprobation in Hispanic American literature. For example, the lower middle class, as portrayed in Blest Gana's masterpiece, *Martín Rivas,* appears both displeasing and amusing. Their brazen crudities and ludicrous attempts to ape the aristocracy are exposed in the activities of the uncultured family of Doña Bernarda Colera, a widow of about fifty years of age. The widow's eldest daughter, Adelaida, is good-looking but has a hardness in her expression "which shows a calculating mind and repels confidence." She wishes to marry a well-to-do *caballero,* just as the romantic adventuress of a drama, for "amongst middle-class people, who are not acquainted with our salons, a caballero, or, as they call it, a man of good family, is a type of perfection."

If any phrase can characterize the general tone of Hispanic American literature in the nineteenth century, it is "liberal-humanitarian." The concepts of progress, intellectual liberty, and individual enterprise, expressed in both verse and prose, herald the emancipation of the individual and are basic to the philosophy of a rising middle class. Also, the themes of enterprise directed toward the welfare of society, equality coupled with *noblesse oblige,* and a large Americanism introduce a humanitarian note not in harmony with the forces involved in the emergence of the wealthy people. In essence, Hispanic American literature pleaded that man in society should be free as long as he respected the liberty of others; expressive of such an ideal, its young writers contrasted in their idealism with the predominant cynicism of the French, German, and Russian treatments of the bourgeoisie in the nineteenth century.

Chapter XIX

LITERATURE AND THE MIDDLE CLASSES

III. The Victorian Period: Macaulay, Dickens, Gilbert, & Co.

Victorian literature turned the spotlight on the middle classes and brought out in distinct outline the practical characteristics of the bourgeois life. In poetry, essays, and novels Victorian pundits repeatedly expressed those three catchwords of the new society—respectability, humanitarianism, and optimism—as summarized, in "the importance of being Victorian."

Respectability had attached itself to the traders in proportion to their economic and political advancement, and had culminated in England with the passage of the Reform Bill of 1832. Moved by the fact that this act of suffrage had been passed without much violence and that the result had not been the expected counterpart of the French Revolution, Englishmen decided that it was henceforth perfectly respectable to travel the highway of reform; whereupon the middle-class individual preened himself and put on a still finer cloak of respectability. Such an attitude, at large in an era of great mechanical changes, imbued the bourgeoisie with the feeling that progress along orderly lines was inevitable. Accompanying this new respectability was humanitarianism, which broke through an otherwise callous indifference only by the assistance of a few high-minded but practical writers and economists. Buoyed up by new hopes, England experienced an age of optimism, an age when people were convinced that great changes were taking place, changes that would make the world better and better. They did not laugh at William Morris when he said:

But listen to this strange tale of mine,
All folks that are in England shall be better lodged than swine.

Before this Victorian age, Lord Byron and Percy Bysshe Shelley, as convinced reformers, argued for Catholic emancipation and for individual freedom, Byron actually giving up his life while trying to help the Greeks in their war for independence. Even Alfred Tennyson (1809–1892), who loved to write of ancient lords and ladies, as well as of England and the empire, had liberal sentiments, believing that the world was moving forward to a better and a finer day. At the same time he questioned whether all this material progress would result in a heaven on earth. In his *Locksley Hall* for instance, he intimated that to improve machines without improving men might lead to progress in a direction opposite than heavenward. Other romantic writers opposed the tendency to emphasize reason, relegating the things of the mind to the domain of science. Humanitarians and advocates of a return to nature, they stressed instead the truth of instinct and intuition. This belief was well expressed in the romantic poetry of William Wordsworth (1770–1850), who proclaimed that

> One impulse from a vernal wood
> May teach you more of man,
> Of moral evil and of good,
> Than all the sages can.

But doubt did not bother most Englishmen. Cocksure, they were convinced that England was the best country in the world and that no age could equal the present. Science applied to commerce and industry would, they believed, achieve progress and perfection. Therefore, the Mechanics Institute was founded in 1823, and a few years later were established the bourgeois University of London and a "Society for the Diffusion of Useful Knowledge." "Get educated, and then get rich quick" was the typical English middle-class way to utopia.

No writer better interpreted this energetic age than Thomas Babington Macaulay (1800–1859). In his works he brought out the true Victorian bourgeois philosophy expressed in the famous trinity—Liberty, Utility, and Progress. Frankly materialistic, he asserted that the practical progress of mankind alone counted—all else was irrelevant. Thereupon, he proceeded to preach the gospel of earthly rather than of heavenly rewards, rewards to be obtained only by rugged individualism.

As Luther and Calvin questioned the authority of the pope, so Macaulay questioned the prerogatives of the government. In his opinion the government should confine itself strictly to its legitimate duties and leave capital to find its most lucrative course, "commodities their fair price, industry and intelligence their material reward, idleness and folly their natural punishment." These legitimate duties—the maintenance of peace, the defense of property, the decrease of taxes, and the observation of strict economy in every department of the government—if carried out with thoroughness—would enable the individual to make the most of his abilities and opportunities. Devout believer in individualism, sincere opponent of every kind of interference in economic activity, Macaulay expressed in his essays a complacent egotism which Robert Browning (1812–1889), perhaps unconsciously, reiterated in his famous lines:

God's in his heaven,
All's right with the world.

Two ruling ideas inseparably associated with the new society rose out of Macaulay's philosophy. The first of these is the bourgeois' invincible determination to "get ahead," to compete successfully with his business rivals at whatever cost, in a relentless struggle in which only those survived who were the fittest. This struggle Wingfield-Stratford describes in his *Victorian Tragedy* as a "Universal Black Hole of Calcutta, where God's creatures fight without truce, and trample one another to death for a breath at the solitary window." The second idea is a corollary to the first and at the same time a result of it: a strong sense of individualism, of self-confidence, a conviction of both the moral obligation to, and highly practical value in, unremitting personal enterprise. Under the impetus of this gospel of work were developed energies that overflowed from the business world into every channel of human endeavor.

Side by side with the pious attention to gaining success in the financial world was a scarcely less driving desire for social eminence. This was a distinctly middle-class characteristic, for the aristocracy had no need to rise, and the lower classes, speaking generally, had little wish or hope to do so. To the bourgeoisie belonged a somewhat pathetic faith in what might be called the perfectibility of social status, based on no firmer foundation than the possession of wealth and subject to severe disillusionment when that all too insecure foundation gave way. To give an impression of moving in the upper ranks of society, to form only those alliances of business and marriage which brought increased wealth and prestige, either to fawn upon one's social superiors or to affect no envy of them, and to patronize all the rest—this was indisputable evidence of social importance.

The moral code of the ambitious Victorian middle classes had for its essence "respectability" and for its creed two maxims: first, "It pays to be good"; second, "If you must commit sins, at least don't talk about them." This cult of respectability for its own sake, not preceeding from any inner inspiration, was imposed as a formal discipline from without; therefore, it produced an artificial society whose devotion to false standards was to prove its own downfall. Yet, by what seems a strange paradox, the Victorian period brought with it a new Golden Age in the domain of creative writing, a literary blooming-time comparable both in the number and in the brilliance of the writers with Elizabethan and Augustan times.

These Victorian writers were, as a whole, typical of their age. Preëminently representative of the period in which they lived, they were profoundly influenced by and at the same time made a deep impression upon contemporary society. Themselves middle class for the most part, these intellectuals in their works have given us a true picture of their class. We see in their writings the optimistic bourgeois Englishmen hard at work "translating that optimism in the fact of history." Out of their devout yet practical advocacy of labor arose such worthwhile characteristics as discipline, concentration, and moral earnestness. Qualities such as these not only made possible the material greatness of Victorian England but also helped to make that country the moral and cultural leader of the world.

Work and concentration, backed by religion, furnished the foundation upon which middle-class morals could be built. To later generations this morality appeared shallow, for the Victorians very carefully refused to see below the very thin surface, overlooking vice as if it did not exist. Life must appear respectable, and the purity of the family group must be beyond all question. Yet the Victorians were not hypocrites. They were earnestly and conscientiously seeking after the morality in which they believed. Moral to a degree which has seldom been rivaled, they held to their tenets with an almost unparalleled fidelity.

Victorian writers brought out the dark as well as the bright side of bourgeois life. They pictured many middle-class men as selfish individuals, bent upon following their pleasures, when they could afford them, or devoted to the task of keeping up appearances when they could not. Money and rank meant everything to these "aristocrats." William Makepeace Thackeray (1811–1863) well typifies the mid-Victorian writers who portrayed the middle classes in this way. Keen exponent of satire, he took pleasure in ridiculing the upper classes of English society. In his *The Adventures of Philip,* for example, he satirized the aristocrats so as to please the envious readers. On the other hand, in such a work as *Vanity Fair* he criticized the new society of which he assumed that snobbishness, "the mean admiration of mean things," is the master passion. He took for his subject "the moral middle class," with the design of showing, as he wrote to his mother, ". . . a set of people living without God in the world . . . greedy, pompous men, perfectly self-satisfied for the most part, and at ease about their superior virtues."

Thackeray wrote of the society with which he was best acquainted, the upper middle class of rich city merchants. It was his design to portray the world exactly as he saw it, without sentimentalizing or idealizing, although, as a satirist must in order to accomplish his purpose, he sometimes drew with a blacker brush than the strictest realism would allow. He had a serious mission in writing. When he gave the title "Vanity Fair" to his first novel, he symbolized both the character of the society which he undertook to describe and his own attitude toward it. To him the men and women of the fashionable world struggled and schemed and trampled upon their fellows only to attain something not worth having, a prize of no greater value than the gaiety and glare of Vanity Fair. The members of this class worshipped rank and title; they cared nothing for nor did they recognize the qualities that make a true gentleman. They married for wealth and social position; they lived far beyond their means in order to remain "in society"; they often ran deep into debt without intending to pay; they were generally selfish and heartless. "I don't grudge money when you're in good society," said an indulgent father in *Vanity Fair* to his son, "because I know that good society can never go wrong."

Thackeray's successor as a writer of philosophic bourgeois novels was George Eliot (1819–1880), in whom the moral and philosophical element is heavier and more marked. She represents still a third sector of middle-class life, the rural and provincial, with which she was intimately acquainted. She has drawn a picture of wealthy and enlightened society in a provincial city in *Middlemarch,* which satirizes the modern world's pursuit of false ideas in intellectual ambition, in religious aspiration, and in its blind worship of money and social position. In the town of Middlemarch the principal families were those of Mr. Vincy, the mayor, a silk manufacturer described by Mrs. Cadwallader (wife of a clergyman whose chief interest seems to be fishing) as "one of those who suck the life out of the wretched handloom weavers of Tipton and Freshitt"; his brother-in-law Bulstrode, a banker and "sleeping-partner" in various trading enterprises, and a man who deceives himself with the delusion of deep religious conviction; and the Plymdales, who are engaged in the dyeing industry. The Vincys were the social leaders of the town, at whose parties gathered the professional as well as the business class to spend the evenings in "gossip, good cheer, whist-playing, and general futility," as the young Dr. Lydgate, a new-comer to Middlemarch, said. The great families outside the town, the Chettams and the Brookes, of course did not meet the city society on an equal footing with themselves. The clergyman, however, mingled with both groups.

All the divergent social groups, however, including the prosperous farmers, tenants, and the laboring class in the town, were united by one common bond, the powerful one of conservatism. They resisted equally the coming of the railroad, new theories of medicine, model houses for laborers, the Reform Bill, and too much "moral earnestness," as all dangerous to the settled conditions of life in which they were almost ineradicably entrenched.

While Thackeray and Eliot described sordid wealth and made it hateful, Charles Dickens (1812–1870) portrayed sordid poverty and made it almost lovable. It was his mission, says W. S. Lilly, in his *Four English Humorists of the Nineteenth Century* (J. Murray, London, 1895), to reveal the masses (who a century before had been nothing in the public order and who were fast becoming everything) to the classes and also to reveal the masses to themselves. Drawing upon his memories of childhood and upon his experiences in London as a law clerk and reporter of debates, he took for his theme the London middle and lower classes; and the inimitable humor with which he drew his characters and caricatures soon made him the favorite author of the middle classes. But, as became an earnest Victorian, he did not think it his mission to provide amusement and nothing more. Deeply imbued with a spirit of humanitarianism, he regarded his work toward social reform as of the utmost importance. Choosing as his subjects the downtrodden and oppressed, he sought to arouse the conscience and social sympathies of his contemporaries in their behalf. He became perhaps the most effective writer on social conditions in England. Other intellectuals, it is true, made significant contributions on this subject. Mrs. Elizabeth Barrett Browning, for example, in her passionate poem *The Cry of the Children* and Thomas Hood in the *Song of the Shirt* did much to bring about factory reform. But Dickens was the father of contemporary social reformers. In his works dealing with the lowly in English life he described the horrors of the work-houses, the ludicrous methods of English schools, the endless delays of the courts, and the hopeless existence of the unfortunates sent to prison for debts. His *Oliver Twist* attacked the old poor laws because they created Bastilles instead of homes for the poor.

Dickens' first important work, *Pickwick Papers,* has been called "a middle-class epic." Such it may well be termed, for it is an idealized representation of English life in the great rank of the "medium middle class." In this book Dickens' love of fun appears at its best; Pickwick and his friends are made ridiculous but in such a way that we take pleasure in them without feeling scorn for their foolishness. Where but in that "great semi-educated class" could exist such characters as the cockney Pickwick and his associates, whose pretensions to erudition, sportsmanship, and "gentility" are so delightfully satirized? The crusade against social evils, however, was only beginning and the moralizing tone was consequently less strong in this work than it was in the later novels.

Nicholas Nickleby exhibits more emphatically both the active interest in social reform and the exaggeration of certain traits of character to the point at which individuality becomes submerged in the type. Some examples of the latter process illustrate various virtues and vices commonly associated with the middle classes. There is Nicholas himself, a young man of impeccable virtue, nobility, and industry, educated to be a "gentleman," who is willing to try any sort of work from being an usher at Dotheboys Hall to writing and acting in a fourth-rate London theater to support himself and help his mother and sister whom his father's death has left without resources.

In *Dombey and Son* Dickens paints a very pathetic picture of the hardships wrought upon small merchants and tradesmen as a class by the new methods in business and manufacturing. Solomon Gills, ship's instrument maker, has seen his business fade away to nothing. Unable either to revise his methods or modernize his stock, had he any real desire to do so, he realizes the change but cannot help himself; discouraged, he says:

". . . the world has gone past me. . . . Tradesmen are not the same as they used to be, apprentices are not the same, business is not the same, business commodities are not the same." Competition and "big business" had proved too strong for him.

In this same novel Dickens continues his crusade against the evils of the educational methods, making Paul Dombey the victim, not of physical cruelty, but of the ruthless forcing process that went on at Dr. Blimber's, where young gentlemen of the middle class received what was considered necessary for "polite" education. Not only the curriculum and methods but also the directors of the school are satirized.

David Copperfield, generally considered to be his masterpiece, is the story of a young man of that portion of the middle class which is in comfortable circumstances but not wealthy. Although the hero lives a comparatively uneventful life, he achieves success as a vigorous writer. The reader finishes the book with a gratifying picture of goodness and diligence receiving their reward.

Some Victorian writers questioned indirectly the Victorian reliance on these bourgeois virtues. They saw in the economic development of England forces which stood in the way of everything that was right. These intellectuals, however, were not opposed to the Technological and Industrial Revolutions which had caused social inequalities. They accepted such inequalities as a necessary phase in the economic development of the nation. Their protest was not against these revolutionary changes themselves, but against the failure of society to deal properly and adequately with the new conditions. Disraeli, in *Coningsby* and in *Sybil,* for example, attacked the individualism of a social order in which aristocrats, devoid of any traditional sentiments, and middle classes absorbed in the pursuit of wealth had created a society that had destroyed all organic bonds which used to support national unity.

Certain literary artists could see no good in the Industrial Revolution. Thomas Carlyle (1795–1881) viewed it as a monstrous thing, wholly and hopelessly materialistic, the progress of which was crushing the spiritual instincts of the English people. John Ruskin, the great devotee of art, hated it because he was convinced that it alone was responsible for most of the ugliness in English life. He attacked the industrial developments of the age by demanding a "moral code" in commerce as opposed to the "ruthless competition theory of the Manchester School."

Carlyle despised political economy. In his opinion this "dismal science eliminated the factors of religion and morals from the relation of man to man, and established that relation on a scientific profit and loss basis." It preached that the business of each man was to get as large a share of the world's goods as he could at the expense—strictly regulated by the laws of contract—of his fellow-man. Carlyle believed that the path marked out by such a science was the way to perdition and national ruin. Inconsistent with his opposition to economic individualism was his belief in the necessity of leadership. In his opinion the future of society lay in the hands of the self-made men who rose from the masses. "There is clear truth," he wrote in his *The Hero as a Man of Letters,* "in the idea that a struggle from the lower classes of society . . . must ever continue. Strong men are born there, who ought to stand elsewhere than there. The manifold, inextricably complex, universal struggle of these constitutes, and must constitute, what is called the progress of society."

Regardless of these criticisms, English middle-class society progressed along materialistic lines. After the Second Reform Bill in 1867, a change in that social order became apparent. Bourgeois culture had had its first hardy blooming and the next flowering gave promise of being more unwholesome, if more colorful. For the great majority, economic life was much easier; with less effort needed to make a living, more time was available to spend in considering ways of improving society. The old aristocratic landed class had nearly disappeared; it retained a hold only in a few country districts. Wealthy middle-class men bought landed estates. Marriage across classes became more and more frequent. Peers began to be appointed from the bourgeoisie in the 1880's. Changes in the upper class, both in blood and in ideas, left little to choose between its viewpoint and that of the *nouveaux riches*. Soon society began to adopt middle-class concepts.

An intensified desire to appear well was fostered in the new generation. With increased leisure time, which the greater profits and salaries brought her, the middle-class woman had an opportunity to "improve" herself and society. Necessity of using her spare hours forced her into many strange bypaths. If no other aspirations swayed her, she could at least strive to make the entire family "genteel." Such words as "self-satisfied," "smug," "complacent," "self-righteous," and "suave" well characterized the bourgeoisie. Nothing could astonish this astonishing society. Time to think about something besides business engendered a curious attitude. There was a discontent, in the main unconscious, underlying the "genteel" layer in middle-class life. Many people vaguely felt that something was missing, that life was narrow and often ridiculous. By no profound analyst, but by two keen musicians was this uncertainty best expressed.

W. S. Gilbert and A. S. Sullivan, writing in the last three decades of the Victorian period, poked fun at English middle-class life; but their fun had a sober edge. In beliefs, Gilbert, who wrote the lyrics, was typically late Victorian. He had the hard common sense of the rugged business man; at the same time he was romantic and even sentimental on occasion. He had lost that seriousness about the fundamentals of the "good" life for which the earlier Victorians were noted. He laughed at society and the seriousness with which it regarded itself; and yet, while he was chuckling, he wanted no substitutes. Life was secure. Change could only mean refinement of the details of existence.

While Gilbert never lost an opportunity to satirize Victorian life, he was primarily a playwright, interested in a good story. This fact is shown clearly by the themes of his different plays. Some definitely treated middle-class characteristics and life; the others are merely entertaining tales. *Patience,* ridiculing aestheticism, is an instance of the first, while *The Yeomen of the Guard* falls into the second category. Gilbert never spoiled a plot or any of its details merely to point some ironic truth. However, he had so many chances for satirization that he really did not have to drag in more opportunities.

The opera *Patience* was Gilbert's most serious attempt at true satire. It ridiculed one of the intellectual fads which so occupied society's leisure moments at that time. "Culture" was the magical word to all the middle-class housewives of the '70's and '80's. One phase of this culture was "aestheticism"; Oscar Wilde, who seemed to have had a genuine ability as an advertiser, was this cult's high priest. While it did foster an interest in art, sociology predominated—the simple life was the only life. Its devotees dressed in Greek robes or "poets'" costumes; worldly things such as money or muscles were anathema; a light conversational style was absolutely indispensable. Things were "too—too" or "utterly too—too" or "just too utter." Gilbert explains the brotherhood:

If you're anxious for to shine in the high aesthetic line as a man of culture rare,
You must get up all the germs of the transcendental terms, and plant them everywhere.
You must lie upon the daisies, and discourse in novel phrases of your complicated state of mind,
The meaning doesn't matter if it's only idle chatter of a transcendental kind.
And everyone will say as you walk your mystic way,
"If this young man expresses himself in terms too deep for *me*,
Why, what a very singularly deep young man this deep young man must be!"

Be eloquent in praise of the very dull old days, which have long since passed away,
And convince 'em, if you can, that the reign of good Queen Anne was Culture's palmiest day.
Of course you will pooh-pooh whatever's fresh and new, and declare it's crude and mean.
For Art stopped short in the cultivated court of the Empress Josephine. . . .

In *Iolanthe* Gilbert ridiculed the business men in politics.

He dealt with Parliament and the new middle-class forces which were gradually breaking into this stronghold of aristocratic ideals. The fairies make Strephon, who is a fairy down to his waist, a member and then support him in all his political ideals. The Peers stand it as long as they can; but, when Strephon introduces a bill to open the peerage to competitive examination, they plead to be relieved of the burden of his presence. Lord Mountararat expresses the opposition, "I don't want to say anything against brains. . . . I often wish I had some myself—but with a House of Peers composed exclusively of people of intellect, what's to become of the House of Commons?" Finally the Peers marry the fairies and go with them to fairyland since there is no place left for them on earth if the peerage is going to be composed of only intelligent men. This double satire is typically Gilbertian.

H. M. S. Pinafore and *Utopia Limited* also dwell upon middle-class people and their ideals. In *Pinafore* the father, a sea captain, wants to marry his daughter to a snobbish, wealthy, self-made man. She loves a young sailor and is with great difficulty made to forget her rank and flee with him. Everything turns out well in the end because the sailor becomes captain in place of the father—they were changed by their nurse when they were babies. The self-made man cannot stoop as low as a sailor's daughter, so she is free to marry the young captain. This ending exemplifies a characteristic typical of English middle-class audiences at that time. The youngster rises in rank, which is the ideal of all, but the manner occasions no feeling of strangeness on the part of the audience. So many wonderful material things were happening every day that a changeling coming into his own was only too possible.

In *Utopia Limited,* Gilbert again ridicules English institutions and life. The scene is set in Utopia, a tropical island. Its king sent his daughter to England to study and to bring back English culture because "Great Britain is the greatest and noblest nation in the world." The princess returns with "the flowers of progress," who proceed to remodel the country entirely. The "flowers" are a military and naval officer, a logician who is a member of Parliament, a Lord High Chamberlain to purify morals of the stage, a County Councilor to improve sanitation, and a Company Promoter who teaches them to take advantage of laws of liability and bankruptcy. Each succeeds so well in his field that a wave of unprecedented prosperity results. But everything is too perfect, and the people rebel. The member from Parliament then gives them England's last great gift, party government, saying that this will keep them busy and nothing will be accomplished. With such a plot it is obvious what Gilbert could do. He made the most of every opportunity.

While the plots, with which Gilbert laughed at certain institutions and movements, were clever, his greatest satirization occurred in connection with those typical bourgeois characteristics which so marked the individuals of that class. The self-made man had a very prominent place in Gilbert's librettos. In *H. M. S. Pinafore,* Sir Joseph Porter, K.C.B., Lord High Admiral of England, is one of the famous people in literature who climbed to the pinnacle of wealth and position through hard work.

> When I was a lad I served a term
> As office boy to an attorney's firm.
> I cleaned the windows and I swept the floor,
> And I polished up the handle of the big front door.
> I polished up that handle so carefullee,
> That now I am the Ruler of the Queen's Navee!

The judge in *Trial by Jury* is another type of self-made person very common in middle-class society. While work helped him to rise, yet his success was due primarily to his being a "fast thinker." Plugging away at some task day in and day out did not appeal to him, so he sought some easier way and he was not squeamish as to his methods.

> When I, good friends, was called to the bar,
> I'd an appetite fresh and hearty,
> But I was, as many young barristers are,
> An impecunious party.

I'd a swallow-tail coat of a beautiful blue—
A brief which I bought of a booby—
A couple of shirts and a collar or two,
And a ring that looked like a ruby.

. . . .

But I soon got tired of third-class journeys,
And dinners of bread and water;
So I fell in love with a rich attorney's
Elderly, ugly daughter.

. . . .

Women, also, had aspirations, and for the majority of Victorian maidens their supreme desire was to become the wife of some wealthy man or some chivalrous, romantic nobleman who abounded in the three-volume novels. If one of the maidens, by some freak of chance, did not have this object in life, her parents had it, which amounted to the same thing. Marriage into the upper class was held out as the supreme reward for virtuous maidens. This idea was instilled when they first began to think of beaus and kept up until they were actually married. The propaganda usually had the desired effect. Gilbert wrote as an example:

Gentle Jane was good as gold,
She always did as she was told.
She never spoke when her mouth was full,
Or caught bluebottles their legs to pull;
Or spilt plum jam on her nice new frock,
Or put white mice in the eight-day clock,
Or vivisected her last new doll,
Or fostered a passion for alcohol.
And when she grew up she was given in marriage
To a first-class earl who keeps his carriage!

Gilbert had a great deal to say about the "properness" of the Victorian maiden to whom appearances meant so much. That he had a sense of middle-class propriety was displayed in his plays many times. His heroines were especially solicitous that men should display the correct attitude toward them. An improper advance they resented to the utmost depths of their Victorian souls.

Not only were Gilbert's heroines proper, but they had another characteristic which adds to the sum total of Victorian virtue. They were womanly women. No maiden was worthy of the name unless she was able to give way to her emotions at the proper times. One of them explains, "I was highly wrought . . . and I am but a girl, and so, when I am highly wrought, I faint."

Another instance in which Gilbert made fun of the superficiality of the Victorian social code was in the various "Big D——" episodes. Capt. Corcoran prides himself that

Bad language or abuse, I never, never use,
Whatever the emergency;
Though "bother it" I may occasionally say
I never use a big, big D——

What, never?
No, never!
What, *never?*
Hardly ever!

Gilbert did not fail to ridicule freely and frequently middle-class social ambitions. To be invited to a ball given by a member of the upper class was the dream of every well-to-do bourgeois matron. Such an invitation marked the zenith of her social career, and not only did she benefit, but all her feminine relations gained prestige. Nor were the men always insensible to the glory cast by such an event. In giving parties it redounded immeasurably to her credit if the hostess also could include several titles in her list of guests. The host appreciated the distinction which was given to his business if he could say that prominent among his clients was Baron Fulano de Tal. Impecunious Duke and Duchess of Plaza Toro explain in detail how they aided aspiring middle-class society:

To help unhappy commoners, and add to their enjoyment,
Affords a man of noble rank congenial employment;

Of our attempts we offer you examples illustrative:
The work is light, and, I may add, it's most remunerative!

After the *nouveaux riches* had finally reached the heights of their ambition, they often turned into intensified snobs such as the world has seldom seen.

No better composite picture of the English middle-class "gentleman" and middle-class "lady" can be found than in the Gilbert and Sullivan operas. These people are smug, snobbish, grasping, but utterly human. Gilbert copied them from the models which were everywhere around him; and, while he satirized them, he understood their virtues too. He wanted nothing better himself and suggested nothing new. His laughing admonition to Victorian society might well have been:

Ye butchers and bakers and candlestick makers
Who sneer at all things that are tradey—
Whose middle-class lives are embarrassed by wives
Who long to parade as "My Lady,"
Oh! allow me to offer a word of advice,
The title's uncommonly dear at the price!

During the late Victorian period, however, a number of writers lost faith in their age. In fact, the novels of George Gissing (1857–1903) marked the beginning of a realism and pessimism in English literature that had long been present in French writings. Unlike the optimistic Dickens, who believed that poverty could be remedied by a large-hearted humanity, Gissing regarded poverty as "a desolate, worthless waste on the borders of the Kingdom of Commerce." He did not much concern himself with the workshop or conflicts of capital and labor; but he pictured the world of poverty as a place where envy, jealousy, and revenge are the reigning motives. Thoroughly pessimistic, he viewed socialism as the road to mob murder. At the same time he maintained that if wealth were equally bestowed upon the lower classes it would lead to demoralization. In a sense he, in his novels, represented that pessimism which was to characterize England during the late Victorian period and which was to inaugurate an opposition to many features of the early bourgeois society.

John Galsworthy (1867–1933) and John Masefield (1878–), like Gissing, had compassion for mankind; but like his it was a curiously ineffective sympathy. Surveying the social system of their time, they seemed resigned to its hopelessness. According to Masefield, the best man can do is, like Pompey, to stand fast for his principles and be crushed.

A pessimistic and cynical outlook upon the social order can be found in the writings of George Bernard Shaw (1856–) and H. G. Wells (1866–). Prior to the World War, Shaw with his rapier-like pen and Wells with his shrewd crystal-ball penetration of both the past and the future criticized and analyzed the phenomena of the bourgeoisie. One of the founders of the Fabian Society, Shaw "agreed to give up the delightful ease of revolutionary heroics and take to the hard work of practical reform on ordinary parliamentary lines." He and his associates endeavored to make socialism respectable by repudiating the idea of revolution based on class war and advocating instead the attainment of a new order through education. Hating the hypocrisies and stupidities of the English middle classes, Shaw, although himself a member, became a leading critic of them. He was out to shock society's dearest prejudices, to defy its conventions, and to challenge its whole order. Like Ibsen he goes straight to the heart of contemporary life.

Inclined toward "mild radicalism," H. G. Wells is more romantic and less dogmatic than Shaw. Impressed by the changes brought about by science, he has been constantly trying to save man from the fate of the mechanic who is caught up and crushed in his own machinery. In order to make science a blessing rather than a curse to mankind, Wells has urged the making of men intellectually and morally capable of running a scientific world. Better described as a "parlor socialist," Wells believes that the terrible muddle in which society finds itself can only be cleared up by the creation of an educational process which will stimulate men to such "love and fine thinking" that they will reorganize society in a more humane and intelligent way; then class hatreds will end, poverty will disappear, and men will live fuller and richer lives.

In these latter days, intellectuals are prone to regard both Wells and Shaw as relics of a day gone by, for their ideas are now considered highly innocuous in comparison with modern advanced theories; somewhat cruelly in fact it has been said that Shaw expired in 1900. However, both Shaw and Wells in their efforts to reorganize society have made contributions which are still extremely vital and which will apparently remain so for years to come.

CHAPTER XX

THE NEW REVOLUTION; OR, SO ROSE THE RED

The only true contradictory of Individualism is that common kind of Socialism which proposes to use the power of the State in order . . . to "organize" society, or some part of it. . . . this "regimental" Socialism proposes to interfere with the freedom of the individual to whatever extent the sovereign may dictate for the purpose of more or less completely neutralizing the effects of the innate inequalities of men (Thomas H. Huxley, "Methods and Results," in Collected Essays, *D. Appleton & Co., New York, 1896–1902).*

NATIONALISM, democracy, and secularization of schools were, as we have seen, the crucial issues between the conservative church and representatives of the progressive bourgeois régime. By the middle of the nineteenth century, however, intellectual attacks, fostered by men engaged in a study of the natural sciences, as well as by political writers, struck at the very foundation of Christianity. The religious leaders retaliated by putting the new régime under a fire of criticism.

Natural scientists began the conflict when in the nineteenth century biologists definitely evolved the theories of the cell and of protoplasm as explanations of the organization of living creatures. From these they produced the theory of bacteriology, by which germs were shown to be the cause of many diseases. In the same period students of geology, zoology, paleontology, and the newer social sciences, such as psychology, archaeology, ethnology, anthropology, and comparative religion, by adopting scientific methods and by constantly observing, naming, and classifying, obtained much information concerning man and the earth on which he lived. Startling in contrast to the staid Biblical concepts of the time were the discoveries that the earth was millions of years old and that our ancestors were here many thousands of years ago. These revelations tended to prove that the history of man as related by the Bible was incomplete and inadequate, for the Scriptures covered only a comparatively late and short period of his actual presence on this earth.

Scientists, under the sway of these new doctrines, were the protagonists for an ensuing age of materialism. Spurred by success, some of them became so confident of their ability to penetrate life's mysteries that they promised to abolish crime and poverty, to prolong life, and even to discover its meaning. Some supporters of these "scientific heroes," the philosophers, adopted the quizzical or Missourian attitude and, by their particular turn of philosophy, called pragmatism, advanced the rule that the real worth of moral and religious ideals should be measured solely by the practical effects upon people.

Although at first there was no clear conflict between scientists and churchmen, by the middle of the nineteenth century the way was prepared for a world-wide struggle when scientists brought forth the theory of evolution, which cast doubt upon the historical authenticity of the sacred Scriptures, the very well-springs of Christianity, Protestant and Catholic. The Catholics, however, were not so deeply offended as were the Protestants, who based everything on the Bible, instead of as the Catholics, upon the supplementary teachings of the Church Fathers and upon ancient tradition. The Protestant phase of the struggle continued in America to the time of William Jennings Bryan (1860–1925); and although the battle has died down considerably, an armistice has not yet been declared to this day on the scientific-religious front.

Science, it is the general consensus of opinion, has had the better of the argument. While the churches divided among themselves as to lines of defense, science built up a strong case for organic evolution. It found continuous links of evidence to substantiate the theory. It faced facts. It forced a reinterpretation of the Scriptures according to generations and genealogy. It waved aside any literal possibility that the world was created in six days. It tried to talk in simple, understandable terms to the layman.

The effects of the theory merit attention. After the publication of Darwin's works, his ideas were discussed and popularized by a number of writers. In 1860, one year after the publication of Darwin's *Origin of Species,* Herbert Spencer began his monumental *Synthetic Philosophy,* of which the last volume did not appear until thirty-six years later. Therein, as has been mentioned before, he tried, first, to apply the theory of evolution in the realms of philosophy, psychology, sociology, and ethics, and secondly, to bring out the idea of development and progress. When Spencer maintained, however, that behind everything there must be a power which he called the Unknowable, he caused many Christians to shudder. To them Spencer's way of looking at things tended straight toward materialism, atheism, and hell.

Another shock came when Thomas H. Huxley, a devout follower of the new science, deliberately attacked Christianity. In his *Man's Place in Nature* he tried to show that man was only a transitional stage in the natural evolution from lower to higher types. Criticizing the foundation of revealed religion, he maintained that he could find no evidence of the existence of God. He therefore rejected Christianity, asserting that it was nothing more than a mixture of some of the best and worst elements of paganism and Judaism, "molded in practice by the innate character of certain peoples of the Western World."

Ernest Renan (1823–1892), able French student of comparative religions, supported Huxley in this view. Through his investigations in the Levant he was led to the belief that the Scriptures and Christian theology were but a development—an evolution of primitive fable and myth. As a professor of Hebrew and a clever writer, Renan became the leader of a skepticism which was no longer content to be indifferent toward Christianity. Skepticism became an aggressive force, winning thousands of adherents and greatly weakening the Christian church.

Many devout persons blamed the new order for these attacks, probably because most of the followers of the scientists, especially of Darwin, were middle-class men—professors, lawyers, students, and business men. It was natural, therefore, that the hitherto liberal Pius IX, who ruled as pope from 1846 to 1878, confronted on the one side by this wave of skepticism and on the other by political foes who were attacking the church by threatening to deprive him of temporal as well as of spiritual power, should have taken a determined stand against the bourgeois program, revealing himself in the redoubtable armor of an orthodox knight of the Holy Church.

Wise, honest, and courageous, "the middle-class pope" soon began to perceive that the spread of liberalism in Italy meant the downfall of the temporal power of the church. He believed that should this happen, he would no longer be an independent head of a great religion and would become instead the subject of the secular ruler of Italy. Then the church might split into national units throughout the world, and the unified institution of Christ would no longer exist. This danger was not the only cause for his "desertion" of liberalism; Pius IX was aware of the tendency to emphasize material things. He lived at a time when the revolutionary teachings of Darwin, the socialism of Marx, and the great mechanical inventions were taken as evidence that man was beginning to worship materialism in place of God. Someone, he believed, must direct the movement to save the spiritual side of life; as head of the universal church, he considered it his duty to lead the faithful.

His relentless warfare culminated in the famous encyclical *Quanta Cura* and the accompanying *Syllabus of Errors* (1864). In the former, the pope repudiated many leading liberal ideas and reasserted the supremacy of the church over state in matters of religion and morals. As understood by Catholics, the unity of faith necessitates complete independence of the ecclesiastical authority. Thus the secular state cannot and must not impair its freedom. The *Syllabus* consisted of a collection of eighty propositions dealing with specific religious and political beliefs which the pope condemned. Such bourgeois practices and ideas as Bible societies, secular education, lay control of the church, lay marriages, agnosticism, and free-thinking were condemned.

Many liberals criticized the attitude of the pope toward the new order. Moderates within the Catholic Church feared that he was trying to regain his temporal as well as spiritual power. Numerous Protestants maintained that, far from attacking merely the abuses of liberalism, particularly revolution, he was threatening the very existence of Protestantism. Some enthusiastic nationalists decided that the pope was about to thwart their plans to unify Germany and Italy and their desire to establish political democracy in France and Spain. Thenceforth his followers were called clericals by their enemies and were considered by many bourgeoisie and their allies, the working men, as obstacles to progress, as undemocratic and unpatriotic, thus formidable opponents of liberalism.

Undeterred by these criticisms Pius IX determined to strengthen papal authority and to settle the questions raised by liberalism, called a general council at the Vatican (1869–1870), which was attended by about eight hundred churchmen. Long and earnest discussions occurred which resulted in the definition of the famous doctrine of papal infallibility. According to this tenet the Roman pontiff, when he speaks *ex cathedra,* that is, when as head of the universal church, he defines a belief regarding faith or morals held by that body, he "is possessed of that infallibility with which the Divine Redeemer willed that His Church should be endowed for defining faith or morals; and that therefore such definitions of the Roman pontiff are *per se* immutable and independent of the consent of the Church." In other words, a decision of the pope in a matter of faith or of morals is final, for he is the echo of God's voice.

This doctrine, although it was merely the statement of an idea which had existed for centuries, annoyed the forces which opposed the church. Agnostics, Protestants, and even some Catholic laymen denounced papal infallibility. A few thousand Catholics in Switzerland and in southern Germany left the church and founded what they called the "Old Catholic" sect. A number of French Catholic writers asserted that this doctrine was essentially new and constituted an attack upon the liberties of the Gallican, or French national church, and also upon the power of church councils. But these were minorities; as a whole, the Catholics of Europe were overwhelmingly submissive to the principle of the infallibility of the pope.

Deprived of his rule in Rome (1870), Pius IX encouraged the clerical movement by which Catholics throughout the world were urged to work for the restoration of the temporal power of the pope. Little headway was made at first, because the churchmen were distrusted as bitter enemies of such features of middle-class control as nationalism, secular education, and science. Before the clericals could gain enough favor with the new order to satisfy their aims, this bad reputation had to be removed and they had to get in the good graces of their natural enemies.

Despite internal factional splits, Protestants and Catholics managed to arrange a settlement with the bourgeois order, a settlement which included an understanding with regard to the relationship of religion and science. Aroused by this controversy, various schools of thought had appeared in Catholic and in Protestant countries. One group believed in the orthodox teachings of the Catholic and Protestant churches and refused a hearing to bourgeois beliefs and practices, especially to scientific concepts. Another accepted the new beliefs and became skeptics, agnostics, or atheists. Finally a third group appeared, which sought a compromise between science and religion.

In Protestant countries this last group carried the day, for many Protestants, excepting the fundamentalists, managed to remain Christians and yet to fit the evolutionary doctrine into their religious scheme of things. This they were able to do by recognizing, with reservations depending on their personal degree of discrimination, previously held interpretations as to the meaning of the Bible. Nevertheless, they insisted that the church was the great force in determining morals and conduct on this earth and in preparing man for everlasting life in heaven.

The Catholic church, by reviving the study of the writings of Thomas Aquinas, the great theologian and philosopher of the Middle Ages, reached the conclusion that

> . . . Darwinism was only a hypothesis, which was being confessedly weakened in certain details; that the Darwinian theory, if

true, could explain only the evolution of man's material body, not the creation and life of immortal spirits; that the spiritual side of humanity still belonged to the realm of faith and religion as unquestionably as its material side belonged to the province of natural science; that the possibility of an allegorical interpretation of the account of Creation in the book of Genesis as well as a literal interpretation had always been recognized by foremost fathers of Christianity; and that a subsequent confirmation of Darwinism might even serve to enlarge man's comprehension of the wonder-working ways of God (Hayes, *Political and Social History of Modern Europe,* The Macmillan Co., New York, 1924).

A contributory factor in settling the controversy was the progress of socialism. Many churchmen feared that socialists and anarchists plotted to overthrow not only the political and social order but also Christianity itself. Consequently, churchmen and middle-class leaders tended to unite on the idea of perpetuating a bourgeois society. This *entente* did not mean that all the issues between church and state were settled nor that all churchmen and all scientists had much brotherly love for each other. It did signify that the bitter hostility which existed between these groups in 1878 subsided, largely because representatives of both camps were soon engaged in a struggle against common enemies, the representatives of the New Revolution—the socialists, the anarchists, and other radicals. To suppress these extremists, Catholic political organizations, called center parties, and Catholic labor unions were established in many European countries, especially in France and Germany. Democracy, constitutionalism, and lay education were recognized or at least tolerated by the successors of Pope Pius IX; at the same time many scientists and religious leaders came to a tacit understanding by which science became the monarch of the mundane world while the church retained mastery of the spiritual sphere.

In 1891, Pope Leo XIII, in his famous encyclical letter on *The Condition of Labor,* frankly came out in support of the bourgeoisie in their war upon radicalism. Rejecting the main tenet of socialism—the community of goods—the Holy Father accepted the bourgeois emphasis upon the sanctity of private property, claiming that it was "according to nature's law" and the Divine Law which reads: "Thou shalt not covet thy neighbor's wife; nor his house, nor his field, nor his man-servant, nor his maid-servant, nor his ox, nor his ass, nor anything which is his." Leo also opposed the idea of the class-struggle. "It is ordained by nature," he wrote, "that those two classes [rich and poor] should exist in harmony and agreement." In achieving this end the state should be just toward all—high or low, and promote "private prosperity."

Despite this alliance between the church and the exponents of the bourgeois régime, a certain amount of distrust persisted. Many persons opposed to the Roman Catholic faith still considered the age of Pius IX as significant only in so far as it marked the last stand of that citadel of conservatism, the Roman Catholic church, against the modernism and materialism of the middle-class régime. Supported by a number of scholars, especially scientists, these critics held that the church was medieval and anachronistic, its pretensions to universal supremacy and papal infallibility absurd.

On the other hand, there were those who could see in the antagonism of the papacy to certain aspects of the new order (as, for example, to extreme materialism and to rampant nationalism) a resistance to those forces which eventually might bring about the destruction of the new régime. "For," as Cardinal O'Connell of Boston said in an address in 1930, "luxury, to which wealth often leads, is the first step to decadence and degeneracy, personal and national."

Within the Protestant and Catholic churches, many powerful persons, including the pope, have not yet capitulated to unrestricted bourgeois individualism, for, recognizing the existence of social inequalities, they have held that individualism was partially responsible. This has led them to legislation designed to benefit groups and classes rather than individuals. In the main, both Christian churches gave their support to the established order in preference to following a *laissez faire* policy that might permit radical forces to bring about their downfall. Nevertheless, they were compelled to shift their stand continually in order to protect their positions against the threat of socialism.

Not only in literature and in religion was criticism of the new order manifested; these direct assaults were also supplemented by the indirect implications of utopian schemes. Where dreams of an ideal state flourish, there, one can be sure, a dissatisfied people dwell. So in France and in England dissatisfaction with the bourgeois order was implied by the popularity of cult after cult of reformers. These had as their strain of descent Plato's *Republic* and its early modern progeny such as Francis Bacon's *New Atlantis,* Thomas More's *Utopia* and Tommaso Campanella's *Civitas Solis,* all propounding formulas for an ideal agrarian society. It was not until the French Revolution, however, that plans were made for a perfect industrial order. Concluding that plutocrats as well as aristocrats should be destroyed, Saint-Just, a revolutionary leader, envisioned a society in which both wealth and poverty would be eradicated. During the Directory (1795–1799) another idealist, Babeuf, maintaining that the French Revolution had chiefly benefited the bourgeoisie, organized a Society of Equals for the purpose of bringing about a compulsory equalization of wealth and the abolition of poverty. In 1797 his followers staged an uprising; Babeuf was executed; and his society disintegrated.

In the early nineteenth century, reformers conceived new panaceas. The fantastic Frenchman Saint-Simon (1760–1825), a wealthy idealist much admired today by parlor socialists and social scientists, although unwilling to discard the capitalistic system, proposed that the "great minds," the financiers, the industrial leaders, and the great scientists, should, by means of inventions, scientific discoveries, and industrial improvements, coöperate in a planned movement to eliminate poverty. He believed that a crisis was confronting the French people, a crisis which, he wrote,

> consists essentially in the change from a feudal and religious system to an industrial and scientific system. . . . France has become a huge factory and the nation a colossal workshop. The real temporal power of today is to be found in the industries and the spiritual power in the men of science. . . . All social institutions should have as their aim the physical and moral improvement of the most numerous and poorest class.

"This was a vision from the heights which," wrote a certain historian, "was far in advance of his time." Saint-Simon has come, therefore, to be regarded as the founder of French utopianism.

Charles Fourier (1772–1837), another Frenchman, proposed a plan by which, instead of a central government handling the great business enterprises—a difficult task—France should be split into small groups of families, called *Phalanges,* each of which should contain eighteen hundred members, owning in common the buildings and all the implements for the production of the necessities of life. The total product of their work was to be divided so as to give capital four-twelfths, labor five-twelfths, and talent or management three-twelfths. Fourier's plan was international in scope. Visualizing a confederation of *Phalanges,* with the capital at Constantinople, Fourier soon had followers as far west as the United States.

England had a brilliant utopian in the wealthy liberal manufacturer Robert Owen (1771–1858). Perturbed by the prevalence of poverty, he hoped to regenerate mankind by the formation of coöperative groups which should own and use for their benefit all the necessary means of production. As manager of a large cotton mill of which he later became the chief proprietor, he paid good wages, bettered working conditions, and transformed the living quarters into a model town. To the surprise of fellow-industrialists, Owen's factory, despite additional expenditures, earned dividends as large as before. Many people came to study this unique experiment at first hand. Owen, however, did not confine his attention to local reforms. Converted to socialism, he dedicated his life and wealth to this cause. Writing numerous articles and books, appealing to the crowned heads of Europe, and defending his plan before the American House of Representatives, he was indirectly responsible for the establishment of several experimental colonies in the United States and in England.

Like their Greek and Renaissance predecessors, these earnest utopianists, lost in visions of a perfect society, failed to appreciate the obstacles in the way of imposing a new state upon an evolutionary society. Sentimentalists and humanitarians for the most part, they suggested impractical reforms which bore little or no relation to reality, and concocted panaceas which could in no wise be accepted by human beings possessed of acquisitive instincts. At the same time idealists, by pointing out the imperfections of the existent social order, stimulated men toward envisioning a more perfect state.

Disagreeing with the general methods by which the utopianists sought to change society and believing it hopeless to expect benevolent reforms and concessions to be handed down by the upper groups, some reformers urged militant action in the form of class warfare. Workers, they felt, should take matters into their own hands by organizing political parties and conducting general strikes in direct pursuit of their ends. One of these unsuccessful radicals was Louis Blanc, a Frenchman, whose primary object was to organize a republic in which the wage-earners, by means of universal male suffrage, should possess political control. Control being secured, the workers then were to confiscate the factories and to establish national workshops owned by wage-earners.

From these revolutionary movements rose the apostle of modern scientific socialism, Karl Marx (1818–1883). During his youth Marx saw Germans trying to unify and liberalize their country, the Industrial Revolution penetrating the Rhineland, and the consequent enrichment of a few and the impoverishment of many. Brought up amid the sufferings of his fellow-men, educated in a German university where freedom of thought, speech, and action were stifled, and conscious of the public criticism of the money-making abilities and selfish, unscrupulous characteristics of his fellow-Jews, this prophet of the working man decided to devote his life to the task of revealing social inequalitics and of emancipating "the working slaves." He soon aroused the ire of German authorities because of the radical views which he expressed. Forced into exile, he encountered oppression in Paris and in other continental cities, finally settling in London, where he studied and wrote until his death.

As a student, Marx had come under the influence of Hegel, the philosophical arbiter of Germany. Accepting Hegel's idea "that each period is characterized by the predominance of a 'world people,' who are possessed of a universal idea which must be given to mankind," Marx explained that the cause of changes was not in the ideas of God but in material circumstances—climate, soil, inventions, the economic struggles of classes, and similar forces of man and nature. Upon the fall of the bourgeoisie, it followed from his reasoning that the working men were certain to become "the world people."

No one revealed the current social and economic inequalities better than Marx. With an enormous amount of detail, with logic both penetrating and pitiless, he described the social conditions in the England of his day. As a correlator of social and economic circumstances in Western society during this period Marx was perhaps unrivaled. Although of prime position as a destructive critic of society, especially in his indictment of capitalism, he nevertheless was a great constructive theorist, as evidenced in his analysis of capital and in his outline of socialism. Writing voluminously on economic history and political philosophy, Marx left a strong imprint on almost all the social sciences. To the leftists his name today is a revered symbol.

His basic views on political economy were incorporated in a thick tome, entitled *Das Kapital,* which was left unfinished at his death, but was completed by his colleague, Friedrich Engels. Although sometimes called the "Workingman's Bible," this book in far from simple, scriptural language but with far less ambiguity explains in complex form the cardinal doctrines of socialism as presented by Marx and Engels. These tenets were more concisely expressed in their other works, especially in the *Communist Manifesto.* Nevertheless, in describing the terrible social conditions brought about by the Industrial Revolution *Das Kapital* stands forth as an intellectual monument.

Marx not only exposed the inequalities of his age, but also, in developing his so-called materialistic interpretation of history, he emphasized many significant factors in human activities hitherto neglected by historians. With Engels he wrote in the *Communist Manifesto:*

> The history of all hitherto existing society is the history of class struggles.
>
> Freeman and slave, patrician and plebeian, lord and serf, guild-master and journeyman, in a word, oppressor and oppressed, stood in constant opposition to one another, carried on an uninterrupted, now hidden, now open fight, a fight that each time ended, either in a revolutionary re-constitution of society at large, or in the common ruin of the contending classes.
>
> . . . in every historical epoch, the prevailing mode of economic production and exchange, and the social organization necessarily following from it, form the basis upon which is built up, and from which alone can be explained, the political and intellectual history of that epoch. . . .

In his writings Marx also asserted that certain events would make inevitable the rise of the proletariat, who would end the hegemony of the capitalistic class by seizing control of the agencies of production and distribution, and consequently of the government. The continuous concentration of wealth under capitalism would in time place all property in the hands of a very few, and as a result the exploited classes would unite to overthrow the established order. The communist prophet did not envision a division of property after the overthrow of the capitalists; he advocated its transfer to the state, which would operate the means of production for the direct profit of the world people. Contending that the capitalist, as a stockholder drawing dividends, was an idle drone and as useless as a feudal lord in the eighteenth century, he predicted that in time the capitalist ownership would be destroyed and the salaried clerks of great corporations would become the employees of the government.

Marx, in justifying his beliefs, emphasized the view that labor was the source of all value. Anyone, he asserted, who contributed to the welfare of mankind should have his share in the total output, whether he were an engineer, farmer, street cleaner, teacher, manager, or artist; but as long as men drew dividends from money invested in machines, workers would not get what they rightfully earned. Under his scheme the state would own all the agencies of production, and private ownership would be confined to such personal items as food, clothing, furniture, pictures, and books. All would enjoy the available necessities and luxuries. Oppression and poverty would be obliterated. Why should one-tenth of the population live in luxury over the labor of the other nine-tenths? All should be rewarded or should suffer alike. True equality, real democracy, and human welfare, he said, demanded that the workers unite. They had nothing to lose but their chains, and through unity the world was theirs. The time would come when all men would work and no one would become wealthy at the expense of his neighbor. Then, when all had an opportunity to express the best that was in them, poverty would disappear and individuals would be emancipated from hunger and disease. Marx assumed that thereafter men would be able to live in harmony and brotherly love.

Marxian philosophy was soon trimmed to the winds. As Marx declared, a society would not rise out of the air; it had to evolve out of the prior economic and political order. Unlike the utopians who created a perfect society in their heads, irrespective of all existing conditions, he envisioned a régime which would naturally replace the capitalistic system. Inevitable as the new order was, he urged the workers to organize along class lines, so that they might be prepared to take the lead when the time was ripe for revolution. Those upholding his ideas formed socialist parties throughout the world. Many thought that the promised millennium was at hand when the Bolsheviks seized war-torn Russia and began a government based on Marxian principles.

A great number of his followers as well as his opponents misunderstood certain of his statements. One of the most common misconceptions was the belief that, from the beginning, he wanted violent revolution; in reality, in his early works he merely suggested widespread social reform by legislative action. But later, as a result of his study of the Paris Commune, Marx wrote a treatise in which he advocated the dictatorship of the proletariat attained, if necessary, by violent methods. Applying his economic interpretation of history, he held that, just as the great French Revolution had destroyed the bulwark of feudalism and paved the way for the rise of the bourgeoisie, who consolidated their gains by the revolutions of 1830 and 1848 in France, so the disturbance of the Commune of Paris (1871) marked the rise of the proletariat against the new repressive bourgeois order. Marx then set forth in this study the belief that a minority, creating a strong government, had to rule during the transition from capitalism to socialism; a dictatorship by the proletariat was an essential prelude to the establishment of true socialism.

Undoubtedly one of the keenest critics of the bourgeois régime, Marx believed that to a large extent motives of all kinds were determined by the economic positions of the people who held them; each class of persons, whose interests were similar, constituted within itself an intellectual cosmos with a politics, a metaphysics, and an art of its own. He came to the realization that the romanticism, the idealism, and the revolts of the early nineteenth century were largely bourgeois movements; that is, the merchants, manufacturers, and the financiers were fighting the last vestiges of feudalism. He also believed that the new social system, called capitalism, resulted in a large-scale exploitation of the working classes. Machinery and credit had enabled the bourgeoisie to replace the feudal lords as the masters of the state. That capitalism would eventually destroy itself was the recurrent note in his writing.

Another form of radicalism—anarchism—challenged the premises of capitalism. Like socialism, it was engendered by the Industrial Revolution and arose out of more or less systematized theories on the part of middle-class reformers as to how poverty and its attendant ills could be exterminated. But it differed from socialism in that it would abolish entirely all government and give complete freedom to the individual.

Anarchism had as its nurturers two brilliant advocates: the Frenchman Pierre Joseph Proudhon (1809–1865) and the Russian Michael Bakunin (1814–1876). Proudhon's ideas came from two sources: first, the evils France had inherited from the Industrial Revolution; second, the spirited opposition of the proletariat to the middle-class régime of Louis Philippe. Losing faith in all governments, Proudhon wrote *Qu'est-ce que la propriété? (What is Property?)* (1840), answering his rhetorical question with "La proprieté, c'est le vol." ("Property is theft.") Strangely enough, however, he did not favor public ownership of private property. Every man should have an equal right to use property as his personal possession. Every man should enjoy the full benefit of his labor. Authority in any form is anathema. Self-determination, or self-government, is the best means for an orderly society. "No more parties," he said, "no more authority; absolute liberty of man and citizen." Like Rousseau, Proudhon also believed that man was fundamentally good but was corrupted by civilization. Thus, if individuals could get rid of "man-made laws" and live together, not limited by supreme authority but only by voluntary yet legally binding force of contract, a perfect social order would be attained, for men, inherently just, would then obey contracts, which they knew to be necessary. Wrong-doing would be abolished, and complete individualism would make the world a veritable paradise.

Bakunin outlined a more militant form of anarchism. Living in autocratic Russia and exiled to Siberia because of his ideas, he not only disregarded the past but also became a staunch advocate of terrorism. He said:

> The future social order must, from top to bottom, be made only by free association and federation of workers, in association first, then in communes, in districts, in nations, and finally, in a great international and universal federation.

These were essentially the ideas of Proudhon. To them Bakunin added the conception of revolution, or of violence, as the inevitable method by which the old order would be destroyed and the new established.

Another French radical, Louis Auguste Blanqui (1805–1881), seemed to have adopted Bakunin's ideas. Like many Jacobins of the French Revolution, Blanqui urged a policy of extreme governmental centralization, which was to be made possible by the dictatorship of the proletariat. Not only was a violent revolution necessary, but also it was to be achieved under the guidance of an intelligent faction which was proletariat at heart. Regarding the evils of bourgeois society as far from rational, he decided that utopia was possible only if private property were abolished. His program attacking religion as well as capitalism was revolution, atheism, and communism.

It is not strange, then, that in the nineteenth century the middle classes and the church, who at first tended to oppose each other, united in common opposition to the radicals. For, with Marx predicting the rule of the proletariat, with Proudhon advocating the abolition of the centralized political government, with Bakunin expecting violence, and with Blanqui believing in the leadership of an intelligent minority of the proletariat in a revolt to overthrow capitalism and Christianity, the way was being prepared for Lenin and Trotsky. The attack upon Western capitalism, the New Revolution, was in the making.

Chapter XXI

THE NEW NOBILITY

Aristocratic society is based upon an unwritten compact to maintain a certain standard of manners and conduct within its pale. To this end wealth is merely a means; it is only in a plutocracy that it is regarded as an end in itself (Wingfield-Stratford, The Victorian Sunset, *Wm. Morrow & Co., New York, 1932).*

Ogre of Main Street, Big Business of the twentieth century set out to devour its heroic but petty bourgeois adversaries and to build its own stronghold—Wall Street. Big Business, however, was but an old giant wearing a new mask, for its ancestry lay in the economic past of the centuries before. No more was the plutocrat inevitably the scion of the great commercial classes or of wealthy landowning aristocrats such as those who dominated England during the early nineteenth century. The man of wealth was no longer necessarily the heir of wealth. The time was come that the great industrial and financial captains emerged from the ranks of the petty bourgeoisie to rule the state.

To the French Revolution the new power owed a fundamental debt for it broke down the caste barriers of traditional and artificial distinctions between classes, forcing a readjustment of social conditions so as to give to everyone, at least more than in the past, a fairer chance according to his natural abilities—the creed, in other words, of liberty, equality, and fraternity. It was, consequently, from this time on, feasible for the ordinary *entrepreneur* to rise to equality with the long-reigning business barons. On the heels of the French Revolution, the creation of democratic nations in England, France, Italy, and the United States with the concomitant weakening in strength of the feudal-commercial alliance and the authoritative or absolute state made possible the "hands-off" or *laissez faire* policy in business. Too, the Industrial and Technological Revolutions gave opportunities to those sharp-witted enough to capitalize on them. Finally, the principle of nationalism, protecting and encouraging as it did both domestic and international economic enterprise, provided safe and profitable markets for the ambitious adventurer.

From these changes steamed a new nobility able to take its place on equal terms with the old nobility of entrenched plutocracy. No wonder that self-made men and gigantic business enterprises mushroomed into existence. Individualism apparently was now destined to produce an age of super-capitalists along autocratic lines, with all power centered in the hands of the ruling group at the top.

By 1900 these captains of industry and financial lords were the aristocrats, or as more frequently called, the plutocrats of the new social order. As capitalists and industrial barons they lived in mansions and penthouses. They practically controlled economic life. Men and machines were their puppets. Machinery and credit enabled them to replace the feudal lords as the masters of the state. They constituted the new nobility.

It is true that most of these aristocrats did not possess the noble titles of Marquis, Count, and Duke; but they did gain such dignities as Privy Councillor, Chancellor, Secretary of the Treasury, Chairman of the Board and such distinctions as honorary or student degrees in letters, law, or science. The masses honored them as Captains of Industry, Coal Barons, Industrial Dukes, Steel Kings, Engine Builders, Financial Lords, the "Powers that be"—the "Boss." Dynasties appeared, such as those of Rothschild, Morgan, Rockefeller, Mellon, and Ford; and the populace regarded these moguls of finance and industry with the same worship, reverence, fear, and hatred as their ancestors had the barons of old. Cynics could well point out that the ordinary person was so dependent for food, clothing, and shelter upon these tycoons that he was no whit different from the serfs of old. A New Serfdom indeed!

Could this control endure? According to Karl Marx, the system which the plutocrats dominated was truly capitalistic; each manufacturer would try to outsell the others, with the result that there would be a constant stimulus to more efficient methods of production. But the more efficient an industry would become—the faster the machines were able to work and the fewer people were needed to tend them—the more workers would be thrown out of jobs; that is, the more commodities produced, the fewer people would be able to buy them. To market at all under these conditions, one would have to undersell his competitors; that would mean more efficient and more expensive machinery, fewer workers, fewer people again able to buy what was being produced. This situation would cause—had already caused—a crisis about every ten years. The more efficiently goods were manufactured, the more money would be needed for the plant, and the larger the plants would become. Thus the industries would keep growing and the empires would keep merging until each industry would become one great unified plant with centralized control, and the money which kept them going would have to be concentrated in the hands of a few capitalists. Some Marxists, however, sat on the sidelines, waiting expectantly to see the ogre topple and smash.

Although all industrial nations experienced this era of Big Business, the pioneers were Germany and the United States. In Germany Big Business became a legitimate phase of the autocratic state. Bismarck, like post-World War dictators, hated democracy and soon set himself against economic individualism. Influenced by the benevolent despotism of the great Hohenzollern leaders of the past and by the neo-mercantilism expressed in the works of such German economists as List, Schmoller, and Wagner, he became a staunch exponent of governmental authority in economic as well as in political matters. Nineteenth-century exponent of the predominance of the state, he insisted that all classes must coöperate in the creation of a prosperous and powerful German Empire, so that all might profit. To achieve this end—even before the industries and factories of Germany were earning great profits—he instituted social legislation designed to give security to the workers. Meanwhile, this practical reformer fattened thin industry and agriculture by protection against foreign competition, by financial subsidies, and by favorable legislation.

Germany's late economic growth helped her in obtaining a share of the large world trade, for the Germans—not handicapped by the English conservatism which refused to discard time-worn machinery or to depart from traditional business methods—were able to move rapidly in both agriculture and industry from the small-scale standards of medieval society to the large-scale organization at the basis of twentieth-century Big Business.

The people, accustomed to tendencies toward consolidation, entertained no suspicions or fears concerning trusts. Hence, by 1914 a great part of German economic life, especially in the chemical, coal, iron, and steel industries, was organized into consolidations called cartels. These were powerful associations of firms in which members preserved their separate existence and individuality but agreed to coöperate with one another in the control of output, prices, and markets. This form of syndicate was advantageous in that it eliminated waste, economized effort, and checked cut-throat competition. On the other hand, it led to the concentration of financial and economic power in the hands of a few big industrialists and bankers, who, by manipulating prices, credit facilities, and production, took advantage of the helplessness of the masses of people. Nevertheless, cartels were spreading rapidly in all fields of production by 1914. The government worked hand in glove with these associations in their attempts to extend their markets abroad and to monopolize those at home.

Before the outbreak of the World War, the German business plutocrats, as a result of this industrial development, were in a position to challenge the supremacy of the landowning aristocrats, the junkers. Like their English brothers in the fight over the Corn Laws, these German capitalists in 1912 objected to the high tariff on foodstuffs which enriched the junker landowners and brought about a rise in the cost of living. Organized to abolish high tariffs, reduce taxes, and lower the cost of living, the business interests appealed to the proletariat for support. Consequently, in the elections of 1912, the conservative agricultural groups were badly defeated. Big Business was in the saddle, riding high, wide, and handsome.

By the late nineteenth century the United States reached the era of "Big Business." As in Germany, the government in America did much to encourage economic enterprise. Following the Civil War, a great "banquet" was held. At this feast the common farmer got tender giblets, while the capitalists obtained the rest of the turkey. In other words, the Homestead Act permitted farmers to acquire 160 acres of land after five years cultivation; while such capitalists as Collis Huntington obtained from the government railway land-grants—vast empires for nothing—immediately.

Railway capitalists, however, were not the only representatives of Big Business. American faith in private initiative resulted in the rise of great concerns in the various fields of industrial and commercial endeavor. After 1880, although production increased, the number of independent mills, mines, and factories declined, dropping 30 per cent within a decade. Great trusts, or combines, developed, which tried to squeeze out the small *entrepreneurs* and to create monopolies. Trusts appeared in such things as railroads, steamship lines, mines, oil, steel mills, textiles, and foods. In 1899 there were over three hundred and fifty trusts, with capital amounting to over $3,000,000,000; in 1915 there were over a thousand, with a total capital of some $30,000,000,000. At the opening of the twentieth century finance capitalism—control of many corporations by a few powerful banks—marked another stage in the concentration of economic power in the hands of a few. A new section of the present-day nobility now rose to power—that of financial barons, such as J. P. Morgan.

"Good times," the culmination of Big Business, stimulated the whole population. All over the country, in the towns, the farms, and in the growing cities, people stirred and awakened. Railroads were pushed across the plains. "Great coal-fields from which was taken food to warm the body of the giant, were opened up in widely scattered sections of the country." The phenomenal success of the new princes of wealth, the Morgans, the Rockefellers, the Fricks, and the Goulds, defied the laws that had submerged the trading classes. They were merchants dealing in great things—steel and iron, railroads, factories, and oil fields. To them the accumulation of wealth apparently had become the sole aim in life. "It was a time of hideous architecture," writes Sherwood Anderson in *Poor White,* "a time when thought and learning paused. Without music, without poetry, without beauty, in their life of impulses, a whole people, full of native energy and strength of lives lived in a new land, rushed pell-mell into a new age." "Work to go ahead" was the slogan in the seventies and the eighties. The section hand on the Union Pacific, the miner in Pennsylvania, the wage slave in a New England factory, and the town banker and merchant on Main Street were encouraged by their wives to do everything well. "Show them that you can do perfectly the task given to you to do, and you will be given a chance at a larger task. Some day when you least expect it something will happen. You will be called into a position of power."

"Salvation on earth," became the great objective of these nineteenth-century rugged individualists. Utopia, or earthly heaven, to the individual was wealth. "Boys," writes Anderson, "who in the schools had read of Lincoln walking for miles through the forest to borrow his first book . . . began to read in the magazines and newspapers of men who, by developing their faculties for getting and keeping money, had become suddenly and overwhelmingly rich." Horatio Alger was the biographer of the period; from "Rags to Riches" was the universal theme.

By the turn of the century gigantic combines and huge fortunes had made the capitalists or plutocrats the aristocracy of the day. These "self-made men" dominated all social life with their wealth. But, before they were able to assume genuine standing, they had to import tutors from Europe in order that all traces of their lowly ancestry as small farmers, merchants, and stock-jobbers could be removed and social graces, befitting their newly attained positions, be acquired. Naturally, they were fond of exhibiting themselves in the "market places" where the masses could look on with reverential awe. Why be rich, asked these plutocrats, if the garb of obscurity could not be cast aside? "Into the large cities of the East," writes Beard in his *Rise of American Civilization,* "there moved an ever growing army of those who had gathered from the mines of California, from the forges of Pittsburgh, from the forests of Michigan, from the . . . mountains of Montana, wealth beyond the dreams of Midas."

While Big Business promoted widespread prosperity in Germany and in the United States, it contributed to the gradual economic decline of a great rival—England. This decline was first evidenced by a protracted depression between 1873 and 1888. During these years a general lowering of prices in agriculture and industry brought ruin to many capitalists, stockholders, and farmers. Unemployment struck so rapidly that during the height of the depression one man out of ten was without work. Imports increased, and, what was even more serious, British manufacturing supremacy was challenged by foreign countries. This state of affairs the Victorians could not ignore.

Numerous inventions in the iron and steel industries help to explain England's industrial troubles. In the eighties science enabled cheap steel to supplant expensive iron as the basic material of trade. Thus, English iron production received a serious, if temporary, setback. German and American industries expanded rapidly, and, to compete, England was forced at great expense to scrap the obsolete machinery in her iron-manufacturing plants.

In the seventies and eighties British industry suffered when Germany, Holland, and the United States adopted the gold standard. As a result of this action the total amount of money in use was reduced. Lacking good mines to replenish the gold supply, England experienced a definite falling off in prices, which in turn discouraged business enterprises. Construction in the field of transportation declined. Europe was no longer placing large steel orders to be used in the building of new railroads. A boom in steamship construction had come to an end. Ships were larger in size and fewer in number, and every inch of space in the boats was used to advantage. The revival of shipping competition through the development of merchant marines by means of subsidies and other governmental aids in

France, Germany, and Austria, for example, contributed to the decline of British shipbuilding and British shipping.

Nationalism in other countries did much to retard British trade. Bismarck, influenced by patriotic motives, became a protectionist, and by tariffs he practically closed German markets to certain British goods. Consequently, free-trade England was afflicted by a double misfortune: exclusion of some of her manufactured products from all countries adopting a protective tariff and the submerging of her unprotected markets by cheap goods manufactured in other industrial nations.

Agriculture as well as industry suffered during the depression. Free trade enabled foreign countries, especially the United States, to flood British markets with quantities of grain. Agricultural prices fell, and the English farmer, who was paying high rents and had invested considerable capital in the development of his farm lands, was unable to sell his products profitably. Thousands left the farms and went to the cities. Many became small farmers and existed by raising perishable products such as vegetables, fruits, and even flowers. The large landowner tried to survive by adopting the latest labor-saving devices and farming on a large scale. Agriculture in England had received what seemed to be a permanent setback.

In 1895 the Conservatives, who had replaced the Liberals in control of the government, decided that the revival of imperialism would end the depression. They therefore looked overseas for markets, raw materials, and economic opportunities. They fixed their eyes on South Africa, where gold had been discovered. There Cecil Rhodes had become a millionaire from his gold and diamond mines. The Boers alone stood in the way of complete British exploitation of that region. Soon, the imperialist seeds which Disraeli had sown were bearing fruit. England, now conscious of her destiny, was convinced that the British Empire was the world's greatest instrument for good. With Conservative approval, the war broke out between the Boers and Great Britain in 1899; by 1902 the Boer states had lost their independence and were a part of the British Empire.

Despite labor troubles, industry experienced a definite economic recovery between 1890 and 1914. Imperialistic advances, resulting in an influx of gold and an increase of raw materials and economic opportunities, helped to raise the general price level and thus promoted industrial expansion. British industrial supremacy, however, was never regained. During this period Germany and the United States had continuous economic expansion and "good times"; in fact, their industries developed more rapidly than did those of England. By 1900 the United States produced more pig-iron, steel, and coal than England. British increase in the exportation of cotton and machinery was not as great as it had been in the past, and the tendency on the part of foreign customers to use local deposits and to substitute oil for coal indicated a possible diminution in the coal industry.

At the opening of the twentieth century England was dependent upon foreign nations for food. Her population was over three-quarters urban and unable to live upon necessities raised at home. She therefore had to rely upon her shipping, her investment resources, and her exportations to pay for this imported food. Competition in these fields by foreign states, however, made it increasingly difficult for Great Britain to maintain a satisfactory balance of trade.

To compete with the great industrial combines or cartels of Germany and to end cut-throat competition at home, British industrialists finally decided to establish great corporations. The first of these formed in the early nineties was the huge Brunner-Monod Salt Union and consisted of about sixty-four competing firms. By 1900 the Coats's Sewing-Cotton organization had been established with a capital of 10,000,000 pounds and a virtual monopoly throughout England. Imitations of the German cartels and the American trusts sprang up in England as the movement in favor of large units of production gained headway. Shipping "rings," whereby steamship companies made monopolistic agreements in which they divided up the trade routes and paid rebates to merchants who used their lines, came into existence. British industrialists were engaged in a desperate attempt to regain their former supremacy when the World War interrupted for a while the international economic conflict.

Because of its very largeness—war or no war—Big Business

seemed destined to decline. Before 1914 many petty bourgeoisie in all industrial countries opposed the selfish aristocracy. To be sure, these dissatisfied groups admitted that plutocracy had benefited society by introducing technical improvements, labor-saving devices, efficient management, and often lower prices. They admitted, moreover, that mass production had frequently brought luxuries within the reach of the man with moderate incomes. Nevertheless, they maintained, these benefits were insignificant in comparison to the great evil—a new economic serfdom—inflicted upon society by Big Business. This evil, insisted many middle-class men, must be eradicated, otherwise the entire capitalistic system was doomed. What characterized this new serfdom, how the petty bourgeoisie, backs to the wall, resisted it, and how capitalism finally was tested in the crucible of the World War and in the post-war era now remain to be seen.

Chapter XXII

BOURGEOIS BACKS TO THE WALL

The United States and England

The middle class occupies a high and respected position in any society. . . . Destroy it and then is destroyed the backbone of a country (Lewis W. Douglas).

Before the Great Depression, even before the Great Struggle, the middle classes began to feel uneasy about the future, to peer ahead with shaken optimism, fearful of certain vaguely looming forces which might stop their headlong race toward prosperity, prestige, and security. True to the saying that "Uneasy lies the head that wears the crown," some of these heads, especially the petty bourgeoisie, began wagging pessimistically in anticipation of the relentless march of big monopolies.

It was these same business elements who were most uncertain of their destination and their destiny. As classes go, they were quite new, born in the welter of the Religious and Economic Revolutions, grown to a precocious maturity in the cradle of nineteenth-century liberalism, imperialism, international expansion, and general well-being; but, all this once said, they were still on the borderline, still as far from true bourgeois-hood as they were close to the proletariat. A half century before, S. G. Perkins pinned them down as those persons "who possess a capital, either in money's worth or education, but are yet obliged to work for their maintenance. This body is distinguished from the aristocratic or privileged class, which lives or can live upon income from capital, without work, and from the laboring class, strictly speaking, which subsists by wage-labor and possesses little or no capital." Apparently the new middle class included the smaller *entrepreneur* in industry and trade, the small producer of goods, the official and salaried employee, lying between the capitalistic plutocracy (trust bourgeoisie) and the proletariat; the small farmer or owner of land; and such others as artisans, clerks, teachers, and professional people.

What blocked the road for this group was the economic strangulation brought about by the mechanization of industry and the rise of Big Business. Small enterprises, unable to compete with gigantic concerns, sell out. Result: thousands of small shopkeepers, out of work, join the ranks of the wage-earners. The cost of living keeps rising; taxes mount; wages fall; the labor market becomes unsettled; securities act unpredictably. A depression, then another, and another. Those dispossessed, squeezed by these apparently uncontrollable economic forces, become more and more uncomfortable, more and more insecure, and as a consequence more and more dependent upon the financial lords for their livelihood. In the eighties some of the English middle classes, however, like their American brothers before the World War, were quite optimistic. They still believed that there was room at the top; all a man had to do was to keep on the move and make a place for himself. To the English writer, T. C. Vebbel, consequently, the whole middle class, compared with the plutocrats above and the proletariat below, represented "a surging restless mass of individuals always fighting for a place, eager at least to secure as good a one as their parents occupied before them and to give their children the same advantages as they enjoyed themselves."

Handicapping the efforts of the middle classes at large to better their conditions was the fact that they were not able at first to win the workers as close allies. The plutocracy and the proletariat constituted separate orders held together by many ties: by community of interests, habits, and pursuits; by common memories and a common past. With regard to the middle classes the reverse was true. They did not constitute an order or a class bound together by any *recognized* ties or *conscious* of any continuous ancestry. They were unaware of any great brotherhood in which they could find moral support under the pressure of material misfortune. In the middle classes every man was for himself. He knew nothing of his neighbor; the latter's affairs did not concern him. The whole class was an agglomeration of individuals recognizing no common interests or unifying elements.

The economic position a middle-class man had won for himself was absolutely all that he had. If he lost that he lost everything. Therefore, he, more than any one else in society, feared a revolution. "The aristocrat and plutocrat might fight his way through it and ride upon the whirlwind. But the man with a little fortune in bonds or invested in a small business enterprise knew that if political convulsions went beyond a certain point his ruin would make him a pauper or a beggar." Bourgeois life, more than any other type, promoted conservatism. Acquisition of property was the basic aim, and selfishness was apt to be the dominant characteristic in industry and in commerce as well as in social life. Utopia was purely personal—a state where one would be economically independent and socially prominent.

English and American middle classes were unanimous in their dislike of vested privilege. Resentful at these industrial and money pirates, doubting the assertions that great enterprises caused greater employment, lowered the cost of living, and made prosperity possible, the workers and the middle class often combined against their masters. In the United States this alliance resulted in the Populist movement of the late nineteenth century. Determined to protect small property these bourgeois and rural "radicals" advocated government ownership of railroads, telephones, and telegraphs, governmental regulation of monopolies, and reduction of great wealth by the imposition of inheritance and income taxes. In the eighties William Graham Sumner, aware of the antagonism to Big Business, in his essay, "The Forgotten Man" (*Essays of William Graham Sumner,* Yale University Press, New Haven, 1934), urged common action on the part of the little rich, the small farmers, and the workers against the plutocrats. A few years later (1887) the selection of the Interstate Commerce Commission marked the first of a series of state and federal acts designed to regulate Big Business. The Sherman Anti-Trust Law of 1890, the dissolution of the Northern Securities Company in 1903, and similar legislation within the jurisdiction of the states, were a part of this attempt to protect the little fellow against the big boy. By abandoning the policy of non-intervention in business the government did much to prevent the great corporations from dictating the terms on which they would deal openly with producers, distributors, and consumers and enabled the middle classes to retain a large part of their self-sufficiency, independence and security. Big Business, however, was not destroyed.

By 1904 the lineup against monopolies included leaders in American intellectual and political life. Ida Tarbell, in 1904, outlined the unsavory and corrupt career of the outstanding Octopus by tracing the *History of the Standard Oil Company*. Scandals, corruption, and other misdoings involving the trusts were soon a matter of common knowledge. The panic of 1907 in Wall Street brought President Theodore Roosevelt in direct conflict with the capitalists. Calling them "malefactors of great wealth," he became the leader of that middle-class movement against monopolies, known as "trust-busting." President Wilson was the last pre-war leader of the petty bourgeoisie. By means of the Federal Trade Commission, the Clayton Act, and the Federal Reserve System he tried to reëstablish competition, to revive the small independent enterprises, and to destroy control of credit by the big financial lords.

But it was in England that middle-class resentment against privilege reached its zenith. Moved by high taxes and the growing insecurity both of small business enterprises and of jobs, the middle classes united with the proletariat in attacking the landowning aristocrats and the plutocrats. Surprisingly, the alliance brought about an attempt to introduce state-help in economic enterprises. Motivated by the discontent of the masses, many British bourgeois leaders finally realized that the doctrine of *laissez faire* would have to yield to a program of social reform. The upshot was control of the government by the Liberals in 1905. Changing conditions had forced the latter into a position in which their chief concern was turned from debate over political freedom and religious toleration to consideration of the lot of the lower classes, whose condition they were determined to improve even though the individualism of Adam Smith would have to be thrown overboard in the process.

Clever Welsh attorney and "dare devil" statesman, David Lloyd George (1863–   ) became the leader of the bourgeois-proletariat alliance. Reared in poverty, he showed in early youth a violent abhorrence of the privileged Anglican or state church and the selfish "ramparts of wealth," the great land-owners. Scorn and rage grew in his youthful heart whenever he heard the well-known anonymous couplet:

God bless the squire and his relations
And keep us in our proper stations.

Elected to Parliament, he determined to dethrone these "privileged institutions" and to help the masses. As the champion of a more democratic England, he believed that capitalism was doomed unless the condition of the working classes was ameliorated. So he grasped the flaming torch of reform and cried for followers.

The time was ripe. Until 1905 few social reforms involving direct governmental aid had penetrated England. In 1885 Gladstone looked with horror upon "what they [the reformers] call construction—that is to say, taking into the hands of the state the business of an individual man." Imperialism, during the conservative régime (1895–1905), silenced any movement in this direction. Consequently, the only relief the masses had received was in the form of legislation against abuses in the industrial system, usually in the form of factory laws. In 1902 this legislation was unified in a single code comprising the chief laws enacted in the nineteenth century and new legislation designed to improve the lot of the workers. This factory legislation and mining code, passed by Parliament in 1906, forbade employment of children under twelve in a factory, regulated hours of work of those from twelve to eighteen, provided for supervision of factory sanitation, and prohibited employment of women and children in mines.

Factory legislation, however, did not obviate the problems of poverty and unemployment. Many humanitarians, especially Lloyd George, felt that these conditions had to be attacked on a broader basis. The Poor Law, under which poverty was a crime, and which had no provision for sickness or old age, had collapsed. These liberal bourgeois leaders knew that the precariousness of living must be obliterated. But how could this be done? Without hesitating, Lloyd George accepted the leadership and, like Bismarck, fought the spread of radicalism by introducing beneficial social legislation.

During the eight years preceding the World War, the government tried to give the people security against misfortune. Friendless old Britons in 1908 were granted a small pension at the age of seventy. Those who were sick were aided by an insurance scheme (1911) maintained by contributions of the employer, the employee, and the state. The government was unable, however, to do anything about employment. A plan was proposed whereby in certain selected trades a fund would be set up to support persons temporarily out of work. Many Conservative leaders felt that this plan would encourage idleness, while certain influential labor leaders were dissatisfied with the contributing feature of the project, believing that the worker had a "right to maintenance." Consequently, unemployment legislation was not passed. By enacting other social reforms, however, the Liberal government did give the masses a feeling of economic certainty which they had hitherto lacked.

There were numerous critics of this social program. To the representatives of socialism and syndicalism these reforms were insufficient. Believing that the state should completely abandon the historic *laissez faire* doctrine and engage actively in the solution of labor difficulties, they demanded, as immediate steps, the nationalization of certain key industries and the initiation of graduated income taxes. The Conservatives, representing the landowners and wealthy business groups, also denounced the Liberal program, although for other reasons. They claimed that the provisions of the reform acts, especially unemployment insurance, resulted in higher governmental expenditures, which the government met by overtaxing the landowners and industrial leaders.

Lloyd George, when he introduced his budget bill of 1909, had launched an attack upon the landed aristocrats and wealthy capitalists. In his opinion, these property owners were best able to pay a considerable part of the taxes levied by the government. "The ownership of land," he said, "is not merely an enjoyment, it is a stewardship. . . . Why should I put burdens on the people? I am one of the children of the people." In this budget Lloyd George used all of the old taxes, such as those on income, inheritance, liquor, and tobacco; and in addition he placed heavier taxes on large incomes and on liquor licenses. A plan for taxing land was innovated whereby the government appropriated a part of the "unearned increment." A tax was imposed on the increase in value of land not due to improvements, upon undeveloped and idle real estate, and upon incomes from mining holdings. Those who inherited or were given lands were to pay a special levy, but no taxes were to be imposed upon property used for agricultural purposes.

Indignation to these proposals on the part of landowners and wealthy middle classes rose to such a pitch that many sincere Christians were surprised that "Heaven" did not strike dead such a wicked man as Lloyd George "before he could accomplish his fell purpose in the ruin of his country." Supported, however, by the masses, this astute reformer succeeded in passing his bill through the House of Commons by a tremendous majority. The House of Lords, however, disapproved of this unparalleled taxation and claimed that the budget was "something more than a money bill." Therefore, even though the House of Commons had passed the bill, the Lords decided to delay its enactment by refusing to sanction it before it had been referred to the people at a special election. This stand of the House of Lords resulted in the passing of the Parliament Act of 1911 by which the House of Commons received virtually complete authority, the nobles merely retaining the right to delay legislation by a limited veto power.

In addition to opposing social reforms Conservatives long disapproved of the education of the masses, believing that knowledge would foster much dissatisfaction and radicalism. Under Gladstone, however, the famous Forster Act (1870) established a national system of popular education. In 1902 a bill was passed which transferred control of the state schools from local authorities to the county or borough council. Private institutions were to receive government support. The two systems (private and public schools) were coördinated in relation to the school population, and both were held to the same standard of work. This Act aroused the disapproval of those who believed in secular education. Laws passed between 1876 and 1899 governed other matters, such as compulsory attendance for children under twelve years of age. In 1906 Lloyd George, supported by Laborites who advocated secular education, introduced a bill which recognized only state schools as a part of a national educational system. In these institutions there was to be neither religious instruction nor a religious examination for teachers. The bill was vetoed by the House of Lords.

These reforms, together with the law providing for the care of the unemployed, were a departure from the old principle of *laissez faire*. To most Conservatives, Lloyd George was simply conforming to the desire of the Laborites and Socialists to take much that concerned the Englishman's daily life out of the hands of the individual and put it into the hands of the state. In reply to this accusation Lloyd George and his Liberal followers declared that, unless the government intervened to aid those who could not help themselves, socialism would supplant capitalism. Expounding the doctrine that, if the poor need assistance, the rich should pay, the bourgeois Liberals therefore erected in England a framework for state socialism. By so doing they hoped to eliminate the privileges of plutocracy, improve the lot of the proletariat, and check the decline of the middle classes.

Chapter XXIII

BOURGEOIS BACKS TO THE WALL

Europe

Just as, therefore, at an earlier period a section of the nobility went over to the bourgeoisie, so now a section of the bourgeoisie goes over to the proletariat. . . . The lower middle class, the small manufacturer, the shopkeeper, the artisan, the peasant, all these fight against the bourgeoisie, to save from extinction their existence as fractions of the middle class (*Marx and Engels,* The Communist Manifesto).

EUROPEAN nations, as well as England and the United States, were faced by vital social deviations prior to 1914. Unlike the English-speaking people, however, the Europeans recognized a definite bourgeois predicament and tried to face it. "Everyone today," said a European administrator in 1896, "is interested in the material and moral improvement of the working class, and rightly so, because the cause is just, and the future of society is concerned in it. But the maintenance, the prosperity of the middle classes is a cause no less just, and the general interest requires that this cause should not be ignored."

Before the turn of the century a gradually increasing number of governmental officials and economists were aware of the business situation. Economic liberty and technological and industrial developments in the nineteenth century had endowed men with capital, especially the active, bold, gifted, shrewd individuals. They were able to concentrate in their hands the manufacture and transportation of goods on a large scale at a cheap price. Aided by advertising and often by questionable political machinations, they had formed trusts and cartels, which had frozen out the little fellow. Reaping tremendous profits by means of these virtual monopolies, the industrialists pointed the way to the even more unscrupulous financial capitalists of the twentieth century, with their holding companies and investment concerns.

Concentration of products, rendered possible by scientific progress and economic liberty, brought into being the large department stores. In these vast caverns of merchandise the consumer saved both time and money, for Big Business aimed to sell everything in one place at a "favorable price." Indeed, "motorized power" in the twentieth century enabled Big Business to manufacture, to sell, and to invest on a large scale. The small industry, store, and bank seemed destined to disappear.

The law of concentration, however, was helpful to the proletariat. It enabled them to organize by bringing them together in large concerns and making them first craft, and then class, conscious. Consequently, they formed unions to aid in obtaining better wages and working conditions, and coöperatives to enable them to purchase necessary articles at cheaper prices. These coöperatives, like the department stores, injured the small merchant. In short, by 1914, Big Business, Big Stores, and Big Coöperatives threatened the very existence of the petty bourgeoisie. Lacking sufficient capital, political power, and organization, this class, discouraged, faced a very uncertain future.

Concentration of wealth and the growth of Big Business were accompanied in industrial countries by a decrease in numbers and in wealth of the middle classes. Small business enterprises simply could not compete with the great corporations. They were unable to purchase raw materials in large quantities and thus to obtain the discounts given to the corporations. Sufficient credit not being available, they could not improve their concerns by the introduction of the latest machinery. Consequently, they were unable to meet the low prices of the large companies in the sale of goods. For these and other reasons many small merchants and industrialists were forced out of business, and most of them became members of the propertyless, jobless, or wage-earning classes.

Exponents of Big Business, however, doubted this disaster to the petty bourgeoisie. In their opinion, capitalism offered the "little fellow" new opportunities, such as advertising, installing, distributing, and repairing the goods produced in large factories. Moreover, there was still a great field for the small manufacturer in the production of artistic goods which could not be made by machines. Nevertheless, the majority of men belonging to the middle classes felt that Big Business was responsible for their economic perplexities.

This decline of the "little fellows," in the opinion of many people, threatened the very existence of the capitalistic order. A harmonious society, according to Senator Cooreman of Belgium, required that "a stable middle class exist to connect the capitalist and the wage-earning groups." The decline of the petty bourgeoisie constituted a problem as important as that of the working class. "Indeed," he maintained, "the disappearance or the weakening of this intermediary group would be disastrous to the nation and to organized society."

This statement of the condition of the middle classes well described the situation in the rich industrialized countries in 1908, according to an Italian writer, Magaldi. In certain parts of Italy, he asserted, the middle classes, especially the small merchants and manufacturers, were becoming less important and, unless something were done, that class would soon disappear. "Therefore, we must study this bourgeois problem, try to help this bulwark of our society, and endeavor to harmonize the relations between the various social classes, so that a reign of justice and social peace will be achieved."

But the "little fellows" were not passively accepting their threatened extermination. Even while Magaldi wrote, the bourgeoisie, backs to the wall, often submerging class differences against a common foe, were stubbornly resisting further inroads and, at times, even making sorties into the enemy's camp. Progressive Belgium led all the European states in attempting to stave off class extinction. More methodical, more liberal, and more scientific than Austria, France, or Germany, she slowed down, repulsed, and then advanced against the political malefactors.

As far back as 1878 the process of common coöperation began when guilds of business trades were founded, composed of workers and small owners and resembling the medieval corporations, to be followed in 1892, by the "General Syndicate of employees, business men, and owners," with a membership of 8,000. Numerous associations were organized for the study and defense of bourgeois interests, culminating in 1899, when a bureau was subsidized in Belgium for the express purpose of promoting economic and professional associations or syndicates among small business men and industrialists. In the next nine years, four great congresses of the middle classes, meeting in Antwerp, Liége, Ghent, and Nemours, scrutinized the scientific and economic aspects involved in stabilization of the bourgeois order. Royal decrees and national investigations followed, all with the objective of finding means for improving conditions for the middle classes. One result was that in 1903, the Belgian Parliament set up a department to promote technical education, mechanization of industry in small concerns, national professional associations, and trade syndicates. Another forward step was the royal decree of 1906 whereby a Bureau was formed to deal with middle-class problems in connection with the Ministry of Industry and Labor. This organization gathered and classified information concerning the small trades and business enterprises and the economic condition of the persons belonging to them.

All kinds of activities affecting the middle classes were considered by the Bureau. It studied the laws dealing with these classes everywhere, prepared new laws and regulations, and saw that all legislation was enforced. It investigated such problems as the professional training of children and young people in schools, offices, stores, and homes; technical procedure and useful employment; ways and means of acquiring raw materials; methods of selling goods; associations of economic character formed among artisans, employees, small industrialists and business men; credit institutions and taxes; and the other "encumbrances of the middle classes." By means of numerous lectures and publications the Bureau did much to popularize various measures designed to help the business classes. Unions of professional men, syndicates, and various coöperative societies were encouraged, especially the organization of credit institutions to help the "little fellow."

Professional congresses, backed by the Belgian government, grew more prolific. In 1905 eleven assemblages were held, representing such industries as baking, lumber, iron, printing, plumbing, wigmaking, and watchmaking; and in 1907 occurred an International Congress of breadmakers, shoe manufacturers, painters, tailors, watch and jewelry makers.

Governmental investigations of economic and social life also delved into the situation of the petty bourgeoisie. Austria, in 1893, Germany, in 1895, and Belgium, in 1902, appointed commissions to undertake this work. These commissions considered such matters as education and professional training, businessmen's organizations, introduction of useful machinery, the holding of expositions, the matter of credit, patent legislation, customs duties, and pertinent business jurisprudence and legislation. They published volumes on these and such other subjects as auction sales, voluntary liquidations, abuses of usury, legislation limiting personal liberty, free travel on railroads, bankruptcy, and expansion of public works.

While Belgium took the lead in the movement to preserve the middle classes, other states were not far behind. As far back as 1877, economic license had been decried in Germany by certain bourgeois representatives in the *Reichstag* who pleaded for the limitation of individualism and the renaissance with government aid of industrial coöperatives or guilds in which the relationship of the masters, journeymen, and apprentices would be regulated as in medieval days. Many guilds were formed; and in some parts of Germany all industries, even though they did not join the coöperatives, had to obey the guild rules. In short, these organizations ran the economic life of the community. Life blood was injected into middle-class enterprises by the systematic organization of credit facilities. As early as 1850, the government formed the "Prussian central banks of coöperative associations." Industries carried the principle of coöperation further by purchasing the raw material and machinery in common, then selling the products jointly.

In fact, as these efforts illustrate, the middle classes, even though they lacked political power, possessed real economic vitality in Germany. Nevertheless, Big Business, as usual having the upper hand, pushed the "small fry" gradually down the ladder. Consequently, at the turn of the century, the petty industrialists and bourgeois merchants were fighting to retain their enterprises and struggling against the tide of heavy taxes which was constantly beating them back. They shouted in vain to the government for aid, but in their opinion the government seemed more concerned with the difficulties of the proletariat than their troubles.

This attitude of partiality to the proletariat and comparative indifference to the petty bourgeoisie struck fire, as was typical in all Europe, from the Catholic Center Party. Its leaders insisted on an investigation which would throw light on the defects of commercial training and the conditions of the merchant syndicates; and they suggested that a determined attempt be made by the *Reichstag* to ascertain the needs of the small merchants, artisans, and traders. Their policy, known as *Mittelstandspolitik,* gave rise in 1907 to an association of middle classes called the *Deutsche Mittelstandsvereinigung.* In a meeting held that year the delegates discussed a wide variety of significant subjects, such as the need of middle-class representation in the government, the necessity of getting the *Reichstag* to back legislation dealing with credit, stimulation of the building trades, extension of the pension system, insurance of private employees, measures in favor of widows and of orphans, and formation of a chamber of labor to regulate such matters as strikes and boycotts. Supplementing this assemblage, in the same year, a general congress of corporations and trades, known as the *Allgemeiner Deutscher Innungs und Handwerkertag,* gathered at Eisenach. The partisans dealt largely with the labor situation and encouraged the establishment of federations of owners to curb conflicts and strikes. They investigated the matter of credit in the building trades. They suggested the election of more artisan representation in the *Reichstag* as well as of more delegates representing the bourgeoisie. They sought successfully for the establishment of an imperial Bureau of Trades; in Prussia, Bavaria, Württemberg, and Baden such organizations soon appeared.

Austria experienced a middle-class movement, the main manifestation being the establishment by law in 1883 and 1887 of the coöperative idea. To a lesser degree Holland, Switzerland, England, and the Scandinavian nations nurtured sentiments for betterment of the position of small business men. In 1907 a national congress of the petty bourgeoisie was held at Amsterdam, consideration being given to credit, bourgeois organizations, and such similar matters as before enumerated. Meanwhile, the Dutch government instituted a general investigation of business conditions to consider especially the friction of the professions, the purchase and sale of goods, unfair competition, and legislation. In England, the disorganized trading classes managed to establish in 1906 a defense organization and a paper, *The Elector,* to fight socialism.

Not until 1905 did France produce a real middle-class offensive. Earlier evidence of similar discontent, however, can be found. Following the fall of Napoleon, large stores were established. Small shopkeepers soon protested. A certain number of retail business men tried to meet this new competition by grouping themselves into "workhouse units," toward which each merchant would contribute his share of the rent and other costs of upkeep in proportion to the size of his place. The object was to give the public the benefits of concentration, variety, quality, and quantity of goods. But these groups, called the *Palais Bonne-Nouvelle,* and the *Bazar de l'Industrie,* failed, largely because the various merchants refused to coöperate. Fear of the Big Stores, however, persisted, taking the form in 1880 of an agitation to tax them. Similar attempts were made in 1883 and 1886 without success. In 1887 the *Crise Commerciale,* a newspaper, was founded, and proceeded to oppose the "monopoly of several business firms" and advocated the closing of these by high taxes. In 1888 a syndicate or league for the defense of the interests of labor, industry, and commerce was started, and its newspaper announced a program of resistance "to financial feudalism which is constituted by monopoly without restraint by the capitalists whose *Grand Magasins de Paris* are the most flagrant expression." The league planned, by protecting the middle classes, to give the salaried people and workers an opportunity to obtain positions and to become employers.

A Commercial and Industrial Party was organized and was followed by other associations which, besides arbitrating disputes between members, investigated tax accounts, old-age pensions, and the purchasing of goods in common. Economic unions were formed to fight large firms which sold on credit and by subscription (installment buying). However, in 1905 the first large-scale middle-class movement rose out of general objection to the government's income tax, when an association for common defense, composed of more than 1500 syndicates with over 600,000 members, was established.

Before the World War, France was worried about "feudalistic capitalism which was growing, the middle classes who were dying, and the proletariat who were crowding into cities and towns." Although certain writers maintained that the petty bourgeoisie were not on the decline, most of them believed that if Big Business continued to expand the middle classes would disappear and a collectivist or socialist society would be the final result. To save themselves from ruin and France from socialism the bourgeoisie began to organize. By 1910 they had formed the Society of Social Economy, had established newspapers, and were advocating political and social changes. All measures were designed to help the small landowner, the small industrialist, and the small merchant and professional man—the independent, autonomous producers.

As a result of these measures, the French business men before the war were engaged in a desperate attack upon Big Business. The Association for the Defense of the Middle Classes, founded in 1907 in France, dedicated itself to the goal of reawakening the bourgeoisie, spreading propaganda against current abuses and in defense of human rights through lectures, pamphlets, assemblies, and congresses. The abolition of monopolies and heavy taxes was its chief aim. Bills designed to change tax rates so that the plutocrats would pay a more just amount, and measures levied against governmental regulations and against monopolies were discussed in the legislative houses.

Better business schools, effective business methods, abolition of price cutting, limitation of selling on credit, and prompt collection of bills were some of the aims of the potent middle-class organization.

Money was needed to lubricate the rusty wheels of bourgeois enterprises. Small industries did not have the means of renting or purchasing new machinery or labor-saving devices. Filling the want, "Popular Banks," in which the little business men owned stock, were set up with the purpose of furnishing them ample credit.

Between 1903–1909 the "Save the Bourgeoisie" campaign became international. The leader was Doctor Boediker, a German who had been deeply interested in social legislation for workers. Under his guidance an International Institute for the Study of the Problems of the Middle Classes was established at Stuttgart in 1904. Non-political, this Institute now resolved to investigate the situation of these classes in other countries and the methods adopted to improve their conditions. All governmental acts and documents relative to the types of associations, syndicates, and credit institutions being established were to be collected. In short, the Institute was to assemble all material pertaining to this investigation.

This organization had representatives, honorary and active, for the European states. Apparently, the society was of European origin and concern; its membership consisted of delegates from Prussia, Württemberg, Bavaria, Saxony, the "Sovereign German States," Austria, Belgium, Spain, France, Italy, Luxemburg, Holland, Switzerland, and Russia. These representatives met annually in general sessions which consisted of meetings of the central committee and also gatherings of the members.

Prior to the outbreak of the World War, this Institute made considerable progress in its study of the middle classes. Committees investigated the situation in the various countries of Central Europe and wrote valuable monographs on such subjects as credit for the business men, "professional unions," and the latest and best methods in such bourgeois activities as tailoring, merchandising, lumber-selling, butchering, and baking. To facilitate the spread of the latest information on business methods, prizes were offered for the best essays on the use of credit and business practices, on buying and selling, on the commercial and financial technique of large stores, and on the relations between producer and consumer. A monthly bulletin enabled the members to keep in touch with what was going on in all countries. Finally, all laws affecting the bourgeois interests were studied and beneficial changes were recommended.

International Congresses, designed to save the middle classes, were held at various times. The first meeting was at Liége in August of 1905. Doctor Boediker, first president of the Institute, also presided over the Congress, and representatives from the German Empire, Prussia, Saxony, the Grand Duchy of Baden, the Free Cities of Lübeck, Bremen, and Hamburg, Alsace-Lorraine, Austria, Australia, Belgium, Bulgaria, China, Spain, Hungary, Italy, Luxemburg, Mexico, Holland, Portugal, and Rumania attended the inaugural meeting. At this Congress such topics as professional training education, the improvement of machinery, the study of the technique of department stores, and the credit situation as affecting the middle classes were discussed.

Between 1905–1909 congresses were held at Vienna and Salzburg. The second meeting at Vienna of the International Congress of the Middle Classes, under the patronage of the International Institute (1908), was especially outstanding. In addition to discussing thoroughly professional education and coöperative mercantile and industrial organizations, this assembly considered rural and urban credit, the protection of regional home industry, housing for the middle classes, insurance for the aged and the incapacitated, and the relation of trades in regard to the building industry.

During the first decade of the twentieth century International Expositions (or Fairs) and International Congresses were staged for and by the bourgeoisie, lavishly displaying its activity, industry, progress, and achievement. For example, at the Liége Exposition in the early twentieth century the professional associations of the middle-class trades had exhibits. The National Federation of Bakers demonstrated mechanical baking in action, showing the electrical machines, which the government by lectures, publications, and direct subsidies was trying to introduce in bread-making. Tapestry masters, upholsterers, and furniture-makers—all had beautiful booths. In the exhibit of the watchmakers' association alone hundreds of thousands of francs had been invested by the small industries. In addition to the displays of the professional organizations there were numerous exhibitions of "tools of the bourgeois trades," showing the latest motors and machines. Inspired by this particular feature of the fair, Count de Mailáth declared: "The domestic hearth and the occupations offer greater and purer happiness than ever before." In his opinion the machine age would witness the rise, not the fall, of the small business man.

These various expositions and fairs were significant because they indicated that by 1907 the interests of the middle classes in the leading European countries were far from unforgotten. Through bourgeois movements and bourgeois representation or domination in government, the various leaders were determined to preserve the business interests and thus to save the capitalistic system. They realized by now that failure would mean a large restless proletariat and a small potent plutocracy. Then the revolution predicted by Karl Marx might occur, and the established order be overthrown.

In 1914 the bourgeois movement seemed to have as its objectives the removal of oppressive capitalism and the checking of organized labor. These were to be achieved through control of the state by "little fellows" or by erecting a bourgeois "state within a state." Thus the middle-class organization, although its aim was chiefly economic, could evolve to a point where it would be dominantly political. Many far-sighted men, however, maintained that their organization should not try to ruin Big Business by unfair legislation and by appeals to the government for aid. They realized that the state could destroy the large concerns by heavy taxes; but they also saw that high taxes would be a danger to all. Therefore, the middle classes should merely ask the government to give them the aid that the workers had received. In other words, the state should investigate conditions, obtain information, and help the little traders form their organizations, so that they could compete with Big Business. In order thus to compete, however, the "little fellows" should study and imitate the methods of Big Business and, by buying and selling in common and by arranging for ample credit, be able to reduce prices and fight the enemy on even terms. Thus, by forming associations and by adopting the methods of Large Scale Industry, the middle classes, many believed, would survive. As real bourgeoisie, therefore, they alone, their backs to the wall, must work out their own economic salvation from this industrial serfdom.

Big Business at first adopted an indifferent, if not a sneering attitude toward this flurry of activity by the petty bourgeoisie. Warm advocates of competition within the nation, the great industrialists seemed determined to eliminate the less fit and to establish a concentration of wealth through monopolies which would depersonalize industry and would dominate the nation. Entirely out of sympathy with the bourgeois liberals who wanted to give the little fellow a chance, these ambitious and often unscrupulous plutocrats probably felt that they, as the nobility of capitalism, were to head a capitalistic hierarchy. Moreover, these new aristocrats did not fear the little Babbitts, because the latter were dependent upon the banks for credit and the banks were practically controlled by the plutocrats. Well organized and in control of public opinion by their indirect influence through advertising in the leading newspapers, the plutocrats actually believed that they were the salt of the earth.

In their international competition, however, certain buccaneers of Big Business encountered stiff opposition. To prevent such foreign rivalry in their home markets, Big Business in the United States, Germany, France, and other states had its governments pass protective tariffs. But there was always the danger of financial crises and depressions, accompanied by a fall in prices, a decline in consumption of manufactured goods, and an increase in unemployment, poverty, crime, and radicalism. Nevertheless, Big Business, blinded by the Almighty Dollar, refused to recognize the need for any thoroughgoing reform. Enthusiastic advocates of that kind of liberty and individualism which had originated in the jungles, they reached out for markets and plunder. Imperialism to them seemed to be the only way out; partly for this reason the second outburst of modern expansion came in the third quarter of the nineteenth century. This newer imperialism may be defined as Benevolent Piracy. Far transcending the older form in virulence and subtlety, it was less concerned with the acquisition of subject peoples and territories than with the control of their raw materials, mineral resources, markets, and economic opportunities and potentialities.

Although the costs of these imperialistic ventures, especially of wars, were borne by the many, only a few enjoyed the direct profits. Such groups as exporters, importers, shippers, and those imperialists dependent on colonial raw products and markets, as well as manufacturers of armaments, uniforms, and materials used in colonial development, benefited greatly. Enormous profits, which were reinvested in other imperialist ventures, often accrued to financiers and bankers. Colonial administrators and their families, explorers, adventurers, and missionaries were prone, for various reasons, to support foreign interference in "backward" countries. To promote the acquisition of naval bases and strategic frontiers and the erection of buffer states, military and naval men encouraged imperialism as a mode of defense. Moreover, the display by imperialist powers of large armaments enhanced the prestige of certain men and their personal opportunity for distinction and advancement. Statesmen, such as Disraeli, Ferry, Chamberlain, and Theodore Roosevelt, by appealing to the imperialistic-nationalistic enthusiasm of their patriotic countrymen, improved their own political fortunes. However, the people as a whole—especially the petty bourgeoisie and wage-earning classes—received but indirect and often only theoretical rewards. Usually they were assured that their business, their work, their wages, in fact their entire standard of living, depended upon the maintenance of foreign, including colonial trade.

Unfortunately, this imperialism was accompanied by that

brand of secret diplomacy which frequently resulted in bloody and costly wars. By 1914, Europe was divided into hostile camps maintaining a precarious balance of power. Fearful of the consequences, Big Business as a whole did not want a world war. Therefore, it attempted to settle all imperial rivalries, including the contest over the Near East. But the plutocrats could not control the economic antagonisms and hatreds which constantly endangered the maintenance of the status quo. And when the war finally broke out, nationalism, which had contributed so much to the rise of the bourgeois order, caused most men of all classes, plutocrats, "main streeters," proletarians, and socialists to rally and support their governments. Western civilization had again plunged itself into another historic tragedy—"a struggle of right against right"—the World War.

Chapter XXIV

CAPITALISM IN THE CRUCIBLE

When war ceases, the sense of human brotherhood will be stronger and "heroism" will no longer mean to kill, but only to serve, or save, our fellows (Andrew Carnegie).

War is the crucible of mankind. When cast into its seething caldron nations, people, theories, ideals, beliefs, prejudices are subjected to such a confusion of forces that the ultimate residues are unpredictable. Political and economic eruptions seem to follow in its wake with indefinite, unexpected, frequency. Society seems to simmer uneasily, taking an endless time in settling down.

So the great World War was a titanic struggle of "nations, peoples, theories, ideals, beliefs, prejudices." In it capitalism was put to the test of fire with an outcome left to be described by the historian of tomorrow. In it the middle classes played their typical part; ardent patriots and full of ringing liberal ideals, they gave their sons, their money, their abilities, their enthusiasms to the cause of making the world safe for democracy, i.e., safe for themselves.

Soon, very soon, however, they began to have a foreboding that Sir Edward Grey, Foreign Secretary of England, was right in 1914 when he said: "Whatever the issue, one thing certain is that it will end in ruining industry, commerce, and the power of capital." As the costs pyramided, it became evident that some one would have to foot the bill; by previous experience the middle classes well knew who that would be. Finally, when in 1918 the Central Powers collapsed before the superior human and material resources of the Allies, the bourgeoisie found themselves face to face with the reckoning.

False optimism deluded them at first. With peace the world

apparently was facing a new era. Democracy had been saved; Autocracy had been overcome; Utopia awaited mankind. International and internal debts, falling prices, financial chaos, and radicalism did not daunt the victorious Allies. The only concern of the shortsighted bourgeois representatives seemed to be the territorial and financial settlement with the enemy. Germany and her allies must pay. The result was that Prize Bourgeois Blunder, the ignominious Treaty of Versailles, a document of guilt, robbery, and shackles, which has kept Europe in a state of irritation to the present day.

More even than this spirit of *revanche*, the Russian Revolution of 1917 disturbed the equilibrium of the European bourgeoisie. They welcomed the first phase of the uprising—the overthrow of the old régime—but, when the Bolsheviks obliterated the socialist-bourgeois-provisional government of Kerensky and announced the establishment of a communist state, the bourgeoisie saw that a threatening red cloud had appeared upon the horizon, that they were in danger of being overtaken by a political storm. For, whenever and wherever the economic effects of the war tended to aggravate social unrest, there communism appeared. Determined, therefore, to check the spread of radicalism and to find new fields for economic exploitation, the Allies at the peace settlement developed national sentiments and set up a bulwark of independent states along the Russian frontier. In doing this, they destroyed economic unity in Central Europe, so that financial chaos followed inevitably. The Western bourgeois powers found themselves confronted, as a result, by political, economic, and social problems in that part of the Continent, as well as by the "Russian menace."

Meanwhile, the Russian middle classes (after the Bolshevist Revolution) suffered tremendous hardships. For the first time in history these people, together with the landed aristocrats of the old régime, became the victims of a vengeful proletarian class. Thousands were killed, were exiled to Siberia, or were forced to flee Russia. Most who remained lost their property and their position, and lived in complete poverty and obscurity. A few, possessed of technical skill and willing to conform to the new order, obtained positions as bank officers, engineers, technicians, scholars, and diplomats. But they were the exceptions. Most of the bourgeoisie became the "Dead Souls" of the twentieth century, people without a country.

Currency inflation in almost all the European countries was another direct consequence of the war. One of its first effects was to change the standard of living of the middle classes. This did not, however, affect all sections in the same way. That part of the monied classes which was in a position to pass on the increase in prices to others and to take advantage of the depreciation of the national currency profited greatly. Business men, who could raise prices to meet the fall in the value of money and at the same time use the depreciated currency to pay off their debts, made good use of their opportunities. Owners of real estate also profited by the lower value of money to liquidate their mortgages.

On the other hand, all those who had fixed incomes, or, like the professional men, those who were not in a position to raise their charges as fast as the value of money declined, were being economically strangled. As prices went up, they had to reduce their expenditures more and more, and this could not be done without lowering their standard of living. In Germany, and to a lesser extent in France, England, and Italy, even those who had been very well-to-do before the war found themselves hard pressed.

In France, the cost of the war and of reconstruction produced an inflation which worked great hardships on the middle classes. An examination of the fate of a hypothetical family, having a fortune of 500,000 francs in 1914, will make the situation clear. While in 1924 the total estate of the family would be about the same as in 1914, its income, allowing for the decrease in value of certain investments and the increase in value of others, would be 30,000 francs as against a little more than 23,000 in 1914. The misfortune of this family would reveal itself in the calculation of relative expenditures. In order to maintain the standard of living which, in 1914, cost about 14,000 francs, this family would have to spend 40,000 francs in 1924. Thus a family that had in 1914 a surplus of about

9,000 francs which it could reinvest, if it maintained the same standard of living in 1924 would have a deficit of about 10,000 francs. French middle-class families that were comfortably situated before the war and in the habit of saving a part of their income, by 1924 found themselves in a situation where

> The children can only get a free education, they must go to the local public school; the mother has to cook, wash dishes, scrub, sew, iron, without the help of a servant, even a charwoman; the father is never able to offer the family any recreation—vacation in the country, travel, theater, not even the cinema; and if death, or illness, or house-moving should occur in the family, the budget would be unbalanced for years. In short, it is a situation comparable to that of a workingman (Chilly, *La Classe Moyenne en France après la guerre,* A. Tardy, Bourges, 1924).

Some French speculators and plutocratic industrialists managed to make big profits, but the petty business classes as a whole experienced a definite economic setback. Unable to carry on their enterprises or to live on incomes derived from their various professions, a number left their activities and "became bartenders and bell boys" in order to eke out an existence. Teachers enlisted in the army because the pay (which included free clothes, trips, and articles at reduced prices) was better. An instructor, in becoming a doorkeeper for one of the leading hotels in Paris did this, he said, because he could purchase good food and more books and thus live better physically and intellectually. Abstract research, which made possible such scientists as Pasteur and the Curies, no longer offered the scholar even a living wage. Consequently, many French intellectuals actually feared that there would be an end to scientific progress.

In 1921 pessimistic predictions were the vogue. The ruin of the middle classes seemed inevitable to many; and, inasmuch as the bourgeoisie by their thrift, their sobriety, and their patriotism had built France in the nineteenth century, they believed this social collapse would bring about the fall of their beloved nation. Determined to prevent this catastrophe, bourgeois "Civic Leagues" were organized to stamp out the strikes of the proletariat and to maintain "law, order, and security." A General Confederation of Intellectuals, consisting of engineers, doctors, and other members of the professional classes determined that they would not be crushed between the two extremes—the plutocrats and the proletariat. Therefore, they formed an organization to safeguard their interests. Later, energetic royalists and fascist groups bid for the support of the middle classes. These elements, claiming that the Bolsheviks were worse than the Jacobins of the Great Revolution and that the plutocrats were more foolish than were the newly rich of the Directory, begged for the support of all "loyal" Frenchmen.

The bourgeois landowners as well as the business man was injured as a result of the World War. Prior to the struggle he had leased his land to tenants and had lived off the income. Since the war, inflation and high taxes had forced him to take back the land and try to work it himself. Unable to do this, he often lost his property. As a result, the great conservative bourgeois farming class, brought to the fore during the French Revolution, was practically wiped out of existence. Meanwhile, the bourgeois peasant, or small farmer, also found it difficult to pay taxes. His sons, unable to purchase farms or find work in cities, were a matter of much concern to the peasant whose farm was too small to divide among his heirs.

Despite these hardships, the French bourgeoisie never lost heart. Convinced that they were the "chosen people," they faced their problems realistically and confidently. This attitude is brought out brilliantly in Antoine Redier's novel, *Léone,* in which the strong conventional brother speaks to the weak unsocial sister as follows:

> We are bourgeois, Léone—we belong to the class of men that carry humanity on their shoulders. It is true that the peasants helped win the war. They fought bravely under our orders and by their hard work they fertilized the soil. But they are servants; we are the masters—we, the bourgeoisie, alone are equal. Therefore we should be worthy of our position and fulfill its obligations. Other classes are strong—but so are we. The working men have their numbers, the financiers their money, the farmers their land—while we

have wisdom; we are the rational people. At the present time the common people and the plutocrats tend to become robbers—even gangsters. We alone—influenced by solid traditions, knowledge, and experience—are the honest people. We carry in our "solid heads" the welfare of the nation. Bitter opponents of violence, however, we will impose our law only by means of our intellectual strength and moral rectitude.

Inflation in England did not go so far as it did in France, mainly because of the English policy of taxing rather than of borrowing during the war. Nevertheless, the English debt was expanded tremendously. Although every effort was made to deflate the currency and to keep the prices down, the years immediately following the World War saw the English middle classes in a seemingly desperate predicament. House rents, equivalent to two hundred and fifty dollars before 1914, by 1921 had risen to three hundred and fifty dollars. Taxes that were ninety dollars in 1914 were three hundred dollars in 1929. Cost of foodstuffs was more than three times what it had been in the period before the war; prices of clothing had doubled.

The middle classes gaze on this terrible increase in prices with a rising despair. . . . "They have to pay for the increased cost of their children's schools by further limitations on their own necessities and pleasures, and by spending what little money they have accumulated for old age" ("Collapse of Britain's Middle Class," *Literary Digest,* May 1, 1920; 33-34).

A contemporary stated the situation realistically when he wrote: "The middle class is damned, we are crushed between the 'upper ten' and the organized workers."

Pride tended to accentuate the difficulties. For years the bourgeoisie had enjoyed an adequate standard of living. Their children were educated in private schools. Their homes were large and comfortable. They could buy what pleased them. They did not have to skimp. The entire family could spend a vacation in the country or at the seaside. They had the freedom of security. Despite the unfavorable economic plight, they tried to carry on. The very appearance of poverty, many of them still foolishly considered, was a crime. So, frequently worse off than the workers, they starved in silence and refused to take advantage of the governmental aid given the poor, in the form of public schools, sick benefits, old-age pensions, and the dole.

It was difficult for the middle-class man to realize that he was worse off than the worker, that perhaps his whole individualistic philosophy would have to be scuttled. He had been taught that "a man's economic position depends upon himself." In this above all else he placed faith. When he finally discovered that he was in reality just one of the masses, despair settled over him. Self-complacency and self-initiative vanished. Before the war he often said, "I am going to do what I jolly well please and be hanged to anyone who interferes with me." In 1920 he frequently sighed with a helpless shrug of the shoulders, "I suppose I've got to put up with infringements on my liberty." He had lost his old-time superiority and confidence.

In Germany the middle classes were hit the hardest by this inflation. There the bourgeoisie constituted a powerful class, consisting as they did of small *entrepreneurs* in industry and trade, simple producers of goods (artisans and farmers), and small shopkeepers and tradesmen. Moreover, their views and interests were adopted by such other groups as the peasants; public officials; private salaried employees; unsuccessful members of the free professions; doctors, lawyers, teachers (the intellectual proletariat); upper sections of the working classes (the aristocracy of labor); the union leaders and officials. All of these groups suffered as a result of the decline in the purchasing power of money.

By the end of 1923 inflation had proceeded so far in that country that those whose property or income was fixed in terms of pre-war marks had lost everything. Pensions, rents, interest on bonds, and fixed salaries, which was the form taken by the wealth of a large part of the middle classes, indicated little. Before the inflationary period, an income of 50,000 to 100,000 marks would place its owner—remember the How Much Theory?—near the top of the middle classes; by the end of 1923 it was necessary to have an income of 50,000 billions to 100,000 billions in order to maintain an equivalent position. Literally, German money was not worth the paper on which it was printed.

The bourgeoisie with fixed incomes derived from interest and rents and even the section whose income was secured from more flexible sources, such as fees and salaries, found it very difficult to keep up with the rapid and continuous rise in prices. Savings lost practically all of their value, pensioners and *rentiers* starved, families formerly well situated had to discharge their servants. They were forced to eat less well and in some cases hardly at all. Moreover, they were unable to buy clothes, not to mention the many small luxuries which went to make up a comfortable existence. Hundreds of thousands of German middle-class men, women, and children had to depend on charity for their existence.

While the process of inflation was breaking down the standard of living of the middle classes of Europe, it was not hitting the other groups so hard. During the war the plutocrats had made great profits. Large-scale industry had developed considerably, to a certain extent at the expense of the smaller businesses. When the war was over and inflation set in, the big capitalists were in a position to get rid of their bonded debts. Many small business men and farmers did not experience great hardships. True, they lost their reserves, such as cash, investments, and insurance; nevertheless they managed to retain their stores and farms. Nor did the wage-earners suffer. During the war those working men who were not in the army earned large wages and lived well in spite of the rising prices. When inflation started and the men who had been in the armies returned, there was a certain amount of unemployment, in some countries a considerable amount, but even then the workingmen were not so badly situated as the members of the middle class. Any one who could find work could demand wages more or less proportionate to the cost of living. Even in Germany, where prices rose so rapidly that it was impossible to keep up with them fully, the wages of labor kept much more closely in line with the cost of living than did salaries and fixed revenues.

It was in this period that the middle-class agitation against the too prosperous laborer and the war profiteer began. Poorly paid professional men and starving *rentiers* were enraged when they saw bricklayers more prosperous than they and when they heard of the luxury in which the big business men and war profiteers reveled. The contrast between their actual and their former position in society caused these middle classes to feel that they alone were suffering and bearing the cost of the war. From 1919 on, article after article appeared in the magazines pointing out the plight of the middle classes, stressing their great contributions to the advancement of contemporary civilization, pleading with or commanding the state to do something for these deserving people, and threatening dire consequences to the whole social fabric if nothing were done to raise the middle classes to their former pedestal.

One of the chief reasons for this sudden bourgeois self-consciousness was the imminent threat of social revolution. From one side came the danger of the total absorption of small and medium sized businesses by the big industrial and financial concerns, which would mean the end of the "independent" middle-class merchant or manufacturer. From the other side came the danger of a communist dictatorship, with its accompanying destruction of the middle classes. The success of the Bolshevik Revolution in Russia was taken as a warning that unless "social stability" was safeguarded by vigorous measures which would defeat and destroy the revolutionaries and support the stable elements of society, Western civilization was doomed to disappear in the turmoil of a red terror. The revolution in Germany, which might so easily have been disastrous to the propertied classes served to intensify the movement for protection of the status quo in other countries.

In every state of Western Europe the government was forced, mainly by middle-class agitation, to take cognizance of the social situation brought about by the economic and political changes which followed the war. In the small nations, such as Denmark, Sweden, Norway, and Holland, the prosperity of the middle classes also "gave way to a more and more depressing poverty." Governments were aware of the precarious position of this group and feared the results of their disintegration. At the same time, those in authority had to guard the welfare of the lower classes because of the dangers of discontent from the proletariat. Finally, there were the interests of the potent capitalists to be considered. Each country tried to meet its problems in its own way, with varying results.

Germany was one of the first states to experience a crisis. The end of the war found that country a defeated and exhausted nation. After the abdication of the kaiser, it was without its traditional leaders. In the midst of chaos the Social-Democratic party was the strongest power. As this organization drew its main strength from the influential trade unions of the country, it was a working man's party and might have seized the opportunity offered by its position of dominance to carry out a thoroughgoing socialist revolution somewhat on the Bolshevik model. Whether the reason was over-devotion to democratic ideals, doctrinaire aversion to violence, genuine respect for property and other middle-class institutions, or fear of failure because of foreign intervention, the Social-Democratic party did not attempt to set up socialism in Germany. Instead, it brought forth a liberal, democratic republic.

The establishment of this government saved the German middle class from the menace of Bolshevism. Even with the ballot in the hands of the working men and women of the country, the bourgeoisie could and did manage to retain a large share of political control. Indeed, compared with their power under the empire, they may be said to have augmented considerably their influence on the actions of the government; for the German middle classes comprised nearly half of the population of the country. Their power, directly through the ballot and indirectly through the influence of bourgeois ideals on the Social-Democratic party, safeguarded most of the rights of property and prevented the socialization of commerce and industry.

There were, however, certain problems about which the middle classes could do very little. Of these, the policies and actions of the Allied powers were especially disturbing. The Treaty of Versailles, drawn to benefit the victors, dealt Germany a staggering blow. In Europe she was deprived of 25,000 square miles and 6,000,000 inhabitants. Her loss of raw materials and mineral resources was serious, involving 45 per cent of her coal, 57 per cent of her lead, 65 per cent of her iron, 72 per cent of her zinc. From 12 per cent to 15 per cent of her agricultural products and 10 per cent of her manufactures were also lost as a result of territorial readjustments. Abroad, she relinquished her entire empire, with an area of over 1,000,000 square miles and a population of 12,000,000. Her foreign concessions and privileges were swept away. The German merchant marine shrank from 5,500,000 tons to a paltry 400,000. Furthermore, German business was saddled with the tremendous burden of the reparations. Fixed in 1921 at $31,500,000,000, the reparations represented a great stumbling block in the German republic's path to reconstruction. Even when the charges were later reduced, they remained large enough to loom as an apparently insurmountable obstacle to economic and financial rehabilitation.

Willing or unwilling, Germany could not meet the Allied demands. Many of her great markets, notably those of France and the United States, were at least partially destroyed by the erection of tariff barriers. The loss of foreign markets and the poverty of the domestic market so reduced economic activity in Germany that the collection of the reparations became possible only by sapping the very capital of the country. You cannot squeeze blood out of a turnip, the old saying goes; but, one might add, you can eat the turnip. And foreign creditors were doing their best to gobble it up.

In such circumstances there was little that the German government could do. For years the country hovered on the brink of economic ruin. Commerce and industry were almost at a standstill; unemployment grew steadily; taxes cut deeply into the resources of all those who were not dependent on charity. The liberal democratic government lived by compromise, taking from one group to give to another, then taking from the second to give to a third, and so on in circles. At the same time it tried to satisfy its creditors, paying with promises so far as possible and with money only when unavoidable.

During this period of compromise, unrest and dissatisfaction was growing in all classes of society. Unemployment caused great distress in both the middle and lower groups. The government attempted to offset its effects on the lower classes, but it could do very little for the bourgeoisie. Even the stabilization and restoration of the mark to its pre-war value did little if anything to help the middle classes; it was too late, their savings and investments having been used up during the long period of inflation. Nor were the upper classes satisfied. The former nobility was still interested in restoring the kaiser or one of his family to the throne. The capitalists, the Big-Business men, looked with disfavor on the republican government because it seemed to lean toward organized labor by trying to regulate trade and to cut into capital's profits in order to provide for unemployment insurance, old-age pensions, and other social reforms.

The result of this general dissatisfaction was the growth of organized opposition to the democratic, compromising republic. A communist faction broke off from the Social-Democratic party, as it had done in Russia. A nationalist organization appeared, and a National-Socialist party began to form. All of these groups, although their aims were different, were agreed on the desirability of overthrowing the republic at the first opportunity and of setting up a dictatorship of one kind or another. In the midst of this agitation, the Social-Democratic party, which had become an organization of the conservative working men allied with liberal members of the middle classes acting in more or less close coöperation with such groups as the Catholic Center party, was trying to keep the republic alive. This precarious balance was maintained through the relatively prosperous years of the middle twenties, but the economic depression which followed brought a new intensification of discontent which finally crushed the republic.

In post-war Italy the social situation was similar in a number of ways to that in Germany. Although Italy had been on the victorious side in the war, she was not satisfied with her treatment at Versailles. The Italian people were sure that their government had been negligent. Furthermore, while not to the same extent as in Germany, inflation had taken place in

Italy at least enough to raise prices and bring heavy pressure to bear on those who lived on more or less fixed incomes.

Unlike Germany, where the Social-Democrats in no way menaced the security of the middle classes, the chief danger to bourgeois Italians in the years immediately following the war was the revolutionary movement. In 1919 many radical agitators, chiefly socialists, began to urge the seizure of the factories by the proletariat. By the fall of 1920 the movement had reached its climax, with more than six hundred factories in the hands of the workers. At the same time the revolutionists were gaining rapidly in parliamentary strength.

During this period the Italian middle classes were not inactive. When the workers took over the factories, they found themselves unable to run them. They could get no help from the factory managers and technical experts; they could get no credit for raw materials; and they could get no business men to buy their goods. In this way the movement to take over the factories and the means of production was defeated by the action of the middle classes without the help of the state.

The do-nothing attitude of the government in the face of the economic and political crises, added to the loss of prestige which it suffered as the result of the Treaty of Versailles, succeeded in turning a large part of the middle classes against it. With this antagonism went a growing scorn for democracy. The Italian property owners began to feel that no democratic government would do anything more than talk and compromise. Frightened by the power shown by the revolutionists in their attack on the factory owners, hard pressed by the rising cost of living which was the indirect result of financial instability, and weakened by the continued concentration of wealth in Big Business, the middle classes wanted drastic action; they demanded firm and powerful leadership. This desire for domination was fulfilled by Benito Mussolini and his followers, the Fascisti, when they placed themselves at the head of the middle-class-proletarian reaction against plutocracy, democracy, and communism.

Democracy, according to the ideology of this ex-socialist, was a failure. It had merely enabled the privileged classes, by means of the sanctity of private property, to bring slavery and wretchedness on themselves. Inasmuch as under democracy the helpless masses merely existed for the profit of a minority of bold people, the lower classes were doomed to a life of misery and poverty. The state, therefore, constituted the only hope of these disorganized individuals. In fact, it was the only means whereby the petty middle classes and the proletariat could express their will and have their interests defended. Before their prosperity could be assured, however, the most dangerous foe of the nation—communism—must be obliterated.

Since the revolutionary movement was already on the decline when Mussolini came to the front, it was easily and rapidly suppressed. The Fascist fighting squads merely supplied the finishing touch in the destruction of a movement that had been crippled at birth by the spontaneous action of the business elements. Nevertheless, Mussolini acquired the reputation of being the saviour of Italy. Middle-class men and a large number of peasants and workers poured into his organization. In October, 1922, Mussolini staged the Fascist march on Rome. Backing him were people of all classes, tired of a parliament in which the three parties—Socialist, Catholic, and Fascist—scorned to support the government, tired also of ministries for a day. So, when the man who had "saved" them from the menace of communism claimed that democracy was dead and that only authority could make Italy a powerful and prosperous nation, the middle classes were in the vanguard of his *coup d'état*.

Confronted by the evident power and popularity of the man, King Victor Emmanuel III requested Mussolini to form a government. A cabinet was soon assembled, and the Fascisti were in control. In the years that followed, Mussolini proceeded to build up his Fascist state in which all classes, under the rigid control of the government and the Fascist party, were to cooperate for the greater glory of the Italian nation. Thus, while the German middle class was attempting to solve its problems through social democracy and compromise, the Italians were trying to do the same thing through despotism and centralized rule. Employers and workers were organized into separate federations, dominated by Mussolini, which represented such types of activity as industry, mining, the trades, commerce, transportation, banking, credit institutions, and the liberal professions. Collective bargaining between employers and employees was permitted, but the government, prohibiting the use of the strike, was the last court of appeal.

In the meantime the English middle classes, whose dominant position in the state had long been the envy of their brothers in other nations, were having serious difficulties in maintaining their status, both as individuals and as a group. Their problems, like those of similar groups in the Continental nations, were both economic and political. The economic situation, however, was not as bad as that of Germany, nor was the political situation as tense as that of Italy. There was no anticipation of any fundamental changes either in politics or in economics. The question to be answered was whether the English middle classes would peacefully decline under economic pressure or whether they would, just as peacefully, succeed in readjusting the post-war situation to something like the pre-war state of things.

The election of 1918, in which Lloyd George and the Coalition cabinet remained in power, indicated the spirit of unity brought about by the war. Quite conservative on the whole, this government attempted to forestall any economic depression by enacting measures very much in line with the traditional English policies, except for an import duty on certain manufactured products, which was designed to protect British industry from the competition of countries with depreciated currencies. The middle classes, who constituted an integral element of Lloyd George's support, apparently underestimated the importance of the serious dangers confronting them. But, as economic difficulties continued to intensify, as over 2,000,000 men and women were out of work by the summer of 1921, as the government conceded the inevitability of a system of doles for the unemployed, as it tried to halt flagging British trade by a commercial treaty with Soviet Russia, as all these measures and others were fostered in a desperate, unsuccessful attempt to relieve the situation, the middle classes stopped being political bats and scanned the contemporary horizon.

What the business men saw apparently induced changes in their thinking, with the result that, as in other countries, still believing in the feasibility of democratic parties as instruments for economic recovery, the middle classes elected conservatives to power but at the same time deserted their previous tool, the Liberal party, for the new and more progressive Labor party. Apparently, the commercial and industrial groups had split, some going to the right, some to the left.

This lack of decision in the British electorate was demonstrated by the course of English politics in the next two years, culminating when the Conservative Prime Minister, Stanley Baldwin, attempted to revive England's falling trade and industries by a protective tariff. The tariff principle was acceptable to a part of the electorate, but to the majority, which was not yet ready to abandon England's tradition of free trade, it was anathema. Consequently, in the new elections of 1923, the pendulum of power swung from the Conservatives, past the Liberals, to the Laborites. The latter, with Liberal support, formed the first Labor ministry, with Ramsay MacDonald as Prime Minister.

The British Labor party, like the German Social-Democratic party, was in theory a socialist group, basing its membership and policies on the trade unions; and, like the Social-Democrats, lacking complete control of the government, it was unable to introduce actual socialism. While Labor was in office it did nothing that was very disturbing to the middle classes, except its last act of consequence, the recognition of Soviet Russia. It did not carry out its proposed capital levy on all fortunes above 5000 pounds sterling, nor did it nationalize the mines and railways. MacDonald, the Prime Minister, expressed his attitude when he said, "Our Labor government had never had the least inclination to try short cuts to the millennium." This was a soothing sentiment dear to the timid middle classes.

Chief efforts of the Labor government lay in the fields of foreign conciliation and in improvement of domestic and international trade. To further these ends at one and the same time, MacDonald finally extended *de jure* recognition to Soviet Russia. Despite the moderation of the Labor government in its other policies, this act of friendliness toward a power whose constant and open purpose was the undermining and destruction of bourgeois states brought about MacDonald's fall. Not even the prospect of economic benefits could induce the Liberals and their bourgeois supporters to countenance Soviet recognition. In the election which followed the withdrawal of Liberal support from Labor the Conservative party gained a clear victory. The pendulum had swung back.

From 1924 to 1929 the government of England was Conservative. Since the middle classes had apparently deserted the Laborites definitely, the mandate of the Conservatives was clear. They had the support of the English business groups in a policy of recovery without concessions to revolution, whether in the form of nationalization of mines and railroads, high income taxes, or grants to labor. But the government had its difficulties with the economic situation, notably with the mining industry, which had been crippled by the falling off of coal exports.

Despite the Conservative program, however, the English middle classes were not yet back to their prosperous pre-war condition. Incomes and salaries were still low; prices and taxes, especially taxes, were still high. As more and more working men swelled the ranks of the unemployed, the government was forced to extend unemployment insurance and the dole. Business men grumbled. They felt that they were being taxed willy-nilly to subsidize idleness—that any man could get work if he would only really look for it. As the depression deepened, the English middle classes, however, in contrast to the Italian, still showed confidence in democratic government. They felt that they had sufficient voting strength to hold the proletariat in check at the polls; and in this they were apparently correct, for the Labor party in its palmiest days had never even approached a clear majority in Parliament. Being still quite strong and reasonably self-confident of a turn in luck, the English middle classes did not recognize the "advantages" of a dictator or of a strong non-parliamentary leader to prevent an attack from below.

Yet the question of the ultimate destruction or reëstablishment of British prosperity was still unsettled, postponed into unreality. With the Conservatives in power, the middle classes sat back, hoping the storm would blow over and that sinking markets would be revived. During the late twenties they discovered that recovery was a long way ahead. Trade depression, war debts, and high taxes were slowly depriving them of the few luxuries "that made life worth living." Ostensibly, they rejoiced that they had returned to the gold standard in 1925 and had arranged a debt settlement with the United States. Actually, they realized that these policies were delaying recovery—that the throwing overboard of the gold standard and the repudiation of the debt settlement might revive industry, reduce taxes, and restore prosperity.

In post-war France, too, the pre-war governmental organization survived unchanged, with the middle classes peacefully maintaining their control of government. Inasmuch as in France the position of this group was threatened more by the general economic emergency than by the attacks of other classes, that country resembled England more than Italy or Germany. Despite some difficult periods, the well-established bourgeois republic was able to carry on without serious trouble until the nation began to feel the effects of the world-wide depression.

During the years immediately following the end of the war, the problems most seriously confronting the French middle classes were the menace of another German invasion, the high cost of living (brought about by the gradual inflation of the franc), and the danger of Bolshevism. In 1919 as a result of this fear of social revolution the conservatives triumphed. These conservatives—French iron-masters (the *Comité des Forges*) and big financial and industrial leaders—immediately influenced their statesmen, Millerand and Poincaré, to carry out militaristic and imperialistic policies designed to prevent German recovery, to expand economically in Central Europe, and to increase dividends. At the same time it was felt that a determined stand against Communist Russia would be sufficient to protect the property of good French bourgeoisie from the danger of confiscation under a dictatorship of the proletariat.

What to do about the inflation of the franc, inflation which was eating into the savings of the middle classes, was not so easy to decide. The cost of military preparations and of rebuilding the whole devastated north-east of the country was unbalancing the finances of the government. Despite the fact that German reparations were supposed to cover the cost, and despite the determination of the French people to see that they did, the reparations question became a political football. When Briand's moderately progressive ministry agreed to grant Germany a partial moratorium, the French middle classes clearly showed their feelings by supporting the conservative-nationalist Poincaré, who replaced Briand as premier. Poincaré's attempt to solve the financial problem by forcing Germany to pay resulted in the expensive occupation of the Ruhr. In 1923 the French, confronted by the menace of real inflation, began to swing once more to the left.

By the middle of 1924 the control of the moderate government was endangered. As the French currency continued to fall, the bourgeoisie were becoming more and more vehement in their demands for restoration of the full value of the franc and for its stabilization. A "radical" politician who depended for his support on the moderate members of the business elements, Premier Herriot did not wish to antagonize the well-to-do by levying the heavy income and excess profit taxes advocated by the Socialists. Though ministries fell and rose again revamped, the situation grew worse. Finally, there was the inevitable reaction, and a National Union ministry was organized under Poincaré in 1926.

Although Poincaré's ministry was predominantly conservative, the members took radical action to save the financial situation. New taxes were levied, governmental expenditures were reduced, and salaries were cut. By December, 1926, the situation had so far improved that the franc had risen from 48 to 25 to the dollar. At this point Poincaré stabilized the franc, giving it one-fifth of its pre-war value. The stabilization of the franc at this low figure was a great blow to the bourgeoisie, for many of its members had invested their capital in government bonds—obviously those who had bought before or during the war lost four-fifths of their property outright. In spite of these losses, however, they favored stabilization for, though they regretted inflation and were determined never again to be caught by a fall of the franc, they wanted order and security above all, and if losses were necessary prerequisites, they were willing to pay the present price for the future gain.

In general, the future had very little to offer the bourgeoisie. For, whether it was France, Germany, Italy, England, or the smaller nations—Russia being the exception—capitalism in the late twenties was still in the crucible and the middle classes were still awaiting a final reckoning.

CHAPTER XXV

THE GREAT WORLD DEPRESSION

Of all dangers to a nation, as things exist in our day, there can be no greater one than having certain portions of the people set off from the rest by a line drawn—they not privileged as others, but degraded, humiliated, made of no account (Walt Whitman, Democratic Vistas, *1882).*

WHEN, in 1929, the great World Depression settled its economic pall over all nations, the post-war repatching and rebuilding of the social structure by the middle classes availed little, and bourgeois governments seemed in danger of being stifled by radical and revolutionary doctrine. Once more the middle classes were subjected to the strains of economic distress and the pains of "subversive" agitation. Once more they were forced to look for a passage to progress.

In watching their search for a way out of the economic maze, we must remember that the depression business classes were not the same as those of the decade before. Economically, the bourgeoisie of 1930 were not a homogeneous group. The chief division had always been between those who were their own "bosses," that is, those who worked under their own direction; and those who depended upon others for their livelihood, that is, those who worked for salaries under the direction of others. This had been true throughout the history of the middle classes; but since the end of the war this factor had become more and more evident. At the beginning of the twentieth century, the tendency toward the concentration of business in big enterprises had already become apparent; in the period after the war, large industrial, financial, and commercial concerns grew rapidly at the expense of the small and medium-sized businesses. The result of this development was a decrease in the number of independent middle-class business men and a large increase in the number of families depending on salaries.

These two sections had come to be called the "independent" and the "dependent" groups. In a certain sense this distinction was valid, but the inference which could be drawn from the words used was false. The "independent" middle classes of the post-war period were only one step removed from the direct dependence on large banks and the Big Business that characterized the salaried officials and employees who made up the "dependent" middle classes. Another division of the post-war bourgeoisie was also made: that which separated them into the "old" and the "new" middle classes. In the "old" middle classes were placed the well-to-do real estate owners, business men, *rentiers,* and craftsmen; in the "new" the members of the liberal professions, and the salaried employees and officials. Clearly, this distinction between the "old" and the "new" was false, for the "new" section had been one of the mainstays of the middle classes for several centuries.

With the expansion of large-scale business all over the Western world, there came an increasing pressure on the "independent" middle classes. The spread of chain stores and the expansion of the mail-order business tended to drive the small or medium-sized concerns off the market. Large enterprises, with their vast buying power, were able to offer the customer a wide range of goods at prices which the small merchant with his limited turnover and expensive overhead was unable to meet. In manufacturing, the tendency was the same. Big plants with enormous production capacities could buy their materials at a lower price and turn out their goods at a lower unit cost. Consequently, they were in a position to undersell smaller concerns.

This pressure on the "independent" middle classes did not, however, bring about a reduction of the size of the bourgeoisie as a whole. Some of the "independents," when forced out of business, did drop out of their class, but their number was not great. The small merchant or manufacturer tended to lose his "independence" rather than his class. He became the paid manager of the business which had once been his but had become the property of some large concern. Thus, one section of the middle classes grew in size, while the other diminished

—the group as a whole remaining at more or less the same level.

At the same time there was another factor working towards the increase of the "dependent" business men. In the industries of all large countries, as big enterprises began to take up a greater percentage of the field, the number of office employees and functionaries tended to grow faster than the number of workers.

The "independent" middle classes, however, did not remain passive in the face of this pressure. At the end of the nineteenth century, as we have seen, they began to organize themselves into groups to fight the large enterprisers on more equal terms. Landowners formed agricultural associations; owners of urban real estate organized tax-payers' associations; small and medium-sized merchants met in coöperatives in order to secure group rates; even office employees in most of the European countries began to organize unions among themselves. The all-prevailing attitude was one of class self-sufficiency. Business men, landlords, and office employees felt that they themselves, through coöperation, could work out their own salvation.

After the war these organizations continued. As the position of the independent small business men became more untenable, more of them joined the coöperative societies, as did the other members of the "independent" middle classes. In general, it may be said that the bourgeois organizations gained rather than lost in membership as a result of the effects of the war on business. There was, however, a change in attitude on the part of their membership. Although they still attempted to help themselves by their own efforts, they began to turn more and more to the government for aid.

This breakdown of bourgeois individualism was one of the important results of the war and the war's aftermath, the great World Depression. Faced by such problems as bad business, high taxes, spread of radicalism and of large monopolies, many Babbitts, for the first time, discovered that they were dependent upon other people and that their home town was not the only spot on the globe. Some of them actually comprehended that their problems were connected with national and even with international affairs.

By the end of the 1920's the experiments in Russia and in Italy were observed by the average person. Economic planning on a national scale was familiar to readers of newspapers and magazines, in other words, to most business men. Consequently, when the depression struck at the economic foundations of bourgeois society, the members were not content to ask only financial stability of their governments; they requested protection and assistance in something they had previously considered to be sacred to individual initiative—private business. The event which led the "independent" as well as the "dependent" middle classes to appeal to the government, and even to demand its interference in economic processes, was the growing severity of the depression. When, in 1930 and 1931, their situation became desperate, they saw that there was no other way out. The government must help them or Big Business would ruin them.

Another factor in this change of policy on the part of the middle classes, other than the grave dangers arising out of the war and the depression itself, was the transformation of their character. Hitherto most members of the "independent" element hesitated to appeal to the government because of their traditional reliance on individual initiative and because of their fear that government interference might result in state control, very high taxes, and a great reduction in profits. Their brothers, the "dependents," however, had no such fears. On the contrary, now accustomed to being under the rule of a bureaucracy, they had nothing to fear from state control. Moreover, they saw that government interference in industry had not harmed the laborer, but rather had helped him through unemployment insurance, old-age pensions, and other social legislation; they were not averse to securing such benefits for themselves. An increasing number of "independent" middle-class men accepted this point of view.

A third factor which caused the bourgeoisie to demand the interference of the government in the social and economic situation was the more and more marked strength of the revolutionary movement. With the lurid example of the fate of "their brothers" in Soviet Russia continually forced to their attention by a partisan press, the members of the middle classes were almost hysterically anxious to prevent the establishment of a communistic or socialistic régime. Since the working classes also felt the depression and demanded that the government do something to protect them from starvation and misery and since the action which they proposed was often in conflict with the desires of the middle classes, the period following the beginning of the depression saw a series of contests between these two groups in society for the control of government.

These forces, especially the growth of Big Business, the economic pressure of the depression, and the menace of socialist or communist revolution, were the impelling causes of the bourgeois movements that brought Europe in the early thirties to a state of jittery uncertainty. Since the relative importance of these influences varied from country to country, the movements which have resulted from them differ in the separate nations. In some cases, as in Germany, other factors had interfered to react upon the strength of the middle-class drive; but in all cases the fundamental motive was the same—the bourgeois fear of extinction.

In England the revolutionary spark was so weak that the middle-class movement of opposition was not touched off. The nation's chief problem was economic. Even more than in the period before the end of the war, the English nation, and especially the English business groups, felt the effects of lessening economic activity. As unemployment became greater and more families were forced to become dependent on charity, the burden on the state became excessive, the drain on finances heavy. New expenditures meant new taxes and these fell with severity on the unfortunate middle classes, who held a good share of the taxable wealth. The result was bourgeois discontent, dissatisfaction with the government, and at least the nucleus of a class antagonism to the working men who were supported by unemployment insurance.

Increased taxation was not the only result of the depression which had its influence on the attitude of the English middle classes; another strong factor was the great scarcity of the type of employment which the bourgeoisie considered suitable for themselves. Chiefly this lack was felt by the younger men, who discovered that they had very little chance of finding work which would pay them enough to maintain proper standards of living and to provide reasonable security for the future. Lloyd George wrote recently:

> One of the most dangerous features of European conditions since the War has been the menaced position of the middle classes. Black coated unemployment has been largely on the increase. The prospects for educated young men, when they have finished their career at the high school and the university, have become most precarious.

Chain stores made it increasingly difficult for middle-class men to find positions. Indeed, "mass production" tended to blot out the solid business men, "who despite their narrow middle-class morality—or perhaps because of it—were worth far more to a local community than a score of employees in a company shop ruled by an unseen board of directors, alien to the town."

On the surface, however, save for the unfortunate unemployed, the English people, about 1926, seemed fairly well off. Wage-earners, middle-class men, as well as plutocrats, had money to spend and even to save. But every one seemed uncertain as to the future. Many realized that this boom was artificial; it was maintained by a policy of "soak the rich" to take care of the poor unemployed. This could not continue, for the income of England had suffered such a severe drop that many people were living off their capital. To stop this waste, the conservative of the middle classes backed Big Business in its attempts to lower production costs, especially in the coal industry. Organized labor reared up in dismay, and struck in 1926. The middle classes helped to break up this revolt by acting as strike breakers. Henceforth, the government—Conservative, Labor, and "National Coalition" from 1927 to 1935—tended to pay less attention to the proletariat and more to the protection of the property and savings of the middle classes.

In 1931 the government embarked definitely on this particular conservative policy. In the elections of that year the Conservatives won a great victory and a Coalition government with labor leader J. Ramsay MacDonald as prime minister and the Conservatives in actual control came into existence. Policies designed to lower the tax burden on the propertied classes by reducing salaries and the dole were inaugurated. Along with these cuts came an economy of expenditures on education and on other social services, "a policy advantageous for balancing the budget, but fraught with grave injuries to the life of the people." As a result, the incomes of the lower middle classes and of the wage-earners were lowered and their purchasing power diminished.

Disregarding a possible collapse of domestic markets as a consequence of these policies, the government in 1931 abandoned the gold standard, believing that this act would stimulate export trade. This radical policy caused surprise throughout England. According to Sir Philip Hamilton Gibbs (*Ways of Escape; a Challenge to the New Generation,* W. Heinemann, London, 1933):

> . . . old gentlemen, and younger men than that, stared about them from the depths of club chairs with a sudden sense of apprehension, with a feeling of "goose-flesh" which did not come with any draught from one of the club windows. It was the chill of doubt that beneath those chairs the ground might not be solid; that all this comfort, this old tarnished splendor, this old England of Pall Mall might have no security but stand over a quaking precipice.

Disregarding these fears, the government in 1932 instituted a protective policy designed to bring about economic recovery. At the farmers' Ottawa Conference preferential tariffs were arranged with the various states of the commonwealth. By thus making the empire an economic *Zollverein,* foreign trade would be practically shut out while British industry and commerce would have a greased inside track. This new economic policy, on the whole, was satisfactory, especially to the upper middle classes. The great burden of taxation was lightened; the actual cost of goods was lessened; and cheapened money enabled many bourgeois house owners to pay off their debts and to hold their heads above water. In short, many conservative Englishmen believed that the gradual economic improvement in 1934–1935 would result in the return of normal industrial and economic conditions.

Francis W. Hirst, conservative economist, seemed to be of this opinion. In his *Consequences of the War to Great Britain* (Yale University Press, New Haven, 1934) he claimed that the standard of living was gradually improving. The luxuries of 1913 were now necessities. Profits of shopkeepers and of the distributing trade had more than doubled. Many small tradesmen kept balances in the bank. Moreover, the middle classes enjoyed their leisure as never before. Sports of all kinds had increased in popularity, and motoring and the cinema were new diversions with deep social implications. In short, the petty business groups were more occupied, more content, and possibly better off than they were before the war.

This conservative program of recovery, however, had its critics. Representing the lower classes and the proletariat (the fourth estate?), such leaders as John Hobson, a moderate socialist, and Lloyd George, an immoderate liberal, questioned the success of the conservative policies. Hobson, for example, maintained that the Coalition program of recovery had actually reduced consuming power and retarded thereby industrial recovery. "The measure of recovery that has actually taken place is in spite of this foolish and false economy." Apparently in sympathy with Hobson's ideas, Lloyd George advocated public works and other governmental expenditures as a means of helping the fourth estate, restoring industry, and attaining true recovery. Both seemed to favor a kind of national socialism or semi-corporate state, in which capital and labor would be organized in such a way as to work for the common good.

The fascist way out also attracted a number of middle-class men. Ever opportunists when their welfare was concerned, a small but aggressive minority joined Oswald Mosley's black bud of fascism, the Black Shirt party, abandoning their policy of minor and gradual changes, peacefully conducted for one of direct, and if necessary, violent action. In 1934 Lloyd George estimated that the Black Shirts had proselyted three per cent of the British electorate. Those who enlisted did so because they thought that peaceful, slow, parliamentary evolution could not preserve for them their position in society and save them from the menace of radicalism. So far, respect for the traditional forms of government and unwillingness to follow in the footsteps of other European countries have acted as a brake on these tendencies in the English middle classes; but how long these checks will remain effective is an open question. The business men of England, caught in the grip of the depression, are struggling for freedom and for their previous status. If the gentle suasions of parliamentary democracy are not effective, they may seek the more violent mandates of a class dictatorship.

In France, the situation of the middle classes is very like that in England. There they, too, are caught in the tentacles of economic forces and are fighting a desperate battle. Fairly prosperous until 1930, they soon thereafter began to feel the effects of economic stagnation. As in England, the business men at first felt that they could save themselves without resorting to violent measures. Through the actions of the government, they tried to preserve their position by isolating themselves from the less prosperous part of the world. Higher tariffs and a system of quotas kept the products of other nations out of the country. Working for the support of the peasants in case of trouble, the urban middle classes placed French agriculture in a fine position by giving the farmer a highly protected home market. The working classes, in whom lay the potential danger of revolution, were taken care of partly through the program of state assistance to domestic industry and partly through direct government aid.

This situation could not last. A nation cannot become an economic hermit. France soon found that she could not cut herself off from the outside world, and that she was therefore bound to become caught in the universal maelstrom. As the situation grew worse, the carefully erected defenses started to crack. Confronted by the problem of high taxes and unemployment, the peasants and urban workers, and members of the great bourgeois bureaucracy began to be dissatisfied despite the efforts that the Chamber of Deputies had made to assure their good will. At the same time, as in England, the middle classes began to realize that the government could not save them.

By 1935 the situation in France had shown no definite trend. The revolutionaries were strong because of the economic crisis, but the plutocrats and the middle classes were apparently stronger because of their political supremacy. Ineffectualness and corruption in the government have indeed led to the strengthening of anti-democratic fascist and monarchical parties of the right as well as the socialist and communist groups of the left, but for the time being at least, the French middle classes have not deserted the side of "moderation" and democracy. Confronted by numerous dangers, such as the threat of new inflation, they stand solidly behind the republican government which has as its mission the defense of bourgeois property and of the bourgeois republic—Liberty, Equality, Fraternity are not forgotten watchwords.

It is in Germany that the middle classes have suffered their severest trials, being weakened there not only by the depression but also by pressure from the groups above and below them. Germany was one of the first countries to feel the depression and was one of the hardest hit. A crisis was precipitated about 1928–1929, when the foreign owners of an enormous amount of German short-term industrial bonds called for their money. German Big Business was forced to retrench and did so by discharging thousands of workers. Unemployment swelled tremendously and to maintain the unfortunates on "the miserable dole" the government had to increase taxes. A general reduction in wages naturally followed. Again the middle classes, who had lost property, investments, and income during the period of inflation faced loss of a part of the one thing that kept them alive—their salaries. Small capitalists and industrialists, professional men, public employees, and other salaried groups were put on a starvation wage-scale. Meanwhile, the youth of Germany faced the future with little hope of jobs which would give them a decent living. "The submergence of the middle class is being hastened," wrote F. A. Ross in "The Passing of the German Middle Class" (*American Journal of Sociology,* March, 1924), "like a toxin, the paralyzing philosophy of despair is spreading insidiously to all parts of the social body, but it has been especially malignant among the middle classes." By 1932 nine-tenths of the German people existed upon wages or salaries; society was being proletarianized; and the competitive system had practically disappeared.

When the German bourgeoisie looked about to see what could be the cause of their desperate situation, they found several apparently relevant reasons. One was the improved position of the proletariat. To safeguard the working men and women, the German Republic had passed laws for old-age pensions, unemployment insurance, and accident insurance. Not content with protecting the working class from exploitation, many municipal governments further provided direct assistance in the form of working men's apartment houses, parks, nurseries, and other facilities. All these had to be supported by public taxation, a large part of which came from those members of the propertied classes who had managed to retain a certain degree of prosperity.

Another apparent cause of the bourgeois depression was the great expansion of big industrial and financial concerns, chain stores, and huge department stores. For some time, and particularly since the end of the war, German industry and finance were out of the hands of the middle classes. The institution of the cartel and of great chain banks had given a small number of large capitalists control of German industry and finance. On the other hand, German commerce had been relatively free from monopoly rule and even in the early post-war period had been one of the strongholds of small *entrepreneurs*. After the war, the tendency toward concentration of management became more and more apparent in this field. Those members of the "free" trading classes who relied on commerce for their independence found themselves driven into the "dependent" groups as their businesses were taken over and they became the employees of the large concerns.

Other alleged causes for the decline of the German bourgeoisie were the increase of communism and the position of the Jews in the country's economic life. Germany's 600,000 Jews, although they comprised under one per cent of the entire population, were said to control the large banks and to dominate both commercial and industrial establishments. In these fields and in the liberal professions they made up a much larger proportion than they did in the population as a whole. The middle classes, sullenly observing and resenting this competition, were not troubled by doubts as to which of these three causes was responsible for their predicament. As their situation grew worse in the years following 1930, they became more and more certain, with the "assistance" of astute demagogues, that the Jews and the Marxists were the suspicious characters in Germany's political wood-pile. If German business was bad and unemployment consequently high, it was because these two groups were turning the foreign countries against Germany. If taxes were high it was because the Marxists, whether Social-Democrats or Communists, were leading the German working men and women astray, persuading them to make more demands on the state. If many doctors, dentists, and lawyers could find no clients and business men were forced to become paid managers in the employ of large concerns, it was because the Jews were usurping the places of Aryans.

As nationalist discontent and hatred of "alien" groups increased, the bourgeoisie began to cluster around a leader who had newly arisen from their midst: Adolf Hitler. Hitler and his National Socialist German Workers party offered an organization and a program which appealed to the bourgeoisie. Disgust with a compromising, ineffectual democracy, suspicion of Big Business, hatred of Jews and Marxists were all represented in the Nazi credo. "We demand," read the National Socialist program, "the creation of a healthy middle class and its preservation, the immediate socialization of the large department stores and the renting of their facilities at minimum rates to small merchants, and preferential state and municipal contracts."

Drawn to Hitler's magnetic oratory, the members of the middle classes flocked into the Nazi organization. Like those of the other European countries they had come to rely for their salvation less on themselves than on the government, so they were all the more ready to support Hitler when they saw that he meant to let no considerations of democracy or of legality prevent him from carrying out his aims. In Hitler the German middle classes saw their saviour, their Leader.

On April 10, 1932, Hitler polled more than 13,000,000 votes as unsuccessful candidate for the presidency, against the venerable incumbent, President von Hindenburg. It was thought that this marked the high tide of Nazi prowess. How wrong, indeed! On January 30, 1933, Hitler was appointed chancellor. On March 23 the *Reichstag* conferred upon him dictatorial powers for four years, during which time the constitution was suspended. Hitler and the Nazi party became the rulers of Germany. Supported by the middle classes and young people who wanted protection and jobs, by the poor peasants who desired the break-up of large estates, and also by the industrialists who believed that the overthrow of the republic would weaken organized labor, Hitler began his campaign to save German capitalism and its dependents from the dangers of socialism, communism, Big Business, and foreign oppression.

The way has been dangerous and difficult. The first attempts, only partially successful, of the Nazi government, were to remove the Jews from their positions and to suppress the revolutionary movement. That the efforts of the government in the field of economic rehabilitation have taken the direction of the destruction of the republican social legislation which favored the working classes and have not seriously interfered with Big Business is not surprising. Hitler's supporters, although many of them are members of the "dependent" middle classes and have little to fear from state ownership, are still too close adherents to their old psychology of individual initiative and private enterprise to favor government control.

Moreover, political problems have delayed fundamental economic changes. Hitler, it is true, organized the "Fighting League of the commercial middle classes" a year before he became chancellor and apparently was sincere in attempting to help the bourgeoisie. But, once at the head of the government, he professed that the interests of Germany as a whole, especially in the matter of foreign relations, forced him to rely upon the support of many powerful plutocrats. To hold the middle classes, it was his policy to abolish the big department stores and the workers' coöperatives, but in this direction he was quickly confronted by tremendous obstacles. Such problems as that of continuing the work of the large stores, the re-employment of their help, and the reimbursing of banks and stockholders for losses incurred when stores were put out of business, prevented him from carrying out this plank in his platform. But he was able to help the peasants by placing them on lands formerly possessed by the junkers and by granting them credit. The cost of assisting the farmer, the status of farm mortgages, and the results of an attempt by the government to raise food prices by tariff protection have not enabled him to produce a complete solution. Nevertheless, he persists in his attempts to decentralize industry and agriculture. In short, the immediate result of Hitler's rise was the ousting of Communists, Socialists, and Jews from many positions and their replacement by Nazi followers. That Hitler wants to help the middle classes seems certain. In general he plans to aid all German groups through the establishment of the coöperative state and the building up of Germany as a ranking world power. At the same time, in attaining these ends he does not intend to violate the bourgeois belief in private initiative or in "law and order" maintained by the central government. In any case, Hitler and his Nazi followers have crossed the Rubicon; they must win or be annihilated.

Like Germany, the middle classes in Austria and Hungary have suffered as a result of post-war inflation, communism, and conservatism. Up to the present the Horthy dictatorship, representing the "feudal landed aristocrats," has oppressed the rather weak bourgeoisie in Hungary, while in Austria a cold and bloody dictatorship has protected at least the capitalists against the assaults of the radicals.

Bourgeois attempts to obliterate radicalism and curb rugged capitalism have occurred since the war in the small as well as in the large nations of Europe. In Sweden, for example, voluntary coöperation and a limited amount of state capitalism have resulted in a distinct improvement in economic conditions. Through the formation of collective marketing, purchasing, and manufacturing associations, the bourgeois citizens of Sweden have managed to reduce prices, to expand production, and to increase the size of dividends. Moreover, by means of a limited state capitalistic program, the government has entered into the control and operation of a number of industries such as railway transportation and public utilities. This public ownership has resulted in a reduction of rates and an increase of income. By these policies, extremes of poverty and wealth have been diminished and the general level of prosperity has been raised.

The most interesting of the post-war revolutions, however, took place in Spain. Two years before Germany submitted to the dictatorship of Hitler, the Spaniards decided to get rid of their monarchy and to establish a republic. This revolution was the climax of the long struggle between church and state on the one hand, and between liberalism and radicalism on the other. Now occurred a complete break with tradition. The old church was stripped of her spiritual monopoly and her secular landed wealth; Alfonso XIII was forced from power; a republic was established; and, with a view to making Spain a country of social justice and equal opportunities, all the wealth of the land was subordinated to the interests of national economy. Henceforth, the state had the right to participate in the development and coördination of industries, to nationalize public services, and to socialize large estates. Work was made a social obligation, and the state was duty bound to protect laborer, farmer, and fisherman. Whether Spain will be able to carry out this program of social reform without resorting to a real dictatorship in order to suppress the communist movement, is a question to be decided in the future. Meanwhile, the present kings of Spain—its bourgeois and socialist citizens—are trying to reach the shores of economic happiness.

To reiterate, in the course of the post-war years, the European middle classes have had to meet two major crises: inflation and the depression. In each case they have been threatened with destruction, but as yet they have managed to exist. One of the most important factors working for their preservation is their flexibility, without which they would surely have succumbed. The pre-war business classes were, on the whole, independent, peaceful, humanitarian, conservative, and prosperous. With the decline of prosperity they have lost their other characteristics. The post-war middle classes have come more and more to depend on the capitalist element for their livelihood and on the state for the solution of their problems. They have also abandoned their peacefulness and their regard for the rights of other groups; they are in a fighting mood, ready for a ruthless defense of their position. The trait that is least evident in these post-war bourgeoisie is their former conservatism. All over Europe they are deserting their traditional policies and showing themselves ready to experiment with new and radical ideas.

The most outstanding examples of this metamorphosis are Italy and Germany. In both these countries the bourgeoisie have abandoned the parliamentary democracies, for which they had long struggled, and put their faith in dictators. Whether France and England will follow the same road remains for the future to decide, for in both countries are fascist parties advocating dictatorships. So far the prestige of long-established democracies has been too strong, and the attraction of the unsuccessful dictatorships too weak. But, in the midst of doubt as to the future of the middle classes, one thing seems certain: the changed conditions of existence have brought about a permanent transformation in their characteristics. The old independent and conservative business men have been replaced by restless, struggling individuals, who feel that their destiny is bound up with that of their nation and of the present social system.

Chapter XXVI

THE OLD DEAL

I have seen corruption boil and bubble
Till it o'er-run the stew
(*Shakespeare,* Measure for Measure).

War depressed the middle classes the world over, and so in the United States it is natural to find the post-war period the history of the efforts, sometimes artless, sometimes crafty, of the bourgeois citizen to regain or to retain the position in the social whirligig which he felt was inherently his. But the road which he was to travel between 1918 and the present was long and difficult with obstacles built for an allegorical Christian; but, unlike Bunyan's Pilgrim, he had no vision of a Celestial City to lead him on; in fact, the farther he went the darker were the clouds in the political sky. The horoscope was unpromising. He had to face situations which, if not essentially new, were unfamiliar, perplexing, decidedly unstable. At times he was threatened with apparent extermination; again he seemed to be on the verge of permanent security. Blown hither and thither by political caprice, he wondered to what port he would be driven.

When the war was reduced to statistics it appeared at first that making the world safe for democracy had been a very good stroke of Yankee business. Many a war profiteer had fattened himself from the proceeds of the slaughter. The number of millionaires during the war was more than doubled. Although by no means all business men had made fortunes during the struggle, still all had cause to develop income tax complexes.

But it did not take the manufacturers, merchants, and industrialists of the country long to discover that they had backed a costly Crusade. The national debt was the staggering sum of billions of dollars and the financial pillars of society squirmed at the inescapable bogeyman of new and higher taxes. It was no wonder that they were not at all anxious to carry out the policies of the idealistic war president, whose message of November 11, 1918, called on the American people to "assist by sober, friendly counsel, and by material aid, in the establishment of just democracy throughout the world," but preferred Warren G. Harding's sentiment, uttered in an address in 1920, that "America's present need is not heroics but healing; not nostrums but normalcy; not revolution but restoration . . . not surgery but security." Restoration and serenity were their watchwords. The din of European conflict echoing in their ears as the middle classes of Germany, Russia, Italy, and other countries fought to stave off extinction, the bourgeois citizens visualized only too easily an American Revolution, uncomfortably close, with dire consequences.

Adding to the feeling of instability engendered by the international outlook was the insecurity of the business situation at home. For the moment prices, salaries, and profits were high; but it was apparent that the end of the war would alter business trends. Manufacturers, merchants, and farmers had piled up huge stocks in anticipation of a great and long European and domestic demand for war materials and for food. The Armistice broke into a bull market, catching many of them overloaded. Nevertheless, spoiled by enormous profits during the war, they refused to accept moderate gains in peacetime. Labor, complicating the situation by demanding the high wages obtained during the struggle, resorted to strikes, especially in the coal industry.

The first efforts of the business classes at the end of the war were directed toward getting the government out of business, reducing taxes, and once more building up the tariff barrier which would prevent competition from a reviving Europe. Although the country was still technically in a state of war, the work of destroying government control of economic activity was begun. Various boards and commissions that had been set up in 1917 and 1918 were abolished. Railroads, which the Federal government had taken over in the crisis, were returned to private management. High income, inheritance, and excess profit taxes were reduced or abolished. The reërection of the tariff barrier was halted for a time by the Democratic president, but that obstacle too was destroyed by the election of the staunch Republican and crony of Big Business, Warren G. Harding. In 1922 Congress passed the high Fordney-McCumber tariff.

Although the government was easily handled, there remained another menace to the position of the middle classes: the strength of the labor movement. The American trade unions, under the leadership of the American Federation of Labor, had given the war their full support and had shown their patriotism. They accepted high wages offered by the capitalists and the government, and in return they refrained from stopping production by strikes or other means. When the war was over, industry slowed down and wages began to decline, while the cost of living tended to remain at the old level or to go higher. The result was a series of strikes for higher wages and better working conditions. The magnitude of this movement, which in 1919 involved some four million men in 3630 strikes, roused the business interests. When they heard of strike after strike and thought of radical Russia and Germany, they saw that such action was "un-American" and were convinced of the necessity of putting an end to it in any possible way.

Action against these strikes and against labor leaders was not meant, of course, to undermine the position of the "good" American working men. It was aimed, as middle-class action always is, against "alien" elements and "undemocratic methods." This attitude was epitomized by Mr. George F. Baer, President of the Reading Railroad: "The rights and interests of the laboring people will be protected and cared for, not by labor agitators, but by the Christian men and women to whom God has given control of the property interests of the country" (quoted in W. E. Payne, *Behavior of Conflicting Economic Groups,* Ellis Publishing Co., Battle Creek, Michigan, 1930). When workers in the steel, coal, and other industries insisted on taking action for themselves, the strikes were broken up by the use of judicial injunctions and, in some cases, by state troops.

Meanwhile, the middle classes turned on the people they believed were responsible for this labor unrest—the Communists. Throughout the years 1919 and 1920 they pursued the "Reds" from one end of the country to the other. The newspapers were full of news of Bolshevist plots against the government and the respectable people of the United States. Descriptions of horrible and immoral conditions in Soviet Russia by "thoughtful" publishers served to keep the American people alive to the bearded menace. News of radical activities in that country kept them aware of the danger at home. A series of bombings in 1919 and 1920 were attributed to the "Reds," and the bearded brute with a smoking bomb in his hand became the symbol of Communist Russia to paid cartoonists in the country. Excitement reached such a pitch that the five Socialist members of the New York State Assembly were expelled in April, 1920, although they had been legally elected, on the ground that they were members of "a disloyal organization composed exclusively of perpetual traitors."

While the "Red scare" was running its course, a situation developed which aroused the anxiety of the middle classes for reasons closer home than the Soviet Union. Business was bad and appeared to be getting worse. The size of the stocks of materials piled up at the end of the war forced a decrease of production. Employment and wages dropped while prices remained high. Retail food prices averaged 207 in the first six months of 1920 as against 146 in 1917 and 100 in 1913. The 1920 dollar would only buy half as much as the 1914 dollar. Although the working class was the first to be hit by the drop in its purchasing power, the less prosperous sections of the business groups soon began to feel the pinch too. The farmers found that while the prices of those things they had to buy remained as high as ever, the profits of farming were destroyed. At the same time they had to meet taxes and interest on the debts which they had assumed during the war. The result was the collapse of the economic structure of agricultural areas. After 1920, no matter how prosperous the rest of the country, the farmer was clamoring for relief.

Those members of the lower middle classes whose incomes

were fairly stationary—the salaried employees and the professional men—were in a position almost as bad as that of the farmer. They found themselves unable to meet the high prices. They could not maintain their old standard of living. Convinced that they were useful citizens and that society owed them a better living, many of them, when they heard that a bricklayer, on an hourly basis, was earning more than a high school teacher, concluded that civilization was indeed coming to an end. Periodicals of the period were full of their warnings and appeals.

In 1921 and 1922 the economic machine was badly run down, but by the end of the latter year it was regaining momentum. Business was improving, prices were declining, and wages were rising slightly. True, the farmer never really recovered from the effects of the post-war deflation, but the other sections of society did, and he was soon all but forgotten in the rush to take advantage of the ever-increasing prosperity of the country.

In the midst of these "good times," on August 3, 1923, Calvin Coolidge became president, following the sudden death of the genial Warren Harding. "Quiet, thrifty, industrious, and staid, Coolidge never shocked anyone by advocating strange or radical things; nor did he ever hold back when he saw the majority moving in a definite direction." As governor of Massachusetts he had gained headlines by calling the militia to put down a policemen's strike in Boston. This staunch defender of "law and order," who was "dull and insistent as duty itself" and who "thoroughly approved of the Ten Commandments" (John Corbin, "The Laborer and the Lady," *North American Review,* September, 1922), became the ideal head of a bourgeois "safe and sane" democracy. Economy was now elevated "to the dignity of a principle of government." Prosperity was regarded as the pinnacle of the Republican party's achievement.

The middle of the nineteen-twenties was the high tide of American middle-class prosperity. Probably never before in the history of mankind had a people been so well off. The world beat a path to our door, seeking to divine America's superiority. While Europe still struggled with the aftermath of the war, with every major country in financial and political straits, the United States marched serenely along, piling up wealth and making most everybody happy. The working men here lived more comfortably than the bourgeoisie in Western Europe, and Americans enjoyed what was to European eyes almost unbelievable luxury. A Frenchman wrote in 1928:

> If we realize that the ordinary working man (in the United States) earns $3.00 to $5.00 per day and the qualified working man receives as much as $15.00 to $17.00 (1925–1926) we will not be astonished to learn that the American wage-earners are enjoying real prosperity. This prosperity enables them to insure themselves against accidents, to own their own homes, and in many cases to become partners in the factories they have been working in, or to buy shares. In 1923, 16 per cent of the workers of the United States Steel Trust were shareholders and nearly 100 per cent were shareholders in Procter and Gamble. A popular conservative democracy is bound to develop in this country.

One reason for the great prosperity of the American economy during this period was the debility of Europe. The war had cost the nations of Europe millions of men and millions of tons of materials. Much of the industrial machinery had been destroyed. Reconstruction involved a demand for huge quantities of food and materials, a need which could be supplied only by America, the sole large country to be untouched by the war. It was this great European market that enabled the United States to right herself so quickly after the Armistice. Peculiarly, however, it was American money that the European nations used to buy American goods. To the ten billion dollars in war debts, the United States began adding billions more in trade loans.

Uncle Sam was generous, but Europe was an ungrateful debtor. From 1923 through 1929—the period of our largest peace-time lending—out of over seven billions borrowed, foreigners used only two and a half billions to buy our goods, the rest going for internal improvements. Thus the major part of the loans did not promote production in this country and was not laid out here for wages and farm products.

Another factor in "American prosperity" was something of local origin—the great development in the technique of advertising. During the middle twenties, sales promotion became a science, the science of applied psychology. "Sales resistance" was discovered and systematically battered down. The American people were "persuaded" to buy more and more until it became almost impossible to resist the attack of an expertly planned campaign.

But without a certain aid, even the greatest of salesmen would have been impotent, for, measured in terms of the prices of commodities, the wages and salaries upon which most Americans depended for their income had hardly risen above the pre-war level and they did not have the cash to buy much more than they had in pre-war days. "Easy credit"—buying today with the money he would earn next month or next year—was the American's godsend. Installment buying, the easy-payment plan, the budgeting system, the deferred buying plan—here was the new foundation of the American market. An office worker who wanted a home in the suburbs had no need to wait until he was old and grey and had saved at least a good part of the price. He could marry the girl of his heart, pay a few hundred dollars down, move into his Norman-French cottage, and pay off the balance of his debt "like rent." He could likewise buy an automobile, a radio, furniture, jewelry, clothes, and a honeymoon, provided he had a job or could get friends to be co-signers on a note whereby he agreed to repay the loan, plus a goodly interest, in monthly payments extending over a period of twelve, eighteen, or twenty-four months. Mortgaging the future became the popular pastime.

Of this system of high pressure advertising and installment buying the automobile is best representative. At the end of the war the motor car was still rather a novelty. People somehow managed to get from place to place without it. In 1919 there were fewer than seven million private cars registered in the entire United States. In the next ten years the salesmen and the bankers got to work. An automobile became a symbol of success. The middle-class man without one was out of the pale. He was no longer on an equal footing with his neighbors. The man who could not discuss the relative merits of different makes by examples from his own personal experience was isolated socially; he had nothing to talk about with his neighbors, his friends, his colleagues. The automobile became, for short trips, almost the only respectable method of conveyance. Legs were becoming vestigial. The horse and buggy was on the way to the museum. Even last year's car was looked at scornfully and superciliously by the owner of the latest model. By 1929 there were over 23,000,000 passenger automobiles registered; an increase of more than 300 per cent in ten years which showed how indispensable it was to own one. Today there are over 25,000,000 registered cars in the United States out of the world total of 35,000,000.

It was in this period, too, that the radio became a household necessity. On November 2, 1920, the Westinghouse Electric Company opened the first commercial broadcasting station, KDKA, in East Pittsburgh. Public interest developed slowly but, under the careful guidance of the press agent and the sales promoter, it soon picked up. The shift in public attention is shown by a comparison of the number of magazine articles on Radio. In the *Reader's Guide* for 1919–1921 there was one-quarter of a column of articles on Radio; the volume for 1922–1924 had more than nineteen columns of articles on this subject. In 1935 there were estimated to be over 18,000,000 radio sets in the United States.

Wide ownership of radios and automobiles illustrated the general prosperity of the country and particularly of that section that had sufficient standing in the community to gain easy credit, namely the middle classes. But there was an even better indicator of material prosperity during the twenties—the gradual ownership of great industries, heretofore in the hands of the great capitalists, by many small investors. "Since the start of the (income tax) record in 1916, it appears that there has been a major shift in the ownership of industry from the people of large incomes to those of moderate means." This aspect of the development of corporations is most significant. Not only does it clearly demonstrate the prosperity of the middle classes, but it also points to an important adaptation of that group to the newer developments of the capitalistic system. An examination of the three largest non-financial corporations in the country shows the extent of this change in recent years. In 1902 American Telephone and Telegraph had 12,000 stockholders, Pennsylvania Railroad 28,000, and United States Steel 120,000. Even the depression did not halt the process. In 1931 American Telephone and Telegraph had over 600,000 stockholders, Pennsylvania Railroad 241,000, and United States Steel more than 170,000. Nor was this state of affairs confined only to these corporate giants. "The estimated total of all stockholders of all corporations has grown rapidly, from four millions in 1900 to some eighteen millions in 1928."

Middle-class ownership of industry was reflected in the development of a new phenomenon, the Booster. The men who owned the common stock of the great corporations or ran businesses of their own modeled on those large enterprises were proud of their accomplishments. They wanted the world to know of them, and they found that the best means of attracting attention was to make a big noise. In every community of any size or importance the business men began to gather together in order to spur themselves on to greater achievements and to tell the world about them.

These gatherings took the form, usually, of eating clubs. Some met at luncheon, others at dinner, and still others at breakfast; but their main purpose was always the same and this was *not* eating. Perhaps the most famous of these organizations, certainly the oldest and best established, was the Rotary Club. Founded in 1905, it spread rather slowly until after the war. At that time it began to expand. By 1931, membership in the affiliated Rotary Clubs of the nation had reached 150,000, the organization had even spread abroad, and this same year there existed 3000 Rotary Clubs in forty-four nations, most of the foreign ones being concentrated in the countries of Western Europe. The Lions and Kiwanis were organizations similar to Rotary. Founded in 1917 and 1920 respectively, by the end of the twenties the affiliated clubs could be numbered in the hundreds, the Lions reaching 1200 and the Kiwanis 1800 by 1929. Upon approaching a town the first thing the traveler often sees nowadays is an array of signs advertising the presence of these groups.

Meeting together, usually once a week, the members set themselves the task of praising business and justifying it. At all times they emphasized the ideal of service. The good middle-class merchants and manufacturers of America thought of themselves as the forefront of civilization and the highest products of Christian endeavor. To prove this, they were fond of showing that they were following sacred precedents in their activities. Fred F. French, a New York real estate man, managed to justify the aggressiveness of salesmanship by quoting the Scriptures. He told his salesmen "there is no such thing as a reason why not. One evidence of the soundness of this belief may be found in the command laid down in Matthew, 7:7 by the Greatest Human-nature Expert that ever lived, 'knock and it shall be opened unto you.' " The executive and the efficiency expert were justified by Bruce Barton in *The Man Nobody Knows,* which was a best-seller for the years 1925 and 1926, when he wrote of Jesus: "He picked up twelve men from the bottom ranks of business and forged them into an organization which conquered the world. . . . Nowhere is there such a startling example of executive success as the way in which that organization was brought together."

The men who read these books and agreed with the sentiments expressed knew that they themselves were not perfect. They realized that business was not purely unselfish service to the community. But to say anything against these concepts was to be a "knocker," which was an offense against the community second only to being a Bolshevik. The man who could not accept with thanks the blessings showered down upon him by business, the man who would not "boost" his home community above all others, was worse than useless—he was subversive. If he were not native-born he "ought to be sent back where he came from."

Nevertheless, there did exist, even in the period of great prosperity, when the middle classes thought that society was approaching the peak of perfection, a group of men who claimed that they saw flaws in the contemporary world. This group was made up of a number of people who considered themselves to be artists and intellectuals, although the middle classes were never quite convinced of the validity of their claim. The foremost leaders were H. L. Mencken, Sinclair Lewis, and Theodore Dreiser.

As early as the post-war campaign against the "Reds," Mencken was beginning to make himself heard. In the *New Republic* of September 8, 1920, he published a statement of his views in the satirical style which was to make him famous among "advanced" Americans as the greatest of Babbitt-baiters:

> The class that I belong to is an inferior sub-class of the order of capitalists. I am not rich, but my ease and welfare depend very largely on the security of wealth. If stocks and bonds become valueless tomorrow, I'd be forced to supplement my present agreeable work with a good deal of intensely disagreeable. Hence I am in favor of laws protecting property, and am an admirer of the Constitution of the United States in its original form. If such laws can be enforced peacefully, i.e., by deluding and hornswoggling the classes whose interests they stand against, then I am in favor of so enforcing them; if not, then I am in favor of employing professional bullies, e.g., policemen, soldiers and Department of Justice thugs, to enforce them with the sword. . . . I am thus in favor of property and would be quite content to see one mob of poor men (in uniform) set to gouging and hamstringing another mob of poor men (in overalls) in order to protect it . . . I incline to the Right, am a Tory in politics, and trust in God.

In the same year appeared Sinclair Lewis's *Main Street* and two years later his *Babbitt*. Both books made a deep impression on the American intellectuals as exposures of the smug, self-satisfied, limited life of the middle classes. It became the fashion among those who thought themselves people with superior brains and culture to despise the terrible American bourgeoisie, who had all the bad characteristics of his European counterpart with none of the latter's redeeming features. When, in 1923, Mencken and George Jean Nathan brought out the *American Mercury*, the ranks of the critics of big middle-class America were further solidified. They then had a means of keeping their view of contemporary life continually before the public eye, and did so for the next decade. Of course, the Rotarians *et al.* tried to shout them down as knockers, the Secretary of the California Better-America Federation, for example, attacking *Main Street* because it "created a distaste for the conventional good life of the American."

Some of these attacks, however, did reach a vulnerable spot in the armor of the middle classes. Such criticism touched the minds of the wives and daughters of the business men. With the spread of the use of electricity and electrical appliances in the home and the growth of such institutions as the commercial bakery and laundry, these energetic women found that they had less and less to do. With the help of the vacuum cleaner, electric iron, washing machine, and the use of mechanical appliances in the kitchen the housekeeper for a small family, even without servants, could not find enough work to occupy her entire day the week round. Some women went out into the masculine world of business and tried to earn their independence; but the majority either could not or would not do this and had to look elsewhere for interests.

To occupy the leisure hours of these restless ladies of America there developed the institution of the club. In the period of the twenties the country began to be covered with women's clubs for producing plays, for hearing literary lectures, for playing Mah Jong or bridge, for attracting artistic and intellectual stimulation from all sides. Thus the women came into contact with the point of view that their husbands were escaping through absorption in money-making. They met and heard the anti-bourgeois intellectual; they learned that they were provincial, smug, conceited, and that there were a number of apparently charming people who thought very little of them because they lacked refinement. Had any group but the aggressive and self-reliant American women been subjected to such treatment, it might have surrendered to the inevitable and dropped the attempt to absorb culture. It took more to daunt the American wife and mother; she simply went out to "get" it by hook or crook.

Developing out of this determination to be well informed came two movements. Those who could afford to pay high for their education seized upon their husbands and children and took them off to Europe, the home of culture. If they could not induce any reluctant male to accompany them and to play the part of baggage-master, they were not dismayed; they went alone. Nothing could keep them from the fountain-head of civilization. So great was the rush that by 1928 almost half a million people were going abroad every year. The capitals of Europe were full of Americans looking for culture, romance, and liquor. They were warmly welcomed, for they spent about $650,000,000 in 1928 alone.

Those who could not go abroad for their introduction to civilization stayed home and read books. Non-fiction was the vogue, and mention of the best-sellers tells the story. H. G. Wells's *Outline of History* headed the list in 1921. Next year Hendrik Van Loon's *Story of Mankind* and J. Arthur Thomson's *Outline of Science* were the best-sellers. In 1923 prosperous America was feeling the need for social poise and correctness, and Emily Post's *Book of Etiquette* filled the bill. When, in 1927, the desire for deeper culture was making itself felt, Will Durant's *Story of Philosophy* was far and away the best-seller. Many people discovered, for the first time, that libraries had non-fiction shelves; that books could be purchased for a dollar; and that a ticket to the opera was not beyond the average purse.

Complacency now characterized all groups within the middle classes. Anyone who questioned anything connected with the status quo was frowned upon or ignored; whereas a writer, who revealed the faults of the proletariat and praised the bourgeoisie, was applauded. Especially welcome was Wilbur Cortez Abbott's *The New Barbarians* (Little, Brown and Co., Boston, 1925). In this volume the author warmed the hearts of all bourgeois folk from the millionaire capitalist to the village grocer by emphasizing their humanitarianism. Referring to the charitable activities of these men, Abbott wrote

> . . . on the corner-stone of every building devoted to the public service you may read their names; in the subscription book of every good work you will find them; in the lists of boards of directors and

benefactors of every institution which seeks to make the world a better place to live in, they are inscribed.

Another factor that brought about the decline of criticism was the great prosperity of the period. When every one was living on the fat of the land it was hard to obtain an audience that would listen to plans for a different sort of society. The intellectuals themselves found it difficult to remain interested while stocks soared and business boomed. By the end of the twenties the desire to get rich quick was supreme. The stock market was the cynosure of all eyes. The Old Deal, as far as the middle classes of the United States were concerned, was still a good deal.

Chapter XXVII

THE NEW DEAL

... Here is a society that manifests the most extraordinary contradictions ... dire poverty walks hand in hand with the most extravagant living the world has ever known ... strong men by the million walk the streets in a futile search for employment ... racketeers and gangsters with the connivance of public officials fasten themselves on the channels of trade and exact toll at the end of a machine gun ... consumption is subordinated to production and a philosophy of deliberate waste is widely proclaimed as the highest economic wisdom ... an ideal of rugged individualism, evolved in a simple pioneering and agrarian order at a time when free land existed in abundance, is used to justify a system which exploits pitilessly and without thought of the morrow the natural and human resources of the nation and of the world (George S. Counts, Dare the School Build a New Social Order? *The John Day Co., New York, 1932).*

IN 1928, the citizens of the United States elected to the presidency another "self-made" business man—Herbert Hoover. Famous as a result of his relief work in Belgium during the World War, this successful mining engineer was expected to continue the conservative policies of his predecessor and to extend prosperity all along the line. A typical bourgeois individualist, he favored a minimum of domestic legislation and permitted a maximum of tariff protection so that Big Business could continue to grow. Prosperity, he actually believed, would then be enjoyed by all classes. Meanwhile, the desire to participate in this race for wealth affected Americans of all stations in life. Literally millions invested their savings in stocks and bonds, disregarding the warnings of Mellon and other keen business men that the stock market was dangerously inflated.

In the diffusion of prosperity—which meant prosperity for all but the unemployed—certain unscrupulous plutocrats were quick to take advantage of the amazing scramble for wealth. The country seemed to be theirs for the asking, for the middle classes were so interested in the acquisition of stocks that they abandoned the vigilance which for nearly forty years had protected them against the interests seeking the concentration of wealth and consequent power.

Intelligent leaders of Big Business, however, remembered such results of outraged public opinion as the Interstate Commerce Act of 1887 and supplementary legislation. Under the cloak of bourgeois benevolence, therefore, they desired to safeguard their privileges. Utilizing the method of their feudal ancestors, they hired faithful "vassals"—efficient executives, crafty lawyers, and unscrupulous bankers—to help them bring a large section of the middle classes into a voluntary relationship of bondage through the purchase of stocks and bonds. By the sale to the public of various corporate securities yielding small "cash" and large "stock" dividends, important sections of the middle classes and even of the proletariat were brought into this new feudal system. The interests of these bond-servants and their lords seemed to be identical. No longer wage-earners (serfs), these "New freemen" were partners in the great estate. Meanwhile, some members of the New Nobility, by huge salaries, fat bonus payments, and other methods, literally and, sad to relate, legally, looted the estates and robbed their new partners.

Most remarkable was the attitude of middle-class men during this whole affair. Because they imagined that they were better off than before, because they actually believed that they were successful stockholders and speculators, they submitted to the growth of corporation power, became intense advocates of rugged individualism, and actually condemned governmental regulation of corporations. Blindly, they accepted this new economic feudalism that promised eternal prosperity, failing to realize that they were being deprived of their traditional independence, their vaunted liberty.

Few questions were asked during those days of "paper fortunes." Few wondered what would happen to the dependent middle classes if by any chance this prosperity came to an end. Few tried to explain just why the rest of the world was suffering from constant depression, social unrest, and political dictatorship, while at the same time the United States was gaily prosperous. It did not seem significant to many people that the European nations, in order to restore prosperity, were raising tariff walls designed to shut out American products. Nor did anyone hazard the guess that perhaps corporations and super-corporations, erected by finance capitalism aided and abetted by the middle classes, seemed to be bringing about Marx's doleful prophecy of the inevitable concentration of wealth and power in the hands of a few. And, finally, even those few who predicted a collapse of the stock market and a general business depression failed to point out the lack of those factors, such as free land where men could make a new start, that had acted as safety valves at other times. No! the middle classes really believed that a materialistic utopia was just ahead, despite the fact that throughout the world economic stagnation, growing unemployment, and earnest radical agitators menaced the very existence of the capitalistic system.

It is hardly necessary to describe the frenzy of speculation which held the country in its grip during 1928 and 1929. The memory has remained vivid despite the passing years. Preceded by the Florida boom and crash of 1924 and 1925, the great bull market really got under way in 1928. Unlike the Florida affair, which had been more or less limited to the East, the market of 1928 included people from all parts of the country with money to spare. Whereas in 1919 the branch offices of Wall Street brokers had numbered only 500 for the whole country, in 1928 there were 1192 and the number was still growing.

Undismayed by the warnings of conservative bankers and market experts, and by the action of the Federal Reserve Board in raising the discount rate, the public pushed the price of stocks higher and higher. Buying only to sell again, people paid no attention to actual values but gambled on a quick rise. More than a million Americans are estimated to have held stock on margin during the summer of 1929.

With business actually languishing and stocks at four or five times their real value, trouble was inevitable. Certainly, the smart bankers and brokers were not very surprised when the bottom dropped out of stocks. The result was immediate disaster. Thousands of fairly well-to-do people who had been playing the market in the hope of making fortunes were wiped out overnight. Banks whose assets were in the form of stocks and bonds soon began to feel the pinch. A weakening of the financial structure of the country did its part in further damaging already stagnant business. The Depression had arrived. Widespread unemployment resulted, conservative estimates placing the number of men and women seeking jobs in 1930 at 6,000,000 and in 1933 at 13,000,000. Bread lines were longer than ever before as men from all walks of life faced starvation. In many cases farmers found themselves unable to pay their bills or to meet the interest on their mortgages; merchants could not satisfy their obligations to the banks; investors received reduced dividends; and bond coupons were not honored. The wheels of industry ran slowly and the business machine functioned poorly. In March, 1933, economic conditions became so critical that President Roosevelt, shortly after his inauguration, proclaimed a national bank "holiday," whereby all banking operations were suspended pending the enactment of financial legislation by Congress. So tense was the situation that the assumption of war-time powers by the president seemed imminent.

The collapse of prosperity laid bare the weakness of the American economic system. As long as they had been able to earn and save, business and professional men seemed to be in fine condition. But the advent of the depression made clear the changes that had taken place in the national economy since the war, changes which were very much to the detriment of the middle classes as they had been constituted. The most important shift was one that has already been mentioned: the growth of the corporate form of business organization. Its significance cannot be exaggerated. American Telephone and Telegraph Company for example and other industrial giants controlled the processes of manufacture and reduced considerably the importance of the small factory owner. The merchant was attacked in his field by another type of corporation, the chain stores. In this field the corporation had not lagged behind its industrial fellows. Say Berle and Means (*The Modern Corporation,* The Macmillan Co., New York, 1933):

> From 1919 to 1927 sales by chain store groceries increased 28 per cent while sales of five and ten cent stores grew 160 per cent. The rate of growth of these chain stores is so far in excess of the growth of total retail sales as to represent a noteworthy encroachment of corporate upon private enterprises in distribution.

The effect of this development was to drive the middle-class merchant out of the field. To quote *Middletown* by the Lynds (Harcourt, Brace, and Co., New York, 1929):

> A swarm of chain stores is pressing hard upon the independent dealer, who had things far more his own way in the nineties: during an apparently characteristic ten months from April, 1924, through January, 1925, three Middletown clothing stores and one shoe store were taken over by selling agencies having at least one store in another city, and four new chains entered the city with one or more branches.

Other indications of the importance of the corporation are plentiful. Statisticians claimed that "at least 78 per cent . . . of American business wealth is corporation wealth," and that "85 per cent of all corporate wealth in the United States is owned by only five per cent of the corporations."

Under the circumstances the character of the American middle classes was bound to change. As the corporation advanced, the individual business man lost ground. When a store was taken over by a chain, the store owner, if he remained in the business, lost his independence and became a salaried employee. The same was true in the case of the absorption of factories by great industrial corporations. The competition of the tremendous corporations was often more than the small factory owner could meet. Forced to sell or go bankrupt, these little men tended to fall to the level of the salaried manager. An indication of the prevalence of this development is the growth of the so-called white-collar class in recent years, as given in the *Monthly Labor Review* for March, 1934. In 1870 the 300,000 white-collar workers made up 2.9 per cent of the country's gainfully employed. By the twentieth century their number had risen to 2,000,000 and they accounted for 7.5 per cent of the country's workers. In 1930 the number of white-collar workers had risen to 8,000,000 and they constituted more than sixteen per cent of the country's gainfully employed. Describing this decline of the independent business men, Lewis Corey in "The Crisis of the Middle Class" (*The Nation,* August 14, 1935) writes:

> The relative scarcity of independent enterprisers is most striking—only 3,300,000 in a middle class of 12,500,000: one out of four [in 1930], compared with three out of four sixty years ago. . . . Today [1935] there are not more than 2,700,000 independent enterprisers—a loss of three quarters of a million in six years. . . . The middle class is a small minority of the people and the enterprisers are a still smaller minority of the class. Ours is decidedly not a nation of business men.

Big business, destroyer of the old independent middle-class man, was rapidly making the United States a land of dependents—workers, salaried employees and professionals. Nearly three-fourths of the 12,500,000 members of the middle classes in 1930 were salaried employees. In 1935 they numbered about 11,000,000. In fact over eighty per cent of the 52,000,000 gainfully employed in 1935 were dependent upon jobs for their means of livelihood; "the exact opposite in the America of a century ago." Writes Corey: "Ours is decidedly a nation of dependent workers."

While the country was prosperous and business was good, the white-collar workers and the small independent business men found nothing about which to complain. Interest in anti-monopoly and anti-corporation legislation had dropped to a very low level. But when the depression arrived these groups began to notice their position. These low salaried workers did not suffer as greatly as did others, but they knew that times were bad. The average weekly earnings of office employees in New York State factories rose from $36.94 in 1929 to $37.48 in 1930, despite the fact that payrolls in general had dropped, but in the next year they began to follow the general trend. In

1931 the average weekly earnings of this group declined to $35.49, about the level of 1926, and in 1932 New York State office workers were back to the level of 1921, with great drops in the number of employees.

The small business man, even in the most prosperous times, had not been able to build up a very large reserve. With the curtailment of business he began to lose his profits and, having nothing to fall back on, was forced into bankruptcy. These failures so weakened the small independent banks that for a time the whole financial structure of the country seemed on the point of collapse. The final disaster in that case was avoided but the situation was little improved by the Bank Holiday of 1933. Even the formerly prosperous upper middle-class families were forced to give up golf club memberships, to sell their automobiles, and to borrow on their insurance policies. Their sons and daughters had to be called home from the colleges where they had been sent to absorb culture and make good contacts. Indeed, the world of the bourgeoisie was crashing down about its head.

In the face of the crisis the American business men were forced to appeal to the government. Two years before, they would have clamored against any such interference, but their character and psychology had changed. Depression had already taught them something. The small employer, the professional man, the white collar employee, all were beginning to realize that as individuals and even as groups, they could do nothing themselves to avert their being crushed by the great corporations and by economic stagnation. By 1932 they were ready to abandon their traditional reverence for rugged individualism and to put themselves under the guidance of centralized authority. The members of the middle classes were so frightened by what they saw ahead, so anxious to avoid the destruction of all their standards, that the cry of socialism and radicalism raised by the reactionaries could only make them shudder slightly as they pressed forward to the support of Roosevelt and his New Deal.

In what ways did the New Deal propose to aid the middle classes? In the words of President Roosevelt, it was designed to destroy the new feudalism. "Practices of the unscrupulous money changers," he said in his Inaugural Address on March 4, 1933, "stand indicted in the court of public opinion. . . . They know only the rules of a generation of self-seekers. They have no vision, and where there is no vision the people perish." "We must get back to first principles," he wrote in *Looking Forward* (The John Day Co., New York, 1933), "we must make American individualism what it was intended to be—equality of opportunity for all, the right of exploitation for none."

Judge Seabury of New York thus interpreted the relation of the New Deal to the American people: "The administration at Washington," he said, "is endeavoring to give intelligent leadership to the great middle-classes of this nation which, up to this time, have stood mute but unrepresented while their interests have been ground between the upper and nether millstones of highly organized groups representing capital and labor." If we would achieve industrial democracy, he concluded, the principle of representative democracy must be introduced into the great key industries of the nation. Schuyler Wallace in *The New Deal in Action* (Harper and Brothers, New York, 1934), however, presented the best short definition of the New Deal when he wrote that "Avowedly experimental in its character, the New Deal was formulated for the three-fold purpose of halting the deflation, preventing the proletarianization of the middle classes, and introducing a better balance in our national economy."

Taking office in 1933 President Roosevelt tried to carry out this program. Financial aid was given to heavily mortgaged farmers and home owners; banks and insurance corporations were extended support in order to save the investments of the middle classes; and the deposits of the small depositors up to five thousand dollars were guaranteed by the government. The president also attempted by legislation to protect investors from dishonest security racketeers. By various acts curbing production he raised the price of farm products and thus tried to help the farmers. He also favored the drawing up of codes of fair competition designed to protect the independents from such unfair practices of Big Business as selling below cost. Finally, by means of various public relief projects, unemployed middle-class men and women as well as the proletarians were given work.

What has been the effect of the New Deal upon the middle classes? Primarily, it seems to have brought about further divisions within that group. With business conditions improving because of or in spite of the New Deal, the upper middle classes, especially those dependent upon Big Business, have joined those plutocrats who are definitely hostile to the New Deal in demanding a return to rugged individualism as a prerequisite to the real return of prosperity. Ardently, they champion "historic capitalism . . . with its deification of the principle of selfishness, its exaltation of the profit motive, [and] its reliance upon the forces of competition." Meanwhile, the lower middle classes, such as the small shopkeepers and the struggling professional groups, are in a difficult position. Either they must cling to the bourgeois tradition of "respectability and individualism" and join the upper groups, or they must leave their class and merge with the proletariat. Some of the bourgeoisie wonder if there is not another way out—can they not stand alone?

Apparently, at the moment, a split is taking place in the middle classes. Many are joining the camp of the rugged individualists, hoping for the best; others are supporting certain "liberal" bourgeois leaders, Super-Big Dealers such as Father Charles E. Coughlin and his National Union for Social Justice, Doctor Francis E. Townsend and his Old Age Pension Plan, Upton Sinclair and his Epic group, and the followers of the late Senator Huey Long with their Share-the-Wealth Plan. Perhaps, like Technocracy, these too will have their day, and others spring up to take their places. Meanwhile, numerous middle-class men back President Roosevelt, believing that he can protect them against the two extremes—Big Business and proletarian radicalism.

By 1934 Big Business and its camp followers were determined to destroy all enemies. First, with the support of practically all bourgeois groups, the powers that be turned their guns on the proletarian radicals, the communist, and tried to drive them underground. Next they concentrated on the New Deal. Backed by the courts, by their hirelings, by a large section of the press, and by some of the intelligentsia, the exponents of Liberty succeeded in getting most of the New Deal declared unconstitutional. They rejoiced as the Supreme Court seemed to rally to their campaign cry of "State rights" and "Save the Constitution." Meanwhile, President Roosevelt had continued his assault on the feudal barons by bringing about the passage of legislation to curb the power of the public-utility nobility, to give security to the aged and the unemployed, and to increase the tax load on the new aristocracy.

The outcome of this struggle is in doubt. Of the guesses as to what the future may bring, none perhaps is more astute than that of Charles A. Beard in his *The Future Comes: a Study of the New Deal* (The Macmillan Co., New York, 1933). Beard prophesies that President Roosevelt and a sympathetic Congress will be elected in 1936 by a vigilant bloc of workers, lower-class men, and bourgeois agrarian supporters. Under their domination the Constitution will be amended to increase governmental economic authority and the veto power of the Supreme Court will be limited. Thus America will prosper! Roosevelt's adversaries disagree with this. They predict the failure of the New Deal as a result of extravagance and excessive taxes, and exult in a return to prosperity through the reestablishment of good old rugged individualism—"the road which alone," according to one interpretation of the words of Thomas Jefferson, "leads to peace, liberty, and safety."

Apparently bourgeois control of the policies and machinery of the government may not unravel the dilemma confronting the middle classes. How will it be possible for them to curb the plutocrats and at the same time to check organized labor? These petty bourgeoisie—small shopkeepers, farmers, tradesmen, professionals, and others of that general class—have clung desperately to their independence and to their constantly dwindling possessions. Angrily, they have backed the plutocrats in opposing the demands of labor for higher wages and shorter hours. Alone, they have been helpless to oppose organized labor and therefore have welcomed the support of the monopolists, even though the latter have been more dangerous a foe to the bourgeoisie than are the wage-earners. Groups of plutocrats, petty bourgeoisie, farmers, working men, and skilled workers merge in common opposition to the Communists, fearing that these radicals will deprive them of their property and of their wages. This "red scare" alone unites the various groups within the capitalistic system and by so doing enables the plutocrats to continue with "their land expropriation by means of taxes, customs duties, interest, and monopoly prices; while constantly waving the red flag in front of the little fellows and promising assistance in the event of an attempt on the part of the radicals to introduce a policy of 'expropriation by violence.' "

Many people are of the opinion that a definite change is occurring in the American attitude toward life. Young men and women are no longer worshiping at the shrine of the self-made man. Like the Indian, he is a vanishing American. Today's young people want to *live*—not simply to *accumulate*. They desire security, a living wage, independence. They are hostile to the individual who has made a million, and rather skeptical that he got it honestly. True, they realize that Big Business is not entirely a closed corporation or a hereditary dynasty. The office boy may have a chance to become president of the company, but even if he should he will only be a cog in an irresistible machine; like a cardinal in the Catholic church he will be part of a vast organization, his life dedicated to its impersonal existence. The young careerists of today have their eyes open to social and economic conditions. Theirs was no education on the Horatio Alger way to success. They have a more realistic credo: "It is not what you can do that counts; it's who you know." They are not afraid to speak up in meeting about "pull," and "graft," and "dirty-work." They are not blinded by book-learning to real-learning; the percentage of political fools born every minute is steadily decreasing. More and more, the young persons of today are aware of the true economic divisions instead of the propaganda-political classifications. They know that there are groups in society which, intent upon immediate advantages and rewards, disregard all interests save their own. They know that between these forces are the middle classes, unorganized, split into antagonistic groups and therefore impotent. They know that of these middle classes they themselves constitute a vitalizing element with their restlessness, their ambitiousness, and their practical idealism. They know that upon them may depend the future of our society.

Chapter XXVIII

LITERATURE AND THE MIDDLE CLASSES

IV. America: Franklin, Lewis, Dos Passos, & Co.

Offshoot of the mother country and like her long after the bonds of union were severed, the United States had, at least up to the outbreak of the Civil War, no distinctive interpretation of its middle classes that might set them off from England or for that matter from any growing industrial country. Her bourgeoisie had the same worship of thrift, the same puritanical tendency to moralize, the same although perhaps intensified devotion to liberty, the same restless energy and enterprise peculiar to the middle station all over Europe. Babbitt was over a century in the future.

In young America, Benjamin Franklin (1706–1790) might be regarded as the father of American bourgeois concepts. True, such beliefs as he expressed had been previously elaborated by such European writers as Alberti and Defoe. Nevertheless, his *Poor Richard's Almanac,* containing paragraphs and maxims upon business, moral conduct, and thrift, constituted the "bourgeois Bible" of the majority of American farmers and business men in the nineteenth century.

Franklin probably emphasized certain middle-class precepts more than did European writers. Perhaps no other early intellectual equaled him in giving practical advice on how wealth could best be acquired. He emphasized constantly the idea that God would help only those who helped themselves. Industry, therefore, was the way to economic salvation. "Trouble springs from Idleness, and grievous Toil from needless Ease . . . whereas Industry gives Comfort and Plenty and Respect." Frugality was another well-worn virtue stressed by Franklin.

"Beware of little Expenses; a small Leak will sink a great Ship . . . Fools make Feasts, and wise Men eat them." Prudence, as well as frugality, he said, should be followed. "But what Madness must it be to run in Debt for these superfluities . . . when you run in Debt, you give to another power over your Liberty."

In the early nineteenth century certain writers, however, tended to oppose this emphasis upon the utilitarian way of living. Ralph Waldo Emerson (1803–1882), in his well-known essay on *Self-Reliance,* called upon Americans to develop their personalities and not to stress the material side of life. Henry Thoreau (1817–1862) also expressed this idea and urged the necessity of getting away from the blighting influence of property and from the materialistic life in general. "A man is rich in proportion to the number of things he can afford to let alone," he said. Most Americans, however, followed Franklin's rather than Thoreau's line of reasoning.

In the decades immediately following the Civil War, the United States experienced an agricultural and industrial expansion which more than justified the accepted maxims of Benjamin Franklin. Democracy passed into the hands of the middle classes who were busily occupied in establishing a plutocracy. Opposition to material development on the part of nineteenth-century writers seemed ridiculous to the triumphantly dominant American business men. The early idea of beneficent progress, "which was the flower of the doctrine of human perfectability," was now interpreted as material expansion with constantly augmenting profits; and the concept of democracy was defined as the right to use the government as a whole for the benefit of the few. Men judged success in terms of money amassed. Enthusiastically they accepted such fetishes of mature capitalism as the worship of physical bigness, quick movement, staid morals, and the sense of material power.

Despite this worship of practical things there were some intellectuals who questioned certain features of the industrial age and even dared to ridicule the middle classes. Foremost of these early literary critics was Wendell Phillips (1811–1884). In his lectures, delivered in the early seventies, he pictured private capitalism "with its dehumanizing profit motive" as the arch-enemy of a worthy civilization. In his opinion there could be "no adequate civilization, no Christianity until coöperation has displaced competition," and men had achieved economic as well as political equality. Phillips was a radical who frankly said he was not afraid of revolution. He believed that in America it would be fought at the ballot box but, "if it must come to bullets, so be it." He thoroughly approved of the radical plans of the Paris Commune and ardently defended revolution in a Phi Beta Kappa address delivered in 1881. Fortunately for Phillips, his conservative listeners did not take him seriously, for as one said, "It was a delightful discourse, but preposterous from beginning to end."

Criticism of the established order appeared in the writings as well as the lectures of the nineteenth-century intellectuals. William Dean Howells (1837–1920), recognizing the essential tragedy inherent in our social and economic maladjustment, gently satirized his age in such novels as *A Hazard of New Fortunes, The Rise of Silas Lapham,* and *A Traveller from Altruria.* In *The Rise of Silas Lapham,* Howells thus described the wealthy middle-class Laphams:

> They were quiet, unpretentious people, religious, after the fashion of that time, and of sterling morality, and they taught their children the simple virtues of the Old Testament and Poor Richard's Almanac.

Both Howells in his novels and Clyde Fitch (1865–1909) in such a play as *The Climbers* brought out the social ambitions of rich Americans, their beliefs that "money buys position at once," and that the new aristocracy of wealth should be merged with the old aristocracy of blood. One very stimulating exception, however, to the literature depicting the desire of the rich American middle classes to ascend socially is found in George Horace Lorimer's *Letters of a Self-Made Merchant to His Son.* The merchant, John Graham, is head of the firm of Graham and Company, Pork-Packers, Chicago. Having decided to send his heir, Pierrepont, to Harvard "to get a little of the education that's so good and plenty there," he determines to safeguard the youth by occasional letters full of soft-headed bourgeois advice. One of the letters, occasioned by the rumor that Pierrepont is knocking humbly at the door of society, warns him against such foolishness:

> Everybody over here thinks we haven't any society in America, and a power of people in New York think that we haven't any society in Chicago . . . you've got to be a descendant to belong, and the farther you descend the harder you belong. The only difference is that, in Europe, the ancestor who made money enough so that his family could descend, has been dead so long that they have forgotten his shop; in New York he's so recent that they can only pretend to have forgotten it; but in Chicago they can't lose it because the ancestor is hustling on the Board of Trade or out at the Stock Yards. I want to say right here that I don't propose to be an ancestor until after I'm dead. Then, if you want to have some fellow whose grandfather sold bad whiskey to the Indians sniff . . . when you come into the room, you can suit yourself.

Around 1890 the American upper bourgeoisie, the plutocrats, began to be criticized not only as social climbers but also as oppressors of the lower middle classes. But the Spanish-American War at the close of the nineteenth century tended to submerge internal troubles through a revival of patriotism. By 1903, however, the muckrakers were again attacking plutocracy where its joints creaked. A group of writers, including Henry George and Charles Edward Russell, "popularized economics and made the liberals conscious of what was going on behind the closed doors of directors' meetings." At the same time a number of political leaders, typified by Theodore Roosevelt, Robert La Follette, and Woodrow Wilson, endeavored to direct the political machinery to democratic ends.

Frank Norris (1870–1902) is typical of the pre-war writers who in their works pictured the designing ends of the trusts and the "cruelty" of plutocracy. The stifling influence of Bigness in the form of the trusts and in the security of the middle classes, especially in the rural sections, is the theme of *The Octopus*. The scene is California about the turn of the century. There the railroad trust (the Octopus) grasps in its tentacles the small wheat growers of the San Joaquin Valley. By rebates, cut rates, dishonest lobbying at Sacramento, and pressure brought to bear on the State Railroad Commission the independent growers are reduced to the status of completely dependent economic serfs. One of the characters, Dyke, ruined by a change of railroad rates after he had made contracts for the sale of his crops is thus "commiserated" by the barkeeper of the saloon where he had sought forgetfulness in drink:

> "Do you blame us now," cried [the barkeeper], "us others, the Reds? Ah, yes, it's all very well for your middle-class to preach moderation. I could do it, too. You could do it, too, if your belly was fed, if your property was safe, if your wife had not been murdered, if your children were not starving. Easy enough then to preach law-abiding methods, legal redress, and all such rot. But how about *us?*" he vociferated. "Ah, yes, I'm a loud-mouthed rum-seller, ain't I? . . . talk about moderation! And you, Dyke . . . discharged employee, ruined agriculturist . . . wait till you see—at the same time that your family is dying for lack of bread—a hundred thousand acres of wheat—millions of bushels of food—grabbed and gobbled by the Railroad Trust, and then talk of moderation."

Such a speech and many others like it in similar novels seemed to suggest an early realization of a present general expectation —the danger of an economic extinction of the lower middle classes and a union of its members with the working men against their mutual oppressors, the upper middle classes and the capitalistic plutocracy.

It was not until about 1920, however, that the American social system as a whole became subjected to truly biting criticisms. For this sudden trend in literature the World War was responsible. After the Armistice many Americans were shocked to learn that the youngest world power was not to be allowed to make over civilization. Sadly, they realized that the struggle had not made the world safe for democracy, nor had it been a war to end wars. Shorn of its halo of idealism, the World War stood forth to these intellectuals as an imperialistic struggle of nations and men. Affected by the changed point of view, the literature of pessimism, which had been noticeable before 1914, became a literature of ridicule and realism. Such writers as Booth Tarkington, Winston Churchill, Theodore Dreiser,

Charles A. Beard, James Truslow Adams, Sinclair Lewis, Upton Sinclair, and the pre-depression H. L. Mencken have since subjected the middle classes to sharp satire.

All phases of bourgeois life are attacked by these twentieth-century intellectuals. For instance, Churchill in his novels lays bare the selfishness of the profit motive; Upton Sinclair, "the revolutionary sleuth," attacks bourgeois conservatism in American universities; and H. L. Mencken "resorts to farce and burlesque for methods adequate to express his contempt for American democracy." These authors especially condemn the heartless, blind, and never-ending struggle for wealth which characterizes this gilded, machine age. Tarkington, for example, in the prologue to a trilogy of novels entitled *Growth,* writes:

> The smoke is like the bad breath of a giant panting for more and more riches. He gets them and pants the fiercer, smelling and swelling prodigiously. He has a voice, a hoarse voice, hot and rapacious, trained to one tune: "Wealth! I will get Wealth! I will make wealth! I will sell wealth for more wealth! My house shall be dirty, my garments shall be dirty, and I will foul my neighbor so that he cannot be clean—but I will get wealth! There shall be no clean thing about me: my wife shall be dirty . . . but I will get wealth!" And yet it is not wealth that he is so greedy for. What the giant really wants is hasty riches. To get these he squanders wealth upon the four winds, for wealth is in the smoke.

The attacks on the social order, however, are best brought out in the works of Zona Gale, Evelyn Scott, and Sinclair Lewis. Of these Sinclair Lewis is the most famous delineator of middle-class foibles. His satire "is a searching criticism of the bourgeois ideals and habitat, its tyrannical herd-mind, its poverty-stricken materialism." His *Main Street* sketches the small town; his *Babbitt* diagnoses the prosperous small city; and his *Arrowsmith,* in the course of a vivid picture of the medical profession, presents a vertical study of American life from small town to metropolis.

As pictured by Lewis, the ordinary business man is remarkably homogeneous, irrespective of the locality and the size of his city. He earns between $2500 and $10,000 a year. He practices the virtues recommended by Franklin. He is conservative in politics, business, and religion. In his opinion vested interests are sacrosanct. He has no conception of real beauty; no appreciation of literature, art, or music; no knowledge of the vivid past and no interest in a fascinating future for mankind. He seems to be the one a European writer had in mind when he said that socially America is "European nature in the raw, namely: modern man as he is, apart from ancient traditions, ancestral customs, inherited memories, or a great past." This same writer, Count Hermann Keyserling, in *America Set Free* (Harper's, New York, 1929), regards Babbitt as a twentieth-century equivalent of Molière's *bourgeois gentilhomme.*

Unquestioning complacency, according to Lewis, is the most predominant characteristic of this society. In his opinion the ordinary representative of it had recently emerged from the American peasantry—for he explodes the theory that there are no peasants—or from the lower urban masses. This middle-class man has experienced an evolutionary change and apparently is satisfied to rest on his laurels, to leave to his children the continuation of the rise to a higher level.

Babbitt is perhaps the best-known literary example of a modern tradesman. He is a *realtor*—not a *real-estate man*—of the city of Zenith in a middle western state. The author follows his activities for about a year and a half, during which Babbitt speaks eloquently for the modern business man. His Ideal Citizen, for instance:

> Our Ideal Citizen—I picture him first and foremost as being busier than a bird-dog, not wasting a lot of good time in day-dreaming or going to sassiety teas or kicking about things that are none of his business, but putting the zip into some store or profession or art. At night he lights up a good cigar, climbs into the old 'bus . . . and shoots out home. He mows the lawn, or sneaks in some practice putting, and then he's ready for dinner. After dinner he tells the kiddies a story, or takes the family to the movies, or plays a few fists of bridge, or reads the evening paper, and a chapter or two of some good lively Western novel if he has a taste for literature, and maybe the folks next-door drop in . . . Then he goes happily to bed, his conscience clear, having contributed his mite to the prosperity of the city and to his own bank-account.

Evidently Babbitt thought some of his class—but very few—were materialistic. Here is his praise of American spirituality:

> Trouble with a lot of folks is: they're so blame material; they don't see the spiritual and mental side of American supremacy; they think that inventions like the telephone and the aeroplane and wireless—no, that was a Wop invention, but anyway, they think these mechanical improvements are all that we stand for; whereas to a real thinker, he sees that spiritual and, uh, dominating movements like Efficiency, and Rotarianism, and . . . Democracy are what compose our deepest and truest wealth.

Finally, he summarizes American æsthetic appreciation:

> In no country in the world will you find so many reproductions of the Old Masters and of well-known paintings on parlor walls as in these United States. . . .
>
> In other countries, art and literature are left to a lot of shabby bums living in attics and feeding on booze and spaghetti, but in America the successful writer or picture-painter is indistinguishable from any other decent business man.

The middle classes of the small town in Sinclair Lewis's *Main Street* were basically similar to their fellows in the large cities. These suburban business people, however, were even more self-complacent than their despised city brothers. Perhaps the reason was that had they been able they would long since have escaped to a larger place; or perhaps it was because they enjoyed a measure of importance comparable to that of Lords of the Manor and were thus blinded to the fact that they were not aristocrats but merely bourgeois residents in rural communities. At any rate the following is an enumeration of their standardized notions:

> All socialists ought to be hanged.
>
> Harold Bell Wright is a lovely writer, and he teaches such good morals in his novels, and folks say he's made prett' near a million dollars out of them.
>
> People who make more than ten thousand a year or less than eight hundred are wicked.
>
> Europeans are still wickeder.
>
> It doesn't hurt any to drink a glass of beer on a warm day . . .

The farmers want too much for their wheat.

The owners of the elevator-company expect too much for the salaries they pay.

There would be no more trouble or discontent in the world if everybody worked as hard as Pa did when he cleared our first farm.

That bourgeoisism in post-war America was the philosophy of many professional as well as business men is illustrated in the literature of the time. Sinclair Lewis's *Elmer Gantry,* is an example, but a patently overdrawn study, even for satire, of a pharisaical, immoral clergyman who worships the Idols of the Market Place. His *Arrowsmith* deals with the commercialization of the medical profession. Winston Churchill describes the conflict between religion and business in his book *The Inside of the Cup* while Willa Cather in *The Professor's House* considers the influence of business in relation to education, particularly to public education. Sinclair Lewis was especially apt at drawing bourgeois "ideals." A large income, a large bank-book, a big house, an expensive automobile—these were the things the business classes strove to attain. Salvation on earth meant physical comforts, and the criteria of success, as stated before, was Bigness. Babbitt loved Zenith because it "was big . . . and he respected bigness in anything; in mountains, jewels, muscles, wealth, or words." Standardization, as well as bigness, was his boast. "With all modesty," says Babbitt, "I want to stand up here as a representative business man and gently whisper, 'Here's our kind of folks! Here's the specifications of the Standardized American Citizen.' " Tarkington, in the prologue of *Growth,* also revealed this dominating characteristic of the new industrial age when he wrote:

> . . . But there was a spirit abroad in the land, and it was strong . . . a spirit that had moved in the depths of the American soil and laboured there, sweating till it stirred the surface, rove the mountains, and emerged, tangible and monstrous, the god of all good American hearts—Bigness.

A few pages later, speaking for plutocracy, he apotheosizes Bigness as follows:

Give me of thyself, O Bigness;
Power to get more power!
Riches to get more riches!
Give me of thy sweat that I may sweat more!
Give me of thy Bigness to get more Bigness to myself.

Some writers, however, frankly opposed this worship of bigness. John Gould Fletcher, an American poet who lived in England, was unimpressed by the skyscrapers of his native land and thought they were symbolic of false standards. In *Skyscrapers* he asked:

What are they, then, angels, or demons,
Or stone?
Deaf sightless towers
Unendowed yet with life;
Soaring vast effort
Spent in the sky till it breaks there.
You men of my country
Who shaped these proud visions,
You have yet to find godhead
Not here, but in the human heart.

Edwin Markham, in *Man-Making,* also warned that big things may house little men:

We all are blind until we see
That in the human plan
Nothing is worth the making if
It does not make the man.

Why build these cities glorious
If man unbuilded goes?
In vain we build the world unless
The builder also grows.

A number of writers questioned the value of standardization. In other countries there were long-established and deeply cherished local customs, traditions, even pleasures and sports. But the vast expanse of the United States, in which a single language was spoken, had been particularly amenable to the irresistible high-pressure salesmanship of the machine age and mass production. The Babbitts in city and town dressed alike, ate the same canned foods, saw the same talkies, and read the same news from country-wide agencies. Babbitt would be the same in "Ohio or Montana, in Kansas or Kentucky or Illinois . . . or in the Carolina hills."

The influence of this standardization, according to novelists, had an unfortunate effect on two factors that might otherwise have contributed new vigor to the future American. The first was immigration. Willa Cather in her novels of immigrant life regretted that the second generation of colorful Southeastern Europeans was soon Americanized. This shattered a romantic belief of at least one poet. In his poem, "Scum o' the Earth," Robert Haven Schauffler predicted that a potential Chopin or Dvorák or Dante passing through Ellis Island would be destroyed because of the lack of culture in America.

According to some of the novelists and other writers, the second factor that was stifled by standardization was an unawakened native culture and aesthetic appreciation. But how could it come to life without encouragement, without sympathetic guidance? What could one hope for, intimates Sinclair Lewis, from an environment like the following?

> Main Street is the climax of civilization. That this Ford car might stand in front of the Bon Ton Store, Hannibal invaded Rome and Erasmus wrote in Oxford cloisters. What Ole Jenson the grocer says to Ezra Stowbody the banker is the new law for London, Prague, and the unprofitable isles of the sea; whatsoever Ezra does not know and sanctions, that thing is heresy and wicked to consider. . . . Our railway station is the final aspiration of architecture.

Evidently Edgar Lee Masters in his *Spoon River Anthology* had little confidence in standardization, for in describing the misguided yearnings of Frank Drummer of Spoon River, in a humorous but pathetic epitaph, he wrote:

> Out of a cell into this darkened space—
> The end at twenty-five!

My tongue could not speak what stirred within me,
And the village called me a fool.
Yet at the start there was a clear vision,
A high and urgent purpose in my soul
Which drove me on trying to memorize
The Encyclopedia Britannica!

It is undeniable that these pictures as a whole are unfavorable to the middle classes. Are the pictures accurate? In the first place, they were produced at the time of national disillusionment. Lewis in particular was frankly satirical, yet with all his bluster, is not George Babbitt a lovable character? What of *Main Street?* Does not the following description of it by Professor Canby sound the right note of reasonable optimism regarding it and the whole American middle-class scene?

. . . From the window one sees a jumble of ugly brick walls, a sky tainted by coal smoke, signs offensive in vulgarity as in ugliness. Yet beneath is a good sort of people busy supporting families that are cheery as often as mean-minded, as often interested in China, child welfare, good books, and happy conversation as in the price of stocks, the sins of their neighbors, and alcohol. In short, no Main Street is just as it looks to any individual at any given moment of mood and time.

Some recent delineators of bourgeois humdrummeries refuse to accept even this friendly interpretation. Of these, John Roderigo Dos Passos (1896–) is perhaps outstanding. A university man, he was profoundly shocked by his experience in the ambulance service during the World War; out of his intense reaction against the brutality and lick-strip of war came such works as *One Man's Initiation* and *Three Soldiers*. More than the cry of a liberal whose sensitivity had been outraged, these books held the beginnings of his social philosophy. Hesitantly, gropingly, Dos Passos associated the oppression, brutality, and horror of war with some weakness in the existing social order and with the selfishness of powerful economic forces. In his volumes he has evolved a form of novel which is reflective of the complexity and confusion of modern America, particularly of its middle-class elements. He has found that society could no longer be adequately portrayed in the story of a person or a family, nor can it be understood if isolated from the dominant forces of the generation; consequently, he has invented a literary technique making use of the "newsreel" and biographical sketches. The "newsreels" indicate the wide range of events and topics which reach the consciousness of the ordinary American through the medium of the press and popular song. They also expose the confusion of values, the juxtaposition of the important and the trivial, the often shocking incongruities which are characteristic of modern life. The following extracts are picked more or less at random:

Isadora Duncan's New Happiness

IWW trouble-makers overran a Garibaldi birthday celebration at Rosebank Staten Island this afternoon, insulted the Italian flag, pummelled and clubbed members of the Italian Rifle Society and would have thrown the American flag to the dirt if

White Potatoes Show Weakness

Six Unclad Bathing Girls Black Eyes of Horrid Man

Goodby Broadway
Hello France
We're ten million strong

capitalization grown 104% while business expands 520%

HAWAIIAN SUGAR CONTROL LOST BY GERMANS

Biographical sketches, on the other hand, give unity of interpretation to the two volumes, *The 42nd Parallel* and its sequel, *Nineteen-nineteen,* in which Dos Passos brings out most effectively his view of the middle classes. In his books appear as heroes such figures of the labor and revolutionary movements as Big Bill Haywood, John Reed, Randolphe Bourne, Joe Hill, and Wesley Everest. Here also is presented Dos Passos's sympathetic but critical estimate of reformist leaders such as Theodore Roosevelt, "the happy warrior"; Bryan, "the boy orator of the Platte"; La Follette, "fighting Bob"; and Wilson, "Meester Veelson." They picture liberal idealism, rather regretfully, as an ineffectual protest.

To point out the importance of the "newsreels" and sketches is not to minimize the excellent studies of the middle classes embodied in Dos Passos's fictional characters. These people represent many lanes of American life. Perhaps the majority of them, whether they come from behind the counters of department stores or from the comfortable homes of wealthy merchants, are callous to human values and totally devoid of social idealism. Bred in a society which offered them no convincing standard of value other than material success, they measure life by appearances.

One of the sharpest pictures Dos Passos drew of this hard, money-loving type is of the Merivale household in *Manhattan Transfer*. Its philosophy was summed up in the advice Jefferson Merivale, the father, gave to his orphaned nephew, Jimmy Herf, a youth oppressed by the stuffiness of middle-class existence and uncharmed by the prospect of a successful business career.

> I have not noticed that you felt sufficient responsibility about money matters . . . er . . . sufficient enthusiasm about earning your living, making good in a man's world. Look around you . . . Thrift and enthusiasm has made [self-made] men what they are. . . . And don't forget this, if a man's a success in New York, he's a success!

Not all of Dos Passos's middle-class characters, even in the business world, are of this harsh, practical attitude of mind. A rather appealing portrait is that of the humble Thatcher. Here is an individual whose sincere respect for the old substantial virtues is stronger than his desire to get on in the world. He is a certified accountant, a stable, hard-working, devoted family man. His philosophy is revealed in his refusal to gamble on the exchange when a friend urges him to take a sure flier that may land him in easy street.

> "Hell man, you don't want to be in this damned office all your life, do you? Think of your little girl."
>
> "I am, that's the trouble."

"But Ed, Gibbon and Swandike has started buying already at three cents . . . The market'll go crazy on it . . ."

"Unless the fellers doin' the dirty work change their minds. I know that stuff through and through, Viler. . . . Sounds like a topnotch proposition. . . . But I've examined the books of too many bankrupts."

Viler got to his feet and threw his cigar into the cuspidor. "Well do as you like, damn it all . . . working twelve hours a day. . . ."

"I believe in workin' my way up, that's all."

In general, the picture which Dos Passos presents of the American middle class is one of chaos and bankruptcy. To him it seems destined for liquidation. Although the reader cannot escape, he is not left to despair of all order and meaning, for to Dos Passos, this social group is not *all* of America, and, although this class has bungled, Dos Passos has hope that a more reasonable society may still be established out of the vitalizing elements that remain.

Chapter XXIX

EPILOGUE

WHITHER, BOURGEOISIE?

Into this Universe, and Why *not knowing*
Nor Whence, *like Water willy-nilly flowing;*
And out of it, as Wind along the Waste,
I know not Whither, *willy-nilly blowing*
(Rubáiyát of Omar Khayyám).

"The unenlightened workers of pre-revolutionary Russia," wrote Lenin, the Bolshevist leader, "did not know that the Tsar was the head of the *ruling class,* namely, the class of large landowners, who by a thousand ties, were already bound up with a big bourgeoisie who were ready to defend their monopoly, privileges, and profits by every violent means." By 1917, however, in his estimation, the proletariat were keenly conscious of this connection; as a result, they carried through the Communist Revolution.

This large-scale assault on the capitalistic system was made possible by the World War. Mortally wounded as a result of the struggle, the old régime in Russia was easily vanquished by the Bolsheviks who, holding the entire bourgeois system responsible for the world conflict and the inequalities of the time, then undertook to "rescue the property-less man from the bourgeois dictatorship characteristic of capitalistic society." Toward this end, private property was confiscated, industry was nationalized, and a world attack was declared on capitalism, bourgeois and otherwise.

By exposing the glaring defects of the industrial machine and thus providing social and political criticism of the established order, grist for the propaganda mill, the world-wide post-war depression aided the Bolsheviks in their offensive. Prevalent at the opening of the twentieth century, these attacks gained momentum after the upheaval of 1914–1918 and have been increasing ever since. Subjected to steadily sharper scrutiny were the economy, politics, culture, and morality of the bourgeois state. The middle-class order, however, although somewhat altered to meet new demands and conditions, so far has managed to survive this scorching examination and cross-examination of its predominating philosophies.

Both the radicals and the bourgeoisie have made the economic organization of society the focal point of attack. Socialists and Communists have blamed capitalism for all the existing economic evils and particularly have condemned in that system private property, the inequitable distribution of wealth, the operation of industry and distribution for private profit, the exploitation of wage-earners by employers, and the lack of a practical economic plan for the benefit of society as a whole. As a solution they have proposed a new order based upon social control of the means of production, distribution, and exchange —a system which, in their opinion, would guarantee the simple principles of human justice.

Severe, too, in the widespread disapprobation were certain bourgeois intellectuals. But they, unlike the radicals, did not impugn the very system of capitalism; they only commented on its inherent contradictions and apparent decline. Thus, Dr. Harry Emerson Fosdick, one of them, declared:

> Our whole capitalistic society is on trial, for obviously there is something the matter with the operation of a system that over the world leaves millions and millions of people out of work who want work and millions in the sinister shade of poverty.

While another, Professor James Harvey Rogers, wrote in a more ominous vein:

> Thus while the human caterpillars go around and around, the golden spiral winds ever higher and higher its rapidly encircling coils. The dying gasps of capitalism in the constrictor's grasp can all but be heard by one of the world's leading bankers (Montague Norman), while its most renowned dramatist (Bernard Shaw), plumed

and painted, awaits the dance at the funeral pyre. Just as each major expansion period is a new era, so is each violent and prolonged depression the end of our modern industrial civilization.

Pope Pius XI (1922–), in his encyclical on *Reconstructing the Social Order* (1931), criticized the prevailing economic individualism and declared that coöperation between capital and labor was vital if the existing order was to survive. Like the liberal Leo XIII, he defended the right of private property but questioned the right of its unrestricted use. "The very misuse, or non-use of ownership," he maintained, "destroys or forfeits the right itself." Quoting the words of Leo XIII—"The earth even though apportioned amongst private owners ceases not thereby to minister to the needs of all"—Pius frankly advocated a just distribution of wealth by means of state regulation. "Domination has followed free competition," he continued, therefore "free competition and still more economic domination must be kept within just and definite limits and must be brought under the effective control of public authority, in matters appertaining to this latter's competence."

Onslaughts on the political order were decidedly pronounced. By 1933 the principle of democracy itself was under fire. In Italy, Poland, Yugoslavia, Russia, Turkey, and Germany there were open dictatorships. In other countries dictatorial governments were concealed by democratic labels. Woodrow Wilson's ideal of "making the world safe for democracy" had not been realized. In the opinion of many, democracy, which offered numerous opportunities for demagogy, was the underlying cause for the sorry state of the world's affairs. Too often, these critics asserted, incompetent politicians surrendered to the whims and prejudices of the multitude or to the money or power of selfish interests instead of heeding the judgment of competent experts. In France a publicist denounced democracy as the "Cult of the incompetent." In Italy, Mussolini declared:

When the sheep lead the shepherd, when the soldiers of an army can conduct a campaign better than an experienced and technically trained general, when the sailors can command a battleship in action, then democracy will be accepted as an efficient form of government.

Disturbing indeed were the prophecies expounded in literature about existing society. The erudite German writer, Oswald Spengler, in his *Decline of the West,* ushered in a "new pessimism." Arguing from historical analogy, he maintained that Western civilization had reached its apex and was beginning to descend. Charles A. Beard, in his preface to *Whither Mankind,* reiterated Spengler's theme when he asked whether civilization was still rising to a zenith or had already begun to crumble into ruin; apparently he was losing faith in any international solution of our present-day problems. Dr. Beard, in his recent book, *The Open Door at Home* (The Macmillan Co., New York, 1934), however, has presented a nationalist "interpretation of history and policy." As a "little American," he opposes imperialism and favors "the most efficient use of the natural resources and industrial arts of the nation at home in a quest for security and a high standard of living."

Criticism of the order of things was not limited to economics and politics. Science, religion, and morality were also subjected to incessant challenges. Scientific conceptions underwent scrutiny and revolution, theory after theory arising to command investigation, many persons believing that the great intellects were merely playing an abstruse game of shuttlecock. In a period of scientific changes a renewed questioning of the fundamentals of religion was only natural and what with the growing acceptance of the evolutionary theory combined with the intense and widespread suffering occasioned by the economic depression, there was a distinct loss of religious faith and the spread of esoteric cults, of atheism, skepticism, hocus-pocus worship, and what not. Coincident with these movements was a breakaway from the traditional morality in social and sex relations; Walter Lippmann epitomized the situation in his *A Preface to Morals* when he declared that religious sanctions for morality were no longer sacred and that the existing moral structure must find a philosophy based on a rational foundation.

Confronted with this turbulent unrest, the bourgeois ship of state seemed to many in imminent danger of capsizing. It was forced, on numerous occasions, to calk its hulk, to strengthen the ebbing spirit of its panicky crew, to quell mutinies, to select new officers, and at times even to send out signals of distress. The question loomed: How much longer could it weather the storm? Many believed that it could do so indefinitely; theirs was the blind faith that all these black clouds had silver linings, that the sun would break through and brighten the existing order. Apostle of this point of view, Herbert Hoover, ex-president of the United States, summed up the case for capitalism in a 1932 campaign speech, saying:

> If it can be demonstrated that by means of this, our unequalled political, social, and economic system, we have secured a lift in the standards of living and a diffusion of comfort and hope to men and women, the growth of equal opportunity, the widening of all opportunity, such as had never been seen in the history of the world, then we should not tamper with it or destroy it, but on the contrary we should restore it and, by its gradual improvement and perfection, foster it into new performance for our country and for our children.

There was no doubt as to his premises; the first three decades of the twentieth century had indeed witnessed a tremendous lift in the standard of living and a diffusion of culture. The rising flood of inventions revolutionized in many ways the daily existence of the average middle-class person. Greatly increased leisure time permitted the nurturing of culture. Knowledge was more widely distributed than in any other period during the history of mankind. The radio and the automobile made it a small world after all. Hoover seemed right—why tamper with that which had produced so many blessings?

Notwithstanding these remarkable achievements of the twentieth century, numerous Americans were hostile to the outstanding product of modern times—Big Business. In their opposition, these people were influenced by economic changes and by the social upheaval which occurred as a result of the mechanization of industry. Some concluded that real individualism was threatened by the monopolies of Big Business as well as by the collectivism of Communism. The push of industry toward monopoly and the utilization by Big Business of the state to achieve its objectives, through sound money, protective tariffs, and military and naval support for investments abroad aroused the fear of bourgeois liberals everywhere. A propertyless condition, they believed, was the impending fate of the small business men. Moreover, such middle-class virtues as diligence, economy, frugality, and respectability, they felt, had been superseded by speculative cunning, political chicanery, and unscrupulous use of power. Even the home experienced effects of the new mechanical age. No longer was it the center of social and moral life; rather it was just a place to eat, sleep, and keep things.

Moved by these changes, many middle-class idealists lost their traditional optimism. They decided that man could no longer be regarded as a rational creature. Did not modern psychology stress his fundamental irrationality, his gullibility, his susceptibility to emotional prejudices? Neither could the idea of the inevitable progress of the human race sustain them. Consequently, they threw mid-Victorian and Hegelian optimism and the evolutionary thesis of perfectibility into the intellectual garbage can and handed over the idea of progress to paid propagandists and promoters. To those bourgeois "pessimists," progress was limited to Big Business alone. The little fellow was destined to an economic status similar to that of the modern worker or the medieval serf.

No longer was the doctrine of rugged individualism accepted as a panacea for all economic and social troubles. Confronted by the problems of heavy taxes, unemployment, diminishing income, and inability to meet the competition of the large industrial and financial monopolistic units, these bourgeois pessimists did not subscribe wholeheartedly to the belief as presented by the capitalistic press that just "as the savage organized his tribe, for safety and stability, so 'Big Interests' have organized industry, distribution, and mass production, providing for all what was once the privilege of a few." They also inwardly rebelled when some exponent of the present order frankly admitted that "scheming selfishness growing and working in the brain of man little knows that what seems only selfishness is the power of creating a better race and civilization." They believed that this "scheming selfishness," which *may* have made possible the production of cheap automobiles, *did* help to precipitate four years of murder and destruction. They also maintained that this "scheming selfishness" has frequently resulted in overreaching, idiotic, reckless, and unrestrained competition, gambling, and legalized robbery by financial manipulation, which in turn have produced terrible economic crises, called depressions. They felt that despite the "material gains" attributed to Big Business, the little fellows—the middle classes and the proletariat—were gradually losing their property and their jobs.

Desperate as a result of their economic plight, these bourgeoisie refused to accept the idea that the "good old doctrine of enlightened selfishness" would enable mankind to create a better civilization. They even questioned the sincerity of certain representatives of Big Business when the latter described the benefits of an age of "enlightened despotism" whereby the industrial and financial lords would hand down "something" to the people.

Such opposition of these middle classes to plutocracy was based primarily on the belief that the barons of capitalism were not capable of solving the social problems which had been accentuated by the Industrial Revolution. In the opinion of many business men the mechanical and industrial development was concluded. They believed that no further inventions could avoid such phases of the world depression as unemployment. Moreover, they were of the opinion that the capitalistic principle of free competition and selection could no longer work efficiently. Liberty of trade and industry, given by the state to the individual a century or so ago, had been taken over by Big Business and used or ignored, according to its interests. As a result, free trade had practically died out and protective tariffs, designed not to help the people of a country as a whole but to aid particular interests, had been established. Individualism, whereby a young man through his initiative and ability rose to the top, also had been sadly curtailed. It was possible for a few to become executives of large concerns; but most men were functionaries, simply managing a "paternal inheritance." In short, these bourgeois intellectuals were convinced that Big Business had virtually destroyed real individualism.

For the same reason the little business men opposed communism and other radical movements. Sincere advocates of capitalistic beliefs such as private property, the profit system, personal initiative, and thrift, they feared the dictatorship of the proletariat, for they believed it would destroy these canons. In their opinion, Big Business was the lesser of two evils; consequently, whenever the little business men had to make a choice, they usually supported the forces of capitalism against those of communism. Between Scylla and Charybdis they found it hard to steer a middle course.

Faced by the danger of extinction as a result of being caught between the millstones of Big Business and of communism, the middle classes tended to exert their influence in the realm of government. In democracies, such as France, England, and the United States, they supported legislation designed to thwart the power of capitalism and the growth of radicalism. Broadly stated, their program included social legislation to help the workers, laws designed to restrict monopolies and unfair competition, taxes levied upon those best able to pay, nationalist propaganda, and legislation and organizations designed to suppress radicalism.

In certain European countries, as for example, Italy and Germany, the middle classes welcomed dictatorships and the idea of the corporative state. Quickly they appreciated the apparent advantage of a government wherein the emphasis upon national aspirations might destroy all class interests. The patriotism and the romanticism of Fascism and Nazism appealed to many middle-class men; but, more than this, they were lured by the promise that radicalism would be exterminated and Big Business would be curbed. An economic individualism whereby all persons would have the opportunity to develop their abilities for the welfare of the state, was the utopia offered to these business men. Therefore, they accepted wholeheartedly this attempt to revive politico-economic absolutism.

But will Fascism help the middle classes? In the opinion of Lewis Corey, Fascism in Italy and Germany has profited "only the small minority in the upper middle class, which becomes a dominant class within monopoly capitalism. . . . Nothing is changed except for the worse. Fascism is not a new social order; imprisoned within the forces of declining capitalism, Fascism is the old capitalist order become putrid, organizing economic disintegration, mass misery, and reaction into a system."

Fascism was not limited to Europe. As we have seen, the concept of individualism protected and developed by means of the authoritarian state (a dictatorship) was advanced in the New World during the nineteenth-century revolutions. Numerous dictators, good and bad, at least professed to be working for the welfare of the masses, and some of them achieved worthwhile reforms.

Since the beginning of the twentieth century, Mexico has experienced a most thorough national-socialist revolution. Although a republic, Mexico, under the dictatorial control of former President Calles and his successors, obliterated the old aristocratic and clerical régime and inaugurated a plan of reconstruction which, claim its defenders, "embraces the development of agricultural industry, the breaking up of great landed estates, and the establishment of a national system for the generation and distribution of electric power." This revolution has been essentially socialistic in character and has as its objective the economic and social advancement of the peon and the petty bourgeoisie at the expense of the large landowners, the privileged church, and foreign plutocracy.

Similar bourgeois reforms are being adopted in Hispanic America. In Argentina, Chile, Uruguay, and other states, the upper bourgeois industrialists, the lower bourgeois white collar workers, and the landless proletariat have combined with the purpose of bringing about the extension of suffrage, the separation of church and state, the expansion of the public-school system, and the enactment of democratic land and tax reforms.

Throughout the continent energetic attempts are being made to substitute national socialist states for the old aristocratic land-owning régime.

In democracies such as the United States and England the business classes have thus far declared Fascism unpalatable. Confirmed individualists, they dislike the idea of an authoritative state. Moreover, as middle-class men, they hate regulation and regimentation. Nevertheless, an increasing number of them realize that the law of preservation requires that they go into politics and administer the state as they administer their private interests. They admit that the welfare of all is of direct concern to them and that they must plan for tomorrow, not simply for today. While they believe that the principle of enterprise (individualism) must be maintained, at the same time they realize that this liberty must contribute to the common good and not merely to the interest of a few.

However, a large number of middle-class men, especially the salaried employees and professionals dependent on Big Business, have opposed bitterly the intervention of government in the economic sphere of life. But the lower salaried groups, including quite a number of professionals, waver between capitalistic reaction and proletarian radicalism. Like their brothers, however, the plutocrats and high salaried vassals, they want to believe that the individualism of Adam Smith is the only "way of economic salvation." Paradoxically, however, these men know that they cannot rely upon individualism in economic life to solve their problem. In fact, they realize that they must organize if they are to survive.

Today the only successful rugged individualists are the heads of Big Business. Liberty, equality, and opportunity are simply ideals to the average man. Even the economic security, formerly enjoyed by the upper salaried classes and the thrifty bourgeois investors, no longer exists. Economic life is no longer a game; it is a struggle. The cold, materialistic, and unfeeling encroachment of money has erected a barrier in the relationships of mankind. Wealth is the criterion of success, and man is generally measured by what he *has,* not by what he *is*. Political, intellectual, as well as social life has been dominated by this capitalistic point of view. Man is no longer a *some one,* but a *something*. The old phrase, "men, not measures, count," does not apply to twentieth-century society. In fact, men are ruled by "measures." They are a part of a standardized system, wherein their individuality and their character are submerged.

Unfortunately, the average man does not realize this fact. Intoxicated by the phrases of freedom and unity, bound by the worship of a false liberalism, and blinded by the rays of so-called "intellectual progress," he is blissfully unaware of the fact that in reality he is chained and enslaved.

Will it ever be possible for the middle classes to gain real individualism? To achieve the goal, they must undergo a "radical" change. The old picture of the original Babbitt, symbolized by Louis Philippe, with his cumbersome form, his pear-shaped head, his thick neck swallowing up his chin, his prominent belly, and ridiculous frock-coat tightened at the waist, must disappear. In its place must be substituted the portrait of a young man, possessing the trim build of an athlete; the eager willingness to work, produce, and share; and the sharp mentality of a scholar.

Such a complete transformation, however, will be slow. While most middle-class men realize that they are living in an era of change and that somehow they are out of step with the march of time, they fail to change their gait. Clinging desperately to the solid bourgeois virtues, especially the faith in liberty, they fear to look either to the right or to the left. Bewildered, stubborn, and resentful, they stumble on.

Whither, Bourgeoisie . . . ?

INDEX

CITY OF WESTMINSTER
PUBLIC LIBRARIES